e.e. cummings'
- libretto for Uncle Tom's Cabin
- never produced   (42) (43) (73)

Yvor Winters (74)

arts administrator (153)(154)

argument for government support of
the arts   (159)

board's view — (168)

proportionately few male Russian vters
(173-74)

time problem (192)

Wescott's Audubon libretto —
(225-26)

Also by Lincoln Kirstein

THIRTY YEARS

THIRTY YEARS

LINCOLN KIRSTEIN'S THE NEW YORK CITY BALLET

Expanded to include the years 1973–1978,
in celebration of the company's thirtieth anniversary

 Alfred A. Knopf   *New York*   *1978*

THIS IS A BORZOI BOOK
PUBLISHED BY ALFRED A. KNOPF, INC.

*Grateful acknowledgment is made to the following for permission to reprint
previously published material:*

Robert Craft and The Estate of Igor Stravinsky: For excerpts from *Dialogues
and a Diary*, by Robert Craft and Igor Stravinsky (Doubleday & Company,
Inc., 1963).

Doubleday & Company, Inc.: For excerpts from *Balanchine's New Complete
Stories of the Great Ballets*, by George Balanchine, edited by Francis
Mason, copyright © 1954, 1968 by Doubleday & Company, Inc. Reprinted
by permission of the publisher.

Alfred A. Knopf, Inc.: For excerpts from pages 24–5 and 117 of *Themes and
Episodes*, by Robert Craft and Igor Stravinsky. Copyright © 1965, 1966 by
Robert Craft and Igor Stravinsky. Reprinted by permission of the publisher.

Liveright Publishing Corp.: For an excerpt of text material and 8 lines of
poetry (from "The Dance—Powhatan's Daughter") from *The Complete
Poems and Selected Letters and Prose of Hart Crane*, by Hart Crane.
Copyright © 1933, 1958, 1966 by Liveright Publishing Corp. Reprinted by
permission of the publisher.

Newsweek: For an excerpt from an article by Emily Coleman, October 25,
1948. Copyright Newsweek, Inc., 1948. Reprinted by permission.

The New York Times: For excerpts from two reviews by John Martin which
appeared in *The New York Times*, March 6, 1935, and November 22, 1950.
Copyright 1935/1950 by The New York Times Company. Reprinted by
permission.

Library of Congress Cataloging in Publication Data
Kirstein, Lincoln, [date]   Thirty years.   Includes index.
1. New York City Ballet.   I. Kirstein, Lincoln, [date]
The New York City Ballet.   II. Title.
GV1786.N4K58   792.8'09747'1   78–7132
ISBN 0–394–50257–4   ISBN 0–394–73615–x pbk.

Manufactured in the United States of America
First Edition

For EDWARD M. M. WARBURG

and in memory of

A. EVERETT AUSTIN, JR.,

and MORTON BAUM

CONTENTS

ACKNOWLEDGMENTS

This book contains no mention of many persons who, unknown to an audience, have made and still make possible the continuing activity of the New York City Ballet. Since it has no pretensions to any completeness, the introduction of perfunctory paragraphs as token tribute could only irritate those who are not mentioned but surely not forgotten. Thirty years is a long time; many whose work was primary and capital are no longer here. Only the smallest measure of justice has been paid in print to dozens of individual dancers. This is not from lack of appreciation but from want of skill in translating the impact of performances into lively language with the tone of family pride. The ambiguities of praise or lack of it, affection, or a seeming slight, make one helpless to detail innumerable occasions which have given personal delight. However, it became necessary to record a few names so that, if or when a comprehensive history is undertaken, those most responsible may receive proper due.

Edward Bigelow has become, after Betty Cage, key administrator and functionary—at home, on tour, in so many capacities from his early seasons as a dancer and from stage to desk that his duties are too encompassing, various, and intricate to be precisely described. But they have been and are indispensable. Barbara Horgan has served not only as personal aide to Balanchine in his international commitments, but organizes his time so that the home team gets most benefit, without denying his repertory to the domestic and foreign institutions that seek it out. Rosemary Dunleavy stopped dancing to become ballet mistress, coordinator, rehearsalist. It is she who is to be thanked when an evening shoots along seemingly under its own power; the trigger is hers. Carole Deschamps has been invisibly onstage most nights in the last ten years, picking up pieces when anything in the mechanism momentarily cracks.

Mary Porter made sense of an impossible manuscript, full of tiresome emendations and gaffes, so that printers might read it. Mary Barnett, after everyone else, including the author, had abandoned it, put a cold eye on the text and thereby salvaged it for style and sense. Robert Gottlieb of Alfred A. Knopf, Inc., proposed this book. As a boy he was a devoted member of the audience at City Center's old Mecca Temple, where he paid his pennies to sit at the top of a balcony to applaud many of our early programs.

1973

NOTE TO THE SECOND EDITION

It should perhaps be reiterated that this is not a full-scale, full-dress history of the New York City Ballet. For those who seek complete chronological detail with a sampling of critical response, *Repertory in Review*, by Nancy Reynolds (New York: Dial Press, 1977), chronicles not thirty, but forty years of activity. It is an encyclopedic compendium and makes good reading. It spares me from mentioning a vast amount of material that would too greatly expand this present book.

There is no doubt that there is considerable loss in not reproducing the treasury of photographs which made the first edition noteworthy. Inflation would have priced a facsimile out of the market, and one hopes, at least as a half-hearted excuse, that an uninterrupted narrative may have some virtue as a consecutive story.

It may be noticed that the "Postscript," which attempts to bring this story up to date, is set in a tone different from the text preceding it. There is a tone of polemic which one hopes is not too shrill, but which, considering the times described and the time it took to fashion the book's subject, is not unjustified.

In this printing, there have been few corrections or emendations from the first edition. For instance, that closed with a hope that we would soon produce a ballet to be called *The Birds of America*, concerning the occupation of the North American continent. Some five years later we are no closer to producing it, but I have let the hope stand; so we felt in 1973. If there are repetitions of material or ideas, this has been governed by a desire for emphasis, for presenting an idea from another facet.

While several persons, notably those most closely associated with developments here recorded, have read my manuscript, this does not imply, in any way, that they subscribe to opinions herein expressed.

1978

FOREWORD

Theatrical memoirs are always frustrating. Vividness in performance is based on a fast-evaporating amalgam of color and electricity, of physicality approaching hysteria that is impossible to reconstitute or render impressively in words. Shock, surprise, amazement, all fade in retelling. No matter what is described—stage action, song, or dance—it all sounds as if one has read it somewhere before. In the present recital, the text makes suggestions by way of reviving key occasions that contributed variously to the development of an organism which, after nearly forty years, presents itself as the New York City Ballet. These suggestions take the form of quotations from an imaginary diary, such as might have been kept but in fact was not, paired with a running commentary on the diary's telegraphic accounts of historical fact. Many ballets whose antecedent elements are indicated remain in repertory and may be presently seen at the State Theater in New York City from season to season. Many more have been ploughed under, sometime to reappear in subsequent if much altered forms. The emphasis, however, is on extratheatrical factors which furnished background, springboard, or occasion for organization, and on mechanisms which produced dancers and dance works.

It has been noted, not always with approbation, that from its inception our company has held an attitude, indeed a metaphysic, which differs from others not only in philosophy but also in kind. To explain this difference, it has been necessary to penetrate the inscape and morality of those who were chiefly responsible for its birth, maintenance, and achievement. Its development has been eccentric and haphazard but, at the same time, continuous and possibly rational. Hence there may be a temptation to eliminate accidental factors, to attempt to straitjacket chance into a logic of conscious contrivance. And yet, when the normal increment of accident is admitted or even accentuated, there remain principles that were clear from the beginning, points of departure which determined the kind and quality of school and company.

This vein of independence has been interpreted as arrogance; it presupposed assurance in direction even when the means to achieve it were in doubt. From the start it disavowed personalism, the projection of vaunted stars to sell a product. It insisted on erecting a new repertory instead of borrowing prestige from established personalities and known works. It persisted in collaborating with the progressive musicians of the epoch, notably Stravinsky; in using unfamiliar scores, old and new; as far as possible, in commissioning new music to fit current needs and tastes. From the first there was a trinity of aims: the foundation of a school as basis for a company; the creation of a repertory to accommodate an academic style particular to our climate and continent; the construction of a theater which would house such a company and the development of an audience which would maintain it. Initially this might have seemed to be, on the basis of historic precedent, an ambition to found a native school for a national company. As years passed, and several tentative experiments foundered, it grew clear that our country was far too large to be served by a single representative company, and that any audience which would be practical and desirable was less than a national constituency though rather more than a provincial or parochial one. Later, economic considerations intervened; the format of the resultant repertory enlarged to demand a frame too big for much mobility in touring. It became necessary to depend on a stable, localized subscription public. This was possible only in the single largest available metropolitan area which had a geographical center or focus. Hence what began as the American Ballet and toured as the Ballet Caravan resolved itself into Ballet Society and then the New York City Ballet. Deliberate identification with the cultural if not political capital of a nation justified many elements which led to continuity, stability; the elimination of improvisation and the establishment of a family audience.

In the process of building school, company, and theater, a considerable number of persons were involved, many of whose individual contributions were preponderant at the moment but ephemeral over a long run. It is impossible to be just to many. Some emerge in snapshots; their aid was often far greater than the space given them here suggests. Others—for example, Balanchine himself, whose school, company, and theater it has been, is, and will be, and whose contribution and position are self-evident—may seem slighted in favor of less familiar figures.

The form of a synthetic, factitious "diary" was assumed for compactness and symbolic value. Entries indicate key memories that, never isolated, were steps contributing to the sequence of formation and growth. Memorable premieres, brilliant diplomatic galas, are scanted because the preparations which made them possible were more relevant and instructive. Performances are rarely described but only suggested through the atmosphere which surrounded them. In "diary" entries, a frank artificiality extends to present tense and personal pronoun, in an effort to suggest the air of a particular moment and the diarist's age, rather than displaying all in the diffused glow of hindsight. Total honest recall, absolute frankness, is impermissible. Any complete cast of characters reads mostly as dull names printed on a blank page, hardly even applicable to photographs which might identify them. Small or large, they cannot be seen as characters in the dimension of film or novel. The most one can hope for from the "diary" device is that it confers more vitality than statistics or the conscientious amplitude of specialized theatrical histories.

If and when a time comes that it may appear useful or interesting to compile a more complete history of our company, the present synopsis could serve as spine. If every proper name mentioned here were followed to its logical conclusion (involving twice as many persons and places), something approaching fullness might result. This would include a dizzy financial record which might have some value, though its special nature would be unlikely to interest many readers. However, since money occupied somewhat more than half our waking hours, at least a few words must acknowledge the economic factor, as tedious and awkward as it was to consider in our perennial crises. There was never enough money; unlike the situation in socialist states, there never will be. We rationalized this capital realization into something approaching advantage, although it produced constant serious modifications in our planning—notably regarding stage decoration. We have capitalized on a meager decorative style in a dimension that is importantly visual. Two prime considerations have always been music and plasticity, maps of motion based on piano or orchestral scores. Balanchine's ambition has ever been to make audiences see sound and hear dancing. It is a peculiar conjuring act which requires a particular set of conditions. It is not intended to please as many people as are captivated by ball games. The ensuing "diary" is a shorthand chart of a process which still proceeds.

New York City
JULY, 1973

THIRTY YEARS

Ma took us to the Lyceum. We sat in Uncle Mart's box. Red and gold; everything, red and gold. Drapes on this box, the front curtain; red. Gold fringe flopped when the curtain went up and down. Hundreds of people singing, whirling. One man in a black moustache, red-and-gold uniform, sang; not very funny. A lot of girls kicked very high in black garters. They were fast. Ma says I should say rapid, or quick. "Fast" is wrong. They moved faster than any bodies I've ever seen.

An uncle, Martin Woolf, controlled the Lyceum Theater, a provincial opera house built in the Teutonic taste of the sixties, a not too distant cousin of the San Carlo, Fenice, Maryinsky, as well as my ideal for a State Theater which Philip Johnson would build us fifty years later. *The Merry Widow* was performed by amateurs for charity; its cancan was a shocker. "Fast" then implied loose behavior. My first contact with stage dancing introduced me to a preoccupation, commitment, or addiction. Cocteau named it the "red-and-gold disease." The malady, obsession, advanced state of unease, indeed dis-ease, was compounded of passion for the preposterous, the tease of perfection which was an impersonation of grandeur, or in exalted cases, the superhuman and heroic. Sex, also, is an expression of intense physicality; the restraint, release, and control of mind and muscle. At the Lyceum I also saw Otis Skinner in *The Garden of Allah*, but my sister's fingers clamped across my eyes while Haji, the beggar, was drowned in a small octangular pool bubbling with real water. The gurgling was acoustically perfect; the sound was more horrible than any sight might have been.

JUNE, 1916: *Boston*

Ma has gone to the Russian Ballet at the Opera House and would not take me. I am too young. I am nearly ten. I would not understand. I would, too! Miss Prescott explained everything. Scenery is painted like a signboard; it's not supposed to be real. A blob on the wall means: a fly. Russians are the best dancers in the world. Their best dancer is Nijinsky. He flies because he has bones like a bird. I will never forgive Mother.

I've never known exactly why I was not allowed to see Diaghilev's company on tour. Later I suspected it was because Nijinsky, in blackface as the golden slave in *Schéhérazade*, made love to a white harem queen. Miss Prescott was my teacher in public grade school. She wrote children's books and explained the basis of post-Impressionist painting from colored illustrations in the ballet's souvenir program, which I *was* given to look at. Nijinsky's feet were, of course, no different from mine, except that he was a trained acrobat, among other important capacities. Fifteen years later, when I was working on his biography with his wife, I learned that in all probability Nijinsky never appeared in Boston at all because of a sudden indisposition which was an ominous warning of his increasing illness. His stand-in, Alexander Gavrilov, substituted for him unannounced. However, an image of him, fleshed out by colored reproductions of Bakst's costume sketches, was a spark that set me off. For years I tried to find onstage the magic that I was robbed of here.

JULY, 1919: *Lake Sebago, Maine*

Chris says I could be a dancer if I worked. She is a very good dancer, but she says not as good as her teacher, Isadora Duncan. I work out with her each morning before diving class. Some boys think I'm silly, fooling with Chris. I'm serious. Dancing is not hard; you have to feel free and keep time. Chris says it's by breathing, not by counting. Anyway, I'm chosen to be Pipe Bearer. I don't dance; I just hold the pipe. Then Cap lights it and hands it to the Chief Cub. It looks silly practicing walking and handing over, but it's not as hard as half gainers or jackknives.

At a boys' camp, a girl friend of the director had been one of the first Isadorables. She taught rhythmic exercises disguised to look as little as possible like dancing. Marking my interest, she confessed that actually a few steps further on would almost amount to "real dancing," and that if I truly wished, I could be a dancer. This seemed like admittance to a secret society. She also prepared me as hierophant in a ceremony, around a campfire, in which younger boys were admitted to a higher order. From this I recognized something of the ritual essence of bodily movement—designed for repetition, hence: repertory. Also that there was a superior element in spectacular performance even without a red-and-gold interior—that it could happen equally well in a clearing around a pinecone fire in Maine woods. Later the meaning of the cant theatrical term "camp" would be clarified. It may have derived from induced hysteria of congregations at evangelical camp meetings on the banks of middle-American rivers in the nineteenth century. "Camp" applied to a quality of impersonation, an imitation of heroic gesture, a parody of sacred mad behavior, an ironic or sarcastic criticism of advanced narcissism; the recognition of which would be a kind of antibody diminishing the more humorless sepsis of the red-and-gold disease.

APRIL, 1920: *Boston*

Nat Woolf called; Ma let me go with him; he's seen Pavlova in New York; she is the greatest dancer who ever lived. And Nijinsky? Nat says great dancers are women. Symphony Hall was full; lots of applause, but it was not a real theater. A rigged-up gray curtain; no red and gold. Pavlova in her *Syrian Dance*; trousers and a tall hat; she moved fast but couldn't jump. Nat says this number is a miniature version of *Schéhérazade*; made for concert halls, not opera houses. Ma is letting me go tomorrow night too. As for her *Dying Swan*, Nat says it is "grotesque."

Dr. Nathaniel Woolf was the son of that uncle who owned the Lyceum in Rochester, and my first cousin. A junior at Harvard, he became my aesthetic mentor. Enthusiastic, in love with theater and poetry, an excellent student, he took a medical degree but hardly practiced. His childhood was tragic, his career aborted; he was able to exile himself in Europe, where he touched fringes of the backstage world. He appears fleetingly in the published diaries of Harry, Count Kessler, the German patron of Diaghilev and

Gordon Craig. In my European vacations from college he fed me gossip of the Ballets Russes and gave me a relish for fashion and novelty, as well as a certain skeptical attitude toward accepted models. Once my mother took us both to *L'Africaine* at the old Metropolitan Opera. There was an elaborate ballet in the house's Italian tradition, which he pronounced appalling. Heretofore I had no notion that anything in a format so splendiferous could be in "bad taste." My mother scolded him for spoiling my "pleasure," but this gave me much to think about. His assumption of proprietary interest in theater rubbed off on me; he presupposed he had the right to say what he liked and do as he pleased. Licensed or not, he suggested that participation in the production of art was possible, even by such alien amateurs as we were. From him I realized that theater was not simply a "pleasure" but a matter of appreciating, making, and performing. His inherent interests and kindness, ambiguous existence, and inconsequential end had a cautionary effect. Dilettantism could be attended by mortal danger from the red-and-gold disease, and was a depressing symptom of some of that malady's fringe benefits.

I watched Pavlova with Nat Woolf in Symphony Hall five nights running. Before this exposure, I had a vague idea that dances were somehow improvised according to the "mood" of dancers on their every hearing of the music, and took "inspiration" for method. But on watching the professional repetition of identical figurations night after night, I began to realize that there was something like design in dance, comparable to musical notation or a rationally laid-out palette. Structure was as important as personality or expression. "Soul" was a word then uttered far more than now; it began to have a specious sound. Craft, skill, pattern supporting the dance began to suggest themselves, and "personality" seemed a suspicious ingredient.

JUNE, 1922: *London*

My brother and I were in bed; it must have been around one or two. David woke us up. He gave us some of the girls' yellow-and-orange pyjamas. We went downstairs; Lydia made us do some easy steps in the garden. In the studio, lots of people. George was rather disagreeable but too sleepy to mind. We got through the dance more or less, thanks to Lydia. It was embarrassing but I enjoyed it. Lytton gave me a drink. Maynard is going to marry Lydia; no one seems surprised.

My sister, Mina, had taken a house in London, together with Henrietta Bingham, daughter of Judge Robert Bingham, owner of the Louisville *Courier-Journal* and later ambassador to Great Britain. The two girls, some ten years older than I, were involved with the Bloomsbury group, among whom was the masterful economist and architect of artistic patronage, Maynard Keynes. Lydia Lopokova, the most brilliant of Diaghilev's soubrettes, had become a star of the post–World War I seasons. I could not know that at this very moment, in Leningrad, her brother Feodor Lopukhov was rehearsing with a young fellow student, Georgei Balanchivadze, for an experimental program of revolutionary ballets. Although there were a number of well-known characters in and out of our house, they were taken for granted. Lytton Strachey meant more to me as the model of his huge, lanky portrait by Henry Lamb than as a writer. David Garnett had dedicated his second book to my sister. "Bloomsbury" never seemed to me special or snobbish; rather it was the shifting site of an endless party taking place at various houses all over London and in the country. Art, gossip, or opinions about art seemed its main occupation.

Maynard Keynes showed me an exhibition of Gauguin at the Leicester Galleries and demonstrated the difference between a "good" Gauguin and a "bad" one. Or at least, he made it clear that he considered there was this difference. Heretofore I had assumed that any and every Gauguin was per se of prime importance. He disconcerted me by saying that pictures were also negotiable securities, signed like bank notes or bills of sale. To him the fact that they had other values besides aesthetic or romantic ones accentuated their primacy as historical, social, and economic properties. Any appreciation of art became more complex than the simple acceptance of a personal talent. Gauguin, whom I'd been given as an advance-guard champion, now retired to the status of some minor old master.

Later I would take rooms in Russell Square, and come to know a number of the personages who were for their epoch a concentration of opinion makers and taste masters. Those I knew best were minor members, but these, and one in particular, had a major effect. He was a sculptor, son of a Lord Chief Justice who disapproved of his sculpture. Stephen Tomlin gave me the run of his studio, let me watch him draw from the nude, work with his clay, and play at being serious, disinherited, and in the vanguard. He also let me put gold studs in his boiled shirt when he went into another world of formal "society"; from him I learned the polarized compatibility of High and Low Bohemia. Intimacy with studios gave me a certain security when I later dealt with artists.

JUNE, 1926: *London*

Diaghilev is bankrupt; Lord Rothermere will put up no more money; he must play in a vaudeville theater; Stravinsky has deserted to Ida Rubinstein. Anyway, the present theater is dreary and smaller than the Lyceum in Rochester. I expected more. Not much dancing; not enough dancers. But one exciting moment. In *Firebird* the magician Kastchei was made up as Genghis Khan; Mongolian, with long fingernails like gilded claws, a frightful vulture. In a fantastically evil way he manipulated the others. Afterward, to a restaurant; there he was, among other dancers. I wanted to ask him for a drink, but didn't dare.

I entered Harvard as a freshman in 1926, having worked for a year in a stained-glass factory, since it was thought I should learn something concrete before college. Because my father was self-educated, he was both respectful and suspicious of "higher" education unless it had some practical basis. The stained-glass shop taught me something about technical method and expert execution which applied to other forms of expression. I came to consider familiarity with digital mastery, combined with instruction in the materials of painting and the means of rendering, as the basis of critical judgment.

My parents let me spend most summer vacations in Europe;

attendance at Diaghilev's seasons, mainly in London, became increasingly the focus of my interest. In most ways I was uncertain of any vocation. I wished to be at once painter, poet, and professional horseman. My models were traditional rather than progressive, although I was involved with Edward Warburg and John Walker in the Harvard Society for Contemporary Art. It took me some time to realize that "being a painter" was not painting, nor did "being a poet" produce good verse. It was roles or impersonation rather than the lodged activity that attracted me.

I attached myself to the fringes of ballet and Bloomsbury without real contact. The dancer who had appeared as Kastchei was George Balanchine. When I asked about him I was told that he was an excellent dancer with bad lungs, that Diaghilev had confidence in him as ballet master and choreographer, that he lived with Alexandra Danilova, that he had a personal life apart from Diaghilev's intimate court.

I spoke bad French, accumulated a smattering of gossip that served as a key to superficial entry into closed worlds. Then, curious and energetic Americans were something of a curiosity to Europeans. We could penetrate shut circles with reasonable ease. I was fascinated by what I could not decipher of the ballet world. What I discovered was neither reassuring nor interesting. There must be something beyond personal tension, jealousies, financial insecurity which made what I saw onstage as dancing come to life, although this would elude me for years.

Meanwhile the vague figure named Balanchine gradually assumed more definite shape as his responsibilities and reputation grew. But he was never starred as a performer and infrequently appeared. However, I was not much interested in star personalities. They seemed to have only a single limited self to sell. There were no canonized ballerinas, and at that time Massine, Dolin, and Lifar represented star values to the exclusion of everyone else—except Parisian painters, upon whom Diaghilev was forced to depend since he had no strong company of dancers in depth. Deprived of a Russian source or seedbed, Diaghilev enlisted Picasso, Matisse, Derain, Rouault, de Chirico, Tchelitchev, Max Ernst to produce designs that were more impressive than much choreography. But the combination of painted cloths and theatrical movement igniting the final Diaghilev seasons was a disturbing ferment, a delicious torture, which upset all my anticipatory speculation in the months when I could not see them. I complained in the borrowed fashionable formula, but I was addicted, as in a love affair.

DECEMBER, 1927: *New York*

Tony's speakeasy, West 52nd Street, the first I've been in. Seems like the cozy back room of an Italian restaurant. You're let in by being inspected through a hole in the door; perfunctory gesture; no danger. The whole place, the cabin of a pirate ship, like *Treasure Island*. Everyone knew each other. I felt like the cabin boy in the barrel, overhearing a conspiracy. Gin confused the picture. Muriel Draper, the most extraordinary female I've ever met. In London she was known as the White Negress. She wore a gold turban and sat with a powerful black man, Taylor Gordon, a singer. She looked me up and down as if judging a horse. She was shameless; immediately intimate, but did not try to scare me. Taylor Gordon gave me a drink, and left for Harlem. Mrs. Draper told me to sit in his chair; asked me what I wanted to be? Be? Rather than do. I tried thinking this through: I, well, I wanted —to be, a dancer. She said: Well, you won't; you're too old, too tall, too rich.

Muriel Draper, whose papers repose in the Collection of American Literature at Yale, awaits a biographer who will do justice to a capricious, flamboyant, influential, and now forgotten American woman. A New Englander from Haverhill, Massachusetts—her father was allied with Alexander Graham Bell in early inventions— and an ardent feminist, she liberated herself past the wildest dreams of any Unitarian suffragette. Before the First World War she grew up in Italy and England, and married Paul Draper, who had an exquisite tenor voice and sang *Lieder* better than any other American. They were parents to one of the best dancers in the most musical idiom of tap. Muriel's memoirs, *Music at Midnight*, have not half the quality of her conversation but tell much of her years as hostess before she lost fortune and husband and found Marxism. She returned to New York, supported two small sons as an interior decorator, and wrote weekly about house decoration for *The New Yorker*. Although she was well connected socially, independence was her main concern. She made consequential theater out of her poverty and, in a mad decor of furniture and objects salvaged from thrift shop and warehouse, for twenty years conducted what may have been the last valuable intellectual salon in New York.

NOVEMBER, 1928: *Cambridge*

Muriel up for the Harvard-Yale game, staying with Mother in Boston. Worried; after all, she's twenty years older than I, but marvelous with Father. We got as far as the stadium; Muriel decided she'd seen enough football. To Concord; Walden Pond; we put a big stone on the cairn. To Lexington. Mrs. Ames was in; she lives in Hawthorne's Old Manse, was resting on a laying-out couch. Hawthorne's grave in the late afternoon. Muriel spoke of Nijinsky, whom she knew at Bar Harbor when he was working on a ballet to Bach. She knew Diaghilev. She knew everybody.

I learned more from Muriel Draper about art and life than from five years in Cambridge and London. Before knowing her I had contact with the Big World at one remove; she seemed the Big World itself. There was hardly anyone, from Samuel Courtauld and Bernard Baruch, Lady Rothermere and Lady Cunard, Anne Morgan and Mrs. Willy Vanderbilt, to Jacques Rigaud and Marcel Duchamp, Elie Nadelman and Carl Van Vechten, Gilbert Seldes and A. R. Orage, Henry James and Charles Demuth, Edmund Wilson and e. e. cummings, whom she had not known or did not know—intimately. She was also close to anonymous characters whose histories were equally fabulous for me and even more preposterous, since their provenance was more exotic, their habit less familiar. I was a conventional product of class-conditioned, so-called higher education, knowing nothing but Cambridge, Concord, Boston, and a self-exclusive fraction of London. Now I found myself immersed in Manhattan with a passkey to boroughs as fascinating as Balzac's or Proust's *faubourgs*, which in many ways I felt that New York in the late twenties resembled. It was the site of a continuous educational holiday which stretched from Oyster Bay and Tuxedo Park to Harlem, from Robert Chanler's house on 19th Street to Robert Locher's on Staten Island.

Muriel told hard truths: I would never be a painter, professional writer, dancer. My gifts, such as they were, applied to organization; my talent, if any, was toward tasty management. Puritan New England gave her a conscience in the line of Margaret Fuller, Harriet Beecher Stowe, and Jane Addams. For a decade from 1927, she was a dominant companion and influence. Later she sloughed off such nugatory matters as the life of art, the warmth of friends, or intoxication in music. She became a passionate Communist, with or without a party card, involved in international congresses, traveling to France and the Soviet Union in awkward and perilous times. Although she came to watch ballets we produced, after I married just before the Second World War we saw each other less. But it was she who led me in my directions of most possibility, who gave focus and meaning to my dissipation and inconsistency. She indicated not what I thought I wanted to do, but finally what I wanted to be.

AUGUST, 1929: *Venice*

Agnes Mongan disagrees about El Greco. She thinks his elongations derive from conventions of Byzantine painting learned as a boy in shops of Cretan ikon painters. I'm sure it's myopia or astigmatism, but, after spending a morning with San Marco's mosaics, perhaps she's right. Tried to get into San Giorgio dei Greci, where Greek merchants worshiped, and Greco must have too, but its front was draped in black and silver for a funeral. Sun dazzling; impossible to see inside except candle flames against the ikonostasis. A sacristan assumed we were mourners. He would have let us in but we felt shy. A basso intoned the service, like a solo from *Boris Godunov*.

For my junior year at college I had what amounted to a vacation in Florence. I had been working on El Greco for my senior dissertation. Previously I had traveled through Spain, visiting every church in which he'd worked. Now I tried to retrace his steps from Venice to Rome before he was employed at the Escorial. My two "favorite" artists (or personalities from the past) were Domenikos Theotokopoulos, the Greek, and William Blake. My two favorite paintings were Greco's *St. Maurice and the Theban Legion* and Blake's *Glad Day*. The first incorporated a big corps de ballet of male dancers in skin armor. The second was a sunburst emanating from a youth who proclaimed the Creator's eternal dawn.

My choice of two philosophical painters was neither conscious nor exactly accidental. My tutor in college was S. Foster Damon, a vastly erudite Blake expert, whose knowledge of metaphysical literature excited me more than any other teaching at college. I would learn to rationalize my choice of two mystical artists, one in the tradition of Greek Orthodox Holy Wisdom, the other an inheritance from Jakob Böhme and Swedenborg, but what essentially attracted me was the Mannerist elegance of the male nude. It was more about style than sexuality, although polo players, fencers, and acrobats were more concrete models than any ballerina I had so far seen. I could not make much of El Greco as a person; the pallor of his historical presence never became flesh in my mind; but Mannerism, a tension of opposites, I recognized as the quintessential style of academic ballet. The impersonation of grandeur, the reduction of Michelangelo's grand manner, or *maniera*, to a possibly humane theatrical scale, indeed, Giovanni da Bologna's *Mercury* itself, incarnated the essence of what was most focused for me in stage dancing.

In 1929, I considered the ballet as a province apart and closed to me, particularly after a Covent Garden season of Diaghilev's ballet which was distinguished by a reprise of Balanchine's *Apollon Musagète* and the premiere of his *Prodigal Son*, with collaborations from Prokofiev and Rouault. Whatever direction I was to take, it would be in the line of painting, possibly in art history. Also, I loved horses and learned to box badly; and somewhere in my fantasy still loomed the idiotic notion that dancing was not excluded.

The day following our failure to enter the Greek church, Agnes Mongan, my tutor in Italian painting at the Fogg Museum (and recently its director), and I took the train to Padua to inspect Giottos and Mantegnas, returning by way of the Brenta Canal.

Here among other Palladian villas lay La Malcontenta, filled with frescoes by a painter who may have had connections with El Greco. Agnes had bought a London *Times* at the station, and we learned to our amazement that yesterday in Venice we had all but attended the obsequies of Sergei Pavlovich Diaghilev, who had died on the Lido some days before. At La Malcontenta, the owner, Alberto Landsberg, was extremely courteous, if abstracted. He had not known of our coming but showed us the villa, let us inspect the frescoes, left us alone to look. However, we had broken into a situation of private distress, and leaving, we sought to apologize. As we walked down the stairs of Palladio's portico, we encountered the Russians who had gathered for Diaghilev's funeral. I had never before seen Lifar or Dolin offstage. The silence of personal grief was almost audible; there was no more splendid background possible for the immediacy of this end of an epoch. The positive absence of a princely presence from this palatial yet domestic decor was intensely poignant. Here was a fusion of life, death, and theater, which elevated one afternoon into the sunset celebration of an era. Returning to the Venetian skyline and seascape, the monumental combination of man-made architecture and the Adriatic, we felt the wizardry of imagination and humane capacity.

FEBRUARY, 1932: *New York*

I know Fokine thinks it's ridiculous. I only want to learn the structure of his teaching, but he thinks I'm some sort of mad millionaire (like Ida Rubinstein) who dreams of dancing. Do I want to start an "American ballet"? I do, but of course this sounds crazy. I am incapable of lifting a leg. However, as an exercise in free will (the most recent Muriel Draper has given me), I persist. Also, I write down exactly what Fokine says; it will be a book, if he gives me an hour a day.

I broke away from Beacon Hill, Cambridge, and Concord largely because of Muriel Draper's magnetism. Harvard, for me, was a summation of the lively residue of the nineteenth century. There I learned how to look hard at pictures and objects, to use a

library, to sense the proximity of powerful minds. Dante with
Charles Grandgent, French romanticism with Irving Babbitt,
metaphysics with Whitehead, Coleridge with J. L. Lowes seemed
to tap the long sequence of a living tradition at its source. I also
helped edit a literary quarterly called *Hound & Horn*, which enjoyed the patronage of both T. S. Eliot and Ezra Pound. Our
Harvard Society for Contemporary Art introduced Picasso as well
as Buckminster Fuller, Sandy Calder, and Isamu Noguchi to
Harvard. A great influence was John Brooks Wheelwright, son of
Boston's last civic architect, a truly properly improper Bostonian,
an odd combination of devout Anglican and active proto-Marxist.
He was a philosophical poet of power, an exciting adviser to me
and other young men.

Beacon Hill was historically attractive, but Murray Hill opened
possibilities that made home tame. I explored New York as a
foreign country, and through Muriel Draper gained insight into
high life, night life, and low life. While directing such postgraduate
studies, she heightened and focused my purpose; she made clear
what I wanted to be and do—something connected with dancing. I
realized that ballet for me as a performer was out of the question,
but two aspects of the human body in action and repose seemed
open. I continued to draw from the nude model, and I learned to
box at the West Side Y.M.C.A. from an ex-lightweight who was a
fireman at a nearby firehouse. Sometimes I spelled him when he
needed a night off. Through him I met a galaxy of exotic characters
who preserved me somewhat from the dangers of class conditioning and too shy a life. Also, I became involved with Muriel
Draper's nascent Marxism and flirted with a number of passive
Communist theorists and active organizers.

But my main interest was dancing, and painfully I placed myself under Fokine as the most eminent practitioner of the art and
skill in America. It was he who, early in our century, precipitated
the original choreographic revolution which Diaghilev framed to
show the West. Although he was repudiated by the advance guard,
I found him a living monument and talked to him for hours. This
resulted in a small book published in England which did not entirely displease him, although he was a vain, resentful, disappointed
veteran who could see nothing in any work save his own, and
whose restricted taste was that of his early youth. He thought I was

wasting his and my time. Nevertheless, my opuscule on Fokine served as a passport, legitimizing my dilettante predilections. It showed I had some, however borrowed, authority in an area which was largely closed to aliens and in which authority seemed to descend by physical apostolic succession alone. By birth, training, or merit I could never belong, but by association with Fokine, something might rub off on me. Indeed, at first I had a notion of an "American" ballet centered on Fokine. Since 1917 he had enjoyed numerous chances of his own; apart from sporadic commercial success on Broadway, he had done little after breaking with Diaghilev except teach two generations of American dancers. Also, there was Madame Vera Fokine, an imperious beldam who emerged from time to time to register disdain, which Fokine himself kept in restraint at least while he talked to me. Yet I absorbed from his *barre* exercises a modicum of what is necessary in the schooling of professionals. I learned the consummate logic in the progression of academic exercises from first steps to ultimate virtuosity.

DECEMBER, 1932: *New York*

Difficulties with Romola Nijinsky. Legal problems over her passport. Spent the day at Ellis Island. No more money. Tea with Mrs. Vanderbilt; she will help again, but for absolutely the last time. Romola is desperate. Took Vaslav's notation theory and had it photographed. Gave her back his manuscript and a copy. She says I am a thief and will sue. I apologize; we are reconciled. Privately I think I did right. Anyway, we got plastered with Ma Garrett. Another séance. Romola asked certain questions through Little Blue Bell. Whole morning in dictation. To the cemetery. In spite of everything we laughed a lot; Romola is great fun and very brave.

Having served a brief, modest, and anxious apprenticeship as amateur chronicler of Michel Fokine, I soon became attached to the wife of Vaslav Nijinsky. She came to America to support her husband (then in a Swiss sanatorium), and enthusiasm landed me as her amanuensis. For the next three years I was occupied trying to adapt her memoirs as a book and a film. I had not been permitted to see the original Russian Ballet on a stage, or Nijinsky in the flesh. But now, in service of some private personal and public historical necessity, I was able to relive in its immediate dimension the whole saga of Diaghilev's early seasons through the eyes of a principal participant.

Quite apart from ballet, the epic of Romola Nijinsky's unique, fantastic survival makes a marvelous recital. In the first days of her American adventures she met the influential agent Elizabeth Marbury, as well as Anne Morgan and Mrs. W. K. Vanderbilt. Her life was a succession of desperate ploys, built on persistence, imagination, thin air, and spiritualism. She arrived in New York with the coffin of a friend who had died in Indonesia, and saw that it was placed in a receiving vault in Woodlawn. A notable trance medium, Mrs. Eileen Garrett, was Romola's constant and intimate companion. Psychic research was an adjunct in preparing the biography of Nijinsky. Various lacunae in documentation, or anecdotes where memory failed, were filled out capaciously by consultation with an ancient Persian and his control, Little Blue Bell.

During all this my life became so trying that death held no terror. I grew increasingly fearful that Romola would precipitate herself past our terrestrial plane onto another that she deemed more promising. A part of me was living by proxy in the aura of the initial Paris seasons of the Russian Ballet. Another part was attending peculiar séances which chilled me because the tangential or fragmentary truths they even seemed (often enough) to hit upon were moderately impressive, but had no relation whatever to my own interest or experience. Hence I took the manuscript of Nijinsky's unpublished book on dance notation, which seemed to me to contain the key to unimaginable treasure, and had it secretly photographed against her continual threats to destroy it and herself. There followed a procession of lady lawyers who made me seem like a criminal ingrate, when I felt I had acted like a knight in shining armor.

Behind *all* this was the benevolent patronage of Mrs. Willy Vanderbilt, with whom I had become friends. She did not then appear so ancient, although she could easily have been my great-grandmother. She had adored Vaslav Nijinsky and relished observing late developments in his drama. I knew nothing of her own story and little about New York "society," so I later read Dixon Wecter's history for background. In her lovely house on Sutton Place, with its China-export wallpaper and a broad view of the East River, she encouraged my dreams for an "American" ballet. Later she gave us money. I gave her Wecter's book, and reading it, she told me she discovered in a footnote something she'd quite forgotten: in her youth she had been briefly engaged to Franklin Roosevelt's father.

MARCH, 1933: *New York*

To see Fred King for his scrapbooks; to Mr. Bernays for his. Reports that Hurok has bought Diaghilev's properties, and is reconstituting the Ballets Russes under de Basil's management. Depressing. This means no chance for an American ballet; all money will be siphoned off for the Russians. Fokine produced his Bacchanal (*Tannhäuser*) in a Brooklyn state armory for a benefit for White Russian charities. Scenery: a huge howitzer covered by tarpaulin. This is what ballet in America comes to.

Frederick King had been the theatrical editor of the *Literary Digest* for many years. His collection of clippings, photographs, memorabilia led to my own scavenging. His records of the American tours of the Russian Ballet provided some random accuracy for Romola's romantic portrait of Nijinsky which was finally published. Bernays had been employed by Otto Kahn to publicize the American tours following Diaghilev's appearance at the Metropolitan Opera. The Italian management controlling the Met was terrified lest the Russian somehow might exert control over the Opera, and to prevent this, systematically sabotaged the American tour upon which Diaghilev had counted to maintain his troupe away from Europe during the First World War. Otto Kahn covered the losses. Madame Nijinsky had given me a highly glamorous account of Diaghilev's world; Bernays provided a succinct record of infighting and sharp dealing which was quite another side of historical actuality. A sharper picture of what actually occurred prepared me, to a degree, for my own imminent involvement.

Following Diaghilev's death, in the early thirties succession fell upon various companies, commencing with the foundation in 1931 of Les Ballets de Théâtre Monte Carlo. The company was under the patronage of the Princess of Monaco and the direction of René Blum and Baron de Guinzbourg. Balanchine and Boris Kochno, the artistic directors, then invited Léonide Massine to join them. Portions of the former repertory were inherited, and the debut season, sparked by the triumph of Balanchine's *Cotillon* and *Concurrence*, was a resounding success. The collapse of ballet, which Diaghilev's disappearance in 1929 had at first promised, had not come to pass. Resurrection was achieved. I had no notion that there was already schism in the organization of the revived company in Monte Carlo, that Balanchine and Kochno, who to a large degree were responsible for its inception, would be leaving. Friends who had been in Paris told me of the excitement aroused by the renascent activity. I was torn between curiosity and disappointment. While I had no right to any sort of proprietary resentment, the Russians had scored again and the chances for an "American" ballet seemed to me that much further off.

JULY, 1933: *Paris*

Pavel Tchelitchev's studio. A working model for his new ballet, *Errante*, for Balanchine; seven strips of white paper. Costumes, magnificent; bodies alone, as if designed by a Renaissance draftsman, merest indication of decoration; overall nudity. He treated me like an idiot child, but was encouraging, since I was enthusiastic. He brought out recent pictures; as he said, serious work. Theater is only a game. As for Balanchine—certainly gifted, but essentially a musician. No visual sense; can't tell red from green. Diaghilev took him to a museum once—but it was hopeless. Theater is not dancing, not music, but a mad *salade russe*, which ends up where all food ends up; an amusement. It relaxes him, but not as activity for serious artists.

I was taken to Tchelitchev's studio by Monroe Wheeler, who had known him for years, from the time Gertrude Stein first interested herself in his painting, before they inevitably came to quarrel. For Diaghilev, Tchelitchev had designed the ballet *Ode* by Massine in 1928, with Nicolas Nabokov's score, in a decor which for the first time used light instead of paint, with the addition of projected films. He had survived his exile, first in Kiev and then for more years working in theater from Constantinople to Berlin, where Diaghilev first saw his work. Despite his disdain of theater, he was the theatrical wizard of his time. He used the stage as a laboratory for preparing his canvases; yet his reputation as a scenic artist would overwhelm his prestige as a painter, causing him to abandon ballet and all theater in disgust.

At our first meeting he asked me what I wanted; I told him: to create an American ballet. This was idiotic; Russian ballet has not been Russian for twenty years; there's been no French ballet for fifty; nationalism in any form is nonsense. He spoke excellent idiomatic English, laced with a heady amalgam of current slang and casual obscenity. When I exposed my big hopes and small experience, he told me not to get mixed up with Fokine or Massine; they were part of a past. If I was to persist in such folly, Balanchine was the only possible choreographer; at least he was not brainless; simply—tasteless. Tchelitchev would supply enough taste for all; this was his speciality. Balanchine had no fixed taste. Good and bad taste were equally reprehensible. Everyone had *le bon goût*; the French worst of all. They are starving from good taste, which is simply the good taste of cooks or dressmakers; *comestibilité*. It's what ruined French art: eatable taste; everything for the stomach; nothing for the mind. He invited, or rather commanded, me to come to the Champs-Élysées Theater, where Balanchine's new company was rehearsing.

JULY, 1933: *Paris*

Virgil Thomson tried to explain the wars that exist here. At the Châtelet, the Ballet Russe de Monte Carlo (under Massine) is having a big vulgar success. At the Champs-Élysées, Les Ballets 1933 under Balanchine are enjoying little popular success, but great prestige. Massine thinks Diaghilev is still alive and lives off Diaghilev's old formulae. Balanchine is musically oriented and, at the moment, music is indeed more interesting than painting; except for two stage designers who prefer to be considered as painters, Tchelitchev and Christian Bérard, both appropriated by Balanchine. Also, he's latched on to Bert Brecht and Kurt Weill, fashionable German exiles with Communist leanings now supported by Parisian society. Virgil knows of my interest in an "American" ballet, but he made clear the importance of money: whose money? how much? how certain? Balanchine, for example, seems currently to have an unlimited amount and throws it around like a drunken sailor, but his source is English and they never patronize anything for long. There is no future for him; for Massine there's a big financial future—not alone in Europe; more so in America.

No one has understood the politics of lyric theater, painting, or musical institutions as well as Virgil Thomson. His intelligence is analytical, surgical, cheerful, realistic; it is optimistic in spite of an unsentimental manner which is the passionate reverse of enthusiastic. Instruction from him let me see many factors in depth; his portraits of persons were objective and unromantic; his attitude toward the plans for a company I hoped one day to form, helpful and cautious. He paid me the compliment of assuming that what I declared I wished to do could be done. In Paris I was dazzled by theatrical activity which for the first time I saw at first hand. He undazzled me. He revealed the skull beneath the skin of personages whom I tended to take on trust from their reputation. He showed me many ways to do what I wanted.

I did not have enough cash of my own to do much but travel. My father had humored me in providing partial support for *Hound & Horn*, a magazine with which I was no longer involved, since it had been largely taken over by men with a more genuine interest in abstract ideas than I would ever possess. I never thought of myself as an intellectual, but as an artist or athlete. Virgil's insistence on money gave me the opportunity to decide whether I was serious like him, or silly like my cousin Nat Woolf.

Actually, I had an ally as far as money went—an ambivalent, unwilling, but generous friend, also my classmate in college. It was he who made my presence in Paris and my conversations with Thomson and Tchelitchev not entirely irrelevant. Edward Warburg was the youngest son of Felix Warburg, an old friend of my father's and a business associate of Otto Kahn's. Felix, himself a distinguished amateur and patron of the arts, had a particular interest in Italian tempera panels, Rembrandt etchings, German *Lieder*, and chamber music. In our freshman year of college Eddie and I found ourselves living in the same dormitory, on different floors of Gore Hall. His friends were flashier than mine—boys who made good clubs and good grades. Lacking a vocation, he early found one, that of clown. Overshadowed by powerful parents and three older brothers, he discounted his own genuine qualities, playing at mimic and jester in the theater of his own life. Later he would teach for a while, but his true genius was for the organization and implementation of charity and philanthropy.

Eddie Warburg commenced generously with me on a small scale, which was then an enormous help. His later large support permitted us to make promises that led to first steps without which nothing could have followed. Forcing him as hard as I could, and gaining five years' support, I finally exhausted his patience and interest. Thirty years later on the few occasions when we met, we would greet each other effusively, even apologetically, as if we had both been involved in a mutual disaster which good manners alone could patch up by forgetfulness of what had actually happened. And much of the first years of our joint venture was indeed disaster. Eddie endured failure with grace; he was bullied, abused, ridiculed; he was made unhappy, not willfully by either Balanchine or me, but rather by circumstances in the historical process of our venture. In any case, when I had nowhere near enough money of my own, he let me use much of his. This made it easier to think of approaching George Balanchine with a bit of conviction.

But how was I to get to Balanchine? What, concretely, might I offer? There was little to be done before his own season opened, but now I had the good counsel of Virgil Thomson, Monroe Wheeler, and soon enough, Tchelitchev. Also, we had formed a shadow plan which promised some amorphous stability, although it was roughly designed and weakly supported. A. Everett Austin (Chick to his friends) was building a new wing on the Hartford Atheneum, of which he was director, having been appointed as soon as he finished training at the Fogg Museum under Edward Forbes and Paul Sachs. He had a passion for theater, included a charming small stage and auditorium in his new building, and for the gallery, purchased Serge Lifar's collection of sketches for the most important Diaghilev ballets. Chick and I conceived the notion that Hartford—or at least his museum—would be the perfect place to install a ballet school and a ballet company which might eventually serve a nation. Nothing could have been further from actuality, as it happened, but with Eddie Warburg's guarantee of at least two years' help toward putting us on an institutional basis in a respected public museum, I was given two tools powerful (and dangerous) enough to hoist us with our own petard.

The closer I found myself to the furnace of activity, stoked by various characters and situations attached to the immediate production of ballet, the more intoxicated I became. Using the flimsiest support as my strongest arm, I involved or precipitated Warburg, Austin, and myself with a blind conviction and impersonation of authority which should have surprised us all had I retained any objective insight. Both Warburg and Austin were in America; communication was by ship or letter. I took this as an excuse and told myself I had a free hand to act, although there was no condition or principle upon which negotiation could proceed. I had not even spoken to Balanchine, who had absolutely no notion of my existence. I knew that for a meeting I could count on Tchelitchev, who in some occult way seemed to become our third partner. He had been intimate with Gertrude Stein, Virgil Thomson, Monroe Wheeler, and other Americans; he felt his own future would be in New York, and he was right. His judgment was not hasty, and he thought nothing, including my ambitions, impossible. In more ways than one his ardent instinct made them probable.

JULY, 1933: *Paris*

Dress rehearsal of *Les Sept Péchés Capitaux* at the Champs-Élysées Theater. Wonderful scenery by Caspar Neher. Lotte Lenya and Tamara Toumanova in a doubled singing-and-dancing lead. Edward James afraid of anti-Communist (or, Virgil says, anti-Semitic) demonstrations. Tchelitchev furious because rehearsals of *Errante* are delayed by (needless) elaboration of Neher's decor. Threats of postponement. James is demoralized, interested only in ballets in which Tilly Losch (his wife) appears. If it were not for Dimitriew nothing would be accomplished. Balanchine stays invisible. I never know where he is, since he is never onstage.

After Diaghilev's death, Balanchine worked for films and Sir Charles B. Cochran's popular revues in London, but even Maynard Keynes was unable to obtain a permanent work permit for him. Had he stayed, he might well have been involved in the birth of that company which, with the developed talents and muscle of Marie Rambert, Ninette de Valois, and Frederick Ashton, resulted in the Royal Ballet. Instead, he became ballet master for a season with the Royal Danes in Copenhagen and was then offered the Paris Grand Opéra. There was even talk of his joining Anna Pavlova in America, to invent dances that would somehow be updated versions of *The Dying Swan*.

At the end of 1932 (I had no notion of how it all came about) Balanchine and Boris Kochno, having initiated the Monte Carlo successor to Diaghilev's company, found themselves dismissed. The new power was one Vasily Grigorevich Voskresensky, promoting himself as "Colonel Vasily *de* Basil," an ex-military policeman whose approach to theater combined the ablest features of desk-sergeant and huckster. Not for him a wan career as taxi driver as it was for many other White Russian émigrés. He parlayed muscular shrewdness into an egregious but solid position as successor to a truly princely impresario. As the poor man's Diaghilev he has his niche in theatrical history through the thirties and forties. Like most policemen he believed control is superior to creation. Balanchine already had his fill of such discipline. Diaghilev's benevolent or malevolent despotism had been, however, a valued education. The young dancer and choreographer had also endured long apprenticeship under the strictures of Serge Grigoriev, the ex-dancer who was Diaghilev's regisseur, and whose omnivorous memory held the relics of Diaghilev's repertory for de Basil's manipulation. I could hardly have known it, but my two firmest allies in attracting Balanchine to America were de Basil and

Grigoriev. Without them and their insistence on a ferocious commercial policy, I would never have seemed to offer Balanchine that total license which, while wholly meaningless, promised whatever liberty means to an idealist.

When Balanchine and Kochno quit the patronage of Paris and Monte Carlo, they determined to build a proper company of their own, in apostolic succession from their lost leader. They proposed to perpetuate Diaghilev's reckless caprice, passion for novelty, and disdain of failure. Having exhausted what money they first found, they were momentarily rescued by Coco Chanel, Diaghilev's old and generous friend. After spending her money to recruit a company of very young, unknown, and brilliant dancers, Kochno found Edward James. But the kind of venture capital on which investors hardly expected to receive a return, to say nothing of a profit, was forthcoming only for de Basil. However, James enabled Balanchine to bid farewell to Europe—for nearly twenty years—in a style of which Diaghilev might have been proud.

Edward James was the diminutive, supple, and elegant heir of Mrs. Willy James, one of Edward VII's most preferred hostesses. It was he who was now backing Balanchine's Ballets 1933, partly for his wife, Tilly Losch, a lovely Viennese who had been the dancing partner of the mime Harald Kreutzberg. James was in the tradition of monumental English eccentrics whose manias, taste, and money have enriched the mythology of art patronage since the eighteenth century. He had now come into a fortune derived from his father's collection of worldwide railroad stocks. In West Deane, his Sussex house, the marble entrance hall was hung with a hundred antlers. On one wall was the gold button which King Edward had pressed to release an electrical impulse signaling the completion of the Canadian-Pacific Road.

Vladimir Dimitriew, whose name was new to many, presumably served as Balanchine's "manager." A former secondary basso from the Maryinsky Opera, he had in 1924 organized their common flight from Leningrad. During Diaghilev's life, he had settled for a new career as photographer. More recently he had taken over Balanchine's affairs. Methodical, hard, strong, honest, professional, courageous, he did much to madden Edward James, but also to launch the season. It was clearly indicated that if ever I

was to reach Balanchine, it must be through Dimitriew. Tchelitchev hated him, while granting his usefulness. After the Revolution he had been a croupier in a gambling casino. I would come to
fear him, to admire him, even to be fond of him. At that time he
seemed merely one more, possibly the worst, obstacle.

But the actual performances of the ballets were a parade
of brilliant artistic successes, notably Tchelitchev's *Errante* (for
Tilly Losch) and Christian Bérard's *Mozartiana* for Tamara
Toumanova, then a sixteen-year-old baby ballerina whom Balanchine had discovered in a White Russian school the year before. In
addition to the collaboration of Brecht and Kurt Weill, André
Derain made two of his most beautiful scenic investitures for *Les
Songes* and *Les Fastes*. Night after night there were premieres
which were the epitome of Parisian advance-guard taste of that
particular vintage year—1933. The essence of one ephemeral season was distilled and sprayed about, like an expensive, novel, and
fastidious scent over a capricious public expressly primed for it. A
wholly Parisian phenomenon, it could never have been repeated
with anything approaching its original panache in any other town.
When the ballets were taken to London, Edward James would be
chagrined by their lack of comparable éclat. He would miss Perret's
beautiful theater, designed for dancing, as well as a snob public
which could be excited to argue about new ideas and unknown
dancers.

Les Ballets 1933 was my veritable introduction into Russian
ballet. It would be the model for our American venture, and no
very logical or sensible one. What the median international audience would pay for was what it remembered or could properly
project from Diaghilev seasons; this is precisely what Colonel de
Basil, Massine, and the Ballet Russe de Monte Carlo provided
for the next two decades. That I then scarcely foresaw. I was too
ardent in my enthusiasm for Balanchine, enhanced by concrete
examples he now gave night after night of his fantasy and ceaseless
invention. Everything he did spoke for the present, of immediacy,
by surprise, with brilliance: for 1933. There was a magical transference of private caprice onto a public platform. Studio talk and
studio planning were projected in a heroic dimension, far larger
than life. Everything was intensified through the physicality of the
dancing itself, through the power, athletics, and lyricism of ballet's

language. This was where I wanted to live. This was what I wanted to do; here I was learning how it should be done.

To Tchelitchev's, to tell him how wonderful *Errante* had been. He cut me short and said that half was Balanchine. No real dancers; no chance for magic, like films could make. But with little, a great deal can be done if analyzed; the chief thing is analysis; relationship of everything visual to earth, air, fire, and water. *Errante* was made out of air, fire, and light; nothing of earth. As for Balanchine, his is a complex case. A Georgian, half Moslem, half orthodox, essentially oriental. He has TB in one lung, will die in three years, and adores girls; this is important since The Dance is Woman—Terpsichore, *La Danse*. I said something about Nijinsky. "Pfui, you're another one in love with Nijinsky. He wasn't man, or woman. He was an intelligent bird; not about earth, about air. He couldn't stand earth. He tried. *Le Sacre* finished him. Too much earthiness. He flew; not a man but an angel; sent for a time. Not sick; he wished to leave. Earth's no place for saints or angels." Much about Diaghilev; I can't repeat it to Romola Nijinsky or use it for her book. Although Balanchine likes girls, his is an angelic vision; dancers are sent (like Toumanova) for his purpose. He has a normal advantage in liking earth (the world). Diaghilev said of all the boys he'd known, Balanchine had imagination most like Nijinsky's; that is, his province was plastic movement, conquest of air in space by time. Did I know any mathematics? I got into college by memorizing the first five books of Euclid. "You are illiterate; you understand nothing without geometry. *Apollon* was non-Euclidean geometry. My dee-ar boy; if you want to make ballet—take Balanchine. Only possible with him. No one else—now." But what if he dies in three years? In God's hands. Exhausted, I wanted to leave. "But why you have to go? I have not finished your lesson." I had some sort of rendezvous; some sexy affair? No; only Virgil Thomson promised to take me to Bébé Bérard, whose painting and decor I admired. Tchelitchev produced an approximation of (real?) rage. If I liked Bérard I was not a serious person. Bérard took opium, was a friend of Cocteau's (a disease in itself), an amateur's miscarriage of Aubrey Beardsley, good only for perfume makers and couturieres. If I went to see Bérard, I need not see Tchelitchev again. However, I left and met Bérard; it was worth it.

Pavel Tchelitchev has suffered from an ambiguous reputation. In life and after, he was admired, feared, and envied as a ferocious wit and fantastic decorator. Since he was a sworn enemy of official Surrealism, he never shared in the scandal or prestige of its politics as a clique or academy; yet his free-floating, serious, whimsical rhetoric fatally suggested some likely connection. It accentuated a systematic derangement of the senses, as he said, *sur mesure et par commande*, fantasy by formula, hysteria on demand; substructures touched the rational and metaphysical, while academic Surrealism "comes out of the tube; lies flat on the brush." His huge allegorical *Hide and Seek* in New York's Museum of Modern Art is the canvas which (after Picasso's *Guernica*) is most purchased in reproduction. When young students ask for it, however, they refer to it more often than not as "that picture, you know—about Life," rather than remembering the name of its artist.

Tchelitchev was an aristocrat who had long become a citizen of world capitals, a magician with a phenomenal gift of digital mastery and verbal invention. His sole mistress was, as he said, Mrs. Nature, a metaphor appropriated from him by Wystan Auden, his friend and admirer. In an age of haphazard improvisation, his fantasy fed continually on vividly observed anatomies of animal, vegetal, mineral, and celestial worlds. To be sure, he was "impossible"; he loved impossible colors—the gorgeous chromatics of sunsets, autumn leaves, orchids, jewels, and hummingbirds. He liked dancers and loved to dress them, chiefly by undressing them, but cared little for their dancing once he'd costumed them for the stage. He respected Balanchine but lamented his disinterest in the visual—except for three-dimensional plasticity. He adored the painting of the past; his ideal was the arcane imagery and superrational composition of Andrei Rublev, Piero della Francesca, and Mikhail Vrubel, whom he considered his master.

In spite of personal brilliance, or perhaps due to it, Tchelitchev never promoted his own gift with that seriousness which is a commercial requirement for negotiable success. He was thought to spend too much time on fashionable ladies and handsome young men. He worked like a demon; the boys were his models, students, slaves, and cooks; the ladies his patrons and fashion plates. Also, dressing them relaxed and amused him as well as served him for sketches or research toward his more determined invention. Arriving in New York, he announced he would find me "the keys of the city," which I certainly lacked. In his view, the keys to that particular citadel were in the custody of Mrs. Pleydell-Bouverie, daughter of Lady Ribblesdale, who had been born Alice Astor. He painted a penetratingly melancholy picture of her, which frightened her so much that it was found only after her death. As in many of his portraits, he saw deeply into character with an uncomfortably prophetic or X-ray eye. In time she became our ballet company's important friend and patron, but by then Tchelitchev had removed himself to more impersonal, private, enigmatic preoccupations, far from theater, fashion, and our world.

JULY, 1933: *London*

With Romola, from Holland, after failing to finish Nijinsky's biography. Arnold Haskell will help us find a publisher. The opening of Ballets 1933 at the Savoy. Romola says it is like a school performance compared with the best Diaghilev season. Rumors about Edward James suing Balanchine. Romola will bring me to Balanchine. At Hungaria Restaurant, she said it might be a good idea for her to marry Serge Lifar and star him in a film about Nijinsky, which would sell the book and support Vaslav in the sanatorium. Balanchine's in love with Tamara Toumanova; her mother thinks she is too young (sixteen) to marry; besides, Balanchine will not live long. Romola gave me a sealed envelope with the date of his death, provided by Ma Garrett via Little Blue Bell.

The considerable Parisian success of Les Ballets 1933 was not repeated in London. The Savoy Theater did not have either the cachet of historical association or the physical apparatus of Le

Théâtre des Champs-Élysées. English audiences were not as coherent socially or as advanced in artistic taste as the French. The
tension in management was no help. If anything pleased Edward
James more than patronizing artists, it was suing them. He was so
aroused by legal excitement that he was quite capable of hiring two
sets of lawyers to sue each other in a case for which he would
ultimately pay all costs. He scarcely promised much as a stable
influence. The very name of his company, attached as it was to a
single year's date, guaranteed no succession nor much future. All
was not well between his wife and him, and while I could not know
half of these factors, they were preponderant in Balanchine's final
decision.

I finally met Balanchine, in the kitchen of a house leased for
the London season by Kirk Askew, an excellent art dealer whom I
knew from Harvard. I made a headlong onslaught; what Balanchine thought of an anonymous youth who in exaggerated desperation proposed an entire future career in half an hour, he did not
say, except that he must think it over. I consoled myself that, at
the least or most, it was not absolutely impossible. He was not in
the best of health and had no personal security whatever. But since
we had met, he now knew of another possibility. Also, he owned
half the repertory of the 1933 company as his share. I was not then
aware that he had a mentor and partner in Vladimir Dimitriew.

LATE JULY, 1933: *London*

Batts Hotel, Mayfair. Tea, a lively revival of Edwardian life.
Three debutantes from the West Riding, with plumes in their
hair, dressed for presentation at court, resembling ballerinas in
Balanchine's *Cotillon*, as dressed by Bérard. Waited from four-
thirty to six in rising apprehension. He arrived at six, tired. His
first dancer was ill; he would have to perform tonight. He was not
in practice. He was disarmingly frank. There was little in Europe
to hold him. As for the Paris Grand Opéra, this could go to Lifar.
As for de Basil's Ballet Russe de Monte Carlo, it was Diaghilev's
repertory. He had offers from film and commercial theater; these
were not ballet. On my part, I offered only a steamship ticket, and

the possibility of the Hartford museum. He was polite and remote; we could meet again. I wrote long letters to Chick Austin
and Eddie Warburg, more enthusiastic than honest.

From Warburg I obtained money for steamship fares. From
Austin I extracted guarantees ensuring immigration and the legal
right for two aliens to be employed in educational capacities. I now
met Vladimir Dimitriew, whom I found to be Balanchine's self-
appointed agent and manager, twice Balanchine's age. With him
was Kyra Blank, a charming ballerina; with Balanchine must come
Pierre Vladimirov. (Vladimirov was the eminent dancer who followed Nijinsky at the Maryinsky Theater, and married Felia
Doubrovska, one of the last of Diaghilev's soloists, and a graduate,
with Alexandra Danilova and Balanchine, of the old Imperial
School.) Teachers, after all, were necessary to form a school and
company. This was far more than I'd anticipated, although I could
see its sense. Balanchine was exhausted after the Paris and London
seasons; he needed rest. Dimitriew had little confidence that I
would do much; with these additions to our roster, my initial enthusiasm somewhat declined.

Dimitriew gave me the name of a town in France where they
had been invited to spend a vacation: Nègrepelisse. The name took
on an occult significance. I was to return to America; if I could
manage something effective, he would proceed with local legalities.
Nègrepelisse? What could it mean? A moor's fur cape? In the next
weeks, waking in the middle of the night, I would try to decode the
name as if it held the clue to our future.

I took Romola Nijinsky to the seashore, delivered her to Arnold
Haskell, who, having completed her biography, arranged for its
English publication. In New York, I went straight to White Plains,
where, on a tract of land as large as a duchy, the Warburgs held
state in considerable grandeur. Armed with photographs of the
1933 dancers, I tried to sell Eddie on the absolute necessity of
Balanchine's immediate importation. His father, a sympathetic,
urbane, grizzled gentleman, received me courteously. The fantasy
of ballet was within the realms of his imaginings, if not of his
interest. There were, after all, pretty young girls involved.

In Hartford, I was welcomed with understanding and excitement by Chick Austin, who understood exactly what I was talking

about and who promptly devoted himself to making the entire improbable plan come true. He showed me the new wing of his museum, of which he had been the virtual architect. It was at the time one of the most progressive designs in the United States, severe, elegant, with a surprising combination of contemporary rectilinearity and a splendid baroque marble fountain splashing in an open central court. In his own office each wall and the ceiling were painted in a contrasting color, then a shocking innovation, borrowed from the Bauhaus. He had just purchased excellent examples of those new painters whose work I had seen in Paris, including Bérard, Dali, the brothers Berman, and Tchelitchev. His small theater, with murals by Kristians Tonny, would be (to my eye) perfect for ballet performances. Austin's own house, which he had designed himself, was a delightful Palladian villa set in a site very like a Brenta canalscape. His generosity and excitement made everything seem not only easy but inevitable.

But what was happening in Nègrepelisse? Rumor flew as to the imminent arrival of de Basil's Ballet Russe, as well as Serge Lifar's personal company. When these loomed as threats on our horizon, I did not have the generosity or foresight to recognize that such importations could only familiarize America with an alien art, that only after considerable exposure to ballet as appreciated in Europe could this country be willing to accept any kind of indigenous effort.

With the ostensibly secure backing of Hartford as an institutional anchor, Warburg seemed disposed to guarantee the full amount of money needed. He was willing to head a corporation, which ensured a legal entity. Nègrepelisse was notified. Dimitriew's telegrams were succinct; he insisted on rigorous conditions, but these were not exorbitant. They were mainly about security in the eventuality of failure, and a return trip to Paris.

NOVEMBER, 1933: *Hartford*

Two Italian sisters who keep a dancing school gave an interview to the *Courant* saying that bread is being snatched from their mouths by Bolsheviks. They attacked Chick Austin for making tax-exempt premises available for a nontaxable enterprise in order to put them out of business. The last straw. Dimitriew and Balanchine announce they're leaving for New York (probably Paris); Chick has spent considerable on lawyers, public relations, etc., all of which might damage his position as director of the museum. Thank God we have money in escrow to ship the Russians back to Paris. Also, Balanchine is coughing badly and only consents to see a wisewoman, who bleeds him with leeches. In despair I called Warburg, who asked me to White Plains. His father was extremely pleasant.

Dimitriew and Balanchine had, between them, decided not to return to Europe come Hell or high water. However, they had hardly left that continent to immure themselves in Hartford, Connecticut. As for myself, I had precipitated a first formal failure and, worse, seemed to betray a friend. I had promised Chick Austin some real issue for all his guarantees of institutional bulwarks. I had never questioned that Balanchine would be anything but content in a provincial American landscape. I had not foreseen the angry reaction which intrusion of foreigners would provoke.

When crisis came, I ran off to New York with my Russians, leaving Austin to endure the consequences of ragged explanations, inconvenience, and humiliation, besides his own genuine disappointment. I acted as if in the military dilemma of *force majeure*. Conventional loyalty may have required another course, but here was an act of God and my historic or objective responsibility lay not to a closed past but a future possibility. Later there would be far more ambiguous and awkward failures, more serious and anxious betrayals. In the great world of power politics, money, and property, convenient legalities accommodate treachery. In the small world of theater, traitors are former friends or lovers. While ruptures seem more piercing, they are also more ephemeral. However, they cost bad nights, shabby reputations, and hard feelings.

JANUARY, 1934: *New York*

Opening the School of American Ballet, 637 Madison Avenue. Balanchine had the walls painted a gray-blue he remembers from the Imperial School. Dimitriew furious about nonaligned

mirrors. I tried to calm him down; at least, finally, we were opening. Americans don't understand the difference between amateurs
and professionals: "*Assez de dilettantisme*"; Warburg and I
are hopeless dilettantes. I anticipated some small celebration;
Dimitriew said there was nothing to celebrate but our stupidity.
About thirty kids turned up, including three boys. Balanchine's
tryout class, which I was wild to watch; Dimitriew insisted I stay
in the office and "superintend." Superintend what? His vile temper. Telephoned Father to tell him we had opened; bad connection. Passed Muriel Draper's house; her light was on. She comforted me about the Russians; they know more theater than
anyone, pretending it's important, knowing it's only play; objectivity permits expertness. They are saved by essential lack of
selfishness, knowing their selves, have a superior sense of identity,
but are more interested in the game than in personalities. Cruelty
is just another act, like love; everything is impersonation; high
camp; they act *as if* it were true. But since there is no independent, objective truth, they impose one which is their choice of
"truth." Lots about "as if"; *als ob*; she gave me Vaihinger's book.
She says Dimitriew is a typical Russian pro and I should learn
from him; I was too drunk or tired to listen.

Dimitriew had been singer and soldier, having served his czar
onstage and in the field. Personal existence had been harsh; education and orientation were Prussian, in the style of the German-
trained bureaucracy which had guided Petersburg policy. He
equated order with honesty, disorder with degeneracy and failure.
When I knew him he was already confirmed in contempt for
mankind as well as theater. Since he was in good health, he intended to make his fortune. This, through the combination of
Balanchine, Warburg, and my father, he did, and within five years.
Meantime he gave full service, educated me in many ways, laid
down governing principles for our school and company. The single
most important thing he achieved was to discover in New York a
young Russian girl from an eminent family. Eugenie Ouroussow's
grandmother conducted one of the famous Parisian salons of the
Third Republic. As yet unmarried, Eugenie had hardly worked before. From her difficult apprenticeship as secretary and aide-de-
camp to Dimitriew, she would develop into a sagacious educator

and administrator who, within a decade, would conduct the most influential academy of dancing in America.

Dimitriew knew that I was drawn to him. He was old enough to have been my father; although we spoke French, he always called me "Boy"—when he liked me. When he didn't, he snarled: "Kirshstayn." He resembled a gray-and-white striped tiglon or liger; his method was Blake's: "Damn braces; bless relaxes." Few were ever relaxed around him, except when he judged we had had as much riddling and needling as we could take. He orchestrated or choreographed both explosions and reconciliations; he would take us to excellent Russian restaurants, to get us drunk. Before midnight tolled, Warburg or I would have signed another check, ensuring the school's existence for another few months. My father understood and admired him; since he considered me a financial idiot, there was some security in Dimitriew's unyielding penny-pinching.

What Dimitriew felt for Balanchine was mysterious. Certainly as a basis, there was comprehension and even affection; he had recognized a boy's talent long before Diaghilev. But when Balanchivadze turned into Balanchine, Dimitriew's attitude became ambivalent. Caring nothing for dancing as such, except as a pretext for a paying profession after he had lost wife and voice during and after the First World War, he never envied Balanchine's rising reputation. What he most disliked in anyone, most of all in artists, was the element of disorder, which also comprised their freedom, but which he interpreted as willfulness, irrationality, caprice, and self-indulgence. His taste was retardative, his curiosity restricted; his energy military and exacting; his spirit cynical. He hated humanity; a primitive species. Theater was a ridiculous gloss on life's absurdity. This approach became demoralizing, despite his great abilities. We rid ourselves of each other as soon as we were able. However, he stuck to his, and our, guns and was responsible for much in our beginning which promised permanence. He grafted iron on our spines when we had none.

We found rooms for our school in a loft building where Isadora Duncan once had her studio, paid for by Paris Singer. One iron post stood stubbornly in the center of a splendid open space, but it could not be removed without the collapse of the entire three upper floors. This column assumed an extraordinary metaphorical importance; its implacable challenge to our whole future seemed to be magnetized, in its formidable uprightness and slim mineral solidity, as every possible negative threat. If it could only have been removed we would have had some eighty square feet of unencumbered floor. This was pine and could easily be patched where walls had been inset. The cost of inserting a steel beam to replace the post was prohibitive. Engineers found no solution; Balanchine was determined that he needed the whole open area. We had put a down payment on the lease of the rooms; letterheads had been printed; we had announced our date of opening. Now we were halted by this single intransigent cast-iron pillar. It was one more in an acceleration of last straws following us since the debacle in Hartford. But a week before we were due to open, Dimitriew went early to the building and tapped the walls. One which we had assumed to be a retainer proved a much later addition. It could be removed, giving us necessary space, although with a slightly different disposition of rooms. Dimitriew installed a movable wall between two studios, so that while one room served as a fairly large performing area, the other could seat a small audience. Thus he would solve various insoluble problems with imagination, efficiency, and dispatch.

I did not pretend to be a ballet student, as formerly with Fokine; however, I took parts of enough classes to understand something of what was required to school a professional. Under Dimitriew's tutelage, I also enrolled as a student of management. When he saw that I subordinated myself to his will and direction, all was well. When Warburg and I felt we were merely being used, and crassly at that, there were tense moments and wounded feelings. These were the times when Dimitriew feasted us and got us tipsy.

Balanchine would tell us Arabian Nights tales of the court of Diaghilev as seen from the slaves' quarters. He had never been as much an intimate as Nijinsky, Massine, or Lifar; he had not been a member of the informal secretariat like Boris Kochno and, earlier, Nouvel, Bakst, and Benois. As for Dimitriew, after bringing Balanchine from Russia to Berlin and superintending his entrance into Les Ballets Russes, he'd become a photographer and led his own life.

Dimitriew was a burden, but among several of his proverbs, he often quoted: "God gives the Cross and strength to bear it." He found in New York the possibility of survival on a scale superior to Paris; he risked a present toward future retirement. He had no money; our parents were rich; we could afford varieties of folly and disorder, ballet being the most insistent. An important aspect of his service was to prevent waste, but we bridled under his yoke. As for Balanchine, he was too occupied with the immediate business of inventing dancers and designing dances to worry much about day-to-day disasters, which were often Dimitriew's didactic exercises. He was making a new life for himself in a new world, feeling independence and possibility. Together we all moved toward some sort of student demonstration, as prelude to the formation of a professional producing company.

MARCH, 1934: *New York*

Work started on our first ballet at an evening "rehearsal class." Balanchine said his brain was blank and bid me pray for him. He lined up all the girls and slowly commenced to compose, as he said—"a hymn to ward off sin." He tried two dancers, first in bare feet, then in toe shoes. Gestures of arms and hands already seemed to indicate his special quality. When I reported this to Dimitriew in his office, he growled: *"Je ne sais rien du tout,"* calculated to crush my too ready approval. Did I know how it would turn out? Balanchine also had his failures; it's not the role of a director to license unproven work. Son of a bitch.

Serenade, to Tchaikovsky's piece for stringed orchestra, was originally devised as an exercise to demonstrate the difference between classwork and theatrical dances for the advanced girls' division in our school. Balanchine's initial choreography in America, it was also an analysis in depth of those elements then available, upon which we might build a company. Later he would invent many plotless works, but he had done nothing like this for either Diaghilev, the Royal Danes, or Edward James. A possible exception was *Apollon,* which, however, had a vague narrative pretext and no corps de ballet. *Serenade* possessed a loose narrative line embedded in the music, but it was more atmospheric or suggestive than logically narrative. There was a central male figure supporting three girl soloists who involved themselves with one another in a linked series of tender, amorous, fractured, or fatal episodes. Yet, rather than any plot, it evoked an ambience in which passion was expressed, denied, or transcended in rupture or loss. It was, in fact, an "abstract" ballet, the most intensely romantic and architectural of its genre since Fokine evolved *Les Sylphides* in 1909 from the earlier *Chopiniana*, which itself derived from a situation corresponding to our own—a schoolroom, or an academic recital projected toward repertory theater.

Balanchine commenced by lining up as many girl students as chanced to be in class on March 14, 1934. On that day there were seventeen. These he placed in military order according to height. One more, a tiny but brilliant dancer (Leda Anchutina, later married to André Eglevsky), slipped into the studio late, a few minutes after he had begun to compose. Her tardy entrance was incorporated, framing her as a first dancer, which, an advanced Fokine pupil, she decidedly was, perhaps the most capable of whom we could boast. At the next rehearsal only nine girls appeared; at another, only three. For them he arranged other portions of action, exactly as if they had been especially summoned and scheduled. The ballet was structured piecemeal, with no time wasted and no energy spent lamenting the nonappearance of individual dancers. Rehearsals were as much lessons as sessions toward composition and repetition. While the purpose was certainly eventual performance, no date was set; we were all too occupied with day-to-day maintenance to consider any definite time for public exposure.

Serenade thus was woven from chance. Given the traditional academic language, which Balanchine employed here in a rare transliteration without inversion, deformation, or parody, he now fitted patterns from his analysis of the music onto a formal sequence largely governed by accident. It was not precisely improvisation, but rather a control or ordering of chance. Recently there has been an aesthetic vogue for an empirical method based on aleatory devices, the throw of dice and coins, the rules of I-Ching. It is a projection of accidental "happenings" intended to seduce audiences into closer identification with fictive acts, or more intimate participation in experiencing them. But this is a reactionary program or polemic, a confusion of art with life. Masters over such ceremonies pretend to act in a godlike capacity, ordaining a "fate" and suspending logical causality, a method which is presupposed as irrelevant, inconsequential, hence presumably piquant. It is not a useful device for those who live by the bloodbank of repertory seasons. In ballet, improvisation, as in *Serenade*, may initially push toward invention, but only on a substructure of an established idiom, and only until the choreography is set. After that, brilliant interplay between acrobatic dancers is too hazardous for the intervention of any untimed or unforeseen surprise. In the "modern" dance, aleatory techniques supplement the gamesmanship of unvirtuosic performers who attempt to substitute shock for structure. More often than not this is only a spry and hopeful simulacrum of steady, lasting, and genuine invention.

A girl tripped and fell in rehearsal, close to the end of *Serenade*'s first movement. This accident Balanchine kept as a climactic collapse by which a genuine minor mishap became a permanently framed controlling excitement, a contribution precipitating but by no means perpetuating chance. At the start no boys were available; when five eventually appeared, three were used. At the start the chief solo role was shared among five girls; parts of it were later combined for a single soloist. There were also numerous novelties of pattern and plastic structure, although the ballet was as much a primer for our pupils as it was a demonstration of economical procedure. In the *pas de trois* there was a device by which a girl, supported by a crouching boy half hidden by her voluminous skirts, seemed to revolve on pointe in slow motion, as if balanced by her own extraordinary tension in control. Asymmetrical units of shifting dancers seesawed in contrapuntal accord; a solo dancer, holding a half of the stage, was echoed by a unison group in unlikely opposition. The prime quality of *Serenade* from the moment of its inception was cool frankness, a candor that seemed at once lyric and natively athletic; a straightforward yet passionate clarity and freshness suitable to the foundation of a non-European academy. Balanchine had not seen Isadora Duncan in her best days, but she had certainly affected Fokine, and one might detect a strain of her free-flowing motion here.

When the curtain rises, the corps de ballet, in a strictly geometric floor plan, are seen as a unison platoon standing at guard rest—or actually, in the first of the five academic positions which are successively assumed in the initial twenty measures of the music. Hands are curved to shield their eyes, as if facing some intolerable lunar light. At the first rehearsals all arms were stiffly raised, but since Eddie Warburg imagined that this resembled the *Heil, Hitler* arm-thrust salute, Balanchine altered it to a more curvilinear, tentative, and vague fanfare of indeterminate gesture.

At this time I had been instructing myself in the basic principles of three-dimensional plasticity, standing as a model for the sculptor Gaston Lachaise, who had also carved a very fine rose-pink alabaster head of Warburg. Lachaise had chosen the identical annunciatory arm gesture which, quite by accident, seemed to be a visual pun on the Nazi greeting. I did not speak of this, although now it was in my mind, but one morning when I came into Lachaise's studio, I noticed that he had removed the right arm from its socket. Later he revised its angular thrust to the same degree as in the ballet. Certain gestures, their mutants or variants, seem to be inlaid in or summoned from the texture of historic incident. Mussolini's public stance had its precedent in D'Annunzio's operatic Byzantine histrionics. The language of gesture may possess visual metaphors, puns, or correspondences which contain subconscious or unconscious connotations arousing very different reactions—reactions quite apart from the intention of choreographers.

APRIL, 1934: *New York*

Dimitriew announced at a "meeting," summarily called, that the School of American Ballet is a *total désastre*; no publicity; not enough students or enough scholarships to attract whatever good dancers exist. Their training is so various that they look as if they are speaking in different accents. Americans are not accustomed to work. Balanchine is interested only in pianos, automobiles, and girls. Warburg is not serious. I am greedy, interested in something produced onstage which must take years and then may be no good. If he had known what he knows now, he'd never have left Europe. Insists on seeing Eddie's father—and mine. Called him in Boston; too busy to talk. Explained (?) everything to his secretary.

From the start Dimitriew made a clear distinction between *the* school and *a* company. In order to toss two separate bones to two different pups, he began to assign school to me, company to Warburg, although our functions continued to overlap. Whatever a school cost, he knew a company would cost more, and Eddie's father seemed a more solid resource than mine. Also, Dimitriew wished to focus our interests and energies on single definite targets rather than let enthusiasm range widely and result in little. He imposed the school on me; actually, he (with Eugenie Ouroussow) ran it and (with Balanchine) the fledgling troupe. In a few years he withdrew from both; our respective fathers made it possible for us to buy him out. I would see him less. His second wife, Kyra Blank, an excellent teacher and good dancer, died. He became a misogynist, his lonely, immaculate apartment empty of love or interest. Depression was his climate and habit—a heavy drug; yet his integrity was unquestionable. My father believed in him, appreciating his efforts to force me into a simulacrum of a solid businessman. My father was remote; communications were siphoned through secretaries; he kept a file on each of his children; papers referring to us held more meaning for him than what we actually did. Ballet for him hardly promised a necessary future, but perhaps, or largely, through Dimitriew's status *in loco parentis*, instead of withdrawing aid to the school, he increased it.

JUNE, 1934: *White Plains, New York*

All morning, trying to redeem the stage, after yesterday's washout. Removed tarpaulins; pools of water; everything soaked. Mr. Warburg inspects the catastrophe and makes jokes; light mist until noon; then sun. No notion whether or not anyone would come back tonight. Quite a few turned up; performance

went better than I would have expected. Estlin Cummings a big
help, morally; he made us laugh. Afterward, a party in the garage.
Dimitriew blows up; ghastly scene.

June, 1934, was doubtless no rainier than average. Months before, we had scheduled a demonstration-debut for our putative
"American Ballet," to take place on the grounds of the Warburg
estate in White Plains. Dimitriew designed a bare pine dancing
floor for the open air. Rain drenched the announced first night; the
second was no distinguished debut for an ambitious venture. Our
one performance was cautiously announced as a "demonstration,"
yet we could not help hoping it might kindle a brush fire which, in
no time, would ignite into a full-fledged company. Three ballets
were presented, two from Les Ballets 1933 which had been brought
over from Paris as part settlement in the termination of Edward
James's venture. *Mozartiana*, handsomely decorated by Christian
Bérard, incorporated some of Balanchine's most mysterious and
touching psychological ambiguities capitalizing on the fragility of
postadolescent performers. *Les Songes* borrowed the atmosphere of
Alice in Wonderland for a series of infantile nightmares. André
Derain designed splendid costumes, including an enormous fringed
rat in which Balanchine was amused to appear on several occasions.
Serenade opened the program.

I was then seeing much of Estlin Cummings, more widely
known as the poet e. e. cummings. My dream was to employ poets
as instigators, as had Diaghilev. I felt we needed our own particular
Cocteau; cummings was a willing candidate. In Paris the summer
before, he had warned me about my flirtation with theater and
with those types whom he named "Rooskies." I had published the
first chapters of his journal to Sovietland (*EIMI*) in *Hound &
Horn*. Now I commissioned him to write a libretto for a
choreodrama based on *Uncle Tom's Cabin*, which in ignorance or
innocence I decided would make the perfect plot for an "American" ballet. Eddie Warburg paid Ben Shahn, who was then
emerging as an easel painter, to make attractive sketches for
scenery and costumes.

When I read Balanchine what Estlin had written, translated
into demotic French, he said it might well be splendid prose or
even poetry, but there were no pretexts therein for dancing. He

recalled that Boris Kochno, Diaghilev's secretary, who had pretensions as a poet, used to provide suggestions for choreography or,
rather, scenes which might serve as libretti. In these rough
schedules there would be always one number labeled "*Promenade.*"
However, Kochno never specified what would actually take place
during this promenading. Ostensibly—"just" plain dancing. In the
eighteenth century, professional French ballet composers mastered
a craft justifying their abstract music. This was the craft of *faire
entrer les danses*—how to introduce pure dancing logically into
what preceded and followed mimic action. Cummings wrote a
prose-poem which has its own interest. Later it was published,
accompanied by some of Shahn's designs, with no reference to its
blighted birth. How could I ever explain to so eminent an author
that what he had written at our command was, for us, quite useless? He convinced himself that this was still another example of
atrocious Rooskie behavior. At the start, however, he was amused
to watch our tentative first steps and comment on them with feline
malice and scabrous slurs.

As for our baptism-by-fire (and rain) in the performance at
White Plains, it received its final thunderclap following a strag-
gling reception for a few well-wishers who returned for a second
night. A pleasant feast had been prepared for our company following the performance. A clean cinder-block garage was decorated
with red, white, and blue bunting; flowers and candles for every
table. Dimitriew, already exasperated by the weather, Warburg's
family retainers, and my nervousness, permitted himself one of the
grandest denunciation scenes since Chaliapin's in *Boris Godunov*.
Were artists to be fed like pigs in a barn? He had known we were
dilettantes with no comprehension of art, but were we under the
gross illusion that good artists were serfs to be served in a filthy
stable? Cummings gravely regarded this display, comparing it to
other operatic extravaganzas he had witnessed. Here, whatever our
amateurishness in performance or production, was professionalism
at a high peak. Here was spectacular behavior marvelously sparked
by Great Nature (the weather), framed in glory (the Warburg
duchy), and projected on a special audience (Eddie, Balanchine,
the dancers). Thus empires are born; enunciation of power as rage.
Bismarck forged Imperial Germany by uniting it in hate.
Dimitriew would merge us in the unity of disaster and a deter-

mined will—if he didn't kill us first. Or, as Estlin suggested, if we didn't kill him.

DECEMBER, 1934: *Hartford*

Dress rehearsal. The spiral decor designed for *Serenade* impossible to hang. This theater is pretty, but built with no space to hang scenery. Bad dress rehearsals may mean good openings; tonight's was worse than White Plains. The ballets are only echoes of what I saw in Paris. *Serenade* seems to fill whatever space it's given. At least there's no hysteria. Warburg was cheerful, delighted with costumes by John Held, Jr., for *Alma Mater*. A year ago, we left Hartford in a mess and everything seems to have turned out, if not perfectly, at least promisingly.

The debut of our "American Ballet" took place in Hartford, as we had originally anticipated, but under quite other circumstances. Patchwork and improvisation are methods of salvage; something had been eventually clamped together which roughly resembled a working organism. Chick Austin and his trustees generously forgave and forgot. Our premiere was not a disgrace; Warburg could feel that his contribution, for once, was more on the side of art than of cash. For he had successfully invented a workable pretext upon which Balanchine based dancing.

In 1934, Warburg and I were still essentially undergraduates, our tastes more or less formed by, or against, that of the Fogg Museum and its fine-arts faculty. We were aware of progressive currents in the visual arts, having founded the Harvard Society for Contemporary Art; we had handled and hung artifacts of many of the chief artists of our time, some of whom we came to know well. Through editing *Hound & Horn* I was involved at least in discussion of a number of general ideas, which commanded my awe if not much of my attention. I had few social or political prejudices or preoccupations, but I was very impressed by two models of behavior—James Cagney and T. E. Lawrence. Much moved by the British tradition of illegitimate or extralegal activity and feudal responsibility, I wrote a short essay on Lawrence's life following the

Arab revolt, and received a reply from him in his retirement. Excited by Cagney's films, I wrote another, for *Hound & Horn*. Cagney responded by coming to watch a ballet class; he had been trained as a dancer. I had notions as to which roles he should appropriate—John Paul Jones (following Melville's *Israel Potter*), Billy the Kid, Benvenuto Cellini, Studs Lonigan. Abstract concepts as exemplified by humanist, Marxist, or agrarian symposia meant little to me, but heroic types in personifications of action composed a dramatis personae for a continuous historical drama which I always found exciting. In attempting to project an "American" ballet, our dependence on native mythology may have been naïve but seemed necessary. Diaghilev himself passed through a decade of extracting color and melody from Slavic folklore with an almost scientific attitude.

So, when we first tried to discover a suitable subject for a contemporary work in an initial repertory, Warburg drew on the world he knew best and liked most, that of an Ivy League undergraduate. Just as I was under the spell of Hollywood ganglands, Arab revolt, and Diaghilev's court, he was magicked by rituals of college eating clubs, big football, and Harvard-Yale games. Forty years ago football was not only a spectator sport but, undefiled by television, a participant ceremony involving choirs of noisy partisans, tipsy old grads, orgies of organized cheerleading, song, and bathtub gin from pocket flasks. Team spirit had no commercial additive, and diminutive halfbacks, shortstops, and strokes were personal champions. While it was acknowledged, particularly by "intellectuals," that the whole athletic mythos was faintly ridiculous, it did provide a genuine and decorative atmosphere. Football formations were, in their way, elementary choreography; a cheerleader was a kind of first dancer, or could be presented as one.

Warburg's notion for a ballet was triggered by turn-of-the-century sepia photographs of football teams posed against sections of the old Yale fence, or grouped pyramidally with the year's captain displaying a pigskin inscribed with the date. We'd all read the inspirational texts of Owen Johnson and Ralph Henry Barbour in prep school. *Stover at Yale, Brown of Harvard* proposed a campy campus silliness ingrained in ritual rivalries solemnly perpetuated by generations of loyal alumni. Eddie's aim was ironic as well as comic—to satirize the synthetic idolatry of athletes and athletics

—and he would be disappointed when Balanchine grasped little if any of this special vein of humor, simply resorting to an old bag of European music-hall and circus gags and tricks.

Eddie's inventions for *Alma Mater* involved an idiotic demigod quarterback and a Salvation Army lass who turned into a *strip-teaseuse*. John Held, Jr., the Charles Dana Gibson of the Jazz Age, designed various undergraduate types in crew cuts, raccoon coats, helmets and shoulder pads, bell-bottom trousers, and flapper regalia. Balanchine was piloted to the Yale Bowl; the tactics of broken-field running, surprise plays, and drop kicks were offered to his ingenuity. We asked George Gershwin for a score. Already overoccupied with Hollywood, he suggested that his friend Kay Swift would be witty and capable, and her score triumphantly vindicated his confidence. Balanchine often said he felt like an American even before he left Leningrad, and he had used popular music for revue numbers in London.

Alma Mater was, at the least, an earnest of pious intentions toward the creation of indigenous repertory. In it we fumbled toward an expression of the male principle as athlete rather than prince or god. Balanchine had already paved the way nearly a decade before with *Apollon*, in which the Sun-Dancer played games with his muses rather than making love to them. Girl cheerleaders and baton twirlers were Atlantic City beauty queens—Miss Americas rather than fairy swan-princesses. Balanchine knew that a small-scale domestic frame was all that so slight a pretext could contain, but his carpentry made it viable, and the miniature song-less musical comedy lasted for several seasons. At the commencement of his American career, he recognized the coltish virtuosity, professional amateurism, contrived improvisation which distinguished our best popular stylishness. Prime examples were Gershwin and Cole Porter, Fred and Adele Astaire, Jimmy Cagney, and Ginger Rogers.

Alma Mater had some importance economically and even politically, because it temporarily proved to Eddie that he had uses past signing checks. Also, I imagined I saw signs and portents by which the ballet idiom might be removed from the elite or epicene European atmosphere to gain a public, not equaling but at least approaching a mass audience as something less than a snob attraction. Sooner than we then could know, Balanchine would be working in Hollywood on a film intended for George Gershwin, who would be dead before he could begin it. Thirty-five years later, however, there would be a genuine collaboration in *Who Cares?* for in that carefully contrived romp, the orchestra stays silent during a tape of Gershwin at his piano. Gershwin had appeared frequently in Diaghilev's circle abroad. Stravinsky's *Ragtime* was an early manifestation of the growing appreciation of Americana. It was Balanchine's unprejudiced catholicity in musical taste which was to give our repertory its special savor; this commenced with *Alma Mater.*

FROM THE *New York Times,* MARCH 6, 1935:

Though totally obscure, it [*Transcendence*] . . . is of far greater interest. . . . It has the quality of phantasmagoria and some of its incidents are of distinct power, but whether for straining for choreographic novelty or again because of its complete unsuitability to the talents of the company, it remains largely incomprehensible. Throughout the performance there was manifest a sense of strain. A young and inexperienced group is being pushed beyond its limits of accomplishment, and thereby the future of a promising enterprise is being seriously jeopardized.

Thus John Martin—practically the first, for four decades the most influential, dance critic in the United States, and historically the best-informed and least self-serving—analyzed our opening in New York. As Warburg had been responsible for *Alma Mater,* *Transcendence* was my responsibility, as far as pretext for decor and danced action went. I had read Sacheverell Sitwell's lyrical evocation of the career of Nicolò Paganini, the quasi-diabolical virtuoso who was a variant of, or twin to, E. T. A. Hoffmann and Franz Liszt, as wizard-performer-composer. At Weimar in 1852 Liszt published his *Études d'exécution transcendante,* in which keyboard acrobacy was pushed to its digital limits. In our early ballet tours we could never be sure of an orchestra; hence we considered music which might be played without too much loss by a two-piano team. I felt sure that Liszt-Paganini, combined as one dancer, was a suitable pretext for unlimited possibility in a musical dance-drama. Pantomime and national dances were genres lacking in our repertory. The fused figure of violinist-pianist might stand as archetype and metaphor for the wizard-performer. A male soloist's whole physique could express the power and control of fingers on ivory keys or bowed strings. In William Dollar, an advanced pupil of Fokine's who was a superb athletic classicist, we had an ideal dancer for this role.

At some central European (Hungarian? Czech? Polish?) peasant gathering, a young girl is bewitched by a wandering minstrel. Fascinated by his mad music making, she deserts her horrified fiancé on her wedding day. Then, appearing as a sinister monk, the mysterious minstrel conducts her through the black rites of a witches' sabbath. In an elaborate *pas de deux* he hypnotizes his virginal victim (a reversal of the hypnotic somnambulism of *Night Shadow* a dozen years later). She is saved at the last moment by her fiancé and his friends. The devil—for it is indeed he—is exorcised. However, at a spring festival which follows, the enchanter-minstrel revives himself as the Year-Spirit, a Jack o' the Green; with the returning April sap or energy, creativity or virtuosity is displayed as both good and bad, lucky and unlucky, ephemeral and eternal.

Ingredients were from a mixture of sources, including the Sitwell biography, Sir James Frazer's *Golden Bough*, Jessie L. Weston's *From Ritual to Romance*, T. S. Eliot, and what Romola Nijinsky had told me of *Mephisto Valse*, a ballet Vaslav prepared with Robert Edmond Jones at Bar Harbor in 1916. This waltz served as our witches' sabbath. In 1928 Bronislava Nijinska had created *La Bien-Aimée*, with music by Liszt, for Ida Rubinstein. Here, a pianist mused over his keyboard, recalling past inspiration, which in turn recalled Fokine's first version of *Les Sylphides*—the *Chopiniana* of 1908. After the massive onslaught of modernism and a canonization of contemporaneity in the middle and late twenties, radical manifestations in literature and the plastic arts, there had come a definite reaction, drawing on the Gothic, Victorian, and Edwardian neoromantics, in which Edith, Osbert, and Sacheverell Sitwell were prime movers. It coincided with centennial celebrations of Franco-German romanticism, distinguished by exhibitions of Delacroix and Géricault and renewed interest in Berlioz and Victor Hugo. *Transcendence* anticipated several works of similar taste and interest: Frederick Ashton and Cecil Beaton's *Apparitions* (to Liszt, 1936), Massine and Bérard's *Symphonie Fantastique* (Berlioz, 1936), and Fokine's *Paganini* (Rachmaninov, 1939).

Transcendence seemed to promise so much that we risked commissioning an orchestration for a small pit band from George Antheil, a young advance-guard composer. He had arrived in 1926 with his "Airplane Sonata" and *Ballet Mécanique*, in which propellers and other mechanistic effects were a precedent for much later and more developed electronic devices. He was a protégé of Ezra Pound, who had proclaimed him in a zealous pamphlet entitled "Antheil, or the Future of Harmony." A solid, small, blond, compact, permanent postadolescent, he hardly fulfilled his early heady notoriety. He all but deserted composition for a dubious career in Hollywood, not a career writing film music but one producing newspaper columns on the place of endocrine glands in the human organism. He was a professional musician, a brilliant pianist, an enthusiastic if disappointing collaborator, *bien rusé* in international musical-theater politics, one of the American vanguard, along with Marc Blitzstein, Paul Bowles, Aaron Copland, and Virgil Thomson (all of whom were to write scores for us), educated in Paris, largely under Nadia Boulanger, who would soon return to New York to employ native material.

The beautiful pen and watercolor costume designs for *Transcendence* were by Franklin Watkins (they are now in the Museum of Modern Art). His heroic murals graced the Rodin Museum in Philadelphia, and he had just won the Carnegie International painting prize. His peculiar personal quality of baroque expressionism and a stormy palette recommended itself to the subject. We found that he wished to work with dancers. I was happy with the quality of his collaboration—particularly Balanchine's Hungarian dances, the mesmerizing *pas de deux*, and William Dollar's frenetic pantomime and acrobatic classicism. Those who have seen Balanchine's *Brahms-Schoenberg Quartet* (1966), which Brahms himself could hardly have imagined without the precedence of Liszt, may find a faint echo of *Transcendence*.

In any case, this novelty, such as it was, had been created from scratch in Manhattan, with absolutely no reference to Parisian precedent. I might take satisfaction from the knowledge that it had evolved at my own suggestion, that it embodied a collaborative effort on high poetic principles, and most important, that it had got itself danced on a stage. To be sure, its libretto offered pretexts too overwhelming for our executant potential at this time. But although everyone else (starting with Balanchine) saw our performances as they transparently were, I often managed to see them as perhaps they might have been. *Transcendence*, a firstborn, remained my favorite of dozens of promising short-lived children engendered over the next thirty-five years.

MARCH, 1935: *New York*

John Martin writes in the Sunday *Times* that it might be a good idea for us to send Balanchine back to Paris, where he belongs. He says *Serenade* is serviceable rather than inspired, that *Reminiscence* was the "real delight of the evening." Nothing could make me angrier. "Here Mr. Balanchine has taken actual dances from his memories of the Russian Ballet and adapted them to his own uses. Here the real abilities of the company get their first showing. . . . On the basis of such technical discipline as is here evidenced fine things can certainly be expected in the not too distant future."

Reminiscence was planned as a ballet to end an evening, an applause-machine concocted after a tested, tasty recipe. Balanchine considers himself a carpenter, plumber, restaurant-keeper, and short-order cook. His professionalism enables him, often with surprising piquancy and variety, to resuscitate *démodé* music. Here he took a suite of dances by Benjamin Godard, whose "Berceuse" from the opera *Jocelyn* was for decades a favorite of palm-court tearoom orchestras. John Martin, covering Balanchine's choice of Brahms's *Liebeslieder Walzer* in 1960, suggested that he might next choreograph pages from a telephone directory. As an accomplished and erudite musician, Balanchine learned musical repertory the way medical students read Gray's *Anatomy*. He has not been deterred by the transient strictures of snobbish good taste. Indeed, if an individual talent, once popular, is currently in disfavor, he has often seized on it for forgotten or unsuspected excellence—as, for example, the piano pieces of Chabrier, lost symphonies of Bizet, Gounod, Ives, and Tchaikovsky; Sousa's marches, Gershwin's songs, and music expressly written for forgotten dances by Bellini, Donizetti, Drigo, and Glazunov.

To me *Reminiscence* represented everything banal, compromising, and retardative in a philosophy of what we should *not* be doing—except its execution by our dancers. It was pastiche, a concession at one remove to the Ballets Russes public, a betrayal of Diaghilev's *avant-gardisme;* ten steps backward. Its success and practical uses were incontestable. As a diploma of technical efficiency, at least, it pleased the managerial powers that would land us, sooner than we might have hoped, at the service of the Metropolitan Opera Association. However, our first New York season had its modicum of prestige success and a recognition of energy and money expended. A Russian impresario was found who agreed to arrange a tour. Warburg allowed himself some natural if unwarranted elation; the tour collapsed in Scranton, Pennsylvania. The matter of picking up pieces, restoring morale, paying bills, offered little amusement to a generous, eager, and fun-loving young man.

MAY, 1935: *New York*

With Warburg to see Edward Johnson, the Met's new general manager. I hardly believed where I was, or how I was talking. He hadn't heard of our disaster. Balanchine was at least a name to him. I explained he'd been hired by Diaghilev in 1924 to do all the opera ballets for Monte Carlo in ten days; he said this was exactly the sort of man he needed. He has ideas about reviving the Met, with some new notions. He liked the name "American Ballet"; he is a Canadian. I suggested we might give one whole ballet program a week on Sunday nights with no extra cost. He agreed. After Hartford, I thought we were finished. After Scranton, again. Suddenly here we are, serving the Met.

Edward Johnson, an ex-tenor of much grace and warmth, an excellent singing artist, was a sympathetic gentleman. My ambition had always been to represent and be supported by an established institution. I was naïve in thinking that one could be found in a year. The Met's offer was providential. We saw all sorts of possibilities, but as yet had no idea of the nature of a structure logically rooted in the routine of a repertory system, employing international singers. Here, first and last, the voice was supreme, with every other consideration secondary. Also, we had not yet encountered Edward Ziegler, Johnson's adjutant, whose experience and power made him the real master of the Met. An indigenous version of Vladimir Dimitriew, he regarded our intrusion into his precincts with a jaundiced eye. Ziegler, like so many able managers, was undeterred by personal interest in the arts, ballet least of all; his duty was to enable the Met to survive during a serious economic depression. We had hardly forgotten that the management of the Met was dominated by Italian singers, repertory, and producers, and that this family was determined to keep Diaghilev out of any permanent local presence. But we were ourselves "American," and Warburg's father was from olden times an associate of Otto H. Kahn, who with Puccini, Caruso, and Gatti-Casazza before the First World War had led the Met to surpass La Scala as the prime opera house of the world.

I fell promptly in love with the whole dusty fabric of the Met. Here history lived, as it must have for nearly a hundred years, in a genuine nineteenth-century house, a dinosaur in amber, static yet breathing. Racks filled with thousands of costumes, an armorer's shop, a wig room, shoes to fit a crusader's army corps, a carpentry shop that turned out everything from stagecoaches to ships in full sail—a hugely efficient machine to equip and produce the preposterous, merged in a heady potion to poison me further with another serious attack of red-and-gold disease. My experience so far had been in small theaters. The vast scale of the Met made me drunk. As for Balanchine, he proceeded to turn out necessary divertissements for the fourth act of *Carmen,* the second act of *La Traviata,* the Bacchanal from *Tannhäuser* with dispatch and often considerable inventiveness. We were not even a failure immediately. To him it was simply another opera house, bigger than Copenhagen or Leningrad, drearier than Paris, less productive than London, less innovative than German or Austrian theaters. Warburg and I were determined to make the best of our luck in actually being employed under such formidable auspices. We were hardly counting on Ziegler's antagonism, or Balanchine's quite different interests and ambitions. These could scarcely be reconciled; but meantime we'd found a haven that I felt was heaven. I abandoned any idea of innovation for the moment; we must show the Met how useful we could be. Night after night, whenever a ballet was included in an opera, I would be onstage, like Johnson and Ziegler, in tails and white tie, a splendid official uniform.

As a safe and modest start, Balanchine took music from *Die Fledermaus*, inserting a big waltz—a sketch, in fact, for the enlarged setting of Ravel's *La Valse* fifteen years later. I was made happy by his acceptance of one notion of my own. The eponymous *Bat* was no single dancer, but rather a girl and boy, each having one huge bat's wing of smoky, spangled China silk which, supported on bamboo armatures, collapsed or expanded, fluttering like proper wings. Balanchine invented pleasant devices; there was a gypsy interlude. A conventional piece had its satisfactory reception. We seemed to be doing what we were there for, and we were being paid as well. What could be better?

DECEMBER, 1935: *New York*

To Tchelitchev's studio, 55th Street and First Avenue. A penthouse turned into a garden. New portraits of Charles Ford and Natalie Paley. Marvelous. He says New York is now ready for him, *and* for us. Insisted I take him to the Met. Stopped the taxi to buy whiskey. He did not want to meet either Johnson or Ziegler but only the chief carpenter. He said to Carl Steinmetz: "I am a mad Russian; in the spring, we will work together. Drink this whiskey; in April, you remember who I am and what I want." Steinmetz amused; I had no more idea than he what Pavlik was talking about. Later he announced we would produce Gluck's

**Orfeo ed Euridice as ballet-opera in the spring. Does Balanchine
know anything about this? "He doesn't, but will."**

Tchelitchev's descent on New York was vital and drastic for all
of us. He brought a desperate urgency, his own big talent and
authority, and stirred up infectious excitement. Immeasurably the
most gifted scenic designer of his epoch, he always used the stage
as a seedbed for more serious easel pictures. Among young models
he found likely aspirants for our school and company. Young painters drawn to his work would be recommended as designers. He had
a notion of total lyric theater in which poets, painters, and musicians would be working for dancers. While he was with Balanchine
he joined in a few memorable collaborations; those talents, other
than his own, which attracted him were rarely congenial to us.
What Tchelitchev refused to realize was our particular sphere of
dance—also the fact that music required little visual appurtenance
beyond the proposal and fulfillment of human plasticity and measured motion. Tchelitchev was so seductive a talker, so apt a wit, so
ingenious a diplomat that he could make his most insane project
sound normal and possible. Since he abandoned theater in America
before we had any chance to give him the resources of a large
format, it will never be known what he might have accomplished
with his more fantastic schemes.

There was one he called *Episodes*, an evening's spectacle involving three archetypes: Don Juan, Don Quixote, Hamlet. Another was *Medea*, a great hill, mountain, or beehive which opened
for the perennial battle between Ants and Bees (Fascism against
Communism). On one occasion we did have an opportunity to
work together on a project which employed the equipment of a big
opera house. The result was the most beautiful visual spectacle I
have seen on any stage.

The choice of Gluck's *Orfeo* seemed modest and rational: a
two-act work employing only three soloists and dancers. In it there
was much music actually written for ballet. It had not been
presented in some years; it contained some of the loveliest vocal
music in repertory. Eddie Warburg would pay for a visual production, while the opera contributed the musical services. This ensured that Tchelitchev might have a free hand. He was not extravagant at all; he loved to improvise with the poorest materials.

Genuine silk and satin were vulgar—worse, these were not legible as richness under stage lighting. *Orfeo*'s scenery was made out of chicken wire, cheesecloth, and dead birch branches. He was distressed because there was no good flying apparatus, since he wanted Orpheus, Eurydice, and Amor to soar up into his marvelous celestial regions at the end of the fourth scene, with wires painted frankly white so they could be read as physical lines of magnetic force.

His splendid drawings, forty of them, are now in the Museum of Modern Art. They appear to be life studies as much as costume design, for he insisted upon as much nudity as was then licensed, with skeletal additions of wings, chains, garlands. His poetics were highly organized around elements of earth, air, fire, and water (mist and clouds). Mineral, animal, vegetable, and aerial; winter, spring, summer, autumn were frames upon which he hung his analysis of the Orphic myth. He was one of the last in the line of High Renaissance artists who used a metaphysical ikonology expressed in alchemy, gnosis, and mythopoetic symbolism.

The noble sobriety of Gluck's score proceeds like an aural mural; only in the Hell scene are there violence and strong turbulent action. The entire production was conceived without an element of paint. Rather, pigment was actually light. All hand-props and scenery were three-dimensional. Backgrounds were impalpable, chosen for their capacity to transmit, reflect, or change light. Everything occurred in air. As far as possible, space was unlimited and the frame itself—two transparent towers of which only the mortar for the masonry seemed solid—would disappear.

When the curtain rose, Orpheus, a big boy in a transparent T-shirt and black trunks, impassive, frozen in grief, watches the construction of Eurydice's memorial monument. Friends and neighbors try to comfort him, bringing reminders of his lost happiness. On crossed beams they drape rags, stack brooms, ladders, pots, ordinary objects of domestic ritual. This homely structure is capped by a cloth with Eurydice's wan portrait on a translucent veil. All except Orpheus himself were covered in gray body makeup, shades of sorrow. Alone, he was presented as both athlete and poet. Across his back was strung a crystal lyre. The groups Balanchine found were reminiscent of pietàs, entombments, depositions, ritual groupings gravely proceeding in flowing plastic sequences.

Hell, the second scene, was a Piranesian prison, cross-bars of which were made of braided barbed wire. At that period the reference to concentration camps was not as legible as it would soon become; we were criticized for injecting polemics into spectacle. Orpheus' crystal lyre seemed to draw blood from red-orange silk flames. Demon guards, masked in horse skulls with manes of serpents, brandishing snaky whips, lashed gangs of chained prisoners suggesting a Last Judgment or Doré's engravings for *Paradise Lost* and Dante's *Inferno*. This underworld was composed of stone and fire, chain and bone.

In the third scene, Orpheus' lyre led him through an airless Umbrian landscape in some timeless limbo. Birch trunks, stripped of leaves, hung in midair over a massive mound or burial barrow. A solemn procession of graybeards, vestals, and adolescent youths offered their meager homage of bone-dry laurel. In this anomalous ambience, dancers were swathed in doubled nettings of blue and violet which read as changeable taffeta, revealing naked bodies inside. Among the shadows of a once living world, figures passed in fluid solemnity, vague as forgotten ancestors.

In the final scene, spread across the wide sky, was a self-illuminated Milky Way, thousands of stars superimposed across the traditional diagrams of Lyra, Dipper, Cassiopeia's Chair, standing out against a vibrating mosaic of tiny stars powdering the black velvet night. Within this vast surround, there were only three figures for the entire scene—Orpheus, his regained Eurydice, and an angelic Hermes-Amor, performing a deliberate interlace of knotty figures at once intensely erotic and plastically splendid.

Eurydice was danced by Daphne Vane, a slight girl of doelike sweetness and fragile pathos, sheathed in mother-of-pearl chiffon which barely veiled her. William Dollar as Amor manipulated his goose-feather pinions with astonishing nobility, combining the roles of protector, guide, savior, a permutation of Hermes Psychopompos, the divine messenger who conducts souls to Pluto's realm. Mercury's wings were set on his dancer's feet. Orpheus was danced by Lew Christensen, one of three brothers of Danish-Mormon origin, all with excellent training by Luigi Albertieri, a famous Italian dancing master. Lew was tall, fair, finely proportioned with a noble head, extremely musical, possessing an acrobat's dignity and innate good taste matching his advanced technical security. Balanchine was happy to say there was no male performer outside Russia who could match him as a *danseur noble*. The male principle in America was then sadly lacking.

No singers were onstage; voices rose from the orchestra pit. The opera was presented without an entr'acte, increasing the displeasure of the Metropolitan's subscribers, for whom intermissions are as pleasurable as performance.

In New York, at the only two performances we were granted, the general responses were titters, yawns, or weak, ironic applause. Our audience was totally unprepared for an interpretation that transformed vaguely familiar myth and music into a heroicized domestic tragedy of artist, wife, and work; hell as a forced-labor camp; eternity as no happy heaven, but a paradisaical planetarium where time and space crossed. Tchelitchev's and Balanchine's marriage of metaphors—Hellenistic, Christian, post-Newtonian—were lost on a public that wanted to listen passively rather than actively look.

To the general audience, the use of allusive imagery, the shimmering incandescence of unfamiliar industrial stuffs and textures, the pervasive eroticism of mime and movement smacked of Broadway or the films—which then, as now, certainly employed more imaginative approaches to sound and sense than the Metropolitan Opera. Edward Johnson was courteously forgiving; Edward Ziegler was confirmed in his lack of confidence in the American Ballet. Hoping against hope, we still thought we might benefit by being attached to an establishment. Olin Downes, the omnipotent music critic of the *New York Times*, found it all "absurd," "impudent"; worse—"meddlesome." *Time* magazine and the rest followed his line. It was generally conceded we had thrown away our golden opportunity.

DECEMBER, 1936: *New York*

Received Stravinsky's piano score and orchestration for *Jeu de Cartes*. Clean calligraphy, ready for the engraver. Warburg says it can't be called "The Game of Cards"; it must be "Poker Party." Balanchine tried it on his piano and found it rhythmically fascinating. Quotations from Rossini. This clinched for me the success of Stravinsky Festival next spring. Ballets to add: *Apollon* and *Le Baiser de la Fée*. To Tchelitchev's to beg him to do one or the other. He refused. After his experience with *Orpheus*, he won't work in American theater again. Wired Stravinsky thanks; asked him to conduct performances. To the Met: in *Meistersinger*'s "Johannestag" scene, boys found Sachse, the director, onstage urging them to change the choreography, so they let him have it, with truncheons. Ugly scene with Ziegler.

When Stravinsky had received Warburg's invitation to accept a commission, he was already at work on a new score, which he then turned to our use. We did not know its subject for months after a contract was signed. Stravinsky credited one Malaieff, a friend of his painter-son Theodore, with developing the *prétexte*, which emerged as three deals in a game of poker. Irene Sharaff set the work in a witty frame: an enormous green baize card table against a corner of which stood, in sharply forced perspective, a huge gilt three-branched candlestick. The pack of cards consisted of twenty-six dancers, drawn from the four suits, plus a joker. Balanchine explained:

> Stravinsky and I attempted to show that the highest cards—the kings, queens, and jacks—in reality have nothing on the other side. They are big people, but they can easily be beaten by small cards. Seemingly powerful figures, they are actually mere silhouettes.*

The danced action followed rules according to Hoyle. In each deal, as Stravinsky said, the situation was complicated "by the endless guile of the perfidious joker who believes himself invincible because of his ability to become any desired card." Abrupt entries of the joker, to whom ordinary causality does not apply, destroyed any presumed sequence in the dealt hands. At the end of every deal,

* *Balanchine's New Complete Stories of the Great Ballets* (edited by Francis Mason), Doubleday & Co., Garden City, N.Y., 1968, pp. 74–5.

giant papier-mâché fingers of an otherwise invisible croupier swept away the rejected cards. A short prelude to each deal (march, polonaise, waltz) was followed by group dances, *pas d'action*, and solos. Deal, bet, and pass were translated into the idiom of classic dancing; cards shuffled themselves at the start of each part. Balanchine was prodigal of invention, to such a degree that Stravinsky, always thrifty, insisted he should repeat one especially ingenious device, because the audience wouldn't have time to appreciate it on its first appearance.

Before his arrival, we asked Irene Sharaff (later to become Elizabeth Taylor's favorite costumer) to design scenery and fifty dresses. We suggested that she study the Tarot and other medieval packs for heraldic fantasy and symbolic sense. When Stravinsky saw her clever sketches, he complained that they placed his music in too particular a historical period, evoking a decorative but specific atmosphere that was the opposite of what he had intended. He wanted the impersonal, workaday taste of the usual card pack, forms and details to be immediately legible. There would be many poker players among the public; they should be able to read the drama in his three deals at once.

Before I had much contact with theatrical working conditions, I was puzzled about an element commonly called "inspiration," a mysterious creative quantity without which nothing good gets done. I became accustomed to Balanchine's readiness in improvisatory composition; he analyzed the capacities of available individuals or elements and made dances from given materials just as a tailor cuts and sews clothes. Afterward these may be worn by others or adapted to other bodies, but "inspiration" more often than not turned out to be accommodation to necessity, making do with what one found at hand. Stravinsky was as impersonal as a surgeon, carpenter, or plumber. Imposed factors were not only acceptable but could be warped into constructs which made the factors more firm and clear. We had only a limited time allotted for rehearsals. Clocks ruled everything, starting with the duration of sections of a score. Stravinsky would sit for six hours at a stretch in our studio, then haul the rehearsal pianist off to his hotel for more work. He was a precision instrument, a corporeal metronome, but neither captious nor inelastic. When he saw that Balanchine needed additional music to permit a desired development, he would promptly decide whether to repeat measures or add new notes. If the latter, the necessary piano part would appear next morning, accompanied by its immaculate orchestration ready for the copyist.

Balanchine was accustomed to make his own piano reductions from whatever new orchestral score he was given. Marius Petipa's dancers had followed the piano alone; they would hear the orchestra only at a final stage rehearsal. Balanchine composed with full sonorities and dynamics already in his ear, and while dancers were frequently surprised to hear what eventually accompanied them from the pit, unsuspected sounds and silences were anticipated. As for choreography, Stravinsky expressed neither surprise nor preference. He had confidence in the partnership; what had now become his method was concentration without waste motion. He exhibited only muscular energy, patience, constant encouraging cheerfulness, no hysteria, and courteous attention. Realizing that when he came to conduct the performance he might have a tendency to accelerate tempi and thus dislocate the dancing, he had our accompanist play faster than his score's indicated counts, tempering them to his own discrepancies. He treated Balanchine like a junior assistant, although on an absolutely equal footing as an expert, since there was a presupposed agreement that the spectacle would be governed by music rather than by any overall concept of stylized movement.

JANUARY, 1937: *New York*

Tchelitchev has pushed Alice Halicka for the decor of *Le Baiser de la Fée*. Coinciding with a snowstorm, Madame Halicka arrived in furs. Rather than sketches, her plans are collages, pasted up from paper lace, tinsel, silk, wood veneer, sequins. The effect of Swiss souvenir cuckoo clocks, *boules-de-neige*, glass balls filled with flakes which, when turned, make a miniature blizzard. The last scene defeats her; the Matterhorn glacier, upon which the hero disappears. Tchelitchev found a solution: a huge net, stretched across the stage, under which cold green light would be thrown in jagged points. The last scene would be a dance on a net.

Alice Halicka was the wife of the painter Marcoussis. She had charming gifts as a decorator and with sophisticated mock vulgarity made naïve pictures from a mosaic of materials, an elevated *Kitsch—la romance capitonnée*—stuffed and quilted. Her proposals for the Alps were composed of tufted satin sprinkled with glitter; her scale was a postcard view of a fretwork chalet, blown up to a travel poster. A danger was that her style might seem a parody rather than a proper frame, so that homage to Tchaikovsky's genius, which was the point of the piece, would appear to be mocked or diminished. The finale, which Halicka found difficult to design since it was in reality an interminable climb up an imaginary mountain, contains some of Stravinsky's most luxurious orchestration, but is so extended that it leaves no scope for building dances toward a dramatic climax. The ballet seemed finished long before it ended. Like the scenery, the score was a mosaic of quotations and variations on themes from early, then-unfamiliar Tchaikovsky scores, including a beautiful manipulation of the famous song "None But the Lonely Heart." This was a favorite of Warburg's urbane and generous father, who was polite enough to assume it had been included for his special pleasure.

But the ballet, in spite of a magical *pas de deux* between fiancé and fairy, did not really work. Alpine village and Tchaikovsky quotations offered a visual and musical landscape which seemed not only *déjà vu*, but *déjà entendu*; at best pastiche, although tasteful and dignified. The work entered the repertory of the Ballet Russe de Monte Carlo during the Second World War; Alexandra Danilova had considerable success in the part of the Bride, as did both Mia Slavenska and Maria Tallchief as the Fairy. Balanchine's group formations for the snowstorm were reborn in a variant when he came to choreograph *The Nutcracker* for the New York City Ballet seventeen years later. The fortune-telling duet looked back to the "hand-of-fate" episode in his *Cotillon* of 1932. Balanchine continually reworked his own veins of invention; many motifs reappear in other guises in the sequence of his invention. This explains why he is so loath to revive works which have not had an immediate or complete effect. But one of the miniature masterpieces of the *second* Stravinsky Festival of June, 1972, was an extended divertissement derived from *Le Baiser de la Fée*.

MARCH, 1937: *New York*

Dress rehearsal of Stravinsky ballets. Warburg's decision to use the Philharmonic rather than the Met opera orchestra certainly paid off. Stravinsky particularly liked scenery for *Apollon*: "*Ça fait riche; très Poussinesque.*" Lew Christensen was everything one could wish. Balanchine threw away his wig. His hair is long enough to be curled tight. Tchelitchev cut away half his gilt leather armor. Improved his makeup; little to do with a head like that but let it shine. At the end of rehearsal, Stravinsky thanked Lew.

I had first seen *Apollon* at Covent Garden during Diaghilev's last season, in 1929. Through repeated experience of it, I gained an understanding of Balanchine's essential attitude about choreography. This differed not only from pre-Diaghilev dance design, but also from Diaghilev's own preference. The nineteenth-century philosophy of stage dancing was dominated by opera-house atmosphere, and before 1850, by opera itself. Diaghilev released it into an autonomous form. It is significant that in the chief national houses over the last half century, important diplomatic occasions have been celebrated in Paris, London, and Moscow by ballet rather than opera galas. Through *Apollon* I came to understand that the classic dance, an expressive idiom in its own right, was not necessarily subsidiary to spectacle, employing equal ingredients of painted decoration, expressive pantomime, and brilliant dancing, but rather an independent language of visual plastic interest based on music unadorned. The preoccupation was with three-dimensional movement measured by opulent rhythm and sonority. And through *Apollon* I realized that choreography clothed the dancer far more than costume, that the essence of important dancing lay in combinations and sequences of linked steps quite apart from intrusions by a star performer's accidental overlay of personality.

Originally, Balanchine had been ordered by Diaghilev to invent a work that would frame Serge Lifar, his last first-dancer. Lifar had the air of a postadolescent, self-indulgent boy of grace and energy, but he was by no means a fully equipped classic technician. Balanchine arranged steps for him which accommodated and capitalized on his limitations, accentuated his brusqueness, set off his strength to such a degree that in his triumph, pattern and structure were eclipsed by personality and idiosyncrasy. Hence an eccentricity in many parts of the female variations, which were organized and designed to be consistent with the unique masculine role, at first appeared as particularly disturbing. Diaghilev, deprived of his Russian source of young dancers in his later years, suffered from a weak corps de ballet. In *Apollon* Balanchine used three ballerinas, not only as soloists but as a super corps de ballet, by means which were astonishingly innovative.

With the exception of a very few ballets still surviving, much of the late Diaghilev repertory from 1917 on substituted amusement for amazement. Ideas, poetic or shocking, with pantomime more or less primary, served as lyric drama. New sounds, the *musiquette* of the Parisian twenties, with its perverse polemical bias, mainly against heavy German symphonizing, was the ensign of Les Six, who repudiated the romantic background (Wagnerism in particular) by cultivating deliberate triviality. This Diaghilev encouraged as novelty, since he manipulated the casual snobberies of Paris like a puppet master. He had been responsible for novelty since his debut; his was a formula for planned obsolescence. *Apollon,* in its apparent modesty of scale (four dancers; strings alone), its melodic insistence and rhythmic compulsion, its strict formal skeleton and heroic overtone, was not grandiose although it framed grandeur. It administered a serious negative electric shock, and what is rare in so deliberate a work, effected a consequential reversal in taste. It was at first offensive to a smart public schooled to expect more and more clever, provocative silliness. Diaghilev knew that what Stravinsky and Balanchine had done was to reaffirm the importance of classicism itself with a neoclassic turnabout that had already been proclaimed by Picasso's renunciation of Cubism and his attraction to Pompeian wall painting. Classic wholeness and order were prime factors. Their constant potential for offering plasticity and temporal analysis depended on measuring lofty melody strong and suggestive enough to compel new and alert rhythmic motivation and resonance.

Balanchine used a number of devices that, at their debut, seemed ridiculous. Today this extension of a vocabulary has been so long and so deeply absorbed that there is no fraction which does not appear logical, gracious, and flowing. In 1929 much appeared quirky, "ugly"; in "bad taste." What it had done was to require new looking and listening. Shocking gesture and movement there had been before, notably in the seminal invention of the Nijinskys —brother and sister. But these had been more easily forgiven, since they were apparently derived from folklore and only decorated the rhetoric of the academic idiom. In truth, the Nijinskys invented from scratch. Vaslav, in no way a humorless or uncultivated innocent, solemnly assured one British critic eager for a briefing on his "inspiration" for *Le Sacre du Printemps* that every step had been devised from original Muscovite documents of the fourth century B.C.! Balanchine could claim no such license for extending a classic language which was almost as well known as counterpoint and harmony. He merely asserted new movement, and the more eminent White Russian critics howled as if he had committed rape. But Gordon Craig, who had hated *Le Sacre* for its sweatiness and oppressive subhuman (or superhuman) energy, left the Paris premiere of *Apollon* before the final work on the evening's program, wishing to preserve in his mind its splendor undimmed by further impressions. This ballet proposing a renovated neoclassicism has in forty years become classic.

In its grave sequence Balanchine carved four cameos in three dimensions. Calliope portrayed the metric and caesura of spoken verse; Polyhymnia described mimicry and spectacular gesture; Terpsichore, the activity, declaration, and inversion of academic dancing itself. These are all subservient to Apollo, animator and driver; they are his handmaidens, creatures, harem, and household. He is the dance master whose authority develops from boy to man to god. Freed from swaddling bands, he feels and flexes muscle, matures into manhood, chooses his foredestined partner; finally assumes his godhead. The muses do not develop; they move in a temporal element which has no history, fixed in their idealized preordained powers. Having expressed their Platonic nature, they are and remain eternal archetypes and values. Apollo, commencing as an awkward athlete, gradually emerges as if from a blunt four-square block, just as the early Greek stone *kouroi* over three centuries grew into the released humane prototype of Periclean and postclassical naturalism. By no accident, Balanchine used quotations both from Hellenistic sculpture (Apollo Belvedere, the Self-Scraping Victor of Lysippus) and from beginnings of the baroque (Michelangelo's *God Touching Adam into Life*). The ballet is not, as it may be read from the piano score, only a series of divertissements. In the orchestra it assumes an urgent dramatic logic, ritual rather than narrative. There is no contest, no *agon*, except between the first dancer, his own body, and his self. Tension springs from anarchic muscular energy transformed into physical and moral grace or order. After the electrifying coda, in which his muses are harnessed (a troika) to the god's chariot, Stravinsky masterfully italicizes the serene majesty in motion gilded by Apollo's sunset apotheosis.

With Lifar, Balanchine had been given a boy who might conceivably become a young man. In America, with Lew Christensen, he found a young man who could be credited as a potential divinity. Praxitelean head and body, imperceptibly musculated but firmly and largely proportioned, blond hair and bland air recalled Greek marbles and a calm inhabitant of Nicolas Poussin's pastorals. Diaghilev had taken the decor from a "Sunday painter" in the line of the Douanier Rousseau. But André Bauchant's naïve canvases were irritating in their clumsy innocence. The aim was to cauterize a worn-out vision of Greece as a century-old archaeological reconstruction. But the shock potential in Bauchant's coarsely feeble paint was wiped out by Madame Chanel's "classic" haute couture costumes, which were contemporary tennis dresses, cinctured by striped men's cravats from Charvet. Long classic tutus were replaced. Chanel's small but apt explosion of chic fixed Balanchine's muses in a space far more immediate and surprising than Bauchant's vapid hills and blossoms.

When it was our turn to plan scenery and costumes, we knew the visual frame must not be assertive but, on an opera-house scale, tactfully splendid and solid. Our models were Poussin's backgrounds from his *Echo and Narcissus* and *The Arcadian Shepherds*. Colors of changeable taffeta drapery came from his *Inspiration of the Poet* in the Louvre. Christensen wore a light, supple, gilt armor of soft kid, with a short crimson silk mantle. His own hair, tightly curled and varnished, was powdered with gold dust. Stewart Chaney, an adroit and responsible designer, contrived a big Poussinesque cave, over which spread trunk and branches of a huge sacred laurel. Realized completely in three dimensions, lit to accentuate a late-afternoon glow, it filled the large stage as a sumptuous background. When Stravinsky approved, we were delighted; indeed it was expensive, but unlike Bauchant's decor, it never mocked the music. Stewart Chaney's (and Poussin's) harmonies of sunrise and sunset, glimmering accents of pewter, bronze, and gold, highlighted a sumptuous adornment to choreography (which, when *Apollon* would be revived twenty years later, seemed to need none; by then it was known as *Apollo*, or *Apollo, Leader of the Muses*).

While *Orpheus* was a milestone in every sense, it had no issue. Spectacle, dominated by a painter's imagination, no matter how appropriate or inventive its dancing, would always remain for us, with few exceptions, beyond need or possibility. Tchelitchev retired, something important disappeared. He established a level of fantasy and achievement by which we would judge all future collaborations; few ever approached his. On the other hand, in our first Stravinsky Festival we found we could count on him for suggestion and support. It also meant that Balanchine's principal adjunct, apart from dancers themselves, would be music, and among the living musicians available, Stravinsky. He was and would be, for us, the most accessible and constant. Balanchine looked back on *Apollon* from a perspective of thirty years

> as the turning point in my life. In its discipline and restraint, in its sustained oneness of tone and feeling, the score was a revelation. It seemed to tell me that I could, for the first time, dare not use all my ideas; that I, too, could eliminate. I began to see how I could clarify, by limiting, by reducing what seemed to be myriad possibilities to the one possibility that is inevitable.*

APRIL, 1938: *New York*

Scandal at the Metropolitan. Two of the dancers were late for performance; not the first time. Mr. Johnson displeased with

* *Balanchine's New Complete Stories of the Great Ballets*, 1968, p. 22.

divertissements for *La Juive*. Balanchine demoralized. He has offers from Larry Hart and Richard Rodgers for a Broadway musical; from Sam Goldwyn for Hollywood. Dimitriew prophesying doom; Warburg fed up. School, O.K. Touring out of the question. A real crisis. Ziegler refused to let me explain.

The genuine *succès d'estime* of the Stravinsky Festival merely delayed the inevitable rupture with the Metropolitan. In the late spring Balanchine withdrew his company. This barely forestalled our dismissal; it was hard to say who fired whom. We took comfort in considering that we preserved a moral advantage. Three years on 39th Street was a fair education in the devious politics and mechanics of establishment theater. We had foolishly imagined that if and when we penetrated such prestigious portals, all our energies and talents would be liberated to operate unhindered in the service of unalloyed creativity. It did not take long to discover that ancient formulae governing international opera-house practice had forged chains which were not to be broken soon. Edward Johnson had hired the American Ballet on the promise of its youth and Warburg's backing, but he was not prepared to support us in ambitious aims for the renovation of dancing in opera, or to permit us a free hand in the development of a ballet repertory within his house. He had neither wish nor ability to impose his instinctive optimism on a staff which had long held tenure, nor has anyone in his position attempted it since. I had known something of the history of opera management and of the current situation in Italy and France, and I knew how thirty years before, Diaghilev had been defeated by the imperial bureaucracy in Petersburg. But I was dazzled by our chance of working at the Met, and rationalized plans by which we could eventually gain our way by persistence, service, or boring from within.

Dancing at the Met was by no means easy for our dancers, who were barely permitted to practice on stage. For example, Lew Christensen was to appear as the partner of Rosa Ponselle in the "Lillas Pastia" scene of *Carmen*. She refused to rehearse; she was saving her voice. She sent her own dancing teacher to arrange her stage business with Lew; she would learn it all, somehow, "later." When they met for the first time onstage and commenced their routine, she seized a goblet of wine (grapefruit juice), quaffed a gulp, and tossed the rest in his face. Then she pulled down his head and smacked him full on the mouth. For six seconds they were locked. It seemed sincere. In the intermission, he said: "I thought she was trying to make me in front of God and everybody." Ballet and opera rarely mix; interludes may be intended to rest the voice but they seldom tickle the eye.

Early in 1936 it had come to me that, all else failing, I had best attempt to form some sort of company by myself. I was personally attached to Lew Christensen and to his fiancée Gisella Caccialanza, an excellent soubrette and strong dancer, the godchild of Enrico Cecchetti, the famous teacher of La Scala. There were some dozen other dancers, including Alicia Alonso, Todd Bolender, William Dollar, Eugene Loring, Michael Kidd, and Erick Hawkins, to whom I felt obligated. I now had no role in managing the school, which had increasingly been turned over to Eugenie Ouroussow. I lacked a vocation. I felt that my recent crash-course in theatrical self-enlightenment under the aegis of the Met must count for something. I decided to organize a small troupe on my own and call it Ballet Caravan. It would be self-sufficient, using a dozen of our best dancers, who would also serve as stage managers and stagehands. We could travel by bus and truck with our own lighting equipment, portable switchboard, drapes, and bits of scenery. In this I had the good wishes of Eddie Warburg. Balanchine was off to Hollywood; Dimitriew regarded the venture with amused if tolerant disdain.

I was not helpless, for providence intervened as it had before and would again, this time in the trim figure of Frances Hawkins, an enterprising, adventurous, and imaginative concert manager, who was then booking Martha Graham and Harald Kreutzberg. The daughter of a distinguished labor lawyer in Denver, she had absconded from Bryn Mawr to perform for several seasons in vaudeville in an acrobatic adagio act. There was little about vaudeville she didn't know; American vaudeville was at once her preparatory school and postgraduate course in theatrical administration. She knew more about touring conditions across the entire continent than I would ever learn; she had excellent taste, and loved dancing. With little to go on—no newspaper reviews to sell us at the start, small capital, and a wildly overoptimistic program—she found some forty engagements for our first season. In the next two years, with no subsidy, she took us twice across the country from New England to Oregon and back.

Ballet Caravan was conceived as a miniature. I had no ambition to make it more than a pilot experiment, something I could manage by myself with the help of Frances Hawkins. Primarily it attempted to produce a new repertory by native choreographers, musicians, and designers working with national themes. Prospective audiences would come from colleges across the country, and we would play in civic auditoriums as we could find them. Musical accompaniment was planned for two pianos; if the music we selected or commissioned was of some intrinsic interest, later orchestrations might be made. Everything was planned for possible enlargement; nothing depended on it. My general aesthetic was based on two bricks: five years of college "art and culture" history, and ten years of attendance at Saturday evening concerts of the Boston Symphony Orchestra under Monteux and Koussevitzky, both of whom had been closely identified with Diaghilev. On this basis I hoped to summon out of the air an "American" style from — something in our atmosphere—literary, musical, theatrical. Films, vaudeville, musical comedy, the popular arts in painting and sculpture—all could serve. Dependence on folklore, a cultural chauvinism, is always the first resort of pioneers in a new province. — I was undaunted by the precedent of Franco-Italian ballet masters who went to Petersburg in the nineteenth century to produce Franco-Russian bastardies. In the *New York Times* John Martin had labeled Balanchine's efforts over the last three years *"Le Ballet Americain."* I was eager to drop the French pronunciation.

Through Frances Hawkins's connection with Martha Graham, and Martha's alliance with Bennington College, we were given an opportunity to open in that fortress of modern dance. Owing to the broad sympathy and generosity of Martha Hill, who in many ways was responsible for the early fame of Graham, Doris Humphrey, and José Limon, Ballet Caravan first appeared in an auditorium usually given over to the dauntless experiments of progressive dancing, supposedly in violent opposition to the academic classic ballet. Our performances at Bennington were no more than open dress rehearsals, but the audiences allowed us the benefit of many doubts, and in an important sense, Modern Dance may be said to have launched Ballet Caravan.

We prepared a repertory of five miniballets in six weeks. For dancers we had the strongest available from school and company, including a handful of ambitious, imaginative boys and girls who saw themselves as future ballet masters or choreographers. It was in fact a small academy; five of these would enjoy big reputations in years to come. Lew Christensen, after his Army service, would be charged with San Francisco's ballet company and school; Erick Hawkins became a vocative theorist of the advance guard; Michael Kidd gained considerable reputation on Broadway and in films; Eugene Loring, after a career in ballet and legitimate theater, settled in Hollywood, where he worked in films and kept a school; Alicia Alonso became the Margot Fonteyn of Castro's Cuba.

We usually appeared in movie houses, whose nervous managers gambled that we would do no worse on off-matinees than bad films. Our tours were a parade of many comedies and a few tragedies. In Burlington, Vermont, we arrived to find competition from an American Legion convention, a county fair, and a square-dance contest. We played to fewer than a dozen people—but Frances Hawkins insisted we play, and the show went on. Bus and truck are the least relaxing forms of travel and transport. To drive three or four hours, unpack, set up, take class, perform, and eat later, if one is not too exhausted, hardly puts a performer's body in perfect condition. But Frances Hawkins, the Christensen brothers, the two girls whom they were about to marry, and many of the others were accustomed to touring in vaudeville. They were already professionals; the younger dancers learned to endure such schedules.

I had no instinct for directing a company and was notably lacking in that quality which the Army calls "leadership quotient." I fancied that an "American" company, such as ours purported to be, should be run "democratically," with everyone doing as well as saying exactly what he felt about everything. Here, at least, I would be free of Dimitriew's ukases. I would not treat my dancers as serfs but as friends, and I was surprised and depressed to find this policy as impractical as it was irresponsible. The dancers soon came to me in a body: either one man must plan and manage, face and solve problems—in short, direct—or they could not perform. Their job was dancing, not administration. Frances Hawkins was busy organizing future tours, as well as her other artists' careers, but she reinforced the company's attitude. Gradually I turned into some sort of director.

Whatever the birth pangs of our Caravan's first season, a second seemed justified. Now, at least, there were some agreeable press notices which Frances Hawkins could edit into a brochure. Balanchine took many of our best members to California for the benefit of *The Goldwyn Follies*, but somehow we managed to divide schedules and resources. Virgil Thomson says in his autobiography:

> My other work of 1937, almost wholly for me a year of theater, consisted of a ballet and a Shakespeare play. The dance piece, commissioned by Lincoln Kirstein for his Ballet Caravan, was a slice-of-life called *Filling Station*. . . . That midsummer I had found in Lew Christensen a dancer and director I knew I could deal with, and in the subject offered us by Kirstein a theme I thought I could at least take hold of.*

Filling Station was the result of an extended analytical process. As Virgil wrote, I'd dreamed up a number of libretti long before there was any company to consider them. When Ballet Caravan came into being, I had a mass of suggestions taken from "American" sources, some popular, others literary—from folktales and balladry to tales by Hawthorne, Melville, and Mark Twain. Before I had a company my notions were grandiose, more operatic or cinematic than choreographic. The existence of the Caravan was a precise determinant: fifteen dancers, a program of three units of twenty to thirty minutes each, little scenery, and two pianos.

Two other constants were Eugene Loring and Lew Christensen. A small, compact, exciting theatrical personality with little training as a classic dancer, Loring had energy and appeal. He wished to become a choreographer. Christensen needed suitable roles in a heroic genre within developed American balletic style— roles equivalent to Prince Charming or Prince Siegfried, knight-errant, crusader, romantic wanderer. These were not easy to translate into native terms. Hawthorne provided grotesque suggestions; Poe, morbid ones; Melville was too grand for our scale. Mark

---

* *Virgil Thomson*, Alfred A. Knopf, New York, 1966, pp. 274–5.

Twain's *Mysterious Stranger* seemed to have possibilities, but its medieval, romantic locale was reminiscent of *Giselle*—a locus which at the moment was anathema. A site in which Jimmy Cagney might be at home seemed to hold the key; he would be comfortable in a filling station.

But the ballet could not be realistic; its style must derive from vaudeville, where Christensen had gained his polish. Visually, comic strips were appropriate. John Alden Carpenter had composed his *Krazy Kat* for Adolph Bolm in 1922, but Krazy Kat danced through a landscape resembling Alice's Wonderland. I wanted an everyday, ordinary setting rendered magical. I made Cocteau's philosophy mine: theatrical, indeed all, lyric magic does not derive from the exotic, fantastic, or strange, but from a "rehabilitation of the commonplace." Paul Cadmus, a painter recently working for Roosevelt's Works Progress Administration, had caused a considerable scandal with his panel *Shore Leave*, which showed sailors ashore behaving in a manner which the Navy Department discountenanced. I was attracted by the exactness and vitality in his Hogarthian scenes of metropolitan and suburban life. He'd worked in an advertising agency and had an ironic eye on industrial civilization. He designed the interior of a filling station in terms of a rectilinear blueprint that might be handed to a builder. It had a big window, a gas pump outside, a neon sign in reverse, the door to a rest room. Except for Mac, the mechanic-attendant, who wore a handsome white uniform of translucent nylon piped in red with a red-and-white cap and tie, the other characters were in the style of comic strips or animated films.

Mac centered the action; he served those in need of gas or a telephone, monkey wrench, or road map. A series of incidents occurred, not unlike those in Robert Sherwood's *Petrified Forest*. There were a tourist family, a pair of acrobatic-vaudeville Mutt-and-Jeff truck drivers, another pair of vaguely F. Scott Fitzgerald lovers, a gangster, and a holdup. At first there was a "tragic" ending; but Balanchine suggested that The Girl, who had intercepted the gangster's bullet and was borne off held aloft, would revive in midair and wave to the audience just before she reached the wings. Virgil, as he said in his autobiography:

> wrote a score made up of waltzes, tangos, a fugue, a Big Apple [the popular dance-fad of the time], a holdup, a chase, and a

funeral, all aimed to evoke roadside America as pop art. . . .
Christensen, as a filling-station attendant in white translucent
coverall, filled the stage with his in-the-air cartwheels and held
us breathless with his twelve-turn pirouettes.*

Besides *Filling Station* we devised *Yankee Clipper*, with music by
Paul Bowles (who later abandoned musical composition for con-
fessional prose) and choreography by Eugene Loring, and *Show
Piece*, with music by Robert McBride to choreography by Erick
Hawkins. The first presumed to take a clipper ship's cabin boy
around the ports of the world on a dance voyage from Salem,
Massachusetts, to Tahiti and back. *Show Piece* was a demonstra-
tion of the flashiest dancing we could muster. Performances in
New York with a good orchestra, under auspices of the W.P.A.
Federal Music Project, put some sort of seal of approval on our
repertory, which in its small scale had a modest appeal through its
consistency and taste.

While *Uncle Tom's Cabin* as transmuted by e. e. cummings
had come to little except its publication (although David
Diamond was later prompted to write a score for it), other ideas
took firmer root. David Garnett, whom as a boy I had known in
London, and whose *Lady into Fox* became a ballet for the early
British repertory, had written an absorbing reconstruction of the
life of Princess Pocahontas. Having finished it, he decided to come
to Virginia and check the site, which we did together. In 1933 one
of many subjects I'd proposed to Virgil was the Pocahontas story,
which Florine Stettheimer, decorator of his opera *Four Saints in
Three Acts*, had also independently proposed. As he said: "For
decor it was splendid, but it lacked drama." Virgil also refused an
offer to collaborate with James Joyce on a ballet based on children's
games (out of *Finnegans Wake*) for the Paris Opéra, and he'd
found nothing to be done with cummings's *Tom*.

In spite of such implied warnings, I was still taken with the
notion of Pocahontas, largely because the figure of the adventurer,
John Smith, whose life she saved but whose hand she spurned,
seemed to be an excellent foil for Lew Christensen as John Rolfe,
the young subaltern who took his Indian savior back to England as
a bride. Elliott Carter, whom at Harvard I had known more as

* *Virgil Thomson*, 1966, p. 275.

classical scholar and mathematician than composer, agreed to write the music. I stipulated that the marriage-finale, in which Powhatan's daughter appeared in an Elizabethan wedding dress, should sound like an "American Indian" version of *Apollon Musagète*. Elliott fulfilled this strangulating condition with genuine beauty. In *Flawed Words and Stubborn Sounds*, Carter's revealing conversations with Allen Edwards (1971), the composer speaks of our ballet:

> *Pocahontas* . . . was my second work to be played pub-licly. . . . The character of the work came from the section of Hart Crane's *The Bridge* in which Pocahontas appears as a sort of "mother-earth" of America. There was an attempt to present this story as seen through the eyes of the English who came as colonialists, and their being saved from destruction at the hands of Nature. At that time the American past was being whitewashed, I suppose in a desperate attempt to make the "melting-pot" idea work. I myself had misgivings about the "colonialist" aspect of the subject, particularly as I have some Indian blood of my own, but hoped to make it a parable of cooperation.*

Just as dealings with e. e. cummings had been unhappy over *Tom*, I had something to regret in my occasional contacts with Hart Crane. When I had been an editor of *Hound & Horn*, overly in-fluenced by the rigors and strictures of R. P. Blackmur and Yvor Winters, whose verse and criticism I took very seriously, we had rejected the subway, or "Tunnel," section of *The Bridge*, at the same time printing reams of verse of incomparably lesser quality. After he was drowned, we made feeble amends by publishing Crane's comprehensive letter to Otto H. Kahn, his generous patron, outlining plans for his magniloquent epic structure.

I watched Crane at Manhattan parties when I came down from college. His behavior after dark astonished, alarmed, and excited me, because had I the courage I might have enjoyed myself much as he did. Crane's friend, the photographer Walker Evans, who took pictures for our earliest souvenir program, told me more of

---

* Allen Edwards, *Flawed Words and Stubborn Sounds: A Conversation with Elliott Carter*, W. W. Norton & Co., New York, 1971, p. 57.

Crane. Crane's epigraph for Part II of *The Bridge* bears the title "The Dance—Powhatan's Daughter," and quotes the earliest English records of the Virginia Indians: "—Pocahuntas, a well-featured but wanton yong girle . . . of the age of eleven or twelve years, get the boyes forth with her into the market place, and make them wheele, falling on their hands, turning their heels upwards, whom she would followe, and wheele so herself, naked as she was, all the fort over."*

The costumes for the ballet were by Karl Free, an exceptionally gifted painter and draftsman, who suffered from self-doubt as drastic as Crane's, and who finished life in the same style. He drew heavily on the wonderful drawings by John White, who landed with the first Virginia settlers, and rendered naked Indians in terms of the English Renaissance. Even more in my mind as visual precedent was Degas' magnificent painting in London's National Gallery of young Spartan girls daring adolescent boys to wrestle. These Greeks are in fact archetypical, perennial, snub-nosed, flat-breasted, lean-hipped ballet students at the start of some progressive and permissive "modern" dance. Divested of any decorative or temporal reference, this might happen equally in forest clearing or ballet studio. Hart Crane saw his small ballerina-acrobat:

> There was a bed of leaves, and broken play;
> There was a veil upon you, Pocahontas, bride—
> O Princess whose brown lap was virgin May;
> And bridal flanks and eyes hid tawny pride. . . .
>
> A birch kneels. All her whistling fingers fly.
> The oak grove circles in a crash of leaves;
> The long moan of a dance is in the sky.
> Dance, Maquokeeta: Pocahontas grieves . . .†

I knew how important Jean Cocteau had been for Diaghilev as poet and publicist for his early Parisian seasons, and I always hoped to find someone who could dream up concepts which dancers might incarnate. James Agee and I had been at Phillips Exeter; he sketched for Ballet Caravan several scenarios, one of which bore

* *The Complete Poems and Selected Letters and Prose of Hart Crane* (edited by Brom Weber), Liveright, New York, 1966, p. 53.
† *The Complete Poems* . . . *of Hart Crane*, 1966, pp. 70, 73.

the working title "Bombs in the Ice-Box." Like so many of his marvelous conceits, this dissipated itself in endless conversation. As for two other considerable technicians and collaborators, Wystan Auden and Chester Kallman, they admired Balanchine, who directed the first performance in New York of their libretto for Stravinsky's *Rake's Progress* at the Met. However, in spite of much talk, we would never have the luck of gaining a balletic *Paid on Both Sides, Dance of Death,* or *Bassarids* for our own repertory. Auden disliked the Bernstein-Robbins *Age of Anxiety:* he reiterated that his services were purely verbal, but his passion for opera and Kallman's feeling for theatrical structure and high-camp continually teased our hard-dying greed for such capital collaborators.

We considered Melville's *Confidence Man;* Henry James's *Turn of the Screw,* from which Benjamin Britten extracted viable opera; *Brer Rabbit; Ethan Frome;* Scott Fitzgerald's "The Diamond as Big as the Ritz"; Thomas Beer's *Road to Heaven;* Carl Van Vechten's *Tattooed Countess.* We were by no means alone in a struggle to impose a native meaning on a recalcitrant alien dance tradition. Ruth Page in Chicago, Catherine Littlefield in Philadelphia, and before all or any of us, Ted Shawn with his cowboy and Aztec numbers, experimented with folkloristic material from barn dance, barroom, roundup, and various native mythologies. Possibly the most successful was no ballet at all but Martha Graham's *American Document,* a broad, masterful arrangement of solos and processions interspersed with spoken documentary quotations, encompassing many of the elements that led to the opening of our continent and the tragic drama of its aborigines.

In face and figure Eugene Loring, the protagonist and inventor of *Yankee Clipper,* reminded me of Jimmy Cagney; both were alike in their stubby strength, concentration, and physicality. There was available the legend of William H. Bonney, bad boy from Brooklyn who was taken west in the sixties to become Billy the Kid and was betrayed and killed in 1881. Through Virgil Thomson I met Aaron Copland and asked him to write a score, which I feared he might consider could be overburdened with folkloristic themes impeding his own imagination. I had already become self-conscious about insistence on imposed Americanisms. However, I took the precaution of leaving on his piano an album of cowboy songs to which he might refer. This he did; a few, "Git Along, Little Dogie," "Old Chisholm Trail," "Bury Me Not on the Lone Prairie," inserted themselves into the most convincing and sturdy ballet to come out of Ballet Caravan. Paul Cadmus had shared a studio with Jared French, whose wall paintings for the state reformatory at Coxsackie, New York, were some of the strongest murals done under the W.P.A. I gave him Theodore Roosevelt's memoirs of the Far West, where as a youth he had been sent for his health. This fascinating book had been brilliantly illustrated by Frederic Remington; from his pictures French drew a series of dashing but simple costumes, as well as a backdrop of tall cacti, which immeasurably enriched the ballet.

Billy the Kid opened in the Chicago Opera House in October, 1938, and had an immediate and lasting success. Billy's Mexican sweetheart was danced by Marie-Jeanne. Perfectly cast and costumed, she was an exquisite personification. Ann Barzel, Chicago's faithful ballet historian and critic, wrote in that December's *Dance* magazine: "*Billy the Kid* . . . marks a milestone in American ballet. . . . Loring's choreography is marked by inventiveness and imagination, and yet his work is never obscure. Loring's inventiveness is shown in the movements devised, whether it be to illustrate riding a horse or pushing West. His details are excellent."

There was the problem of the repeated sound for gunshots, which Copland solved with efficient simplicity. Loring also: the shots precipitated his triple air turns. The good-guy sheriff, Pat Garrett, was naturally Lew Christensen, who resembled young John Wayne disguised as the Apollo of Tombstone. Loring had a real scar on one cheek, which added to the sensitive brutality of his boy-brigand's mask. We invented a chameleonlike character under the name of Alias, who was everywhere and nowhere, an impalpable personification of danger, treachery, menace—admirably danced by Todd Bolender, who would also become a choreographer and ballet master. *Billy the Kid* worked well; when I went into the Army, it was assigned to the Ballet Theatre, through my friendship with Oliver Smith, its cofounder. Before that he had served as an assistant to Tchelitchev. But soon the costumes and scenery changed; Loring no longer danced it, and it took its place as a historical fixture in a standard repertory.

FEBRUARY, 1939: *Milwaukee*

Eugene Loring's hometown. We wanted to do his two ballets, *Yankee Clipper* and *Billy the Kid*; the sponsors refused *Billy*; it was no fit subject for ballet. What most provincial American sponsoring committees want is pocket-size Russian ballet. If it's American, it can't be ballet. However, our success was such that we were asked to do *Billy* should we come again next year.

MARCH, 1939: *Visalia, California*

Sunday matinee. Owing to the presence of the local clergy, and their fear of competition, we were not allowed to dance *Filling Station* or *Billy the Kid*.

MARCH, 1939: *Dallas*

Local critic irritated by my "100% Americanism." Tried to show him that our program was not one of blind chauvinism, but a personal attitude, contrasting with a pervasive Russian ballet domination . . . I had wanted to present *Billy the Kid* here, but because of recent big state celebrations, the sponsors felt they'd had enough Wild West. However, the next night, for the state women's college at Denton, Dallas newspapers sent over critics, and many people from the previous night's audience came too.

MARCH, 1939: *San Angelo, Texas*

Local ranchers particularly pleased by *Billy the Kid*. I feared that they might consider it pretentious of Easterners to show imi-

tations of bronco-busting and gunplay, but they were pleased that
we thought the Wild West a suitable subject for classic dances.

APRIL, 1939: *Toronto, Canada*

Official reception with the lieutenant governor-general, etc.
Canadians would have preferred white tarlatans and Russian
music. Everyone polite and cold as the weather.

While we learned much about the United States and Canada
in our far-flung tours, and more about the organization and maintenance of a theatrical company, I began to realize we'd come to
the limits of our particular operation. Long before, my father had
told me that two kinds of energy determine the quality and character of operations: the energy to establish, and the interest to
maintain. For me, maintenance was far more difficult than initia-
tion. The routine of keeping performance at a high level is as
necessary as the original invention of new work, but it is far more
of a grind. Few of us wanted to cross the continent again, even
under the increasingly favorable conditions which Frances Hawkins's stubborn ingenuity and courage had gained.

Back in New York, we had the irrelevant luck to appear with a
first-rate orchestra on one of those peculiar programs which have
nothing to do with anything except the momentary and inconsequential passion of individuals to indulge themselves in haphazard
hobbies. A middle-American millionaire had conceived a passion
for the melodies of Stephen Foster. He commissioned an opera to
frame two dozen tunes, and since this alone did not seem quite
enough for a genuine "festival," our Ballet Caravan was briefly
attached. We also had skittish conversations about being absorbed
by the Ballet Theatre, which Lucia Chase was now directing away
from the original Russian orientation of Mikhail Mordkin, her
teacher. Our aimless flirtation with the Ballet Theater continued
until I went into the Army. Eugene Loring, taking *Billy the Kid*
with him, did go to Miss Chase and Oliver Smith and produced
other works which, uncharitably, I could not commend.

However, as happened after the debacle of our American Ballet
in Scranton, Pennsylvania, another providential patron now arrived

in the unlikely guise of the Ford Motor Company. In the months of suspended animation anticipating World War II, owing to the weird and willful optimism of some obtuse businessmen, New York City organized a feckless World's Fair. People have often mistakenly believed that dancing on the edge of a volcano puts off the eruption. In our case I was approached by Walter Dorwin Teague, an industrial designer employed by Edsel Ford, to devise a spectacle which, through the ballet vocabulary, would sell their new 1940–41 models. Teague had provided a handsome circular pavilion in gold mirror-and-mosaic. Inside was a well-equipped theater with comfortable seats for five hundred people, a turntable stage, excellent dressing rooms, and a built-in canteen.

The pretext for our dancing was the fate of the horse in the path of the automobile. It added nothing to the history of The Dance, but it was an agreeable exercise and had important consequences. We never knew whether or not it sold a dozen automobiles, but for six months it provided food and rent for forty dancers in two teams that performed an eighteen-minute ballet entitled *A Thousand Times Neigh!* every hour on the hour, twelve times a day. Logistics were complex, but they were solved efficiently. Every dancer had one free day a week; there was a "swing shift" to take up the slack of accidents and replacements. Dobbin, the horse, was made up of two boys, head and tail. He executed a soft-hoof bit of tapping.

MAY, 1941: *Flushing Meadow, New York*

Lunch in a private dining room of the Ford Pavilion, given by Edsel Ford for Nelson Rockefeller on the scale of a diplomatic occasion. Mr. Teague had designed everything, furniture to gold plates, cutlery, and glassware. Nelson, cheerful as usual, bantered with Mr. Ford about spending hard money on ballet. I tried to get a word in about the possibility of a national American company under their joint protection. Naturally it was hopeless.

I had known Nelson Rockefeller since 1931. My preceptors in the fine arts at Harvard had been Jere Abbott and Alfred H. Barr, Jr., who were soon appointed codirectors to plan New York's

Museum of Modern Art. In college, with John Walker, who later became director of the National Gallery in Washington, and Eddie Warburg, we had organized the Harvard Society for Contemporary Art, which has been called a prototype for MOMA. With another classmate, the architect Philip Johnson, we had also been loosely attached to planning a program for mural decoration when Rockefeller Center was being built in the early thirties. A stormy exhibition of invited mural painters at the museum followed, as well as the destruction of Diego Rivera's fresco over the entrance lobby of 30 Rockefeller Plaza. In both altercations I was an observer. Recruited by Ben Shahn, then working as technical and political assistant to Diego, I served as a model for a "typical American Jew" (nose, mostly). For the exhibition at the museum I asked Ben to paint a mural fragment, which he based on Sacco and Vanzetti. (My father had employed Sacco's son as his chauffeur.) I was also attracted to several young union organizers working in the South and found myself embroiled in polemical battles which had little to do with art but a lot with life.

During this confusing if instructive time, in which I shifted from one false position to another, on the one hand scuffling with Raymond Hood, the architect, who feared Rivera's mural might bankrupt the rental agents for Radio City, on the other placating Ben Shahn and various fiery self-appointed protest committees, there was one person to whom I could go for sanity and assurance. This was Mrs. John D. Rockefeller, Jr. In a room next to a chamber in which, at that time, were hung the Unicorn Tapestries, now a glory of the Cloisters, Mrs. Rockefeller would give me tea and toast as she listened to my account of the day's skirmishes. She was a personal friend of Rivera's; she understood Ben Shahn very well; that we all stayed less than enemies was due in large part to her refusal to be frightened.

Occasionally I was asked to stay a night at Pocantico. I once met Nelson's grandfather on the golf course; he seemed as ancient as Amenhotep, but actively demonstrated the virtues of his windbreaker made of layers of paper which, he said, kept the wind out better than any leather vest. Nelson and I admired Gaston Lachaise, the sculptor, for whom Eddie Warburg and I posed and whom Nelson patronized. At Dartmouth, Nelson had thought to become an architect and was knowledgeable and interested in the plastic arts. He helped us in many striking ways from our start, and not with money alone.

In 1941 Nelson was appointed by President Roosevelt to head a new agency, the United States Office for Coordination of Commercial and Cultural Relations between the American Republics. (His short title was Coordinator of Inter-American Affairs.) This office was ostensibly under control of the State Department, but Nelson was hardly contained within an establishment which, so far, had done little to prevent that apathy which his young agency was created to combat. In any case, I acted in innocence of the hazardous and complex tensions at work in exalted political spheres. The dance is a universal language, transcending every local dialect of Spanish or Portuguese. In Washington in a climate of unreal informality, unofficial optimism, and casual friendliness, a loose and quite unbusinesslike contract was contrived for a ballet company which would tour every Latin-American republic save Paraguay and Bolivia. An imprecise document assured us that the Coordinator's Office would pay minimum expenses for this company for half a year; further deficits would (more or less) be underwritten; we would defray necessary production costs, including a number of new commissions.

Later there were tiresome repercussions about money, but Nelson was always our responsible defender. When he was attacked in Congress for spending cash "on ballets rather than bullets," he pointed out that in the midst of the Civil War, Lincoln had ordered the expensive casting of new bronze entrance doors for the national Capitol, to show that he was sure of victory and that the Republic prized and deserved certain immaterial values.

Balanchine and remnants of our American Ballet had finished their stint for Sam Goldwyn in Hollywood. He returned to New York charged with Nelson's commission. In Washington I was given a check which seemed so large that I was as scared as if I had stolen it. The actual amount was rather less than what we now spend in a single season of the New York City Ballet at the State Theater. Anyway, I was so frightened that I became suspicious of my least decision. Dimitriew and Warburg were no longer aides or opponents; I was more or less alone, to make mistakes and face a future that I must guide as I could.

The expedition to South America was not undertaken lightly.

With a grant from the Library of Congress, we were able to take along two musicologists who collected folk-song materials from each country. Through friends at Fordham University I was given letters to several Jesuits who I thought might show me parishes and parishioners—which they did to an extent that our official embassies never would. I learned a sort of Spanish in six weeks. We signed thirty-six dancers, a sizable group for the time and circumstances. Our repertory combined elements from the American Ballet and Ballet Caravan, with notable additions. Antony Tudor invented *Time Table* to Aaron Copland's *Music for the Theater* of 1925. The ballet was a nostalgic reference to the First World War on the eve of a Second. In it Lew Christensen shone as a marine bidding good-bye to his girl on a suburban railway platform, reminiscent of the atmosphere of Edward Hopper's lonely paintings. *Pastorela* was a folk ballet, with sung parts based on an indigenous Mexican nativity play transcribed and adapted by Paul Bowles. By this we hoped to show a veritable goodwill toward Latin-American material. But we discovered, on a tour which did not include Mexico, that Brazilian, Peruvian, and Colombian critics each considered his own culture autonomous, unique, and superior to all others. As far as they were concerned, Mexico was as remote as Siam, though less interesting. Alec Wilder put together a series of his delicate tunes for *Juke Box*, but the jazz element was not convincing when danced. The two strongest novelties, hardly to anyone's surprise, were both by Balanchine—*Concerto Barocco* and *Ballet Imperial*, which persist in repertory after three decades.

JUNE, 1941: *Rio de Janeiro*

Teatro Municipal, a marble monument more antiquated than the Met. Accommodations mostly for scenery made out of paper, locally permitted, but which our lighting equipment tends to ignite. In Ambassador Caffery's box he made no secret of his strong dislike, not of us personally but of the trouble we'd put him to by arriving; the ambiguity of our reception. It was no triumph. Later, Balanchine and some of the kids to a nightclub.

For one bottle of champagne and ice cream they were given a bill for more than a hundred dollars.

Although we were accompanied by an official guardian or nanny dispatched by the State Department to prevent errors of tact and decorum, our connection with Rockefeller's agency was regarded by the ordinary Foreign Service diplomat as distinctly suspect. Ambassador Jefferson Caffery was a classic example of the professional career diplomat. He melted a bit at *Ballet Imperial*, an affectionate pastiche of Petipa, but our so-called modern works convinced him that we had been sent to subvert both his embassy and the continent in time of war. Why had we nothing like *Swan Lake?* The Ballet Russe de Monte Carlo had toured South America the summer before, enjoying vast success with the standard repertory. There was no use trying to explain to Ambassador Caffery our philosophy of national coloration; ballet was an alien contraption; what of it that was useful for export should be limited to an accepted typology. São Paulo was a little more welcoming; we valiantly attempted to work with Brazilian composers and painters. Candido Portinari made a handsome backcloth for *Serenade*, scattering stars in the constellation of the Southern Cross in the manner of Joan Miró. Balanchine invented a Radio City Music Hall version of supposedly native dances to music by Guarnieri. We were taken to some allegedly secret, exotic, underground, magical "samba schools." With all the goodwill in the world we were fish out of water, and chronologically out of luck. The newspapers were not entirely unkind; we could send to the Coordinator's office in Washington some evidence that they had not backed a losing horse. Montevideo was not much of an improvement, but the audiences were more sympathetic.

JULY, 1941: *Buenos Aires*

Flew ahead to prepare the season. Arrived Thursday; company due Friday night. Delays; they arrived Saturday morning. At the dock all girls under eighteen were arrested and removed to a local jail; work permits don't apply. We were importing dancers for purposes of prostitution. Some sort of German-inspired plot? A weekend; unable to find a federal judge, the only person capable of springing the girls. Balanchine insisted on being arrested also. To the Ministry of Justice, but nothing to be done until Monday. Dreary theater, usually used for films. No advance at the box office. Baggage held up at Port Authority, owing to our legal status; loss of three days.

Our girls were eventually sprung, little the worse for wear. Performances at first were largely unattended; however, after the presentation of Tchelitchev's *Errante* and Stravinsky's *Apollo* toward the end of a ten-day season, there was an awakening of interest. Victoria Ocampo and her friend Maria Rosa Oliver gallantly stirred up a brush fire of enthusiasm. Miss Ocampo, dauntless mistress of the progressive literary magazine *Sur*, had survived generations of opposition, censorship, and prison to bring to Latin America the best that was being written there and over the rest of the world. They took me to visit Jorge Luis Borges in an ancient apartment lined with books. But Borges, who knew everything about everyone including us and our repertory, was nearly blind. I was taken to the Teatro Colón and wished we'd the luck to be dancing there rather than in a hideous movie house.

After other big towns, we proceeded by train to Mendoza in the high Andes. There, a terrific blizzard immobilized us for a fortnight, forcing us to miss our scheduled subscription opening in Santiago de Chile. The Andes were impassable; our scenery had to be routed, guarded by two dancers, up and through Bolivia. We appealed to our embassy in Lima, Peru, to send transport planes to rescue us from disaster. In the meantime, to maintain morale and gather in whatever fringe benefits might ensue from our persistence, we gave daily performances at the tiny but pretty municipal theater attached to the Mendoza gambling casino.

One morning on my way to class and rehearsal, I crossed a park in front of the theater, where a gentleman courteously approached and demanded why he should not kill himself. In his hand was a revolver; he spoke urgently but quietly; his seriousness was such that I could hardly doubt his insistence. He had lost the last of his money gambling the night before and was heavily in debt. I had nothing to propose except to suggest in my best Spanish: "When you're dead, it's for a long time." I began to realize that I had acquired a mythical reputation as a mad North American millionaire who amused himself keeping a ballet company performing night after night, in the high Andes, to a handful of spectators. Finally, since the man remained imperturbably courteous but obdurate, I told him that I must get on to my rehearsal. Tattered palms shivered in the ragged municipal park; a broken fountain dribbled; starved dogs skulked. His own hungry elegance matched the faded gilt of casino and theater. It was a scene from some fable by Jorge Luis Borges. In the auditorium when I was watching dancers at practice, I fancied I heard a shot; it may have been an automobile's exhaust or another sharp report. However, this indeterminate incident summarized our South American experience in its indecisiveness, frustration, and blunted impact.

The company, using oxygen masks, was finally flown across, or rather between, the Andes. It reached Santiago nearly two weeks late and from there proceeded north by coastal cattle-boat to Lima, Guayaquil, and Colombia. When we had budgeted the tour, a wholly imaginary sum had been allocated for income. After Buenos Aires, even before Mendoza, it became clear we would never approach half of it. In panic I left the company and flew to Washington to renegotiate with the Coordinator's office. I was an unremarkable negotiator; a general opinion prevailed that the remainder of the tour should be canceled. This meant eliminating Peru, Ecuador, Colombia, and Venezuela. I dealt with Wallace Harrison, the architect, who had been pressed by the national emergency into serving as Nelson's deputy. He wanted to know if the tour so far had been a "success."

Certainly this is the most frightening word in a theatrical lexicon. Success on what basis? We could claim little by way of improving the image of a North American government in a southern continent that had so far been ignored except for commercial exploitation. As for personal success, there was our ballet company, which had indeed performed in Brazil, Uruguay, Argentina, and Chile. In the light of historical precedent, might I not claim that the first tour of a sizable troupe performing at some level of efficiency throughout new territory was a kind of "success"? In the light of newspaper clippings collected and influential persons, many in the political opposition, interested or attracted, what could be estimated as the increment? Was success a cipher, amounting to less money lost than had been witlessly anticipated?

We had been dispatched to stimulate goodwill, not to save cash. We could be considered a success insomuch as we had been chosen to be sent, and by many considerations had been no absolute failure. This seemed to be the single alternative to "success"—the smash hit, big prize, Top Ten, the Oscar. Was there nothing between 100 percent and zero? However, Wally Harrison, among others, had something more like a war to win; while he was a friend and a sensitive man, he confessed that it looked like curtains. Until, as usual, our guardian angel appeared in the grotesque guise of an accident high over Colombia.

Sharing our program of cultural penetration had been a famous tenor and film star. When his plane crashed, a whole string of personal appearances had to be canceled. If, hard on this catastrophe, our ballet's performances were also wiped out, what would be the prestige of our vaunted export culture through the highlands and lowlands of El Gran Colómbia? The Coordinator's office bowed to *force majeure*. The tour was continued; meanwhile our engagements throughout Venezuela were actually achieving "success," which made things easier when it came to sorting out the ghastly financial discrepancies. Nelson and Wallace Harrison made everything as equitable as they could. In fact, on the basis of contacts the ballet had made, I returned to South America within the year, supplied with funds to buy progressive Latin-American paintings for the Museum of Modern Art.

Back in New York, looking over newspapers from the South American journey, I was surprised to find how erudite, warm, and favorable much of the journalistic criticism had been. It was almost too scholarly, on too respectful a level. Perhaps it tended to keep popular audiences away by the very level of its seriousness. Ballet was made to seem as sacred as symphonic music, but not as much fun. Also, we had had little or no advance publicity; our embassies had considered us a sinister nuisance. Worse, we had no famous stars—and worst, our ballets were not remotely Russian.

MAY, 1945: *Bayreuth, Germany*

I was last here in 1923 for the first Wagner Festival since the 1914 War. Mother and I were refused at the best hotel in spite of advance reservations. They said we would be happier in a kosher rooming house. At the end of *Meistersinger* a rapturous audience, joined by the chorus onstage, broke into "Deutschland, Deutschland über Alles." Today, the stage was covered with tarpaulins on account of the shattered roof; Special Services will use it for films and name bands.

In the Army my energies were transferred from theater interiors to drama in the open air. The European theater, at least what I managed to see of it as courier or interpreter, was full of brilliant impersonations, among the most notable being George Patton himself. Headquarters had comic-opera overtones; as far as high-camp went, he was certainly among the more conscious and expert prima donnas of his era. Fringes of his command were extraordinarily permissive. In Normandy, momentarily confined to the Cotentin Peninsula before Patton broke loose at Saint-Lô, we spent happy wasteful hours building a movie theater, or at least transforming a cattle barn into an auditorium. From somewhere came dozens of fat rolls of tar paper which had the texture of dull black velvet. We tacked them up in the barn and inscribed them with linear murals, white-on-black in the Cocteau manner. This bit of interior decoration was achieved in off-hours; before it could be finished, on one electrifying day in late July, four thousand planes blasted a path for Patton, and our unit tore after him to Paris.

MAY, 1945: *Trier, Germany*

Bumped into Lew Christensen. He's in Graves Registration. Bad-for-morale to leave pieces of people around the place; his unit collects them, tags them, and cleans up the landscape. We were both so preoccupied with what looks like the end of war that we had little to say. We touched on plans for what could be done in the ballet; he doubts if he will dance again. No point in reminiscence; the last ten years seem ploughed under.

Lew was awarded a battlefield commission and ended up administering a small German town for another year. I found myself in the Austrian Alps, helping uncover Göring's spectacular cache of stolen art objects, but extricated myself from the Army by early October. I had enjoyed most of it, imitating Ulysses the polytrope, the sly fellow who passed, usually safely and anonymously, from one unlikely occasion to another. I found an interstitial existence not only desirable but possible, particularly for one who had a little French and German, no rank, and an authoritative if elaborately courteous and official manner. In fact, I was giving an impersonation of some type of shady character, possibly from a branch of Intelligence, to which I had no claim whatsoever. This sort of behavior is easy enough in anarchic, chaotic, or extreme situations; hence the Army gave me a taste for exercises of simulacra of free will. I gained an illusion that I might do much as I wished so long as I knew what it was and analyzed the factors. A former weakness for the tentative, accidental, or improvisatory was sloughed off, and with it, much insecurity and doubt. In the service I behaved much *as if* what I wanted to do could be done. And peacetime brought its immediate if momentary euphoria which increased this illusion.

I returned to find our school, under Eugenie Ouroussow, stronger than ever. Aims remained basically the same; we needed to form another company, a new audience; and sooner or later we needed a sponsor for a theater of our own. Through the spring and summer of 1946, Balanchine and I planned strategy. An analytical, conscious operation, it was overly ambitious, including a dozen projects which we never started and as many others which would abort. Perhaps the program sprang more from caprice than caution, but the famine of war years had made us hungry and now we were greedy. Our proposals were often reckless or, I suppose, "pretentious." That is, we would pretend to an impact which would be unprecedented in scope and quality. One thing we never considered was "success." There would be no compromise with good taste or establishment standards; to attach ourselves to these spelled death, as our experience with the Metropolitan Opera had proved. Balanchine and I knew that what had been done in the past had no place in a present or future. We needed fresh attitudes, new audiences, and our own theater; we set about obtaining these according to a rational schedule. We projected a private subscription organization called Ballet Society, Inc., and proposed a six-point program which was sent out in a brochure inviting membership. Some eight hundred people responded. They got quite a lot for the money, and so did we.

FROM THE INITIAL BROCHURE INVITING MEMBERSHIP
IN *Ballet Society, Inc.*, OCTOBER, 1946

PRESENTATION of new theater-pieces, including ballet, ballet-opera, and chamber-opera, either commissioned by Ballet Society or unfamiliar to the American public, as well as individual concert-dancers.

CO-OPERATION with other educational and cultural institutions, to enable the production of performances, exhibitions and publications, difficult or impossible to accomplish alone.

PUBLICATION of books, prints and articles that award to the dance a consistent and serious attention long enjoyed by painting, sculpture, architecture and music.

PRODUCTION and circulation of documentary dance-films recording contemporary activity in ballet companies, individual dancers, and national dances, as well as experimental films using dance as a main element.

PUBLICATION of record albums of music in the performances of Ballet Society, with photographic documentation and full program notes.

AWARDS of fellowships enabling talented young dancers and choreographers to work by themselves or with groups of dancers to develop technically and professionally.

It was something of a triumph that in the 1946–47 season, our eight hundred subscribers received everything we promised them, with the exception of record albums. Also included were a year-book as an illustrated summation of our activities; a subscription to the magazine *Dance Index*; hardback monographs on Nijinsky, Pavlova, and Isadora Duncan; a bulletin; and invitations to demonstrations, rehearsals, and film showings. No tickets were sold for individual performances, which circumvented the necessity for a box office and clerical detail, and we eliminated the press list. If newspapers cared to cover our performances they could subscribe, like anyone else. We calculated that, instead of antagonizing critics (who by and large would be unfriendly anyway), this might pique their curiosity, while they would scarcely ignore productions of such intrinsic interest. We guessed right. We gave away tickets to poorer friends and enthusiasts, among them students, artists, and poets; these were the best propagandists we could pay. Typography and presentation for the initial announcements were elegant; our opening campaign had panache and a calculated arrogance which was attractive. There were no large individual backers; however, we dimly felt that somewhere, somehow, somebody would be waiting in the wings in the guise of a guardian angel, and that there must be some future use for what we presently proposed.

SEPTEMBER, 1946: *New York*

Tchelitchev's studio, with first programs for Ballet Society. Final refusal to do anything himself, except offer criticism. I'd already made commitments—for example, to a designer for *L'Enfant et les Sortilèges*. He snapped that she was a nice enough woman, a good cook, but a total amateur; another example of my irradicable amateurism. He again brought up ideas for *The Cave of Sleep*, his *Medea*, and *Episodes*. We haven't enough money even to start on the costumes he would want. He said: "Very well; take Kurt Seligmann; he is an intelligent man." "Intelligent?" "Yes, you have too much enthusiasm, not enough brains."

Working with the composer, Balanchine had produced Maurice Ravel's ballet-opera *L'Enfant et les Sortilèges* (here translated as *The Spellbound Child*) twenty years before in Monte Carlo for Diaghilev. It had not been given in the United States. The charming libretto by Colette was ostensibly a children's extravaganza; actually it was an extremely sophisticated adult's-eye view of childhood, its terrors and wonders. Aline Bernstein had encouraged me in a variety of ways. She allowed me into her workroom to watch the procedures of a professional scenic designer.

The fact that she could not draw very well in no way impeded the execution of her tasteful and imaginative costumes and stage sets. In fact, the naïveté of her watercolors recommended her talent for the infantile elements in Ravel's ballet-opera, in which an armchair is animated and china teapots sing with amorous cats and dance with a choir of frogs and insects. A twelve-year-old boy soprano sang The Child onstage and moved with the dancers. The solo singers and chorus sat with the orchestra.

A main problem was the theater itself. Lacking any possibility of hiring a Broadway house for a single performance, we rented the auditorium of the Central High School of Needle Trades. It had nothing resembling proper equipment, lights, hanging space, or dressing rooms, and it was available only when school schedules permitted. The auditorium was huge, drafty, unappetizing; the proportions of the stage, which was hardly more than two yards above the floor, were broad and very low. However, it had a certain amplitude; here at least nobody bothered us, and Balanchine as usual forced something unusual out of harsh conditions.

In the late thirties he had managed to save some money working with Dick Rodgers and Larry Hart on Broadway and Sam Goldwyn in Hollywood. He had spent it to commission from Paul Hindemith, then in exile teaching composition at Yale, a ballet for string orchestra in the form of a theme and four extended variations. We had first proposed to use the piece for our Latin-American tour. Tchelitchev designed a series of sixty impossibly extravagant costumes on the *prétexte* of four systems supporting human anatomy—the bony structure and the lymphatic, nervous, and muscular systems. Inspired by Vesalius (with an assist from Gray's *Anatomy* edited for first-year medical students), he boasted to Balanchine that when these were executed and worn they would wipe out all choreography and obliterate music; that the audience would be *bouche bée* at such splendor. The splendid designs for his *The Cave of Sleep* joined others now deposited in the Museum of Modern Art.

The Hindemith score remained unused until Balanchine resurrected it for Ballet Society. Tchelitchev suggested Kurt Seligmann, an erudite painter with a big library of alchemy and magic lore, for decorations. Using a blend of personal symbolism and arcane ikonology, encouraged by Tchelitchev's own insistence on visual aspects, Seligmann swathed our dancers in cerements, bandages, tubes, wraps, and tourniquets, so that dancing became more a dress parade than a display of human bodies in motion. (They were soon rejected for practice dress, as has been the case with *Concerto Barocco*, *Apollo*, and other works of overwhelming choreographic rather than atmospheric interest.) To complicate matters, stage proportions were such that Balanchine was forced to align his patterns largely as bas-relief, in linear sequence across a low, broad platform which had no central focus and which was so narrow that it could barely accommodate dancing in any depth. His finale was a volcanic fountain or atomic eruption of bodies; later he also replaced this with the ending still used today. *The Four Temperaments* (the new title for the unproduced *The Cave of Sleep*) was an abstract kinetic gloss on the canonical medieval concepts of corporal and physiopsychological types—melancholic, sanguine, phlegmatic, and choleric. Todd Bolender, whose supple body and tubular limbs were remarkably serpentine, made a powerful impression as a fluidly sluggish acrobatic mendicant.

Whatever its hazards and discrepancies, Ballet Society's debut was a positive success. The Hindemith, *sans* costumes, entered a permanent repertory to be danced in the next twenty-five years by a dozen companies from Canada to Covent Garden. Now, with a new beginning under our belt, we hunted for a theater which would allow us more possibility. Our audience grew; we seemed to be well on our way—somewhere.

During three ensuing programs we offered a dozen new ballets of varying interest, as well as Gian-Carlo Menotti's opera *The Medium* and his brilliant comic curtain raiser *The Telephone*, which we had commissioned. These were immediately transferred to Broadway for a commercial run. Apart from strict ballet, we introduced some lovely Javanese court and popular dances performed against an opulent transcription for Western orchestra which Colin McPhee had made in Java from a Balinese gamelan. Merce Cunningham and Isamu Noguchi collaborated on *The Seasons*, which had visual perkiness or quirkiness, but John Cage's score (for full orchestra rather than his then notorious prepared piano) sounded no more provocative than Christian Sinding's "Rustles of Spring."

Ever since Bennington College's generosity to us, I had done my best to appreciate the so-called Modern Dance, and we would later be able to work briefly with Martha Graham and Paul Taylor. Their individual qualities of personal intensity and integrity were exhilarating. But I never lost the sense that their idiosyncratic styles derived from accident or incomplete training, that the antagonism of such dancers toward ballet (as they then understood it) stemmed from the historical condition of dance education in the United States when they were learning to perform. Their intense individualism hardly lent itself either to their inclusion in repertory or to their attachment as performers to a traditional company. In attempting to work with them we were prompted by their value as novelty for a ballet-oriented audience, rather than by any charitable broad-mindedness or genuine preference. A single unique personality, however magnetic it may be, when canonized for its own sake, restricts itself within its own accidental limits and tends to repeat itself. As far as repertory goes, works designed to frame an individual protesting theorist dissolve in the hands of other dancers, or wither when the protest loses its immediate polemical bite.

In its first season Ballet Society produced one small but exquisite work that sticks in the memory as something completely realized. This was Stravinsky's miniature opera *Renard*, produced first by Diaghilev in 1929 as Serge Lifar's debut in choreography. Now, Tchelitchev advanced Esteban Francés, a young Catalan post-Surrealist, as decorator. A superb draftsman, having been trained as an architect, he designed costumes for Cock, Cat, Sheep, and Fox that were marvelously executed by Madame Barbara Karinska. The elegant and very witty translation of the Russian rhymes by Harvey Officer, who knew his Gilbert and Sullivan, was easy to sing and understand. On its small scale it was as perfect a production as might be imagined.

FROM THE *Year Book of Ballet Society, Inc.*, 1946–1947:

The productions offered by Ballet Society in its first year combined unfamiliar works by eminent composers with new works by musicians, choreographers, painters and dancers who are embarking on their careers.

The performances of these works were a fusion of professional standards and amateur taste (the word amateur understood in its original meaning of careful selection, a cultivated taste, but an absence of timeworn formulae of production intended to guarantee safe commercial success).

Not in the last fifteen years have so many first performances been offered by a single sponsoring unit in this country. The programs, however, were presented not for their newness alone, but because performing them offered a threefold experience in education. Collaborating musicians, choreographers and painters learned how to work with each other in unsuspected ways; dancers could develop themselves through the performance of the results; while the audience accustomed itself to unfamiliar aspects of the youthful spectacle.

During the war years, Frances Hawkins had worked in New York for the Museum of Modern Art in key positions of management and public relations. Ballet Society had now reached a point when it needed a full-time business manager who might also implement policy and organize production. Improvisation at its most nervous and fitful had been our main strategy since we started. Frances Hawkins brought us not only energy and imagination, but also her wise logic distilled from long experience in the theater. Her first move was to insist that all future performances be held in the same house. Our use of dispersed auditoriums all over town was confusing and accentuated an aura of impermanence and unprofessionalism. Changes from one dissimilar backstage space to another made the construction of scenery awkward and wasteful. Stage floor-space, dressing rooms, and storage had been inadequate. From years of touring vaudeville in every conceivable climate and condition, she had sympathy for the performers' minimal requirements. She searched the city endlessly; abruptly our guardian angel manifested itself, this time in the drab but far from uncomfortable quarters of the City Center of Music and Drama, Inc.

Built at the command of a now bankrupt fraternal order, Mecca Temple on West 55th Street has the pasteboard exterior of a one-dimensional mosque. At that time it was surmounted by a huge gilded tin star and crescent, which the wind toppled to hang by a thread before it was finally removed. Over its proscenium of geometric Islamic tile was inscribed a welcoming *Salaam Aleikum*. The auditorium seated some thirty-five hundred; numerous large lodge rooms made good rehearsal floors. The building had been added to city properties for nonpayment of taxes. Newbold Morris, president of the City Council in Mayor Fiorello La Guardia's benevolent administration, and Mrs. Lytle Hull, who had organized an emergency relief committee for musicians in our worst of depressions, conceived a plan whereby the city would gain, at no cost, premises for a people's theater. The necessary transformation of the house commenced with Leopold Stokowski's broadcast concerts. New seats, a raked floor, and lights were installed. While little could be done to enhance the cavernous interior's moresco-baroque decor, it offered an inexpensive and inviting space. Frances Hawkins hired it for Ballet Society's second season at five hundred dollars a night. Little suspecting it, we had found our first real home in thirteen years.

In charge of City Center's finances, and its virtual if anonymous managing director, was Morton Baum, a citizen of incomparable value. He had graduated in 1928 from Harvard Law School to practice in New York with his brother Lester, a former New York State senator. Morton was special tax counsel to the city and devised the first city sales tax. He was assistant U.S. district attorney under Governor Dewey's racket bustings and was elected alderman in the initial La Guardia administration. A man of consummate warmth, toughness, political sagacity, and sterling integrity, he was also an able pianist and, in the true sense, a musical amateur. At the start of Ballet Society's connection with City Center we never met; he appeared to be a business executive and ordinary lawyer with whom our dealings were casual and official. As relations developed, we came to realize our fantastic luck in latching onto a landlord and legal champion who became a close friend.

At the outset Baum had no knowledge of or even particular interest in ballet. He was familiar with musical literature, operatic and symphonic. He encouraged the fledgling New York City Opera company to balance the standard Cav & Pag ham-'n'-eggs with works unfamiliar to its audience. He sight-read easily at the piano and was knowledgeable in the romantic repertory for voice and chamber music. Most important, he understood that hysteria is concomitant with the arts of performance, that without it—since after all, it is mainly a sign of high spirits or excess energy—nothing of much intensity can be achieved on stage. He knew that "efficiency" lies in the impact of performance rather than in tidy accounting systems. In addition to other prime qualities, he was a genius in the peculiar craft of deficit financing, of raising unsuspected funds in emergencies—which, considering our needs and natures, were permanent. He knew without waste motion how to make do with little or, more often, nothing. Later he would be accused of tyrannical secretiveness. He held cards firmly close to his chest; no one except Baum and Ralph Falcone, his endlessly faithful accountant and accomplice, ever knew in any detail how much cash was touchable, how much was promised or could be counted upon, or how much was owed. Falcone had his own sense of justice; although he worked long hours in the theater, he never endangered his sense of equity in handling finances for ballet and opera: he kept himself clear of any taint of unfairness to either starveling simply by never attending one single performance of either.

Baum (and Falcone) somehow maintained both the opera company, which had been in existence for three years, and now the ballet so that they were not only alive but continuously growing. Most important, Baum, unlike most harassed executives, was accessible; he would always appear at the other end of a telephone, never employing the convenient connivance of a secretary except when he was on the street or in conference. And his long intimacy with intricacies of state and municipal government did the City Center no harm. While official support was, for long, token or vestigial, even this gave City Center some appearance of being the meritorious public-service institution which indeed it became in fact. Apart from dancers and ballet masters, the pair most responsible for guiding the New York City Ballet through its early, most difficult years to eventual independence were Frances Hawkins and Morton Baum.

Before encountering Baum, we had been lulled into an illusion that Ballet Society, Inc., might somehow proceed successfully on its own as a progressive, autonomous organization. Our production program was full, subscriptions had grown, our present scale was so extravagant (at least in proposals) that there was general curiosity as to what in the world would be done with our gross accumulation of orchestral parts, scenery, and costumes after the very few performances we announced and produced. We always answered that the city was full of big, clean warehouses; however, this hardly clarified the vagueness of plans which were to lead somehow, someday, toward a viable permanent repertory. We were so concretely preoccupied with arranging four more evenings of novelties that we had little time to consider an abstract future; that could be left to Baum and Hawkins.

Balanchine projected a three-act ballet based on *Beauty and the Beast*. Ballet Society had presented the American premiere of Jean Cocteau's lovely film made from Madame de Beaumont's fairy tale. Music for the ballet would be by Alexei Haieff, whose *Divertimento* was one of the geniune triumphs of our first season; decor would be by Esteban Francés. This might have been a fascinating work, but Ballet Society had run out of money, Haieff of energy, Esteban of patience. He returned to Spain where, far away from dancers, he could paint in peace.

DECEMBER, 1947: *New York*

To Noguchi's studio with Igor and Vera Stravinsky. Isamu had beautiful scale models of *Orpheus'* decor, which they both loved. Nothing Greek about it or the costumes; Arp- or Miró-like shapes for bones-and-flames. Pluto no devil with horns, but more a King of Death like the Hindu Kali. Handsome lyre for Orpheus, carved in balsa wood. Costumes—embroidered wool, timeless, suggestive of ritual tattoos. Stravinsky thanked him for forgetting about Greece. The music is not "Greek," nor the dancing "like Duncan."

Twenty years before, our Harvard Society for Contemporary Art had given Isamu Noguchi, then a very young Japanese-American sculptor, his first one-man show. It was mainly bronze or brass portrait heads, among which were stylish likenesses of George Gershwin, Buckminster Fuller, and other celebrities; later he became distinguished for his beautiful pottery fired in Japan, as well as exquisite paper lamps and masterfully cut and polished stone figures. He developed a special gift for theater, particularly with Martha Graham and John Gielgud; his carving, modeling, and placement of three-dimensional shapes enhanced the plasticity of the space in which dancers and actors moved. Clear colors were thinly washed over metallic surfaces; these attracted light admirably. He had also a sharp sense for the surprisingly or shockingly appropriate. For the moment when Orpheus, in Hell, finally feels Eurydice's hands placed on his own so that, although blindfolded, he is able to start his long ascent to earth, Noguchi designed a slim pennant-shaped streamer of cerulean blue which sliced the infernal darkness on a musical cue. A glimpse of heavenly sky promised hope for the lovers to regain a living world.

We commissioned *Orpheus* from Stravinsky in the fall of 1946. This collaboration between him and Balanchine was one of the closest since Petipa dictated to Tchaikovsky the precise duration of each section of *The Sleeping Beauty*. For example, Balanchine estimated how long he thought the big duet between Orpheus and Eurydice should take: "about" two and a half minutes. "Don't tell me 'about,'" insisted Stravinsky, with the exactness of cook or carpenter. "It's either two minutes and twenty, thirty, or forty seconds; no more, no less." The action in *Orpheus* and its musical springboard are exceptionally concentrated if deceptively bland. There is only a single sequence of violent and fully orchestrated sonority: the final onslaught against Orpheus by the Bacchantes. Rhythmically this passage was disconcertingly complex; Stravinsky was constantly present, analyzing and authorizing the intricate tempi, while Balanchine composed it for dancing and directed stage rehearsals. The most generous and rewarding of partners, Stravinsky always placed himself at the service of ballet master and dancers. He felt that it was his responsibility to change what he'd proposed if it was neither useful nor legible. All his effects, from the most calm and subtle to the fullest, fastest, or most melodramatic, were structured for urgent plasticity in physical movement, visually as well as aurally.

His early renown, fixed by the overwhelming impression of *Firebird*, *Petrouchka*, and *Le Sacre*, made three later generations of audiences hope for a continual reprise of these same pieces. Utilizing folkloristic material, they employed massive orchestral forces, strange sounds, and rude noises for a first thrilling shock. But *Pulcinella, Oedipus Rex, Apollon,* and *Danses Concertantes* were melodic and, though rhythmically disturbing, "simple" or "small" in format. Audiences accustoming themselves to the signature of one sort of prestige commodity were loath to reexamine or reevaluate his continual shifts of manner and material. Stravinsky programmed his constant self-repudiation, moving always toward new frontiers and disdaining previous formulations, particularly those which had already proved "successful." *Orpheus* was *Apollon*'s heir, not alone in the ancient myth, but in the essence of his music-drama. Although it added brass and woodwinds to *Apollon*'s band of viols, it was not calculated as a noisy smash hit which a prepared public could acclaim at first hearing. Indeed, *Orpheus,* for all its beauties, has never achieved the orchestral repertory, and neither have Stravinsky's symphonies or most of his scores after 1930.

Balanchine conceived *Orpheus* as a ritual ceremonial, in its plangency and pathos. It is rare in the theater for artists of like intensity and talent to work together in harmonious tension. The partnership creating *Orpheus* was a triangulated collaboration in which music, sculpture, and dancing were lightly and tenderly balanced; the result could not but have been recognized as compelling, even in the dominant calm and quiet of its mood.

When Tchelitchev designed *Errante* for Edward James's Ballets 1933, he invented for its finale a surpassing *coup de théâtre*. The archetype Wanderer, having passed through fire, flood, revolution, love, hate—all life's changes and chances—was engulfed in an enormous mass of thin white China silk released from the flies. This translucent, light-reflective spun gossamer mass overwhelmed the hero who was enmeshed in its folds and thrashing against destiny. Meanwhile his alter ego, shadow-twin, or daimon, visible as a silhouette against the blinding backdrop, mounted a loose rope ladder, higher and higher, to skies from which the silken cloud had fallen.

To separate the three scenes of *Orpheus* Balanchine ordered a similar translucent curtain of China silk, but one that would, when necessary, veil the entire stage picture. It would never fall released to the floor; instead its billows, blown by backstage drafts and the motion of dancers, would reveal dozens of bodiless arms dragging Eurydice through its voluminous folds back to Hell. The silk for this curtain cost over a thousand dollars. Having it sewed and delivered to the theater cost even more, and such was our situation that we had no cash to pay for it two days before a dress rehearsal. Frances Hawkins had already raided her own savings; we had spent what there was and could borrow no more. We seldom discussed money with Balanchine (this was a courteous fiction, since he could not help knowing exactly what went on, but it helped morale). Noguchi was a model of patient despair, having been refused further credit from one scenery shop because previous bills were unpaid. Between rehearsals there were emergency conferences in corners of the School of American Ballet. We were approaching that desperate moment when we must suggest to Balanchine that he cut his beautiful *pas de deux*, alter his action, and submit to crass blackouts for the linking music between scenes. We did not notice that Balanchine had disappeared from rehearsal. Suddenly he reappeared with five hundred dollars in cash in each hand and tossed the money to Frances Hawkins. We begged to know where he'd found it; he would say nothing except that he hadn't robbed a bank.

The dress rehearsal of *Orpheus* proceeded far too smoothly for the peace of mind of any superstitious watcher. But with Stravinsky, any irrational or apotropaic fear of disaster was sentimentality; he knew what he was doing and results were not luck but logic. And our guardian angel, marking time, now fluttered in the wings, about to proffer peculiar promises.

MARCH, 1948: *New York*

To Nelson Rockefeller's office, 30 Rockefeller Plaza, to meet George de Cuevas, who married a granddaughter of J.D.R., Sr. An engaging birdlike creature, he embraced Balanchine and offered us the Cosmopolitan Theater in Columbus Circle. It was built for Marion Davies by Hearst and renovated by de Cuevas for his own ballet company three years ago; it's been empty since. Too good to be true. We are to participate equally, except in rental, which he promised free.

Too good to be true it was; the Marquis de Cuevas, like Aladdin's djinn, vanished in a cloud of delicious scent (lime or acacia); he was neither seen nor heard from again. This apparition was typical of a bevy of false starts, disheartening stops—suggestions and projects which in early stages glowed like rosy dawn but faded by dusk, or before any firm contracts could be drawn. Hope springs eternal; no stone was left unturned in our chase after stability in the frame of a permanent house. Every empty film or legitimate theater, on Broadway or off, seemed to hand us an invitation; but even the Cosmopolitan, which de Cuevas had refurbished with luxurious taste, seated only a little over one thousand persons. Frances Hawkins outlined a plan for using it a possible thirty-six weeks, during which we might share the house with a variety of like-minded attractions. Such plans always had to be reconciled with popular prices—a policy to which we were committed, and which seemed never to cover the costs. So we contented ourselves with our haphazard rentals of City Center, trying to forget its shortcomings, congratulating ourselves that we could at least spend two days rehearsing on a proper stage, that we had a little time to adjust lights and organize our irregular forces.

MAY, 1948: *New York*

With Frances Hawkins to Morton Baum's office. Baum congratulated us on *Orpheus*. Asked what we intended to do with scenery and costumes we have accumulated. I was short and irritable, nervous about the money we owed. He took no offense; asked if we would form a ballet company for the City Center, like the NYC Opera. But "I am only one person; there is, after all, a board of directors." We had heard this before, and often, at the Metropolitan Opera.

Mr. Baum did well to temper our hopes for speed and ease in the formation of a company. He had his own problems, financial and otherwise. On his board, in addition to various complications, was Gerald Warburg, Eddie's older brother, a gifted cellist, who for years had regarded me as the chief villain in the American Ballet's catastrophic tour after Scranton, Pennsylvania. Gerald warned Baum hotly against any enthusiasms of ours, which could but lead down the garden path to disaster. In addition he avowed that ballet was an impure form, anti-American, elitist; in fact, not even "healthy." There should be no place for ballet in a decent people's theater. However, Newbold Morris, the nominal chairman of the City Center, could be persuaded otherwise. Sooner than we might have hoped, a comfortable agreement had been drawn and signed. Baum's financial wizardry never exceeded the limits of the possible; after all, he was both tax expert and agile counsel. He was also an acute political analyst and knew how small palliatives might affect broad policy. A loose arrangement was effected to put us under the protective custody of a semiofficial institution, which in turn gave us a chance for further development.

We would continue to cover our deficit, but day-to-day services provided by the City Center's staff would reduce this figure. We would also serve the New York City Opera and thereby furnish additional employment for underworked dancers. Our season was concurrent with the opera's; we performed on Monday and Tuesday (the poorest nights in the week), the opera on Thursday through Sunday. Beggars aren't choosers. We saved on costs of stagehands, orchestra, front-of-the-house personnel, advertising. We were in possession of a considerable and varied repertory which had barely begun to be exploited. We had found a home, or something approximating one. When we prepared future seasons of new ballets, despite rainy weather, Morton Baum held over our heads the sturdy umbrella of the City Center of Music and Drama. In 1933 in London, I had promised Balanchine that by the time I was forty, he would have a company and a theater of his own. So far he hardly had either; the war cost us only a year's delay, but our future was open.

EMILY COLEMAN IN *Newsweek* MAGAZINE, OCTOBER 25, 1948:

It has always been Lincoln Kirstein's purpose in life to "do things nobody else would do"; that, he explains, "is the only reason I exist." . . . Now he finds himself on the same hot seat occupied by so many others. The New York City Ballet must support itself or leave the boards. This season, appealing to a broader public [than Ballet Society], at popular prices, is Kirstein's final stand. "This," he says, "is the last formula I can think of."

Our "season," restricted to weak Mondays and Tuesdays, pulled only fifty percent of capacity. It cost around fifty thousand dollars (which in current money would be roughly three times that). Immediately before we opened, the Ballet Russe de Monte Carlo enjoyed a successful engagement at the Metropolitan, draining the curiosity and purses of many ballet lovers who were accustomed to standard repertory and well-known stars. Our situation was certainly sticky. However, Balanchine was not particularly unhappy; to him profit or loss rarely meant much. He would contrive to busy himself; if one theater seemed shut to him, there was, or always had been, another that was open. Maintenance and continuity would be someone else's job; his was to weld a company and furnish it with new works. If our repertory was in itself a failure, if we did not now possess negotiable properties, if our artistic planning had not justified itself (none of which we believed), then and only then might there be cause for suicide. Morton Baum agreed, and offered us a separation from a subsidiary position with the opera. We would become autonomous; he would grant us our own weeklong "season" the next January. This meant that from now on City Center, rather than Ballet Society, assumed our deficits. We—that is, the New York City Ballet as a company with no legal entity— would be charged only for new productions. Novelties were (and are) what we lived by and for, but *how* we lived would now be up to the City Center.

Through new friends we also began to raise a certain amount of money from outside our own circle. Alice Pleydell-Bouverie loved dancing and dancers; she, her sister-in-law (then Mrs. Vincent Astor), and J. Alden Talbot and his Ballet Associates (a previous benefactor of both Ballet Russe and Ballet Theatre) helped to organize gala evenings. They were usually held at the Waldorf Astoria, which not only gave us some politically important social cachet but also brought in cash. Before this, we had had no position among the hereditary Manhattanites who supported the Met and Philharmonic and might have become interested in a native ballet company. Ballet Russe opening nights attracted flashy audiences, which yielded effective unpaid publicity in the press. Such glamour stimulates public excitement which overflows into the box office on subsequent nights.

We would never acquire much social status; we would never enjoy a well-heeled board of directors, or any legally independent status. The City Center stood *in loco parentis*, and we welcomed both the paternal advice and paternalistic patronage of Morton Baum. He did not wish to spend or waste time on cosmetic socializing, and he spared us the ennui of board interference. We learned that the price of "entertaining" prospective patrons was higher than providing free entertainment for essentially unserious enthusiasm, based on no real interest except the idle warmth of casual personal contact. We aspired to a popular policy; but this was not easy, since we were promulgating an aristocratic form of entertainment. But the idea of combining populist service and aristocratic quality appealed to Newbold Morris and Mrs. Lytle Hull, who after all were so secure in their long public services that they could discount the infrastructure of New York snobbery.

As for Baum, he would always be from the wrong side of the tracks. He suffered over his recent rejection by the Metropolitan Opera, where he had been briefly on the board at the behest of the municipal tax administration. But he had asked too many questions for comfort; covert or clear anti-Semitism was seldom absent from the red-and-gold purlieus of 39th Street and Broadway. Baum would turn this snobbery to his advantage; an affluent section of New York's industrial families was siphoned into the City Center, where he made them feel at home. A people's theater could also be classified as an amusing charity or even an "entertainment" rather than an exclusive social club. Baum magnetized a new audience of second-generation New Yorkers with a long tradition of musical appreciation in Middle Europe—an audience which was scarcely made comfortable by the heirs of Dutch patroons and the Hamiltonian succession of Murray Hill's rich, well-born, and able.

However, from this very aristocracy sprang Alice Bouverie, who threw a considerable weight of fair opinion and prestige our way. In England during the war she had worked in a munitions factory.

She had also been close to the tribulations of a nascent British ballet, which was then enduring most of the hazards that we would, with such rare help as hers, eventually surmount. Her admiration and affection for Frederick Ashton was to have crucial implications for us; her interest in our company was never loudly enunciated; she was shy, born, as she said, under the sign of Cancer; her benefactions, though many and large, were granted sideways, crabwise, apologetically. If she couldn't do more at the moment, she'd try later. Her interest, and that of Mrs. James Fosburgh, J. Alden Talbot, and, later, Joseph B. Martinson, gave us an air of somewhat raffish respectability and a bit of extratheatrical glamour, whether or not it reflected any long-range promise of security. Such ancillary or ephemeral factors had undeniable importance; even a sketch of our story would be inaccurate if it did not acknowledge these people's lively and providential help.

Stability we had not and would not have for another twenty years. In England, with the inestimable advantage of Lord Keynes's patronage, Lilian Baylis, Marie Rambert, and Ninette de Valois were beginning to enjoy the results of their Herculean labors ever since Diaghilev's disappearance. Maynard Keynes's profound attachment to all the arts, and through his wife Lydia Lopokova to ballet in particular, would transform the Sadler's Wells Company by patent into a Royal Ballet. That title was magic; the surreal but numinous magnetism attached, however tenuously, to crowned personages in a constitutional monarchy was an enormous popular advantage to the Royals, both in Britain and abroad. How we longed to touch some of that magic, knowing even then (as Wystan Auden said of himself thirty years later) that we were not Americans but rather New Yorkers, and that our ballet must represent one city in its immediacy rather than remotely personifying a nation.

After a reasonably successful season early in 1949, we faced nine months of layoff. Here again was a threat to our company. As usual, however, there were merciful injections which revived our faltering feet. From Sol Hurok, Morton Baum shrewdly acquired Marc Chagall's scenery and costumes for Stravinsky's *Firebird*, in which Maria Tallchief made an electrifying appearance, emerging as the nearest approximation to a prima ballerina that we had yet enjoyed. And Jerome Robbins, who had studied under Fokine and danced with Ballet Theatre, cast his lot with us for several seasons and created *The Guests* for Tallchief with an acerbic jazzy score by Marc Blitzstein. He also took Leonard Bernstein's symphonic reading of Auden's *Age of Anxiety* and, using ingenious photomontage by Oliver Smith, made a popular piece, although the poet prized it not at all. Robbins's genius for improvised comedy, his canny instinct for the artificed use of the apparently accidental, were also evident in his *Pied Piper* (1951) set to Aaron Copland's Concerto for Clarinet and String Orchestra (1948).

A third, less noticed but potent addition to our forces was Madame Barbara Karinska, who arrived from Hollywood with an Oscar awarded for her costuming of Ingrid Bergman's *Joan of Arc*. The supreme mistress of theatrical wardrobe in our epoch, she now gave us perky tutus for Balanchine's *Bourrée Fantasque*, his second recension (after *Cotillon* in 1932) of Chabrier's piano pieces. It ended with the finale of *Le Roi Malgré Lui* but, alas, without its rousing chorus. For years to come Balanchine kept proposing in vain the production of this opera. The score would be offered, a producer or opera manager would express delight, then nothing would come of it, either here or abroad, although Balanchine continued to design dances after Chabrier and never lost hopes for the whole opera.

Todd Bolender, Lew Christensen, William Dollar, John Taras, and Antony Tudor now began to revive or invent ballets for us. Balanchine welcomed other choreographers, but the fact that, except for Robbins's, their works seldom stayed long in repertory naturally gave us the tag of a "Balanchine" company. It could not have been otherwise, granting his qualities. However, none of the "younger" choreographers who have been asked to work with us have ever publicly faulted him for lack of warmth in offering them whatever facilities of rehearsal or production he could furnish.

Our School of American Ballet was growing from strength to strength. From the start Balanchine had organized a structure of strong instructors from whom he himself had learned. Dancers, however admirable as performers, are rarely gifted as teachers. Usually they are either models of deportment, style, and capacity who can be followed or imitated as a criterion, or analyzers who break down or demonstrate components of efficiency in their motor elements. It is seldom that the two capacities of model and analyst are found in a single master. Pierre Vladimirov was as pure an exemplification of *danseur noble* trained in the early twentieth-century Petersburg school as was then alive. Anatole Oboukhoff graduated from the Imperial School to follow Vladimirov as first dancer at the Maryinsky. It was Vladimirov who had been the Prince Charming of Diaghilev's production of *The Sleeping Beauty* in 1921. Oboukhoff was a strong, even harsh teacher who frequently behaved as if he were training big cats, horses, or poodles rather than adolescent bipeds. He barked commands and corrections like a drill sergeant; his own gestures seemed violent to the point of physical aggression; yet he was the gentlest of men as well as the strictest and clearest of analysts. Muriel Stuart, an English girl recruited and trained by Anna Pavlova, was an excellent classicist who also had a sympathy for Martha Graham's expressivity and free forms outside the academic orthodoxy of ballet. Consequently her teaching added a dimension of movement which prepared the way for Balanchine's outlandish innovations and his violations of classic order when her students came to face these in professional rehearsals. Felia Doubrovska, Vladimirov's wife, and Alexandra Danilova, the last ballerinas of the later Diaghilev seasons, had continued to perform into the thirties and forties as popular favorites. Doubrovska's regal authority and elegance, Danilova's sparkle, humor, and attack, gave innumerable girls and many boys the cool, selfless efficiency that Balanchine would use to forge a new style which, though based in Petersburg, found sharp definition and athletic accent in Manhattan.

In ever-increasing numbers our school produced recruits tailored to Balanchine's taste and requirements. Besides students from the school, there were older and more experienced dancers trained by Fokine, Mordkin, Bolm, and other Russian teachers in Paris, as well as Russian dancers scattered over the American provinces following Diaghilev's tours. These came first to join Ballet Society, then the New York City Ballet. Performers of youth and merit, Melissa Hayden, Francisco Moncion, Todd Bolender, Nicholas Magallanes, and Patricia Wilde, turned into company stalwarts. Audiences at City Center adopted them as members of a family whom they delighted in watching develop from season to season. Very young girls and boys entered our school; within four or five years they joined their seniors on the Center's stage. In one early generation emerged Jacques d'Amboise, Edward Villella, and a brilliant, capable, and strangely personal ballerina of wit, Tanaquil LeClercq, who was the epitome of Balanchine's lyrically athletic American criterion.

DECEMBER, 1949: *Rhinebeck, New York*

To Alice Bouverie's with Freddy Ashton and Cecil Beaton. Bitter cold above the Hudson; roaring fire and enormous English high tea. An album with Rimbaud's drawings, nineteenth-century *carte de visite* photographs of acrobats. Cecil thinks there should be no color in *Illuminations:* all dancers in clown-white. At the end, a huge enlargement of Rimbaud's blotted sketch of street, steeple, and sunburst. After dinner we returned to *Illuminations,* but the staff had everything tidy, stowed away, so Fred gave marvelous impersonations of Pavlova, Sarah Bernhardt, and Ida Rubinstein, with whom he had danced: "a giraffe on *pointes.*"

On leave in Paris during the last year of the war, I had heard Benjamin Britten's setting of some of Rimbaud's *Les Illuminations,* ten pieces for high voice and string orchestra (1939), beautifully played and sung by a contingent of British artists-in-uniform. Britten and the tenor Peter Pears had lived in Amityville, Long Island, in 1941 before the United States entered the war. At that time we were preparing for our Latin-American tour and asked Ben to orchestrate two suites of Rossini's piano pieces called *Matinées musicales* and *Soirées musicales,* to be used as a divertissement to conclude an evening. For *Divertimento*—a name we were to use again—we again used André Derain's delectable dresses designed for *Les Songes,* which was originally produced by Edward James in 1933 and later mounted for our American Ballet. I first met Britten through Wystan Auden; they were collaborating on a folk-opera commissioned through Columbia University's department of music. I admired both words and music, but Britten withdrew his score unpublished, and Auden reprinted only the lovely dialogue of Cat and Dog—"The single creature leads a partial life." *Paul Bunyan,* revised, could have been an attractive repertory piece, but it vanished, one more work ploughed under in two dauntlessly prolific careers. *Illuminations,* on the other hand, would hold the stage from its debut through frequent revivals.

I had known Cecil Beaton since 1927, when he befriended me in London. Ashton I had met through Chick Austin in 1934, after Ashton had come to Hartford for his miniature ballets for black dancers in Virgil Thomson's *Four Saints in Three Acts.* He is a scrupulous, imaginative, highly professional choreographer, an old friend of Pavel Tchelitchev's. Pavel provided him with the perfect dancer to impersonate Arthur Rimbaud: a young Mexican of grace and presence, Nicholas Magallanes. Tchelitchev used him as a model for paintings and sent him to our school, where he found his real vocation. He danced Rimbaud in the ballet biography compacted from the time the poet quit Charleville, through the eruption of the Paris Commune and the stormy friendship with Verlaine, to his abdication from poetry before he'd hardly come of age. Ashton realized half a dozen tableaux fusing harshness, violence, and lyricism which had a genuine ferocious impact. Beaton imagined the performers as a troupe of clowns in a one-ring circus somewhere off the Boulevards—mostly white, pale green, mauve, with metallic accents. His was *le style chiffonnier,* a poor man's chic, framing a meager, postadolescent, half-lit pathos in a tradition which reaches from the brothers Le Nain, through pink-and-rose Picasso, to *Les Forains,* waifs, mendicants, and wanderers of Christian Bérard's ballet for Roland Petit in 1945. Ashton, with his considerable skills inherited from the long tradition of English narrative gesture and pantomime, gave us a European ballet. It was unlike any of our more or less "native" American works and an addition we needed for variety at this particular time. Also, we had our eyes on London for some future connection, a possible contact through hands-across-the-sea programs.

The premiere of *Illuminations* provided us with the pretext for a gala. The British ambassador was present; national anthems were played; John Martin of the *Times* gave Ashton a brilliant notice; Alice Bouverie was delighted with what she had, first and last, brought into being. We were now very conscious of the name we carried and pressed a quasi-official alliance with our city on every opportune or opportunistic occasion.

Later that season we improvised *Jones Beach,* on which Jerome Robbins and Balanchine collaborated. At its debut were Robert

Moses, the redoubtable commissioner of parks who had caused the vast Long Island pleasure ground to be built, and representatives of the Dutch government, since the score was composed by Juriaan Andriessen, a very young Hollander here on a Rockefeller fellowship. His music had not been written for us; he had showed Balanchine a lively diploma symphony, sunny and cheerful as a day on sand and shore. Its first movement we called "Sunday"; the adagio was "Rescue from Drowning," entrancingly danced by Tanaquil LeClercq and Nicholas Magallanes; its allegro was "War with Mosquitoes" (largely by Robbins); the finale, for no particular reason, "Hot Dogs." This was typical of a dozen works which were invented backward. We had spent most of our available money on *Illuminations*. As costumes for *Jones Beach*, we wanted something more festive than the practice dresses which Balanchine increasingly favored. Bathing suits offered approximations of nudity and were available in every shape and color. We approached a well-known manufacturer with a magnanimous offer for the firm to donate undress for a classic ballet; its response was as generous as the ensuing publicity. Apart from rehearsal time, *Jones Beach* in all its topical chic cost hardly a penny.

During our early seasons at City Center, we were in the enviable position of having Leon Barzin as musical director. For Balanchine, the orchestra has capital importance; our scores needed attention, discipline, and dispatch in rehearsal beyond the interest or capacity of the ordinary contract type of Broadway bandsmen. For years Barzin had led the National Orchestral Association, which enabled student instrumentalists and conductors to obtain training and exposure under professional circumstances in series of seasonal concerts at Carnegie Hall. Barzin himself was an experienced viola player. In him Balanchine found an eager colleague with whom he could speak as a partner—a conductor who embraced contemporary music enthusiastically while having a wide familiarity with the entire scope of orchestral literature. Our lighting expert and technical administrator was Jean Rosenthal, who had done wonders for Orson Welles and John Houseman since the days of W.P.A. and the Mercury Theater. She worked magic with patched or rented electrical equipment and rickety portable boards—veterans of the Ballet Caravan tours, which she had originally serviced.

Because of the increasing accumulation and persistence of our appearances, our introduction of piquant novelties, and the incidental social functions of two galas and their attendant publicity, we managed to finish this season with our smallest deficit so far. Our achievement was also due to help from Mrs. Bouverie, Mrs. Astor, and J. Alden Talbot. Morton Baum could face his board of directors with some vindication for his rashness in having taken us on. We had not yet bankrupted City Center; on the contrary, we'd managed to attract a different, often younger audience, open up a new sphere of public service, and create a fresh excitement.

MARCH, 1950: *London*

Frances Hawkins and I wait endlessly for David Webster, absent for the weekend. Negotiations at a complete impasse. Our conditions unacceptable; he doesn't want us at Covent Garden. Onstage, rehearsal for Balanchine's revival of *Ballet Imperial*. Margot Fonteyn and Michael Somes danced beautifully. Frances decides to fly home tomorrow; I'll wait for *Imperial*. Cyril Beaumont's ballet bookshop, Charing Cross Road, with Lydia Lopokova; found postcards of her in *The Good-Humored Ladies*. Heavy tea with Dickie Buckle, editor of *Ballet*. He says that Webster is always like this at first.

The first night of Balanchine's *Ballet Imperial*, invented originally to give us a "grand" Petipa-type work for the Latin-American tour, was, in London nine years later, all it should have been. Beryl Grey, Michael, and Margot were strong and stylish; there were seventeen curtain calls. Finally Ninette de Valois, creator and director of the Royal Ballet, came onstage with George, who was handed a big wreath from the dancers. Frances Hawkins had her ticket to New York in her pocket; she'd be leaving at dawn. She bade good-bye to David Webster, General Administrator of Covent Garden, at the party Balanchine gave in the crush-bar of the Royal Opera House. Webster, all smiles, stopped her farewells; she must not leave London until he had signed our contract. We would appear at Covent Garden for five weeks, commencing the middle of next July, then tour the provinces for three weeks more. His terms were generous; he would even pay half transportation to and from New York: our ultimate condition, which clinched the deal. It seemed too good to be true. When Frances took her leave, Webster said: "My dear, believe it or not, I'm happy to have the New York City Ballet; however, I can assure you London will make or break you." We appeared under the sponsorship of the Arts Council of Great Britain. Our visit was considered a semiofficial exchange for the Sadler's Wells 1949 season at the Metropolitan, where the British dancers had received the greatest ovation in their brief history. To an important degree, an alien audience establishes the artistic, economic, and political importance of a luxury export. Acceptance by a foreign public affixes a convincing seal of prestige for home approval.

We were scarcely "official," however, except by the grace of City Center; and we were far from being royal. Our particular American qualities, no matter how they might be prized in New York, gave no special assurance of being warmly embraced by London. So far we barely qualified as a national treasure. I was apprehensive; England meant much. My real education had commenced there; my criteria of sensibility and intelligence were based on British models, living or dead. Nothing less than absolute victory would bring me much satisfaction. One appearance at Covent Garden was a culmination, beyond which there could be nothing: on this I staked everything. It was ridiculous overexaggeration; I would pay for my lack of historical perspective. But I had not been in London since 1933; for me it was still Diaghilev's town; we would be dancing on the stage of vividly remembered triumphs. My sense of competition was factitious; I was not rational; as Frances Hawkins wisely diagnosed: "He's not crazy, he's hysterical."

JULY, 1950: *Covent Garden*

Debut of *Illuminations*. The Queen is not coming. "Mixed" reception. Fred led us underground to a passage that would take us up into the Duke of Bedford's private box. A steel door

locked us in the cellar. We yelled in unison; finally a night watch-man heard and let us through. Marina, Duchess of Kent, glacial. She was not amused by Ashton's pantomime in which a king and queen have their crowns knocked off, while the mob delights in an orgy. Not the sort of thing Fred would have been allowed to do here. I tried to explain to Her Highness. Fred, delighted. He'll do another piece for us next year. Wired Alice Bouverie "love and thanks," but it was no jolly occasion.

Predictably, the anonymous reviewer of the London *Times* loathed *Illuminations* as much as or more than he had hated *Firebird* at our opening the week before. I responded to his shocked stance far too seriously and felt impelled to draft a letter, with the help of Morgan Forster, a friend from Bloomsbury summers. I was much consoled when complimented on it during a quiet weekend in Cambridge where, at the high table in Kings, one of Forster's colleagues said: "Jolly well done." It might be a footnote to the complete letters of the master of *A Passage to India*, for its tone and terseness were more his than mine:

> Sir,
> Your critic's unfavorable opinion of Mr. Frederick Ashton's ballet, *Les Illuminations*, in your issue of July 21 was, so far as I could judge, not shared by the audience, for the reception was enthusiastic. Your critic is presumably aware of the mixed beauty and grossness of Rimbaud's life and work and it is regrettable that he could only recognize grossness on the stage. As for his condemnation of *The Firebird* I would ask leave to correct him on a point of fact. He states that "The whole ballet was danced without the slightest trace of the atmosphere of Stravinsky's music." He seems unaware that the choreography was revived with the composer's desire and approval and that he conducted the work in the February, 1950, season in New York.

London's reception of our company was doubtless not as drastically ignominious as I chose to imagine. The Opera House for our five weeks sold about seventy-five percent of capacity. Many reviews were sympathetic, some even favorable. What might I have expected? Something vague, impossible, absolute—like death or transfiguration? David Webster now turned into kindness itself; he suggested, and should not have, that we play a sixth week. We did, and should have. In reckless compulsion we even felt obliged to produce a new ballet, *The Witch*, by John Cranko, who was presented to us by Ashton as the best of "young" English choreographers; in return, Balanchine gave the Sadler's Wells junior company Haydn's *Trumpet Concerto*. Neither was remarkable except for the genuine exchange of goodwill prompting them. Our provincial tour was lamentable; ghosts whom I hoped had been laid for keeps in Scranton, Pennyslvania, reemerged howling.

There were compensations, or more precisely, memorable incidents. During an intermission after a performance of *Orpheus* to which I'd asked T. S. Eliot, we spoke of a possible sequel for which his words might conceivably be set by Stravinsky, as he had handled André Gide's *Perséphone*. But Eliot knew of the composer's notorious difficulties with French prosody and Gide's poetics, and was not enthusiastic. A sung prayer for dancers could be imagined, but would take consideration. Eliot, remote, courteous, attentive, thought dancing was sufficient unto itself, requiring nothing by way of words, at least from him. I reminded him of his excellent notices of dancing and music halls when he edited the *Criterion*; he replied that those were "evocation not invocation." There would indeed be a sequel to *Orpheus*, but *Agon* was some seven years in the future.

An enormous party in a huge mansion seemed to revive for a night Edwardian Mayfair in its heyday. It was given to celebrate the coming-of-age of a Marquess of Hartington, and our entire company was invited. I was introduced to Clarissa Churchill, later Lady Avon. She inquired—implying, I imagined, some trickery—how we had chanced to come by Chagall's scenery and costumes for *Firebird*. I started to explain, in overelaborate detail, the convolutions surrounding Morton Baum's negotiations with Sol Hurok over the transference of property which had fallen to him. She cut it short: "What I really want to know is why your dancers can't keep in step." I was puzzled; "keeping in step" implied a Rockette type of paramilitary discipline, whereas most of our choreography was insistently contrapuntal, phrasing deliberate imbalance, syncopation, and calculated offbeats. It was characteristic of my mild paranoia that I imagined her hostile.

In New York we had anticipated a London deficit of twenty-five thousand dollars. Owing to our week's extension at Covent Garden and the provincial tour, we lost twice that; Morton Baum would have to cover it in ways one dared not ask. Arnold Haskell, an old friend from 1933 when he and I collaborated on Nijinsky's biography, gave us in print a generous summation. Richard Buckle, critic on the *Observer*, as well as editor of *Ballet*, rebuked his colleagues for a general "impercipience" toward our manifestations. But the most comforting farewell was small handmade bouquets of red and white carnations bought early at Covent Garden's flower market and delivered to every girl in the corps de ballet, with cards reading:

> In gratitude and with admiration for your wonderful dancing throughout the season from your friends in the Gallery and Amphitheater at Covent Garden. Please come back.

Despite ups and downs, before the company flew back to Manhattan, David Webster offered us a return engagement for the summer of 1952. At that particular moment, such was my manic depression that this was the last thing I wanted. There was no evidence that we would even be in existence by 1952.

The stage floor of the Royal Opera House had scarcely been repaired since its honorable wartime service, and our dancers suffered from cracks and splinters. Maria Tallchief sprained an ankle opening *Serenade*; there were other injuries for which the patched surface was not blameless. But Richard Buckle, with his genius for the preposterous which elevates him to a dukedom of the absurd, awarded us a floral tribute of bomb-site weeds and this citation: "*To those Americans who fell at Covent Garden: July–August, 1950.*"

FROM THE *New York Times* (JOHN MARTIN),
NOVEMBER, 22, 1950:

It was a joyous evening at the City Center last night, for the New York City Ballet company opened its three-week season at the top of its form in three of George Balanchine's best

ballets. There is no doubt whatever that the successful out-
come of the young company's daring invasion of London's
Covent Garden Opera House last summer has done wonders
for its morale, and it has returned to its home stage in the
finest of spirits raring to go.

And what a company it is! Without any stars in the narrow sense of the term . . . it has a brilliant set of leading
artists. . . . Here too is an ensemble of note; there was not
one of them last night who did not dance as if she were herself a ballerina, yet with a feeling for the unity of the group
and the framework of the composition. What more can one
ask of any company it would be difficult to say.

John Martin's conversion to our cause, after his earlier misgiv-
ings about Balanchine and our chances for creating an "American"
ballet, was just as important as our London season, since weekly
news magazines which covered city and nation followed the lead of
the *Times* then, as they do today. However, in 1950 there were half
a dozen papers in New York which regularly sent reporters to dance
events. With due respect to David Webster's prophecy, Covent
Garden neither made us nor broke us. Our financial footing was no
firmer over the long run.

London did, however, add a status which we had not enjoyed
before, especially with dancers who had not been schooled within
our orbit. Janet Reed, a sprightly, swift soubrette, came from Lew
Christensen in San Francisco. She was that American who, for me,
most recalled Lydia Lopokova. Melissa Hayden, with her formidable strength and attack, was already a favorite. Maria Tallchief
stayed as our standard-bearer. Now Diana Adams, with her cool
linear plasticity, joined us; a little later came Nora Kaye, the most
intense and melodramatically effective dancer-mime of her generation. Hugh Laing brought his dark suavity and firm elegance to
Antony Tudor's ballets; Harold Lang captivated everyone with his
jazzy snap and sharpness. André Eglevsky, premier *danseur noble*
of his time, terminated an impressive career after several seasons
with us and later taught a generation of boys in our school.

As we proceeded, reinforced by such experienced artists, the
School of American Ballet continued to provide new soloists who
formed continual support in depth. There were, of course, comings

and goings, enforced by personal sentiment, fate, or history. Edward Villella, on the brink of a spectacular development, having studied in our school since he was nine, disappeared for more than five long and unprofitable years in the Merchant Marine Academy. Nora Kaye had been rapturously received on her initial appearance in February, 1951. For her Jerome Robbins created *The Cage*, which, as he admitted, was a ferocious updating of the second act of *Giselle*. More accurately, it was a manifesto for Women's Lib, twenty years *avant la lettre*, in which Nora mimed and danced a predatory, unprayerful mantis. In this and in Tudor's repertory, she was incomparable. Our aesthetic did not suit her, however. She was a tremendous personality in her own idiosyncrasy and could have been nothing less; we were unable to frame so overpowering a presence in roles which she felt were satisfactory. But her success in *The Cage*, which was due as much to her dancing as to Robbins's design, encouraged Baum to risk our first "summer season" which, in spite of a superstition that "no one stays in New York in the summer," succeeded.

Sol Hurok now offered us a national tour, which we might take as a basic commercial accolade. He had been most helpful in arranging our contract with Covent Garden, and it had been through him that we obtained Chagall's decor for *Firebird*. He planned to have local symphony orchestras accompany us wherever possible; there could be extended seasons in Chicago, San Francisco, and Los Angeles. But when Frances Hawkins and Baum projected actual costs and calculated the amounts that transportation and commissions might subtract from any gross we might earn, and when we considered that our repertory would be unfamiliar and probably unattractive to many new audiences, we decided not to risk it. I had hoped that our company would remain comfortably a tale of two cities, New York and London, which was scarcely realistic or far-sighted. Balanchine, who (always wearing a Zuñi bracelet) had driven across the continent from New York to Los Angeles some dozen times via the Dakotas, the Rockies, and the Southwest, naturally wished our ballets to be seen beyond the Mississippi. Where had all my nationalist sentiment gone? What had happened to the doctrinaire programs backing *Billy the Kid*, *Yankee Clipper*, and *Filling Station*? My nationalism was alive and fairly well at the City Center. But now we knew for sure that we were not Americans in general, but specifically New Yorkers.

APRIL, 1951: *Chicago*

Huge parade celebrating Douglas MacArthur. Handfuls of people in the Opera House. Negative satisfaction of knowing I was right in not wanting to move out of New York. Beautiful studio party given by Ruth Page and Tom Fisher. Chicago is a big town in which nobody lives; hard to get home by the Illinois Central to suburbs after dark; only two theater nights, Friday and Saturday. Baum underestimated losses.

On my return to New York, Baum would give no definite date for our company's further appearance. The City Center was undergoing one of its permanent crises, which continue into our present. There were various anonymous characters upon whom he could call in direst need, but since need was always dire and sources few, he was loath to cry wolf too often. However, within a month we were back at work; Baum had uncovered a new patron in a manufacturer of kosher matzos. All this was long before any real support came from the state or federal government or charitable foundations.

Our Chicago experience was sobering, if only temporarily; we would play there again with better luck for several years on a more or less seasonal basis. The main point of touring, as far as I was concerned, was to employ dancers and so avoid the erosion of personnel and the costs of replacement. Dancers were paid about half the rate of musicians and a third of what stagehands made. Their labor-union history was shorter, but they ate as much as their elders or betters. Soon we were appearing rather regularly in Washington, Philadelphia, San Francisco, and Los Angeles. These jaunts eked out our City Center engagements, but costs mounted increasingly (and continue to mount; over the last decade, for example, the company has been able to leave New York only for foreign tours and summer seasons in Saratoga, Washington, Cleveland, and Ravinia, near Chicago).

In the meantime, at home base in City Center Balanchine completed a series of repertory pieces larger in format than any we had handled before. Ravel's *La Valse* had been in part instigated by Diaghilev, who, when he read the piano score, pronounced it undanceable. Ravel's original inspiration may have been Schubert's piano waltzes from 1823, which Diaghilev could have considered superior. Also, in 1912, Ravel's first version had been used dubiously for dances by Natasha Trouhanova, a dancer much disliked by Diaghilev. For our Ballet Caravan, William Dollar had made a ballet from Ravel's *Valses nobles et sentimentales*, the suite of piano pieces from which the big tone poem was later derived. *La Valse* had later been used for ballet without notable success; it was too brief and abrupt to sustain a dramatic extension which initially it seems to propose. Balanchine, however, adapted the early piano pieces, fully orchestrated, as a prelude to the developed grand waltz.

Diaghilev's original prejudice has some justification; *La Valse* is less a canonization of the waltz as a form than a definition of its cataclysmic disintegration. The big themes shatter, rhythms dissolve, a persistent beat grows tenuous, and as a succession of feverish motifs dissolve, the climax becomes chaos. If there is any substratum of narrative, it lies in the suggestion of dancing on the edge of a volcano. Karinska's skirts and bodices fused a Parisian Second Empire theme with a timeless but immediate present, fixing their permanent elegance so that even the waistlines have not been changed in twenty years. At the start, Balanchine developed oddly "Chinese" gestures in a provocative overture that focused on the soloists' long white gloves and introduced a pervasive mood of heartless ritualized flirtation and broken impersonal encounters. Tanaquil LeClercq, with her exceptional nervous energy, grace, fragility, and pathos, strongly supported by Nicholas Magallanes and Francisco Moncion, ensured its persistence in our repertory. Before this we could not have commanded an orchestra capable of mastering a score so large in scale, but Leon Barzin had strengthened his forces, and Morton Baum permitted us to pack a dozen more musicians into the Center's crowded pit.

We deliberated over the problem of revivals. Certain names of older ballets stick in the public mind, although they may never have been seen. Some of Balanchine's European successes ought to be produced here. A few had entered the repertory: *Apollo*, which would be given new vitality by André Eglevsky and later by Jacques d'Amboise; Prokofiev's *Prodigal Son*, with Rouault's decor newly painted from original watercolors bought by Chick Austin for Hartford; Bizet's once-forgotten *Symphony in C*, which Balanchine had invented for the Paris Opéra in 1947 as *Le Palais de Cristal*. Lacking Christian Bérard for a revival of *Cotillon*, Balanchine revised an homage to Emmanuel Chabrier in *Bourrée Fantasque*. Bérard's decor for *Mozartiana* was lost; we had exhausted his costumes in our own recension for the American Ballet. Balanchine staged *Caracole* from Mozart's Divertimento No. 15 as a replacement for his *Symphonie Concertante*, created for Ballet Society in 1947 and too soon forgotten.

We did not yet have a nineteenth-century work on our roster—no *Sleeping Beauty*, no *Giselle*, no *Sylphide*. We were not a museum of past masterpieces, or a guardian of an "authenticity" which at best is no better than the dubious or radical restoration of once splendid but long eroded paintings. Balanchine's practice of altering his own works from season to season as he saw fit would continue to cause rancor among the journalistic confraternity. He would be governed by prevailing conditions as much as or more than by indecision. Often the determining factors were the presence of new dancers with novel capacities and his own altered insight into choreography he felt could be improved. But then, what of "authenticity" and an absolutely "correct" version? We were dedicated to a fresh repertory suited to new habits, our own audience, dancers we'd trained, and circumstances under which we now operated. We were no official agency; we had no imperial ballerinas to accommodate, or princely patrons to flatter. We could do much as we pleased, within limits imposed by our consistently uncertain economic situation. Often it was practical to be capricious, inconsistent, and irritating.

SEPTEMBER, 1951: *New York*

With Balanchine to Morton Baum's to thank him for fall and winter seasons. He was against Bartók's *Miraculous Mandarin* but consented because of aid from the Bartók Foundation. Orchestral pieces considered—Strauss's *Don Juan* or *Til Eulenspiegel*. Again brought up Brahms's *Liebeslieder Walzer*. Voices too expensive. What about *Swan Lake?* Only the second act is interesting.

Baum was not moved by considering cash for itself; he was interested in repertory which would or would not attract customers. His emphasis was not stupid; he never interfered (directly), but he was persistent. Balanchine had admired the talent of Lev Ivanov even more than that of the far more famous Marius Petipa. Much less prolific, shaded by the Frenchman, Ivanov was equally professional but more musical, less synthetic and mechanical. Ivanov was responsible for the success of Act Two of *Swan Lake* in its 1895 revival, when Tchaikovsky's marvelous score vindicated itself (the initial failure in 1877 was due to a presumed "Wagnerianism" and to lusterless choreography). When we consented to face the idea of presenting *Swan Lake*, Balanchine made it clear that what he intended would be a personal abridgment which, while incorporating elements recalled from Ivanov, would be more his individual homage to Tchaikovsky than any "authentic" archaeological reconstruction. In the twenty years since Balanchine revived the second act, many changes, omissions, and replacements have been made. Sections in the score which Diaghilev and others had eliminated were restored; music from other sections was inserted. The unison quartet of "little swans," an unfaltering applause-machine, was soon suppressed; the male solo variation was changed variously to suit a succession of first dancers.

Swan Lake in whatever version, produced by whatever company, bolsters weak programs. It is the favored role of favorite ballerinas, and a legible metaphor for classic ballet in the minds of people who care little for dancing. It is, in truth, reliable insurance. If we wished to consider a production of *Tyl Ulenspiegel*, then to cover its large risk we must make room for *Swan Lake*. At the moment it seemed a glaring retreat from our staunch principle of resisting revivals, adapting prior prestige to present opportunism. And some of the same people who, ten years before, objected to our insistence on novel or unfamiliar music now considered our use of *Swan Lake* an abdication. Yet Balanchine's production was hardly a revival, although he was inevitably accused of lack of reverence for the Ivanov-Petipa "original," wherever that dubious touchstone was thought to exist. Opinions on any strict choreographic adherence to half-forgotten ballets are comparable to divisions over details of an orthodox liturgy. A gloss considered heretical by one ballet master is taken as a standard of correctness by another. Balanchine considered himself a colleague of Tchaikovsky's rather than a protector of Ivanov or Petipa.

In his design for our production Cecil Beaton took as a precedent sixteenth-century draftsmanship as rendered by Urs Graf or Hans Baldung Grien. Their wiry calligraphy proposed handsome linear patterns of white ink used negatively on dark paper. We had a strong cast—Tallchief and Eglevsky in the big roles, Patricia Wilde and (later) Caroline George in subsidiary but scarcely less brilliant dancing. Balanchine's pattern for the finale was a notable example of intensity accumulated by blocks of cross movement. Our *Swan Lake* turned out to be precisely the sort of success Morton Baum desired. When paired with *Firebird*, our "bird program" served manfully in many mutations. Beaton's stylish setting was too small when we moved to the State Theater. Rouben Ter-Arutunian, inspired by Albrecht Altdorfer, painted a moss-banked forest lake with enchanted-island cliffs; again Balanchine altered Ivanov's design; but the music, as always and everywhere, was an indestructible scaffold for satisfactory dancing.

As for the tone poems of Richard Strauss, we went deeply into *Don Juan* and discussed the ballet endlessly with Eugene Berman, who had interesting pictorial ideas. But, as with *Tyl Ulenspiegel*, the brevity of the piece precluded much development and might have resulted only in a sequence of abrupt or truncated vignettes too compact visually for the scale of orchestration. *Tyl* was produced as a repayment of sorts for our willingness in the matter of *Swan Lake*. It was one of several productions which should have had a long life. Large in format, successful at its premiere, novel in treatment, triumphant in visual realization, with a witty performance by Jerome Robbins in all Tyl's tricky impersonations, it was the most elaborate work we had so far presented at the Center. Esteban Francés's scenery was a clever borrowing from the anxious and fantastic world of Hieronymus Bosch. It received unanimous approval from many who felt that we usually skimped on decoration. The music, however luxurious in sonority, gave Balanchine small scope to exploit characterization or incident. There were no possible musical repeats which might have expanded the opportunities for action. To gain a few more minutes he introduced a prologue accompanied only by ominous drum rolls. Two children were revealed opposing each other, playing on a gigantic chessboard. The boy king, Philip II, deployed a toy armada of model ships; the young Tyl blocked him with a blunt loaf of peasant bread. The Spaniard knocked the bread off the board; fisticuffs followed, and then the first chords of the tone poem were heard. Now Tyl, grown into a folk hero, taunts the tyrant invaders by his tricks and rouses his people against the might of Castile and Aragon. *Life* magazine gave us a double-page spread in color; everything promised a long and rewarding run in repertory. But fire swept our warehouse; costumes, beautiful little galleons, masks, all were lost. Jerome Robbins left the company. But most of all, Balanchine felt frustrated by the scale of the score, so there was neither impetus nor energy to attempt its salvage.

APRIL, 1952: *New York*

Final talk with Sol Hurok over 1953–54 tour. He wishes to reduce number of dancers, take only small ballets, use a half-size orchestra, and include one-night stands. Few dancers eager to go, leaving empty apartments; no salary increase. Eleven rehearsal weeks, thirteen playing weeks, and it's not enough. Trouble over possible European tour; Jacob Potofsky, president Amalgamated Clothing Workers and a director of City Center, resigns from the board because we are invited to Franco's Spain.

Our situation was again awkward. A chance of cashing in nationally on whatever success we had built in Manhattan interested Mr. Hurok, but conditions governing financial feasibility pleased neither Balanchine nor our principal dancers. On the other hand, we were now offered a five-month tour of Europe, commencing in Barcelona. Mr. Potofsky had been a good friend of my father's; we were aware of the justice of his protest as well as the injustices that prompted it. The negative political implications of our appearing in Spain were to be echoed continually over the next twenty years—particularly when we went to Japan in 1958, the Soviet Union in 1962 and 1972, and Greece in 1968. Many vocative persons with indignant memories held that we should have no traffic with former foes or present tyrannies.

From the early thirties I had had ample experience of confrontations between art and politics. In 1932 I arranged a show inviting contemporary artists to paint mural panels which might lead to jobs decorating Rockefeller Center, then under construction. Ben Shahn sent an effective panel, which he could hardly have expected to be chosen, for a series detailing the agony of Sacco and Vanzetti. It showed A. Lawrence Lowell, president of Harvard, gloating over their coffins, and caused exactly the offense that was intended. I was also involved in a rather violent attempt to prevent the destruction of Sergei Eisenstein's Mexican film footage. In 1939 for Ballet Caravan, Eugene Loring had choreographed City Portrait with music by Henry Brant, a proletarian, proto-agitprop ballet with a rust-red guardrail around a manhole as its main scenery, and outraged dancing (if not very outrageous for mass movements) by a furious mob of fifteen. Marc Blitzstein and Jerome Robbins had Leftist attachments, and their ballet The Guests (1949) was an ambiguously compassionate demonstration of what a black friend called "the cluded and excluded."

Years spent in the Army, however, had depoliticized me. Irresponsibly or not, I came to consider politics as a whole and politicians as they affected our company mainly as jugglers of intermittent or endemic apathy. Severe experiences with State Department agencies all over the world taught me that direct involvement with abrasive issues and most attempts to satisfy opposing public opinion would only impede my real business, which was our survival on my terms. The energy or talent needed even tangentially for devotion to valid causes was incommensurate with what energy I had to keep our company working. That we were vaguely considered representative of our city was honor and convenience. That we were to represent the nation's culture overseas in a country where our chief concern was naval bases to control the Mediterranean meant no more than necessary weeks of work. Since we could not presume to affect foreign policy either by going or by refusing to go, I would not let objections, however justified, stand in our way.

MAY, 1952: *Barcelona*, MAURICE RAPIN, *Figaro*, *Paris*, MAY 8:

Symphony in C concludes the performance and introduces the homage. The last strains of music end; a rain of rose petals and laurel leaves starts to fall from balconies and boxes in the upper tier while stage attendants begin to bring in baskets of multicolored flowers to the dancers, grouped around their *maître de ballet*. The whole stage becomes a garden. Now, the supreme and rare tribute that Barcelona shows to admired artists: a flight of doves flies from every direction over the entire auditorium. . . . Eight minutes by my watch, the audience applauded the dancers who by now had almost stiffened "to attention"; Balanchine was visibly moved. It was a great night in Barcelona.

Three weeks before this, such glory could not have been anticipated. We had been irrevocably scheduled to open on Tuesday of Easter Week. Just as "everyone" leaves London for Bank Holiday, or New York over the Fourth of July and Labor Day, so "no one" stays in Barcelona during Easter Week. Annual subscribers to the Liceo Theater's programs determine success. However—and doubtless from political considerations—word filtered down that the provincial governor, diplomatic and consular corps, and local city officials would attend our premiere. Then "everyone" else who was anyone felt obliged to be present. Our repertory was appreciated, the dancers even more so, which was lucky since it gave confidence before our imminent attack on Paris.

There we had been invited to appear at the Palais Garnier for a festival entitled Masterpieces of the Twentieth Century sponsored by the Congress of Cultural Freedom, whose secretary-general was Nicolas Nabokov. As a youth he had been discovered by Diaghilev, and in 1928 he wrote the music for *Ode* (Massine-Tchelitchev). During and since the war, he had served in several of our cultural embassies. In Paris there were numerous impressive participants, including the Boston Symphony Orchestra. But Serge Lifar, who had been ballet master at the Opéra since 1932 (at Balanchine's own suggestion), was offended because his company, a national standard-bearer, had not been invited. Reasons for this glaring omission were personal, political, devious, reflecting no honor on anyone. None of it was our fault; we had known nothing of the circumstances, which were internecine and local. However, owing to the ancient connection of Balanchine, Nabokov, and Lifar, we were vulnerable to attack. In the Parisian fashion there were angry exchanges of letters in the press, which blithely contributed to black-market prices for our premiere. The situation of ballet at the Grand Opéra over the last two centuries has been, at best, uneasy. There have been good times when capable administrations found private individuals who personally covered deficits, but at other times the Opéra has been subject to disastrous political pressure when some official bureaucracy assumed control.

Only recently Paris had welcomed other American and English companies, as well as Roland Petit's young and tasteful Ballets des Champs-Élysées. The traditional, indeed legendary supremacy of French lyric theater—which was a semipermanent actuality in *opéra comique* and in ballet at least from the thirties through the forties of the last century—has long been compromised. Hence there were patriotic critics who, like others in years to come, would be lamenting our lack of soul, or *âme frigidaire*. As Balanchine later retorted to similar Russian complaints: "When you say we have 'no soul,' it merely means our 'soul' is unlike yours." For decades before the First World War, there was universal admiration for *l'âme slave*, which Anna Pavlova personified to an often inordinate degree. Dancers whose most adored role is Giselle incarnate "soul"; it is the blood of Swan Queens.

In any case, we could not have wished for more success than we had at our opening performances both at the Opéra and subsequently at the Champs-Élysées Theater. Stravinsky conducted his *Orpheus* in the presence of the president of the republic. Jerome Robbins's *Pied Piper*, a happy improvisation on Aaron Copland's Clarinet Concerto, was performed on the same program. To a Parisian audience, the gravity of *Orpheus* seemed modest or monotonous. *Le Sacre du Printemps* of forty years before was still the type of Stravinsky which spelled a smash; nothing less loud could be expected to elicit so warm a welcome. Robbins's *Cage* benefited from considerable coverage in the picture press; any number of erotic and quasi-pornographic journals regaled its metaphorical ferocity.

A fortnight at the Florentine Maggio Musicale followed, packing the Teatro Communale's forty-two hundred seats at each performance. There was even loose talk of Florence acting as a permanent host to our company, just as Monte Carlo had served Diaghilev after the First World War. A similar offer had come from Milan after Balanchine had mounted *Ballet Imperial* at La Scala the preceding March. North Italian dancing masters of the sixteenth and seventeenth centuries were responsible for a codification of steps which remain the basis for our discipline. Yet ballet as an institution declined there, and recently has been represented chiefly by sporadic or token activity. However generous Florence or Milan may have been, it was impossible to take their enthusiasm very seriously. Italian audiences are oriented toward voice rather than dancing, and their system of municipal subsidies makes any consecutive program questionable. However, the gossip about these proposals did no harm at home. At least it showed that we were appreciated, and that we might hope for similar but firmer appreciation from our own municipal or federal government.

JUNE, 1952: *The Hague*

Frans Schokkink (*sic*), Burgomaster, The Hague, insists we remove *The Cage* from all programs; two local critics who saw it in Florence decided it was "pornographic" and "shameless." The burgomaster has appealed to our ambassador, who says this is beyond his diplomatic competence. If *Cage* goes, Robbins will withdraw all his work; Nora Kaye will refuse to appear in other ballets. Our embassy wants thirty tickets; none to be had.

Possible censorship made *The Cage* more popular than ever; our engagement was sold out; we were invited to return the following year. The historic progression of permissiveness in theater over the next two decades is exemplified by its development in Holland, where the national ballet companies in the late sixties flaunted frontal nudity as thrilling aesthetic innovation. Balanchine for years had opted for an approximation of the body unimpeded, unencumbered by redundant adornment. However, Lord Clark's distinction between nakedness and nudity is a governing consideration. Balanchine continued to clothe dancers in music, movement, and gesture; frontal frankness has its ephemeral piquancy, but sustains only marginal choreographic interest. Often it represents desperation on the part of dance designers, who judge that a wholly exposed body is more fetching than exposure of their notions of movement. Obligatory shock is as tiresome as the resistance or apathy of conservative subscribers. Ballet, since it involves bodies in close contact, possesses erotic dimensions that have long been presupposed, but after the revolution of Isadora and Nijinsky, bankruptcy of imagination in many "young" choreographers (any male under forty-five) proposes genital display as a substitute for plastic invention.

Our second European tour ended with six weeks at Covent Garden, followed by another at the Edinburgh Festival. Our continental travels had been efficiently promoted by Leon Leonidoff, an experienced impresario who became a foster-father to Balanchine and our dancers. He would devotedly handle our European wanderings over the next two decades. This London engagement was less rousing than our first. *The Cage* was received with unflappable calm, perhaps influenced by the parochial nervousness of the Dutch. Nora Kaye had a genuine success. Even *Swan Lake*, despite its predictable lack of "authenticity," caused little discomfort. The critic A. V. Coton wrote: "In fact it has been much like a season by any other foreign company; more people approve than disapprove simply because it is strange and novel and unlike what they are used to."

If we had been French, our product would have been more appetizing and familiar; the English cherish the suave, cosmetic sagacity of French chic. Whatever their insularity, however fond or firm the bonds of our common language and our hands-across-the-sea, London is closer to Paris than to New York. Even after two centuries and four wars, Americans must bear the burden of having behaved like rebellious or ungrateful offspring whose naïve energy may be forgiven, but whose arrogance is not forgotten. Normal envy, residual resentment derive partly from a difference in the manner by which Americans measure time, and a national discrepancy in notions of speed, pace, grace, and motion. We share the same speech, but spelling, accent, tone of voice, and slang differ.

Before he left Russia, Balanchine knew that the twentieth century needed its own tempi, which were jazzy and syncopated, and that asymmetrical rhythm was deep in the motor dynamism of advanced industrial societies. The nineteenth century dies hard; its stronghold is still a constitutional monarchy, socialized indeed, but as firmly stratified as ever. The New York City dancers epitomize in their quirky legginess, linear accentuation, and athleticism a consciously thrown away, improvisational style which can be read as populist, vulgar, heartless, overacrobatic, unmannerly, or insolent. It is also a style of living which may be interpreted as having small respect for its forebears—its elders and, naturally, betters.

Offering the excuse of my mother's recent death, I did not accompany our company on this tour. I might have served in a social capacity, but I absented myself for a more useful conservation of forces. I detest the ritual of first nights, press conferences, confrontations with friendly or unfriendly journalists. I realized that this was all part of the impresario game, but I wasn't an impresario. I was, and would remain, a buffer for Balanchine outside the theater. In Europe he needed none.

OCTOBER, 1952: *New York City*

No money for scenery for Hindemith's *Metamorphoses*. We need something exotic: Chinese? Balinese? Bought three hundred wire coat hangers on Seventh Avenue. Hung a ladder of them; on it, Jean Rosenthal threw gold light; a spidery pagoda. Problem of insect wings that don't flop.

Hindemith's *Symphonic Metamorphoses on Themes by Carl Maria von Weber* (1943) uses and shifts quotations from Weber's Piano Music for Four Hands, whose theme for the second movement was supplied by an "authentic" Chinese melody quoted from Rousseau's *Musical Dictionary*. This Weber had first used in incidental music for Schiller's *Turandot* (1809). Our ballet had nothing whatever to do with Franz Kafka's horrific parable, although there was indeed a huge and monstrous buglike creature (Todd Bolender) who ambled over the stage in glittering armor. Dancers were bejeweled grasshoppers or mineral dragonflies; there was a skitter and flutter of delicate vibrating membranes accompanying entomological quadrilles. In the three parts of the ballet, costumes changed themselves imperceptibly upon the dancers' bodies, so that what was seen first became entirely transformed. There was little suggestion of growth from egg to extinction, but only of continual mutation in a strange aura which was less oriental or exotic than insectile.

Ingenious and elegant carapaces and wings, which Karinska constructed of wire overlaid with metallic stuffs, were a unique happy solution to a perennial difficulty. Costume wings that carry much conviction are a severe trial to fabricate.

Tchelitchev had been expert in his use of feathers: "Tutus must look like chicken feathers," with no spot plucked bare between legs or at the seat. In his *Errante* he crossed twin wings over the breasts rather than fixing them to the backs of his "angels," a solution found in the cherubim and seraphim of his favorite Byzantine mosaics in the Karieh Djami, Istanbul. In his *Orpheus and Eurydice*, Amor wore a pair of wings scrupulously constructed of genuine goose feathers in graduated lengths. These sprang from the dancer's bare body with convincing naturalism and were based on a structure of feathering borrowed from Caravaggio's *Angel Dictating the Gospel to Saint Matthew*. When we were costuming *Swan Lake*, Cecil Beaton made wings in many sizes and models. The difficulty lies in attaching wings to a bodice so that they seem to spring logically from shoulder blades instead of being crudely stuck on. Later Balanchine and Madame Karinska found a solution that, while eliminating separate wings, seemed more satisfactory. When Rouben Ter-Arutunian redesigned *Swan Lake* to fit the larger stage of the State Theater, tutus were cut high and short in front, sweeping back in a bustlelike gathering of feathery tarlatan. The whole of this filmy bulk of tulle suggested folded downswept wings, yet the mass moved integrally with the body's shift. While

Balanchine pays little attention to most run-of-the-mill costume designers, preferring those who are excellent draftsmen and easel painters in their own right, he is extremely conscious of costume's importance, particularly when it supports choreography itself, as in *Metamorphoses*.

OCTOBER, 1953: *New York*

Inspected scale model for Christmas tree in second scene of *Nutcracker*. City Center's stage is not trapped; the tree must rise from the floor surface. Balanchine insists on a three-dimensional tree rather than painted canvas. Jean Rosenthal's model is built of umbrellalike spokes, lying flat; when pulled up, it springs out in high relief. Estimates run from five to ten thousand dollars. Scared to tell Baum. We order it with no firm figure in contract.

Our 1953–54 season introduced *The Nutcracker*, our first "full-length" work, the most elaborate we had so far attempted. While the music's familiarity, due to Walt Disney's *Fantasia*, led most people to call our ballet "The Nutcracker Suite," we used the entire two-hour score, not the diminished pop-concert version. The budget was high, although physical conditions of the City Center's stage restricted much extravagance in transformation scenes. There was literally no offstage room—no space for marshaling regiments of children in platoons of mice and toy soldiers, no space for storing their artillery and bulky mouse-dresses. Logistics were mapped as for a miniature invasion. The smaller students recruited from our school were silently bivouacked in stairwells and corridors leading up to dressing rooms already crammed with adult dancers. A system of hand signals, relayed by stagehands to prompter parents, hurried everyone onstage, on cue as needed.

The Christmas tree was a triumph of engineering. While in actuality only a half-round, its shivering branches of stiff pine needles jogged thrillingly, loaded with ornaments, toys, and glittering festoons as its invisible spine was hauled up. This always drew storms of applause from small fry who, many for the first time, found themselves in a true theater which could vanquish the notion that magic exists on television alone. In early performances, electrical short circuits of small bulbs wired to the tree contributed alarming special effects; they sparked, sizzled, smoked, threatening to burst into flame. But the branches were fireproof, and eventually the "candles" were put under safer if less exciting control.

The Nutcracker had been patiently analyzed for its style and historic ambience. Balanchine accentuated the bourgeois atmosphere of a comfortable but by no means aristocratic home. Some productions (notably that of Leningrad in 1962) set the opening party in a veritable palace. We placed it in an unassuming middle-class parlor, so that the fantastic sequences might be revealed as all the more surprising and strange. The diminutive Prince and Princess continued to be chosen from the most talented children in our school; many boys and girls who later danced as soloists commenced careers as small angels, mice, or toy soldiers.

When we transferred to the State Theater in 1964, we were forced to abandon Horace Armistead's attractive scenery. A greatly enlarged picture-book production within a three-dimensional gilt paper-lace frame (of molded plastic) was ingeniously designed by Rouben Ter-Arutunian. His huge front curtain, on which a benevolent angel protected Christmas Eve roofs, might have been painted by one of the German Nazarenes. Our gift tree was now nearly twice as tall; at the finale, Prince and Princess are drawn skyward in a sleigh upholstered in tufted satin by a team of jeweled reindeer. *Nutcracker* immediately became a fixture of New York's holiday season, and soon we would be giving more than a month of matinee and evening performances, on convenient early schedules, with three separate relays of adult dancers and as many teams of children. For several years the ballet was a Christmas telecast over the Columbia network. Balanchine continually changed solo variations, group dances, pantomime, and incidental stage business. In early years, Tanaquil LeClercq, a diamonded bouquet as the Dewdrop Fairy, led the "Valse des Fleurs"; Madame Karinska's gilt-bronze, rose-pink skirts for the corps transformed the stage into a revolving bed of Fabergé's enameled roses.

While *Nutcracker* represented a major effort, the year 1954 was also distinguished by three other novelties. These were of primary musical interest and precipitated much arresting and durable choreography. While I was working on *Pocahontas* with Elliott

Carter in 1936, he mentioned the existence of a mysterious and marvelous musician, a businessman living in Danbury, Connecticut, who was perhaps the most original of American composers and a leading innovator of his epoch. However, extravagant peculiarities in the scale and nature of his orchestration exceeded the resources of even the larger symphony societies. This hardly recommended him to our small company, which was then accompanied by two-piano teams or an occasional pickup orchestra. But in the fifties Balanchine, voracious for new music, recalled the name of Charles Ives. Leon Barzin, our adventurous and widely informed musical director, found and combined a suite of his pieces under the title *Ivesiana*. Long before *The Unanswered Question* or *Central Park in the Dark* had become popular repertory pieces, Balanchine's dramatic use of Ives's music drew widespread attention to his rich and eccentric beauties.

When I researched facts about Ives in 1953, the 1939 edition of the *International Cyclopedia of Music and Musicians* (for which I'd written a section on dance music) stated flatly that his scores, "both vocal and instrumental, are based on a polytonality that makes them almost impossible to perform." This opinion was still widely held fourteen years later. Resistance to unorthodox orchestration by instrumentalists is no new phenomenon. In 1911 the Vienna orchestra balked at *Petrouchka* for its "wrong notes"; in the summer of 1972 the strings of the Boston Symphony virtually struck in protest over rehearsing and performing a stubbornly unorthodox score. By 1937 the American Ballet had presented three of Stravinsky's late and, to America, unfamiliar ballets. Our use of musical novelties in a theatrical frame often marked debuts of orchestral pieces which later would be accepted and appreciated for autonomous musical quality, unsupported by any dancing. In *Ivesiana, The Unanswered Question* made a strong immediate impression on audiences. A boy seeks the answer to some insoluble cosmic riddle from a sphinxlike girl who, supported by a tribe of anonymous hands and arms, is never permitted to touch earth. The metaphor of equivocal, otherworldly response to his ceaseless appeal was incarnated in the sinuous soarings and collapses of Allegra Kent, a very young dancer of supple eloquence whose bare body seemed boneless, a kid glove of skin firmed with coils of steel.

At the same time, Balanchine used Arnold Schoenberg's Opus

34, his *Begleitmusik* (1930), for a cinematic scene in some non-existent film. (Stravinsky had drawn Balanchine's attention to it.) He repeated the piece twice with the orchestra, presenting a provocative exercise in the possibilities of separate treatment of the same score. Opus 34 was the first dodecaphonic composition that Balanchine found suitable for dancing. While comparatively simply orchestrated in a then radical twelve-tone system, its sonorities were unknown to ballet audiences. However, the fresh use of a twelve- rather than a seven-note scale impelled a family of gesture that was somehow related only to itself, in uncomfortable or abrasive sequences. These seemed visually as taut and relentless as was their aural basis.

By this time, any public reaction vaguely admitting shock at the music chosen by Balanchine had subsided to welcoming or enlightened curiosity. While the novel or unfamiliar aroused anticipation, their piquancy guaranteed no deep or prolonged attention, nor that suspension of habit which might have made looking and listening less conditioned or capricious. In the first of Balanchine's two arrangements based on Opus 34, he ignored the composer's narrative rubric: "Peril Threatening," "Fright," "Disaster." The music itself, divested of pretext, triggered elliptical or tangential curlicues of action which related only to its own hermetic, sonorous climate. When Balanchine had first tackled *Apollon* in 1928, at the start of his kinetic research of which *Opus 34* was the most recent test, he deliberately inverted an ideal academic idiom against some of Stravinsky's most mellifluous measures. This deformed the open, *en dehors* positions perversely (or as it seemed to many, petulantly) into *en dedans*, the closed or shut accentuation. In *Opus 34*, his assertions of disruption were in an entirely different vocabulary, holding by neither inversion nor deformation any relation whatever to any traditional language. Later some would see it as a first sketch for *Agon*, the serial technique of which Stravinsky would claim, at its moment of composition: "A series is a facet, and serial composition a faceting, or crystallizing, way of presenting several sides of the same idea." Both the Webern *Episodes*—also set to serial music—and *Agon* achieved a place in our permanent repertory, while *Opus 34* was ploughed under.

The 1954–55 season was the first for *Western Symphony* (initially with no scenery and in hand-me-down tutus), which

Hershy Kay wittily and efficiently compounded to Balanchine's bracing prescription, making a formal classical symphony from cowboy themes. We had considered a new version of *Billy the Kid* for the sake of Copland's touching score, but his *Rodeo* for Agnes de Mille was being danced by the Ballet Russe. *Billy* had been conceived more as dramatic pantomime than classic ballet; no one wished to supplant Loring's choreography, which was in the current repertory of Ballet Theatre.

In 1955, Balanchine took another unfamiliar symphonic suite of Bizet's—his *Roma* (1860–1868)—and composed beautiful dancing. It was richly decorated by Eugene Berman in a Piranesian townscape of ruined arches, which at a climax were festooned with colorful lines of tasteful laundry hung in a frame of doors and windows remembered from Trastevere and the Tiber suburbs. Neither *Roma* nor the unsuspected but lovely *Gounod Symphony* of 1958 (a lively parade of metamorphic flower beds laid out by Lenôtre turned ballet master) enjoyed the instant popularity which seemed to justify retention in repertory. They lost out in the unending competition for rehearsal hours scheduled for more urgent or hopeful novelties. Balanchine is so masterfully inventive that if a new work is not immediately popular, he's inclined to forget it. Having exhausted his initial interest in the musical possibilities, he proceeds to something else which may prove luckier and hold public attention longer. Yet what we have abandoned, sometimes too summarily, might make rich fare for some extravagant if unlikely company.

Our reasons for discarding a ballet have frequently been as much accidental as commercial or aesthetic: the disappearance of dancers originally identified with the debut roles, its similarity to later work which seems at the moment more successful, warehouse fires, personal petulance, impatience. But *Roma*, *Gounod Symphony*, Alexei Haieff's *Divertimento* of 1947, the Mozart *Caracole* of 1952, *Bayou* of the same year (Virgil Thomson's charming *Acadian Songs and Dances* with delicious decorations by Dorothea Tanning) were losses regretted by those who prize delicacy of texture or quiet sweetness of expression. The criterion smash-hit "success" also extends to ballet repertory; while we have fought it harder and longer than most, whenever a company works for a popular audience, it is their taste, inertia, or attention rather than the preference of a director which will predominate.

Balanchine preoccupied with roses; more satisfactory than choreography or cooking. Blossoms are perfection, blooming without excuse or complaint; they smell good, die quickly; hundreds of old, plenty of new kinds. Later he called me, having received piano score for Stravinsky's *Agon*; the music was more "appetizing" than roses or kitchens.

In college my freshman adviser had been S. Foster Damon, a supreme authority on William Blake and an early explicator of Melville when *Moby Dick* existed only in a limited edition and *Billy Budd* was an inaccurately deciphered manuscript in Widener Library. Foster's roommate was the scholar John Marshall, who after leaving Cambridge edited *Speculum*, a learned journal of medieval studies. It was Marshall who gave me Joyce's *Ulysses*, Ezra Pound's *First Cantos*, and Huxley's *Point Counter Point*, all of which meant more to me than Whitehead's lectures on metaphysics. Marshall was already a famous chef and later would write an admirable practical cookbook. He left scholarship, to become charged with the support of the arts and the humanities for the Rockefeller Foundation.

Serving as director of the City Center of Music and Drama, Inc., and holding brief authority over both opera and drama as well as ballet, I applied to the foundation for a grant-in-aid of considerable proportions to commission new works, among which were Aaron Copland's opera *The Tender Land* and Stravinsky's *Agon*. John Marshall had a special affection for ballet; his youngest daughter hoped to be a dancer; her goddess was Maria Tallchief, whose photos she enshrined—but she shot up tall and leggy. (Later, failing, in her own eyes, to become either dancer or horse trainer, she found a lasting vocation in one of the severest of contemplative religious orders.) Through John Marshall and his superior, Burton Fahs, the Rockefeller Foundation initiated a patronage of the performing arts which, after this courageous and generous precedent, was later pursued by other important bene-factors.

Ever since *Orpheus*, we had longed for a third work which might compose a full evening's sequence, commencing with *Apollo* and ending with the tragedy of his poet-heir. But all proposals for a narrative sequel were killed by Stravinsky. By this time, through the insistence and persistence of Bob Craft, he had become increas-ingly occupied with the music and method of Arnold Schoenberg, Anton Webern, and Schoenberg's dodecaphonic system. As a point of departure for *Agon*, although the casual ballet-goer would hardly guess it, Stravinsky took two collections of French Renaissance dance melodies and adapted some twelve of them for a dozen dancers, in the twelve-tone scale which would also frame a "classic" *pas de deux* as climax.

Regarding repertory in general, and ours in particular, which is the richest extant in musical quality and variety, it has become habitual to presuppose a precious if precarious factor which has managed to get itself called "creative." This factor, not very ac-curately named, characterizes gifts and a relationship which Balanchine and Stravinsky shared in ways peculiar to both. Each held to an identical philosophy which precluded any consideration that what they were or did was—"creative." That is, neither in-vented *de novo* constructs whose root particles had not previously been in existence. For both men, "creativity" was and is a more methodical process than the opportune discovery of some flagrant chanced novelty. As far as talent, genius, or superior endowment extend, these are only viable to degrees of manipulation of extant elements, which however unsuspected or unfamiliar are always available, offering themselves to the observation and choice of self-elected sensibilities. They believed, as Albert Einstein apparently did, that "God doesn't throw dice"; that Order holds some, how-ever fractional, advantage in cosmic play over Disorder. This imagined Order can be called God, in which case He is seen as Creator outside the dimension of time.

Time, as we clock it, is a fiction or device of our measuring. Before and After are loose concepts in relation to an Order which permanently *is*; God, then, is a detimed source, the sole originator of "creative" energy, before and after whom is naught and all; whose ordering is the one possible irreversible Creative Act. Additions, contributions, selections from such ordering by individual historical brainy bipeds comment on such order but hardly "create" or "discover" anything absolutely "original." Creativity, on the human level, is simply what might be called an *uncovery* of commentary on innumerable facts of measure and order (parts of which may include disorder—chaos, hazard, cruelty, injustice, and death). Stravinsky was savage enough about certain notoriously "creative" contemporaries whom he felt were tasteful, or even erudite, anthologists whose reputations were chiefly based on aggressive idiosyncrasy. Fame formed an ephemeral aura around them which was the unique component that had any claim to having been in a true sense invented or created—however factitiously.

It's no secret that Balanchine is a creature of tradition, that he conserves past uncoveries as well as his own abandoned constructs, frames, contraptions, like a well-pruned forest from which timber may be hewn, planed, and joined to produce new furnishings. His polymorphic style, his "soulless" or impersonal manner, his belief in "angelism"—in elements, human or immaterial, that are on occasion sent—are reflected in methods which are, of necessity, economical. This attitude comes from a long and deep familiarity with a multiplicity of repetitive factors. The more these are manipulated, the more supple and dissimilar they appear, thereby gaining or retaining seeming diversity, surprise—indeed, even "originality" or "inventiveness."

Balanchine's arrant distrust of Personality, the negotiable bundle of negotiable formulae which the *prima ballerina assoluta* is wont to purvey, springs from rigorous notions of what a creator, on the terrestrial plane, may presume to be: in what manner, to what degree, performers may claim to be "creative." Stravinsky has often been accused of mannerism, that is, subservience to the styles of others—predecessors who in their turn adopted preferred habit already iterated. Stravinsky was a prime neoclassicist, subscribing to an academy which extends through the ages, having been taught by prior instructors and models—inventors, uncoverers, joiners. In the perspective (and modesty) of their judgment, these instructors recognized with dedication and gratitude their own descent from precedents which derive from a single stream, always fresh, and more potent than any purely personal rivulet diverted for a moment to green some small patch.

From the earliest times, music and dancing have depended upon mathematics and metaphysics. Recently, however, a borrowing of myth as pretext for theater has often been more a prestige-hunting literary caprice than testimony to superior order. Athletes, instrumentalists, dancers, acrobatic virtuosi who live by their bodies' central control, rather than by their minds' rationale, are rarely counted as "creative," or even as "intellectual." They "express," "interpret," "impersonate"—in fact, Realize. On the other hand, composers of music and dances, like Stravinsky and Balanchine, have supported a virtuosity in body, mind, or fingers by a structuring of ideas, but neither on an abstract level of "pure" mathematics nor in a vein of fashionable philosophizing. There are many systems of geometry more ingenious than Euclid's. To makers of a certain temperament it is important that as measures or counters, they hold historical ideas in a resonance of order and build on them. Finally, this saves time, which in theaters and concert halls must be measured by contract hours or else by time-and-a-half charges for overtime. Knowledge of notions already enunciated anticipates errors; unviable paths have already been marked and need not be tried again. This knowledge is acquired less from fear of failure, or as insurance for success, than from recognition that many proposals have not worked and never will, that others time and again have worked and always will. Attempts to command the unworkable earn prestige for "experiment" and for what, over the last three decades, has been considered the instinctive courage of "originality." Incompetence, stubbornness, vanity, and the greedy acceptance of unthinking critical attention has not contributed much to the standard repertory, but has filled a sizable graveyard with moribund work, defunct organizations, and delinquent promises.

It is often asserted, with that naïveté which awards a facile acceptance to its own ambitions and careless authority, that Stravinsky really "put it all together" only once—in *Le Sacre du Printemps* of 1913—and that, on a different scale but perhaps to a currently more relevant degree, Balanchine did the same only once, with *Agon*. This may be, but neither work exists in solitary self-satisfaction or containment. Elements that in one direction reach back to a pair of Renaissance dancing manuals, in another to Max Planck or Einstein, in another to Webern, Berg, or Schoenberg are braided in a collaboration which should be an admonition to creative, inventive, and original "young" choreographers who imagine that instinct, chance, personality, and loose autodidactic energy are fair substitutes for conscious measurement and concrete knowledge of more than a few faddish styles or systems.

Stravinsky, whose Hollywood home was crammed with marvelous clocks and watches, said: "Portions of *Agon* contain three times as much music for the same clock-length as some other pieces of mine." *Agon* presents more concentrated structural dance material in twenty minutes than most nineteenth-century full-length ballets. These, apart from brief solos and extended *pas de deux*, are padded with filler pageantry in a repetitive roster of parade and pantomime, all in the insistent tempi of 4/4, 3/4, 2/4. *Agon* was the full harvest of Stravinsky's seventy-fifth year, half a century after *Apollon*, which was a first capital proclamation of Balanchine's mature attitude and found authority. In 1968, Balanchine wrote:

> Music like Stravinsky's cannot be illustrated; one must try to find a visual equivalent that is a complement rather than an illustration. And while the score of *Agon* was invented for dancing, it was not simple to devise dances of a comparable density, quality, metrical insistence, variety, formal mastery, or symmetrical asymmetry. Just as a cabinetmaker must select his woods for the particular job in hand—palisander, angelique, rosewood, briar, or pine—so a ballet carpenter must find dominant quality of gesture, a strain or palette of consistent movement, an active scale of flowing patterns which reveals to the eye what Stravinsky tells the sensitized ear. . . .
>
> Stravinsky's strict beat is authority over time, and I have always felt that a choreographer should place unlimited confidence in this control. For me at any rate, Stravinsky's rhythmic invention gives the greatest stimulus. A choreographer cannot invent rhythms, he can only reflect them in movement. The body is his medium and, unaided, the body will improvise for a little while. But the organizing of rhythm on a large scale is a sustained process, a function of the musical mind. To

speak of carpentry again, planning a rhythm is like planning a house; it needs a structural operation.*

MARCH, 1958: *United Nations, New York*

Lunch with Dag Hammarskjöld, 38th floor of the U.N., to meet Birgit Cullberg, Swedish choreographer. Office walls hung with Matisse, Braque, Juan Gris on loan from Museum of Modern Art. He asked if Wystan Auden could not "write a ballet" for Miss Cullberg. He showed us the new Meditation Room with its table altar made of polished iron ore, one of the hardest substances known.

Anyone operating the arts as a public service holds constant and constantly frustrated dreams of encountering a Lorenzo de Medici, a Catherine the Great, or in our democractic republic, at least a Thomas Jefferson, a Theodore or Franklin Roosevelt. American Maecenases like J. P. Morgan, Sr., or John D. Rockefeller, Jr., left rich legacies of visual art, not alone in magnificent panels, canvases, and tapestries but in painted and printed books, written pages, and precious objects. Yet in New York, of all tycoons in his generation and the one after it, only Otto H. Kahn had much affection for lyric theater, and that mainly as an adjunct to the Metropolitan Opera House. The first Roosevelt admired our greatest sculptor and obtained from Augustus Saint-Gaudens our finest gold coinage. In a serious Depression Franklin Roosevelt (through Harry Hopkins) sponsored many excellent artists and even theater projects which (under Hallie Flanagan) included dancing, before a churlish Congress killed its great possibilities as "boondoggling." It is almost impossible to imagine discussing the specifics of theatrical sponsorship or performance with most heads of state, enmeshed as they may be in obligations more pressing than the cultivation of popular taste or pleasures of the mind. None of our elected leaders could compose for the violin as well as Frederick the Great, or execute an *entrechat* as well as Lully's star dancer, *Le Roi Soleil*. Only Jefferson, as an enlightened amateur and student of Palladio,

* *Balanchine's New Complete Stories of the Great Ballets*, 1968, p. 11.

brought a cultivated mind to his commonwealth as a matter of course.

Dag Hammarskjöld was something approaching a philosopher-king. His appreciation of poetry, painting, and skills in performance was neither pretense nor light adornment. He had a warm heart, cool hand, and cold eye; he was born to a manner of life which was luxuriously equipped with ideas and their concrete realization—well framed, well printed, well played. He had little embarrassment or hesitation in talking to technicians; artists did not frighten him; they genuinely interested him, as did scientists, mountain climbers, soldiers, pilots, and politicians. He was happily aware of his position as secretary-general and employed his modest panoply of office at the United Nations toward the furthering of those arts whose exchange might serve international understanding. He forwarded the nomination of Saint-John Perse (the French diplomat Alexis Saint-Léger Léger) for the Nobel Prize, although there was resistance from de Gaulle's Quai d'Orsay at that time. He visited the City Center often, became a good friend of Wystan Auden's in both his official chambers and the seclusion of his home, and lent the considerable energy of his support to our efforts and those of many others.

He was not in any casual sense an easily humorous man. In a personal, even priestly commitment he felt afflicted by this world's evil and presumed himself capable, to some degree, of its alleviation. Indeed, he felt chosen for services and sacrifice. A "sense of humor" usually means quick reaction to the comic, ridiculous, or preposterous, but humors that he possessed were so attuned to endemic horror and tragedy on a global scale that, although he had a ready smile and much personal charm, he found little that was superficially amusing. Nor was he exactly "humorless," but pressure from the world's woes was more commanding, seen from his thirty-eighth-floor windows, than individual appetite. This perspective extended far past his own pleasure. He permitted himself appreciation of pictures and poems as symbolic delectation. He felt that those responsible for the weal of nations do well to acknowledge the healing aspects of art as the purest memorials of men's best hope.

Balanchine, in a fit of what was taken by some to be sheer perversity, now chose to exploit the treasure of our best brass-band master, John Philip Sousa. When asked why, why, why, he replied: "Because I like his *music*." This was not alone for Sousa's famous martial marches, but also for portions of an opera and other forgotten pieces. Hershy Kay, who had done yeoman service for *Western Symphony*, turned his talent to rearranging Sousa's brass choirs for symphonic orchestra with strings and woodwinds. Balanchine carefully indicated the instrumentation. The grand *pas de deux* would be scored not for violins, but for plaintive vinegary brass, with the tuba blatantly predominant. This he saw as a tribute to Dwight Eisenhower, in his senior year at West Point, engaged to Mamie Doud. The ballet was conceived as a musical joke, and *Stars and Stripes* was generally received as such, then and since.

Not by Dag Hammarskjöld. He was a stranger to Radio City Music Hall and the Rockettes in their perennial patriotic drills. He had no comprehension of Balanchine's parodistic irony, his ingenuity in transforming a vaudeville parade into balletic beauty; and in the finale when an enormous Old Glory unfurled itself as a gigantic backdrop, swept by a storm of wind machines, the secretary-general took offense. Such a display approached a call to arms, a shameless exhibition of chauvinist sentiment when Korea still spelled war, and this planet could do with a lot less flag-waving. There was nothing one could do to explain, as a gloss on the background of the ballet. The fact that the finale brought a loud and wryly enthusiastic demonstration, which in itself was a parody of patriotism, was no help. We had to suffer one of the worst pains this side of physical torture—enduring an inexplicably and hopelessly false position. We were not warmongers; we were even gentle censors of preposterous hyper-Americanism. But Hammarskjöld judged that the cause of peace among nations was not served by the blatant effrontery of our imperialist gesture.

Hammarskjöld was also a student of the classics and knew that antique myths of aggression, envy, and revenge were no more legendary than reports in the daily papers. He admired Balanchine's *Orpheus* and *Apollo*; he was a patron of Birgit Cullberg, choreographer at the Royal Opera in Stockholm, and brought us together. She was shy, energetic, appealing. She proposed her already successful melodramatic ballet on Euripedes' version of the legend of Jason and Medea, to Bartók music, for

Melissa Hayden, our strongest dramatic ballerina, with Jacques d'Amboise and Violette Verdy. This legend had prompted the most popular of Noverre's reformative *choréodrames* in many recensions through the eighteenth century all over Europe. Balanchine, as always, was pleased to entrust his company to someone, indeed anyone, other than himself, on the chance of broadening our basic repertory. Miss Cullberg's *Medea* played well enough. There were problems about dragging her two murdered children offstage without scraping their shins; a ruby light which meant murder spelled gelatin rather than blood. *Medea* remained in repertory for some seasons; it was mortally serious and provided energetic exercise for its loyal dancers. It was a European, or rather a Northern European, concept which was not hard for an American company and audience to adopt. Hammarskjöld infinitely preferred it to *Stars and Stripes*. Also, he had performed his function as a Swedish civil servant and world citizen. We had done ours as representatives of a quasi-municipal institution; neither was much the worse for it.

APRIL, 1958: *Tokyo*

In the palace, performance of Gagaku by dancers and musicians of the imperial household. Splendid ceremonials, part religious, part military, of enormous gravity, elegance, and strangeness. A chamberlain took us through the huge greenhouses, with wonderful bonsai, centuries old, arranged in miniature landscapes. A daughter of the emperor at our performance. In the intermission, a private audience. Ice cream, like malachite flannel, but delicious. My left big toe stuck out through a hole in my sock. She regarded it with interest; neither of us smiled.

In those days, the flight to Japan took thirty-six hours. We broke the trip at Wake Island, sleeping fitfully in old Army barracks. Most of our Tokyo performances took place in an arena used more often for boxing than ballet. To hide the scene changes the curtain rose from the floor rather than fell; there was a topsy-turvy quality to the whole town. Tickets had been completely distributed on some mysterious schedule by which few were available for sale, while the auditorium was usually half empty. However, the experience and existence of Japan was so amazing, provocative, and compelling that we scarcely bothered to worry about audiences. That had become our embassy's problem, to manage as it might.

Having been raised in Boston, where from clipper-ship days there had been an exchange of tea and artifacts between West and East, I knew the oriental wing of the Museum of Fine Arts, but its wealth of Chinese and Japanese carving and pictures had always blurred vaguely in my eyes, schooled to look mostly at French or Italian painting. I told myself there was no use trying to absorb the Orient: "East is East." But at boarding school, aged thirteen, I'd made friends with a lean, diminutive Japanese who spoke good English although he'd not been away from home before. In a log cabin in the woods we cooked and ate two pounds of crisp bacon with no drastic result, while he told me true adventure stories about himself and his land. His name was Jujun Saigo; once he played with an imperial princeling around a palace pool, in which swam ancient coral-colored carp. The prince, a twig of his own age, wore a dress-kimono gloriously embroidered with the identical fish. Saigo wished to wear it more than anything in his life. He contrived to trip himself up over the brink; splash! With obligatory largesse, the prince hauled him out, dried him off, and wrapped him in the gorgeous fishy garment. The image of those carp, swimming in silk, stayed in my mind for forty years. Jujun himself disappeared one night, recalled to Japan by his father's death; doubtless to further adventures with carp and princes.

At a pleasant reception given by the American ambassador, conversation grew thin. I asked an obviously Westernized guest the kind of tourist's question that makes natives smile: "Do you happen to know a Mr. Saigo?" This gentleman replied: "Ah, so. He is that gray-haired man there." It was indeed Saigo. This was but one of a train of "coincidences," if such they were, which convinced me I'd come to Japan to fulfill some special purpose, that I'd always been coming, to find a style of life to be embraced with no further persuasion, as if I had always known it.

We were lucky in latching onto Donald Richie, then dance critic on the *Japan Times*, who'd lived in Tokyo since the first days of our military occupation and who was intimately in touch with an area that few foreigners ever penetrate. He held an open sesame to an extralegal, subterranean society which one could barely believe in, yet it existed in a downtown section which had alarming resemblances to the less protected parts of Brooklyn. In Shinjuku, the district in which our theater stood, a submerged life went on under the fierce hierarchy of gangs and fearsome, masterless men, much as it had since the seventeenth century. The Americans had reduced the local police to the status of traffic cops, but Richie knew the men who really ran the wards.

We were invited to watch, at six in the morning, the daily practice of unfledged sumo wrestlers, whose uncropped hair had not yet been tied up in the professional chignon. Big boys trooped in from the provinces to seek patronage, fame, and fortune in this proudly competitive and ritualized sport. Few aspirants ever reached those heights where, forcibly fed like Strasbourg geese, they were enthroned as imperturbable monsters of a majestic championage. Through Donald Richie and his friend, the adventurous publisher Meredith Weatherby, an early intimate of Yukio Mishima and patron of many Japanese writers and craftsmen, I met Masayuki Nagare. An ex-Kamikaze pilot, a sword maker, and now a master carver of the most intractable granite in his islands, Nagare would in a few years be executing important sculpture for the United States. Together we spent a memorable week in Kyoto, where he showed me the entire panoply of surviving martial sports, and not only kendo, judo, aikido, karate, archery, sacred football, and jiu-jitsu, but also water walking and the traditional women's fencing with staff, ball, and chain. Most marvelous of all was nin-jitsu, the skill of samurai espionage: sudden vanishment and bilocation, the art of being seen in two distinct places at once—a mystery to be mastered by all theater directors.

Members of our company became acquainted with dancers and musicians of the imperial household. In the spring of 1959, through Dag Hammarskjöld's diplomatic brand of occidental wizardry, for the first time in a thousand years the oldest ballet company in the world left the palace precincts and their own islands. They performed their splendid sober ceremonial dances first under Hammarskjöld's aegis in the General Assembly hall of the United Nations, and later for a season on the same program with our own company at the City Center. In Washington, Mrs. Dwight Eisenhower received them on a memorable afternoon at Dumbarton Oaks, where they danced in the open air on a reproduction of their own red-and-gold stage against a background of magnolia japonica. For one of their dances they used branches of keyaki, the sacred laurel, one of the many exotic plants in the beautiful gardens endowed by Robert and Mildred Bliss for the nation.

In Osaka we opened a handsome new festival hall, sharing programs with the Soviet State Symphony. This was the finest new theater in which we had so far played. Later we would inaugurate auditoriums in Seattle, Montreal, and Saratoga, as well as our own home in Lincoln Center. There is a special excitement in facing the hazards of untried houses, including unexpected pitfalls which no architect is ever able to anticipate.

As for sightseeing in Japan, there were innumerable marvels, but for me the foremost would remain Noh drama performed in Kyoto's old wooden theater. "Perfection" is a word whose claim and meaning are so subjective that pronouncing it brings on a sense of superstitious awe lest this highest accolade shrink to nonsense. If perfection means anything, it is something approaching the irreducible gleam and wholeness of pure gold, faceted diamonds, or the evening star. Noh is the only theater I'd dare call "perfect" in sight, sound, gesture, symbol, without offending those guardian spirits who estimate excellence in the performing arts. Removed to its proper dimension, far from occidental time and space, yet no more verbally incomprehensible than *bel canto* Italian opera, its essence glows like an even blaze of camphor logs—azure, sulphur, malachite—or the wings of a dragon moth fixed in translucent amber. But Noh defeats rhetoric, and is itself defeated when transferred fragmentarily to the West. It demands its immaculate pine walkway and floor, its own curved canopy and painted pines, its own airless airs. In the West, Noh seems like a beautiful pebble brought home from the shore which loses its sheen in your pocket on the way home.

Once, when I was working on *Twelfth Night* with Katharine Hepburn, she grew impatient at my voluble criteria of perfection in past performances. She held that the term indicates only a state of mind, a splinter from personal memory. For me it was Noh; for her it was the mating dance of Australian lyrebirds she'd come on somewhere in the bush. Sometimes in performances of ballet, energy is glimpsed in crystal fractions of precise movement, attached like invisible silk to music's structure. In the West I have never seen a sustained peak of <u>ordered action simulating emotion</u> that lasts for more than twenty minutes. In Noh, it is visible for hours at a sitting.

JANUARY, 1959: *New York*

With Martha Graham, discussing possibility of a collaborative work half by her, half by Balanchine, in which part of her company could dance in ours and vice versa. Spoke of key characters of feminine distinction so far unattempted, she having already drawn from ancient Greece, the Bible, Joan of Arc. I proposed Alice in Wonderland, which seems to me the essence of Martha's spirit; she thought I meant the Red Queen or Ugly Duchess. But she consented to consider Elizabeth or Mary, Queen of Scots.

I met Martha Graham through Frances Hawkins, her early manager, when they shared an apartment. I had been in college with Erick Hawkins, who, among other roles, danced Powhatan, the Indian chief, in Elliott Carter's *Pocahontas*. He left us to join Graham's company and later married her. I had written an unpleasant piece about her, mainly on the basis of her self-designed solo as the Chosen Maiden in Massine's version of *Le Sacre du Printemps* under Stokowski. (This was the first American-staged performance in an initial proprietary crusade for the classic dance.) However, at Bennington College, where she was artist-in-residence when our Caravan performed there, I had suffered a conversion upon seeing her perform as various personae of an Indian princess in her processional *American Document*. She taught me many things, including the importance of keeping a more humble, open eye on the Orient, its ideas and objects. This had long been one of her vital sources, gained partly through association with Ruth St. Denis. We met again when, under the auspices of Merle Armitage, our Caravan first played Los Angeles in 1938. I knew and admired Louis Horst, Martha's musical collaborator, who had a consuming interest in preclassic dance forms. In my ignorance I had thought that these were the property of ballet alone, but he appropriated them as a teaching system for choreographic structure and made them the ideological basis for his work with a generation of heterodox modernists. My contact with Graham was of some duration, despite temperamental differences which were apparent in the nature of our separate preoccupations.

Around 1952 Balanchine learned about the figure and fate of Anton von Webern. Bob Craft had recently brought Webern's sonorities to the attention of Stravinsky, with whom they became a seminal enthusiasm. Balanchine himself had not so far been attracted by atonal music. To him, as he said, Schoenberg stood as the Albert Einstein of twelve-tone systems, incomparable in his own genre but useless for dancing. Craft was then in the process of recording Webern's entire work, and Balanchine wrote later:

> I listened to everything and liked it. The songs were the best of all, but they were written to be listened to [only, with their words]. The orchestral music, however, fills air like molecules: it is written for atmosphere. The first time I heard it, I knew it could be danced to.*

Stravinsky was asked if, in the end, he did not think Webern's music "too narrow in scope." He answered in words that apply also to his own manipulation of temporal measure and dimensions:

> [Too narrow in scope?] Not for Webern . . . I cannot understand the word in musical terms. Webern's time-scale is tiny, his quantity is minute, the variety of his forms is small, but whether these are measurements of scope I am unable to say. If, for example, scope is also a question of depth and not merely width and expanse, then Webern's can be very great. . . .†

As was his usual method with unfamiliar scores, Balanchine took the Webern piece he had chosen and transcribed much of the orchestration for a rehearsal piano, committing new sound and

---

* *Balanchine's New Complete Stories of the Great Ballets*, 1968, p. 133.
† Igor Stravinsky and Robert Craft, *Themes and Episodes*, Alfred A. Knopf, New York, 1966, p. 117.

structure to memory for prompt use in plastic composition. The title—*Episodes*—had stuck in our minds ever since Pavel Tchelitchev had, before World War II, proposed his spectacle to us and to Martha Graham. He imagined her as a feminine archetype, partner to his troika of Don Quixote, Don Juan, and Hamlet, corresponding to the ideals of Dulcinea the rational innocent, the various women who were Don Juan's victims, a guilty Gertrude, and a daft Ophelia. Like most of his fancies they never achieved the stage, but they stuck in our memories stronger than many sights actually seen. The notion of interchanging dancers shuttling between our two groups was only partially realized. From our side, Sallie Wilson portrayed Queen Elizabeth with authority, while Graham lent us Paul Taylor. For him Balanchine invented a variation of such fey eccentricity within the range of his highly articulated athletic presence that we soon had requests from other "modern" dancers for similar extensions of their possibility.

Episodes I (Graham's section) was based on Webern's Opus 1 and Opus 6 (both from 1909), composed before he'd found Schoenberg's use of the twelve-tone row. The opening *Passacaglia*, followed by his Six Pieces for Orchestra, summarized and canonized the passion of Mary of Scotland's memories as she mounts the scaffold in Fotheringhay Castle. Francis Mason encapsulates the action:

> The setting is austere, a black platform across the back of the stage with steps on both sides approaching it; in the center of the platform stands a black box and a halberd-like heraldic device. The music begins with an ominous plucking of strings. Mary, in black, stands below, tense. Her stiff dress seems both to armor and to imprison her. Suddenly high on the platform, she is free of it, stepping out as a young girl in white to meet her lover Bothwell. She comes down again and her black dress remains standing like an empty cage on the platform, accusing her worldliness. She rejects the crown-craving Bothwell, the love of her life, and is in torment.
>
> Four girls now dress Mary in blood red and she begins her long contest with Queen Elizabeth of England. The music shifts to the *Six Pieces for Orchestra*. The black box on the platform becomes a throne. Elizabeth sits there in burnished

gold. She descends. The two queens play a fateful game of tennis, a formal court tennis.

As Elizabeth wins, she is lifted high. Mary then sits for a moment on the throne. But now the throne is the scaffold. Mary kneels before it, the tall halberd, now an ax, turns in the air and a bright red light illumines her cast-off queenly garb.*

Madame Karinska's spiderweb carapaces and freestanding farthingales worn by the rival queens were simultaneously costumes, props, and scenery. David Hays's austere planes and steps stacked with heraldic emblems were spiky, mineral, as leanly profiled as Webern's thorny sonorities. Too soon, when it became impractical for Martha Graham to appear in our repertory because our separate schedules seldom coincided, her entire section was abandoned. Paul Taylor departed also to pursue his independent course, and there was no one remotely capable of replacing him. His oddly mindless mask, sub- or super-human, the peculiar quality of his cheerful in- or a-humanity implementing a serpentine athleticism, exactly corresponded to Webern's fractured glass-snake noises. We called him the Geek; he had his own sweet and sour individuality; one might have wished he'd been trained early as a ballet dancer rather than beginning, as he did, as a crack swimmer.

The effect of our original *Episodes* (*I* and *II*) cannot be recovered from its present truncated version. Not only was Graham's realization memorable, but the occasion itself—her unique symbolic association with the traditional academic dance—provided an ephemeral piquancy not to be repeated. Balanchine's furiously contorted solo variation for Paul Taylor was a statement of such extreme virtuosic perversity in its angular deformation that it almost seemed an insult to a splendid physique. Not only was the dance, and Paul's performance, outlandishly violent—a prolonged acrobatic motor sequence of anguished sound strung on negative gesture ranging from purr to scratch or buzz to strangle—but it prefaced, in dramatic reversal of mood and meaning, the ballet's finale, changing from his extended solo to our full company. The last part of *Episodes II* is still danced to Webern's praise of Johann Sebastian Bach, in the "Ricercata for Six Voices

* *Balanchine's New Complete Stories of the Great Ballets*, 1968, p. 134.

from Bach's *Musical Offering.*" It is an elaborate structure of elevation and grandeur, wholly divested of deformation or commentary, simply expressing the noblest progression in formal dynamics, a sort of *heilige Dankgesang,* a sacred danced song ending with a tremendous organ chord supported by cymbals. It was an assertion—particularly after Paul Taylor's long preface of madly tortured, whimsically anxious, captiously awkward movement—of rational wholeness and humane order.

Predictably, there were passionate partisans of both persuasions, one group vowing that Balanchine should never have worked alongside Graham and another, even more loyal, grieving that she had betrayed nonconformism by permitting herself commerce with the enemy. Actually there was no formal contact between the two sections. A stage was shared; an orchestra offered a bridge for the passage of two disparate visions, one plastically dramatic, the other plastically musical. An event took place which could not have been achieved without the contact or juxtaposition of such discrete elements. There was no lessening of integrity or intensity in either partner, nor was there the least intimation of competition or comparison. Two teams mutually respected their totally opposed disciplines, and an audience shared the incandescent integrity of a peculiar but satisfactory proposal.

DECEMBER, 1959: *New York*

To Morton Baum's with Betty Cage, to convince him we were about to receive (as of January, 1960) a subvention from the Shah of Iran toward *The Figure in the Carpet.* Again Baum brought up the possibility of Brahms's *Liebeslieder Walzer.* We couldn't produce the Shah or any cash. Short of either, he was unenthusiastic, more interested in *Panamerica;* Brazil and Cuba are closer to home.

Since she had fallen ill and required Colorado's high air, Frances Hawkins had ceased to be our general manager. Her friend and apprentice Betty Cage took on the protean task of being at once labor negotiator, certified public accountant, legal expert, mother superior, confessor, psychiatrist, and practicing witch (white magic). In New York she had worked for Miss Steloff of the Gotham Book Mart. Hence she had come to us well schooled in handling problems of production which involved ideas, artists, money and the lack of it, excess temperament, and hysteria. While not a trained dancer, she was expert in the classical Chinese discipline of Tai-chi and wrote an excellent manual of its exercises. She had more than casual knowledge of I-Ching, the Tarot pack, and other arcane aids for the fate and facts of life. We despaired when Frances Hawkins was forced to leave, since her contacts with Morton Baum had been breezy, close, and tidy. She was parsimonious of time and funds, while keeping Balanchine busy producing as much and as fast as conditions allowed. Now Morton Baum came to trust Betty Cage implicitly and tried not to threaten or trouble us with any more dire warnings than necessary, faced as he was with permanent crises. These were not precisely daily bankruptcies, but closely resembled them. Insistence on penurious budgets was something we'd come to live by after a decade of his sponsorship, but Baum was enough of an artist to know that constant poor-mouthing lessened scope in ingenuity and imagination.

Betty Cage came to us already skilled, and would become infinitely more proficient, in the science and pursuit of the possible and impossible. She was accessible, as was Baum, all day and far into the night. By nature taciturn, quizzical, detached, unflappable, she sensed tension before it flared and judged dressing-room gossip for precisely what it was worth. I might be upset by demonstrations of individual erratic behavior; she remained diagnostic, surgical, placatory. She had never seen a wholly "happy" performer, or any who, because of unhappiness, did less than his best in performance. "Happiness," at least in our odd family, was an ideal spread of milk and honey, a golden luxury we could never afford. She accepted strikes or threats of strikes with equanimity; they would pass, like worse disasters—important personal ones, like broken ankles and snapped Achilles' tendons, and collective ones, like the cancellation of promised patronage. As a substitute for applied "happiness," she offered a patient ear, lively mind, dispassionate style, and rational belief in powers superior to the fevers and complaints of lawyers, bankers, and dancers.

The Fourth International Congress of Iranian Art and Archaeology was to be held in Manhattan in April, 1960, under the high auspices of the Shahinshah of Iran and the President of the United States. In 1934, as our final gesture for *Hound & Horn*, we had issued a plump homage to Henry James, reviving a lapsed interest in the intricate patterns of his fiction. His phrase "the figure in the carpet" was a resonant metaphor which stuck in the memory, to serve now as a possible rallying cry for a demonstration of the mystery of design, at least in one important visual sector.

I had long ago encountered Dr. Arthur Upham Pope, the dean of American scholars in the field of Iranian culture, and fallen victim to his subtle and persuasive enthusiasm. Years before, he had guided Edward Warburg through Persia, so I caught a sense of his fantastic gifts in "seduction" and thereby obtained subvention for his encyclopedic publications on ancient Persian monuments.

Now Dr. Pope showed us an extraordinary construct laid out on a big table. At first sight it appeared to be a scrupulously rendered reduction of the interlace of a famous Ardabil rug. However, it was not painted on a single surface, but rather on half a dozen transparent plastic sheets. Each represented a separate system in the design, and when they were placed in the combined order of the rug's all-but-illegible intricacy, they vibrated as a single rich whole. A map of warp and woof, when "the figure in the carpet" was thus analyzed and demonstrated, it no longer seemed a confused vibration of quivering fields of color on one plane, but a chart in dimensional depth of a formal garden which supported a life of its own. The silk plush calligraphy of symbolic clouds, birds, streams, trees was arranged in a tufted mosaic governing a visionary oasis. Carpets laid down on desert sands were originally fictive gardens; their threaded paths and pools wove pleasure and relief from fatigue and heat. The diagrammatic carpet which Dr. Pope demonstrated to our designer, Esteban Francés, was transformed into dances framed as a Franco-Persian court fete. They suggested the age in which the arabesque of Islamic ornament wove itself into Western European fashion and design, just as the *arabesque*, our ballet position, fixed the place of Islam in a royal academy of dancing at Versailles.

The accompaniment was Handel's *Royal Fireworks* and *Water Music* suites. In a prologue, "The Sands of the Desert," Balanchine visualized shifting dunes, before rain transformed dead sand into live gardens. "The Weaving of the Carpet" was a *pas d'action* in which nomad tribesmen shuttled strands in a metaphor of long, multicolored ribbons weaving back and forth to fill the stage like a huge loom. "The Building of the Palace" framed an imperial reception for foreign ambassadors, including those from Scotland, France, Peru, Spain, and Africa, fitting *écossaise, rigaudon, chaconne, bourrée*, and other forms loosely and fancifully based on folk material in Handel's time. After this parade of national entries, the Prince and Princess of Persia, heirs of the Great Sophy, performed their stylized *pas de deux*. The evening's *raison d'être* was a demonstration of the carpet's figuration in its structural overlays, realized as a sequence of pierced and painted drops which descended, one after the other, to majestic strains which may first have been heard behind a royal barge on the Thames. The audience was instructed, as from a gigantic blackboard, in how carpets were woven in the logical design of their symbolic ornament. For a final *bonne bouche*, in "The Fountains of Heaven" there was a Persian garden, inspired by a miniature from a manuscript *Book of Kings*, with a real fountain from whose multiple jets spouted streams that splashed into a tank (weighing tons). Although the Shahinshah's subsidy never arrived, an assemblage of Iranian scholars were happy for an evening. But the ballet was too unwieldy to maintain. Costumes were cannibalized for other more useful divertissements. While we sometimes spoke of revival, *The Figure in the Carpet* too soon became a wistful memory.

At this time we also busied ourselves, under the guidance of Maestro Carlos Chávez, Mexico's senior composer and symphonic organizer, with an evening of Pan-American dancing and orchestral music, including six representative scores. Balanchine shared choreographic obligations with Gloria Contreras, a Mexican dancer and student at our school. Francisco Moncion, who was born in the Dominican Republic, produced a piece by Villa-Lobos. In 1941 in Buenos Aires, we had commissioned *Estancia* from young Alberto Ginastera, but war had intervened to prevent its production. John Taras, who had been on tour with us at the time, now took music by Ginastera for the basis of a ballet that was perhaps the most convincing of the evening. Jacques d'Amboise used a suite by the Uruguayan Héctor Tosar Errecart; Balanchine chose music from Cuba and Colombia by Julián Orbón and Luis Antonio Escobar. We handed out pretty programs in accordion pleats, printed on brightly colored tissues like those for fiestas and bullfights; but one can hardly pretend that such occasional events are viable for very long after their introduction. However, our attempt to explore new music of quality, with the aid of so capable an authority as Carlos Chávez, had some justification, while it indicated to Governor Rockefeller that we had not forgotten provinces south of the border. Although the scores selected had small staying power, a pleasing variety sprang from valid indigenous material orchestrated with tact, if without commanding theatricality. The experiment was worth pursuing, but it also reinforced the statistics showing that of all the novelties we introduced from whatever source, less than a third stayed in repertory past three seasons; and that of those that stuck, a majority were by Balanchine. Yet novelty did spice our seasons. Increasingly we came to provide liveliness and interest which attracted and held a growing public.

JANUARY, 1960: *Albany, New York*

Special train at Grand Central to bring company to Albany for Nelson Rockefeller's inauguration. Rehearsal of *Stars and Stripes* on a miserable stage in the state armory, accompanied by hammering, bunting, balloons, etc. Nelson looked in to see if all was well; ordered more lights. Spoke briefly to him on need for proper space for state occasions. His ideas for the construction of an enormous complex of government buildings. Program ran late, but the train to New York was held.

It seemed suitable that we appear at his inaugural when Nelson Rockefeller was first elected governor. We performed a similar service, also in an armory, for President Kennedy and later in tribute to Lyndon Johnson. Maria Tallchief and André Eglevsky had danced in the White House for General Eisenhower in 1953; later Melissa Hayden, Patricia McBride, and Edward Villella would entertain Mr. and Mrs. Nixon in the same big room.

On a high political level, the arts in this country have intermittently enjoyed the status of adornment, if never that of a national institution. Jefferson was an amateur of music, Lincoln an acute critic of Shakespearean acting. Mr. Truman, on occasion, played the piano, and he, like Mr. Nixon, enjoyed historical films with

military pretexts. The Kennedys graced their entourage with celebrated performers, and in one of Mrs. Kennedy's early official engagements she had Balanchine to tea in the White House. But
Nelson Rockefeller constantly built and pared his own collections,
realizing that objects have a life of their own, independent of
transient "owners," who are bound by a responsibility of present
arrangement and ultimate disposition. While he had always taken
advice from experts—notably René d'Harnoncourt, Robert Gold-
water, Alfred H. Barr, Jr., and Dorothy Miller—it was his personal
preference which guided his first choice, and usually those secondary ones, which are more revelatory, secure, and final. Some of
this collector's attention he allocated to Balanchine, and through
him, to our school, dancers, and audiences, in ways which he's
never cared to claim. However, he put us on paths of public acceptance and provided a chance for finding our permanent home.
He appreciated what our special or immediate situation merited,
just as he understood differences between Sèvres and Chinese export porcelain, or masks used in the Sepik valley or on a Noh
stage.

Balanchine was reared as a cadet attached to an imperial household. The czar in person gave presents to the younger students in
the ballet school at Christmas parties. Hence Balanchine found the
profession of courtier easy to practice when he became attached to
Diaghilev—who in his own youth had served as *chambellan de la
cour* and knew from experience the hopes and hazards of court life.
In the United States, ensigns of power support a "democratic"
style, but behavior in the vicinity of potentates is often more ser-
vile, insecure, and frightened than it is under the symbolic authority of two purely honorific climates: the lapsed divine rights of
the Court of St. James and those of Kyoto and Edo—where tradition is still strong, succession is by birth rather than election, and
each hierarchical and historical level is defined. In America, presidents are only private persons before election and become so again
after their brief exercise of authority. Thus a president's encouragement of anything as ephemeral or occasional as art in performance
is often capricious, cosmetic, or compassionate, reflecting what is,
at best, loose taste on a level of domestic, intermittent, and lightly
prized populist entertainment. In America we often congratulate
ourselves that art patronage is a private function whose exercise is

personal, an evidence mainly of the patron's current affluence. Often as not it has been neither discriminating nor far-reaching.

Institutional theater in particular, including the musical theater, is a living organism which needs nurture from the hearts and minds of qualified authorities for deployment to people who require such skilled and disciplined service. The accelerating permanent crisis of privately (under-) endowed, charitable tax-exempt agencies, whether these be museums, repertory theaters, symphony orchestras, operas, or ballet companies, can no longer in the last quarter of the twentieth century be supported or even alleviated by systems that suited patronage throughout the nineteenth. Government must eventually presuppose that these arts and skills are no less redundant than other necessaries for the public weal. What Europe with its hereditary and hierarchical precedents offers by way of models is less quality in arts, which one way or another produce themselves come what may, than chances resident in continuity. This only means an advance over accident or improvisation, a degree of security and a decency of social recognition which permits performing artists the minimal but basic status of civil servants. For performers are indeed in public service, working for a large audience and utilized as well for political duty past their own borders.

With our company, a sense of paternal, possibly paternalistic, responsibility and consideration has been as strong as conditions allow, given the economy or society in which we exist. To make attractive or impose what must be an aristocratic, elitist discipline upon an anarchic, permissive, heterogeneous source of material has been one of our school's chief problems and accomplishments. Such arbitrary powers emanating from a central authority separate the goats from the sheep, men from boys, ordinary girls from ballerinas. It is not a position or attitude that accommodates facile affection, mass popularity, or much comprehension from the multitude. It is not at all "democratic," but it has its own electorate, and candidates inclined toward the profession nominate themselves without a constituency other than that proposed by individual temperament and capacity.

Through hundreds of years in which order, security, stability, identity were expressed in a criterion of excellence maintained through the paradigm of public gardens, building, singing, dancing, standards were proclaimed by the location of peak excellence under peak patronage. The product was sometimes inferior to the symbol, but nowhere and at no time during social or political revolution, when the ostensible villains were tyrants or crowned heads, did schools or theaters manifesting art in performance stay shut for long. Lyric theater has been constantly carried as one more blazing decoration contributing to the visible glory of common wealth. In the process, the courtier's skill is no less necessary than it has always been. A consciousness of its proper exercise can be gained through the pages of Machiavelli's *Prince*. A far more useful current guide is offered by the Jesuit Baltasar Gracián, theologian of Tarragona, whose *Truthtelling Manual and Art of Worldly Wisdom* dates from 1653:

> Of Cultivated Taste. It can be cultivated even as the intelligence: the better the appreciation, the greater the appetite, and when fulfilled, the greater the enjoyment. Greatness of spirit is known by the richness of the things needed to gratify it; for it takes much to satisfy a great capacity; just as much food is required for great hunger: even so does the sublime in spirit demand the sublime in matter. The boldest objects of nature fear this judgment of taste; and the finest in art trembles before it: few are the stars of the first magnitude, let appreciation of them be equally choice. Taste and contract have a way of going together, and the inheritance is in line: wherefore he is fortunate who may consort with those who have taste at its best. But neither should a trade be made of dissatisfaction with everything, for that is the extreme of fools, and odious in proportion to its affectation, and its intemperateness. Some would wish God to create another world, and of wholly different ideals, in order to satisfy their crazy phantasies.*

APRIL, 1960: *New York*

Meeting at the Century Club to discuss possibilities of Lincoln Center for Music, Inc. Overwhelming representation of interlock-

* Baltasar Gracián, *Truthtelling Manual and Art of Worldly Wisdom* (translated by Martin Fisher), Charles C. Thomas, Springfield, Ill., 1934, p. 67.

ing directorate from Met and Philharmonic. I suggested that a representative of organized labor be elected to the board; also that the name be Lincoln Center for the Performing Arts, since dance and perhaps film would ultimately be constituents; seconded by Anthony Bliss. Conversation with Bliss about future position of City Center of Music & Drama at Lincoln Center.

The Metropolitan Opera Association had long needed a new home. No one knew better than we the inconvenience and dangers of the appealing old palace on 39th Street. In its last days, we joined with others to try to prevent its demolition. Odds were against preservation or conversion to other use, for good enough reasons. The cost of restoring the structure to conditions that would conform to rudimentary fire department regulations would have been more than half enough to build a new house. If it was converted, by some off chance, it might conceivably have been turned over to a troublesome poor relation (like the New York City Opera company) which hardly deserved such grandeur. And in some vague future, such a poor relation might pose a threat to the Metropolitan Opera's absolute control similar to that which the Met faced when it suppressed Oscar Hammerstein's insurgent Manhattan Company in 1910.

If the Met by itself could have built a new home, it would surely have done so, and there would have been no great need or even excuse for Lincoln Center. The Met had never pretended to be a people's theater; its public ensign was a diamond horseshoe which scintillated on the bosoms of hereditary boxholders whose shares controlled the corporation. However, it was now willing to make common cause with the Philharmonic Society, which could afford to be tired of shabbiness at Carnegie Hall. Like the Met, Carnegie Hall was also ripe for destruction, and likewise faced a spectral threat from some competitive agency if there should be a vacuum left to fill in a big empty hall on 57th Street and Seventh Avenue.

There were, however, minds at work sensible of contemporary social and economic realities, which had changed radically over half a century and two world wars. Otto Kahn, Enrico Caruso, Giulio Gatti-Casazza were gone; no triumvirate of such capacity was likely to appear to command a new Puccini. Opera was maintained, but the Met's leadership had proven more custodial than inspired. Policy was perfunctory, although the need for a new face was admitted. The custodians were forced to consider several new aspects of deficit support for a permanently luxurious operation. Great corporations and their subsidiary charitable foundations gave evidence of interest. In such a shift of basis even an institution from the very wrong side of the tracks like City Center, improvisatory as it was and unlicensed by legitimized status or hereditary prestige, intruded to propose a possible service in combination with older and firmer establishments.

Among other unrelated factors, our association with Nelson Rockefeller, his long and understanding help to Balanchine and me, enabled us to nominate our personal architect for a putative theater which might house "The Dance," at least as so specified in promissory brochures. However, there was no specific mention of any permanent controlling inhabitant, other than the parent corporation. But imminent threats of still another World's Fair, again on Flushing Meadow, offered the governor opportunity to appropriate funds to erect a State Theater in the metropolis itself as Albany's permanent contribution to, and memorial of, an otherwise redundant celebration.

One could have hoped that Lincoln Center, Inc., would have commanded a coordinated plan from one single masterful hand, eye, and brain, whosoever that might be. By any European scale the site was not vast or impressive. But a coherent design would, in the opinion of many, have more chance for an achievement of genuine quality than dispersed notions among fatally divided, haphazard, or competitive talents, each of whom might feel compromised or frustrated by subservience to an inevitably lowest common denominator. Michelangelo's Roman Campidoglio, for example, was approximately the same size as Lincoln Center's plot. So were Jones's and Wren's Greenwich Hospital, the city center of Nancy in Lorraine, and Sir Edwin Lutyen's magnificent solution of the government complex at New Delhi. This is no place to detail the gestation or construction of Lincoln Center, but it is appropriate to mention a few of the salient conditions governing Philip Johnson's accomplishment in realizing his State Theater.

Morton Baum was wary of Lincoln Center, Inc., and with good reason. He had been tossed off the Met board for bad manners in talking out of turn (or talking at all). He knew that a struggle for the ultimate control of the State Theater by City Center would be a battle which could cost much. In an important sense it cost his life, and for this he was ready. It was hardly that Lincoln Center would know how to manage any new theater once they owned it, except to exploit it commercially to the hilt by allowing whatever impresario who might rent it to scale ticket prices as high as possible. Baum acted by fiat, as if he had no board; later he consoled his colleagues by his energy and authority, as he stood almost single-handed against the strongest alliance of social prestige and economic power New York might offer.

Tension that was engendered in the grim fight to save the State Theater for the people of New York (city as well as state), precipitated bitterness which may be forgiven, since one is forced to learn that rage only feeds self-destruction. However, it is scarcely forgotten. One must be thankful for what was finally gained, or rather enforced, by Baum's resilience and wisdom, plus the skill, persistence, and integrity of Betty Cage in the actual formulation of an ultimate contract. Few can be comforted, however, by the graceless façade and awkward interior of the Met, the waste involved in multiple corrections of acoustical faults in Philharmonic Hall, or the manipulation of the repertory theater. Had Lincoln Center been a profit-sharing concern, like those other more important ones controlled by its board members, the shareholders could have called them to strict account. The least I could do was to resign, and with the information I had absorbed, struggle as I might for the autonomy of the State Theater. That we were successful, that Lincoln Center stands and operates, that it has found itself a median populist stance and has come to be accepted as a law-abiding and useful citizen in the community, obviates further repining except possibly by impartial historians of architecture or a society whose time is yet to come.

As for the design of the State Theater, we knew we could never aspire to an "ideal" house, and since we were not footing the bills, must obtain what we could by patience, connivance, and ingenuity. We did hold some important advantages. For one, as far as stylistic or elementary aspects of the new building were concerned, we were our architect's single client. The lawyers, bankers, and realtors of Met and Philharmonic were content to have building committees relieve them of the necessity for reading blueprints and for standing firm on whatever particular hopes they may have had. Apart from technical considerations—which were hardly masterfully handled, in view of the redundancy of glass at the back and sides of Philharmonic Hall, the dubious sufficiency of its acoustics, the pitiful lack of public space acknowledged by the Met, and its failure with mechanical devices such as turntables on its opening—the architects of these edifices were in fact virtually their own clients. A vacuum in their patrons' taste is represented by the cramped and confusing foyers of the Met and the entrance which forces Philharmonic subscribers to crowd narrowly past two sides of a restaurant.

Balanchine and I, on the other hand, knew precisely what we wanted and had no one's objections to overcome. Our taste coincided with Philip Johnson's to the smallest detail, and in details, according to Johnson's master, Mies van der Rohe, lie truth, rightness, splendor. Gadgetry was out; technically ours would be a minimally equipped stage. There would be no hydraulic lifts, no turntables, no elaborate trapping, and only minimal electronic circuits (which so far, except for switchboards, have scarcely proved to have any advantage over manual operation). There would be no glaring glass surfaces on three blind exteriors to increase maintenance and illuminate nothing. There would be an auditorium seating some 3,200, with the least possible number of the partial-view seats which must invariably exist in every theater seating over 1,000. However, there would be "continental" seating: aisles, which contain much of the best viewing space, were eliminated; the space between rows of seats would be ample for passage. A double wall would serve as the auditorium's sound-lock against street and foyer noises. Backstage space was sacrificed, but fairly generous onstage side storage was provided. Although not lavish, the rehearsal rooms and practice studios, with pine floors woven in a system developed by Balanchine, were superior to any theater on this continent. We deliberately deprived ourselves of many desirable amenities, even necessities, toward one positive purpose.

New York in the early sixties possessed no space suitable for welcoming heads of state, conquering heroes, astronauts, and international cultural ambassadors. It had made do with state armories or hotel ballrooms. If the city (and state) were provided with an appropriate space to serve as parlor for the metropolis, the municipality could be justified in contributing to its perpetual up-keep, thereby reducing maintenance costs for City Center. Philip Johnson proceeded to envision the most splendid interior our city possessed since the great waiting rooms of Grand Central and Pennsylvania railroad stations, now defaced or doomed. Plans for the State Theater's promenade went through innumerable changes. In Japan, both Johnson and I had been attracted by the Japanese rectilinear modular systems; thin, beveled supports, rhythmically syncopated; and slender balconies, unrelieved by adornment except for the elegance of their structural materials. Johnson prepared several models, one of which even flaunted a fanciful polychromy inspired by the Momoyama baroque and the lacquered glories of Nikko's shrines and Kyoto's Nijo Palace. Finally, under the lean Miesian aesthetic of "less is more," he reduced the structural elements and their chromatics to champagne-colored travertine, gilt bronze, rose marble, a fourteen-carat-gold ceiling, and gilt anodized bead curtains for the large front windows. Two heroic twin figures, the largest marble pieces ever cut in Carrara to be shipped overseas, were based on life-sized figures by the sculptor Elie Nadelman, of which Governor Rocke-feller had long owned bronze replicas. These gigantic lady acrobats or dancers in repose were set as the sole decoration in the foyer to give it scale and polarize its space. There would be no crystal chandeliers; instead of a single grand staircase which, as in the Met, led nowhere and did nothing except to confuse or further frustrate the flow of people on narrow overhanging balconies, there were two boldly hand-carved stone staircases which permitted the huge un-impeded areas of the foyer to serve as a festive visual fanfare for whatever spectacle was held within.

Certainly there were problems—practical, financial, aesthetic. In order to procure gilt-bronze railings for the open balconies canti-levered out from the curved bearing wall, a shop had to be set up which for a year and a half constructed individual hand-forged panels, each different, in patterns roughly deriving from Jackson Pollock's aleatory "drip" technique. The Nadelman marbles in their glowing metaphorical nudity exacerbated a small but influen-tial group in the Lincoln Center management, at a time when ulti-mate control of the theater was still in doubt. A clutch of hard-hats made wisecracks about big bosoms, and there was even talk of their removal. However, the large hole in the building's exterior wall, which alone was wide enough to admit them to a floor above the street, had been sealed on schedule, and the figures were safe. And over our protest, an orchestra pit had been imposed that would seat only thirty-five contract musicians. This is the number that customarily accompanies Broadway musicals, the brand of entertainment which most cost-conscious realtors, lawyers, and bankers relish. Concrete had been poured, but early one morning Balanchine chanced into the auditorium, crowded with forests of scaffolding, to stage one of the most moving and effective solos of his career. After his immediate threat to withdraw our company from further tenancy if the orchestra pit remained straitjacketed, power drills were brought in to double the space, so that it can now, with discomfort, hold some seventy men. This is about two-thirds the size of the orchestra in any fair-sized European opera house that produces Wagner, Verdi, or Strauss, to say nothing of other "grand" opera. And by this time it was apparent that the State Theater would be shared by the New York City Opera company, under the direction of Morton Baum's dedicated protégés, Julius Rudel and John White.

JANUARY, 1961: *New York*

Lunch with General Maxwell D. Taylor, U.S.A. (ret.), newly appointed director, Lincoln Center for the Performing Arts, Inc. Tried to explain our intransigence relative to autonomy for the State Theater, as well as differences between City Center and Lincoln Center in socioeconomic terms. Failed. The field he now commands is in contest, not in tension; but how to make this clear?

As a constituent in occupancy of a projected performing arts center, it was appropriate that a new full-time director should meet with representative participants. By temperament and experience, I was much attracted to professional soldiers. During the war I'd been on detached duty at West Point and was made to feel wholly at home, lodged with a delightful Engineering Corps officer, whose wayward daughter was a gifted artist and confirmed Marxist. His tolerance of her young pacifist companions, his taste in music and painting, demonstrated that traditional authoritarian discipline was elastic enough, off the field of combat, to accommodate freedom of imagination. Also, I had thoroughly enjoyed myself in the Army; in my hagiology, George Patton replaced T. E. Lawrence. My predilection for histrionics predisposed me to embrace a military ethos, even as ploughshares were forged into swords, or vice versa. And through my West Point contacts, we arranged for deputations of cadets to attend our performances at the State Theater on free weekends. They adorned our theater with immaculate dash and courtesy, like *chevaliers gardes* off duty, waiting on ballerinas at the Maryinsky.

Hence I was charmed and flattered to sit, *à deux*, with General Taylor, expressing admiration for his career and profession as well as anxiety and fear in our present situation. In semiretirement he directed a Mexican light and power company. He had been super-intendent of West Point, would become Army chief of staff; chairman, Joint Chiefs of Staff; adviser to Presidents Eisenhower, Kennedy, and Johnson; finally ambassador to South Vietnam. Why, with such credentials, should he not also be coordinator, developer, public relations officer, indeed, director of Lincoln Center? Perhaps he came to ask himself that insignificant question between bad nights and worse days in Southeast Asia; it was possibly a mercy that he soon took refuge in fields more furious.

General Taylor's appointment was a sterling and characteristic and inevitable response on the part of Lincoln Center's board. It offers a classic example of the behavior of responsible Philistines when they think to take over a province of Israel. Responsible General Taylor was; Philistine he was not. For reasons doubtless dictated by his selfless sense of service, and at the moment lacking a sword, he was called to do what should be done about a situation which was increasingly disorderly and promised worse. The gentlemen who nominated him had no clear idea of such development in its particulars, except that it was damnably untidy. To these trustees, the cost of untidiness leads to iniquity deeper than perdition. Their unique talent fosters control, which is what others might name neatness. Neatness means "success"; waste means "failure."

Apart from managing their own business, they handle the trusteeships of hospitals, museums, or schools, considered as obligatory services, in approximately the same fashion. Under them, professionals, doctors, scholars, teachers learn to know their place and proceed, as they can, according to guidelines of certified public accountancy which characterize no-nonsense control, efficiency experts, cutbacks, etc. But when it comes to "art," beyond those objects which are inert, negotiable, real property—or worse, when it comes to the immeasurable and unpriceable arts of performance—it is almost impossible for them to translate "entertainment" which spells "amusement" into "service." Money is always to be "lost" rather than "spent." If it is "lost," loss spells waste and failure threatens, naturally in the form of bankruptcy.

From a wide experience, Stravinsky had many observations on patronage which those burdened with a disposition of funds to our fifty states might consider:

> Art, to middle-class millionaire politicians, is something to be collected and dowered. And this is part of the reason why our yachting millionaires and racehorse millionaires include so many French Impressionist millionaires but so few musical millionaires: the resalable musical artifacts are comparatively insignificant.
>
> Nor are the cultural economics of other societies more instructive, except for drawing still more invidious comparisons. We can learn from them that musicians have not always been starvelings or in such undemanded supply as they are now. In Sophoclean Greece, for example, musicians' salaries were fixed by law. . . . And in Greece, as well as at Mantua, and Esterház, and Monticello (Virginia), they seem to have been regulated by merit. . . . Jefferson was musically cultivated, by the way, and though he was probably a difficult source of income to his orchestra players, demanding that they should also be gardeners, and so forth, he spent a far greater share of his money on music than the "eleven cents out of every

hundred dollars of disposable income" . . . that his fellow
countrymen are now squandering on the "performing arts."*

What our nation needs is not a plethora of bronze and travertine art centers, nor concentrations of facilities serving communities that can't recruit subscription audiences sizable enough to
support the buildings' heat or electricity. If the federal government
is finally brought to support the performing arts with a modicum of
the money spent annually on West Point, Annapolis, and the Air
Force Academy, one might hope that directors of these three facilities will stay where they are and not be purloined to guarantee a
tidy lack of waste in theaters, museums, studios, and opera houses.
Ex-performing artists, indeed, may be forced to assume the managerial role of soldier, which is no easy impersonation. A time may
come when bankers, realtors, lawyers can no longer offer themselves as convenient bullies or scapegoats. In Britain a sense of civil
service has not vanished with imperial shrinkage. Lessons learned
in the Indian civil service have profited custodial precedents for
many present programs. May our operators benefit from the
lightened weight of Vietnam.

Arnold Goodman represents a type of public servant which,
alas, the United States has found it rarely possible to train or
support. Apart from his qualities as man of affairs and diplomat, he
is a critic with erudition and cultivation. Lord Goodman's tenure
in the bureaucracy of the Arts Council spelled a new period of
stability, sensitivity, and service. He has something to say for state
subsidy (in Britain, a smallish island):

> It does insulate cultural organizations against the totally un-
> trammeled concern of the wealthy or busybodying amateur.
> The Arts Council—blessed be the name—whatever its short-
> comings has from the day of its establishment maintained the
> principle of subsidy without interference. This is not a doc-
> trine of timidity but a doctrine of sense. Its duty is to consider
> worthy recipients, confirm their worthiness, and bestow this
> financial assistance. Whatever the problems and shortcom-
> ings of this system, it shines with splendor by the side of a
> system of wholly private contributions from people who think

* Igor Stravinsky and Robert Craft, *Retrospectives and Conclusions*, Alfred A.
Knopf, New York, 1969, p. 61.

that on that account they have a right to a voice and a judgment on subjects where a lifetime of knowledge is required to express any valid view.*

OCTOBER, 1962: *Moscow*

Rocky Staples, cultural attaché, informed us that the embassy takes no responsibility for dancers, that we cannot charter a private plane from Helsinki or Warsaw, and that in case of our internment, he has no authority to intervene. In the Kremlin at the Palace of Soviets, brilliant performance of *Agon,* with the crowd cheering Arthur Mitchell ("Meech-elle, Meech-elle"). On the way to the hotel, rumbling tanks in back streets. The kitchen made a special effort to provide a feast; the maids frighteningly sympathetic. Betty Cage and I in silent cold sweats. Balanchine cheerful: "I've never been to Siberia." From various correspondents (*Time, N.Y. Times, Paris Soir*), rumors of a military putsch within the Kremlin.

The first Soviet tour by the New York City Ballet in 1962 was preceded by Stravinsky's own triumphal return, which he has intimately and precisely recorded through Bob Craft. When Balanchine arrived in Russia after an absence of thirty-eight years, he usually behaved with mannerly irony and casual *politesse,* but did not make it easy for apparatchiks or hack journalists to claim him as a repentant prodigal. Now an American citizen of a quarter century's standing, he affected the stance of a stranger not simply from another country, but from another century. Although he had left Russia at nineteen, he behaved as if he could recall only prerevolutionary Petersburg before 1914, when he was ten. His brother Andrei Balanchivadze, like their father an honored nationalist composer, was at the airport to greet him. There were touching if crass efforts to involve Balanchine in the historical texture of his origins. A reporter found that Balanchine in his youth had once been in the same room with the eminent poet and suicide Vladimir Mayakovsky, although no word had passed

* Arnold Goodman, *New Statesman,* Nov. 24, 1972, p. 770 *et seq.*

between them. Asked his opinion of Anna Pavlova, Balanchine had to admit he'd never seen her, since she had left Petrograd and performed only abroad during his youth. However, *Pravda* ("The Truth") reported that Mayakovsky had encouraged and influenced the budding choreographer, who had first been inspired to dance by the mysterious feminine soul of Pavlova. Resisting such coloration, Balanchine adopted a slyly antiquated manner of speech, patiently answering hack journalists as if he had difficulty with a barbarous vocabulary or jargon. Postrevolutionary portmanteau words and agitprop slang had indeed penetrated the idiom, but they are no more difficult to decipher than captions on a cartoon.

As for impressions, favorable or otherwise, which our repertory may have made, it is impossible to reconcile what we heard and saw of the response with what could be read in newspapers. Official Marxist dialectic transformed original impulse or personal intention into something which, if not particularly rich, at least was passing strange. In *Agon*, for example, Arthur Mitchell, our elegant black soloist, performed the crucial *pas de deux*, cool as spring water in its dispassionately erotic acrobatics. When Arthur first came to our school nearly twenty years before, a furious father full of antebellum prejudice threatened to withdraw his (pinko-gray, ungifted) daughter if this (black, gifted) boy was allowed to "handle" her—in adagio class. In the *Agon pas de deux* Balanchine had arranged one of his most ingenious serpentine, linked patterns in equal balance between partners of opposite sexes. In certain passages Mitchell's pantherine sinuosity tended to swing the combination into approximately a star turn. In the Muscovite press, however, Balanchine's expression of Stravinsky's mutations of Mersenne and de Lauze's Renaissance dances was interpreted as a Negro slave's submission to the tyranny of an ardent white mistress. Andrei Balanchivadze, in conversation, at least, expressed admiration for his brother's tact, daring, and taste in presenting a white girl and black boy in such an implicit and prolonged design. This element had caused no comment at home in the five years of its existence.

Naturally the townscape of Leningrad made its hypnotic impression. One's sense of the present was almost obliterated by the treasures of the Hermitage: the cabinet of Scythian gold, the felt tapestry hangings recovered from Altai permafrost, Rembrandt's

Danaë and the Golden Shower, the twin galleries of military portraits of commanders in the alliance that defeated Napoleon, the
massive but exquisitely cut vases of semiprecious stone demon-
strating the mineral richness of the Urals. Rossi's lovely small
theater, linked by a bridge from the museum palace, was particularly impressive, for here Diaghilev, on a stage identical with the
Maryinsky's, had rehearsed his dancers for the 1909 Paris season.
Suddenly his foreign office subsidy was withdrawn, and he was
forced to continue for the moment entirely on his own.

From my attachment to Nijinsky's memoirs and from
Balanchine's school-day recollections, we approached the Kirov
Theater as a shrine. We appeared there for a few performances
before transferring to a huge, relentlessly unglamorous sports arena,
but the former imperial opera house presently appeared as a pretty
enough, small nineteenth-century theater. But with shabby
draperies, it was musty and sad, particularly in comparison with
Philadelphia's Academy of Music, built in 1859, which was at the
moment being superbly restored by Philip Johnson as self-instruc-
tion preparatory to planning our own State Theater.

Differences between Soviet and American ambience and possibility were sharply illuminated, particularly in theater. At the Maly
there was a magnificent revival of Meyerhold's thirty-year-old
production of Lermontov's *Masquerade,* with its astonishing
prologue. On big double turntables, revolving against each other,
an entire pack of personified playing cards danced Khachaturian's
polonaise. The pack vanished; from the center of the stage rose a
huge gaming table, its green baize lit by a single overhead lamp,
throwing in dazzling relief a crowd of officers and dandies against
whom the opening dialogue was now heard. There was also a
splendid performance of Chekhov's early *That Fool Ivanov,* played
according to the author's intention (generally ignored in the
West) as a tragic rather than comic melodrama. I was assigned a
formidable companion, whom I was told held the rank of colonel
in the political police. She took me to any play I wished to see. At a
dreary, perfunctory delivery of *The Winter's Tale* at the Moscow
Art Theater, then passing through a drab period, her eyes filled
with tears which flowed steadily from the first declaration of
Hermione's innocence. I stayed stubbornly dry-eyed, impatient,
only willing to stick it out since she was so obviously moved. As we

left, she turned on me like a tigress: "Do you know why you didn't weep?" I risked faint criticism. "No!" she snapped: "It's because you're so *rich!*"

We were permitted to attend classes in the ballet schools, a sobering and instructive experience. In Leningrad we found much that one might expect—strong discipline, expert acrobatic partnering, rather blunt and slow bodies. A frontal static correctness in basic positions of arms and feet governed a lack of plastic fluency; the rigor in constant returns to an initial rigid anchorage in the canonical five positions robbed many sequences of uninterrupted flow. We saw group photographs of graduating classes from the early nineties. Portraits of prizewinners included those of Pierre Vladimirov, Felia Doubrovska, and Anatole Oboukhoff, who at that moment were teaching in our own Manhattan classrooms. There was a charcoal sketch of Georgei Balanchivadze, aged thirteen, costumed as a cupid. The school in Moscow was even more physically impressive, but stylistically the instruction was less to our taste. It was more a national than a municipal institution; we had learned (although this was officially denied) that the best provincial students were siphoned into classes preparing the Bolshoi company, which, while not highest in prestige abroad, is politically more powerful at home.

A remarkable class of Central Asians was filled with extraordinarily supple and handsome boys, twelve to fifteen years of age, strong and Mongol in cheekbone, tawny skin, and black hair. They'd come to Moscow speaking no word of Russian and susceptible to pulmonary disease in city air vastly different from their native steppes. The Asian students had their personal tutors, nurses, doctors, infirmary, and were cared for with the attention we give only to prize athletes or champion colts, which they proudly resembled. It would seem that, out of a class of fifteen or twenty, there must emerge at least half a dozen splendid male soloists, and that over a five-year period, on the basis of such material and conditions, the Soviet Union would be gaining regiments of unparalleled stars. But considering the mass (one-sixth of the world's land) and extent of the Union of Soviet Socialist Republics, and the prestige of classic ballet for both home consumption and diplomatic export, it is notable that Russia has produced comparatively few prime male dancers since the Revolution. In the past, Chabukiani and

Messerer; more recently Vasiliev, Soloviev, and now Baryshnikov are at the peak of their profession, along with Leningrad's defector, Nureyev. It is curious that the astonishingly numerous and promising aspirants in the lower grades of Russia's ballet schools result in so few finished artists, either men or women, of the first rank.

The one sad and implacable cause seems to lie with music: a lack of variety and scope in training, not the somatic body, but the ear; a lack in developing aural capacity as trigger, not alone of bones and muscles, but of imagination, mind, spirit, and governing philosophy as well. While jazz, moderate rock, and other international popular forms were permitted in social clubs and even some public concerts, there was an absolute division in academic instruction between the variety of rhythmic metric which has dominated Western music since 1917, and that which governed the generation of the great Five, Balakirev, Borodin, Cui, Moussorgsky, Rimski-Korsakov, and their succession. The pervasive transformation of Western audition, deriving on one hand from improvisational forms originating in New Orleans, Kansas City, and Chicago, and on the other from the progressive methods of Stravinsky, Schoenberg, Webern, Varèse, Ives, and Alban Berg, had not been licensed to inform the apparatus or legitimate production of Soviet musicians. We did meet a few "underground" composers who, secluded in their apartments, might have bootlegged scores or tapes, and who wrote, for themselves alone, in an arrested idiom wanly following the bourgeois pioneers of the West.

The experiments of a loyal Soviet artist, however, must be governed by ethical optimism, local ethnic melodic material, academic modalities, and supercharged heroics. No deviations from elementary tonality or primary rhythms were permitted to sully rigid habit, either in music or in movement which depended on it. Hence gifted young aspirants from Uzbekistan, Georgia, or the Ukraine were condemned in class and onstage to waltz, two-step, and fox-trot, their feet and bodies chained to 3/4, 2/4, or 4/4 measures. Thus in choreography there was absolutely nothing new in our understanding of the term, past the nineteenth-century repertory, except massive physical parade and prowess. The governing orchestration, with the remote exception of the early, now vaguely licensed Shostakovich, or the broken if unregenerate

Prokofiev, was as bland and hygienic and "positive" as graduation exercises.

Any probing on our part into aesthetics, which are an important element in mechanics, was taken as unfriendly disapprobation. There were countercomplaints that Americans moved too fast, that we could not "interpret" Tchaikovsky; that our beat was heartlessly computerized, percussive, eccentric; in fact, that we had no "soul." No use to claim that our soul, while ticking, was not the same as others ticking to more syncopated tunes. While it was generally agreed (in private) that our training and equipment were "technically" accomplished, the concession was tempered by a tone implying that this quality was mechanistic, dictated by an impersonal, inhumane, or decadent formalistic servility. Our sparceness in decoration and costume was hapless formalism; our androgynous lack of polarization between musculated males and bosomy females was the result of a fatal absence of Socialist health and psyche. Such was the verdict of a large portion of printed opinion, yet certainly not of a vocative public which actually saw what we danced. Nor was it the judgment of that daring band of hopeless enthusiasts who followed our appearances from Leningrad to Tbilisi and Baku, back to Moscow and Kiev, who could hardly see enough of the novelty, strangeness, or freshness of a wholly alien vision and philosophy.

Our season in Moscow, which opened at the Bolshoi and continued in the Palace of the Soviets, one of the world's largest and most comfortable theaters, coincided with President Kennedy's Cuban missile crisis. The tension, indeed the terror, of those few days and nights, without a blow ever being struck in anger, were more demoralizing to me than anything I had encountered from the invasion of Normandy through the capture of Munich. Through it all, Betty Cage and Balanchine cushioned the brunt of unimaginable possibilities with such tact and skill that the danger of our situation hardly percolated down to the dancers, who night after night within the Kremlin's walls heard six thousand voices yell for fifteen minutes after every performance: "Bal-an-chin, Bal-an-chin!"

Among many distinguished guests after our opening at the Bolshoi at an elaborate party held in Spaso House, the splendid residence of the American ambassador, was Khrushchev's son-in-law Adzhubei, at the moment an all-powerful newspaper publisher. He placed himself by Balanchine's elbow apparently eager to offer formal felicitations. Balanchine, seated casually, continued a concentrated conversation with a girl and a boy, two of our youngest dancers. One became nervous in the heat of a human situation within a tense political atmosphere. Balanchine had long complained that we have no one to teach pantomime in our school, whereas Russian students constantly enact roles in dumb show along with their earliest dance training. I began to realize that he was now giving a lesson in advanced pantomime. Evidently Adzhubei recognized this also, for with a wry smile of comprehension he turned away. Balanchine had been so attentive to his two dancers that he could never have been charged with discourtesy.

I had known Sergei Eisenstein, the film director, in New York at the climax of his worst catastrophe. He was unable to retain his right to cut footage of *Que Viva Mexico!* against Upton Sinclair (who had raised the necessary money) and was faced with the horrid prospect of returning to Moscow with nothing to show for months of willful absence. I now became friends with Pera Atasheva, his widow, in a whirlwind intimacy. Every morning after breakfast I'd walk to our embassy to hook whatever rumors were running, then go to her tiny apartment in the back courtyard of a ruinous block of fallen plaster and cracked concrete. Her sitting room was crammed with mementos of Eisenstein, circus days with Meyerhold, Noh masks, Aztec skulls, photographs of Cocteau and Charlie Chaplin, Gide and Dreiser. From her files she extracted my letters dating from the early thirties.

She and I shared crystallized nuts and fruit, herring and eel, during the fear, menace, and excitement of those threatening hours. On the worst morning, opening her door, she asked in a voice drained of sarcasm or irony: "Are we friends or enemies?" I had just passed by an aborted "spontaneous demonstration" organized to splash paint and rotten cabbages against the fortress walls of our embassy's chancery. Crowds, marshaled as far back along the wide avenue as the Borodinsky Bridge, had assembled with sloganed banners, eggs, bottles, moving-picture cameras, and sound trucks. But the weather would not cooperate; there was not enough light for decent filming, so the protest was spontaneously rescheduled to take place the following day. Pera Atasheva and a few of Eisenstein's young followers, who were now editing his theoretical prose in six volumes, could laugh at what would have been his opinion of such grotesque child's play. It was he who had foreseen the most breathlessly inventive *ciné-vérité*; he who had organized the entire city of Petrograd to shoot *Ten Days that Shook the World* (portions of which are filed in archives from Leningrad to Washington as authentic films of the 1917 Revolution). In farewell, Madame Eisenstein gave me his wicked sketches of Nijinsky and Diaghilev, which are now in the dance collection at Lincoln Center.

Performance of music and dancing aside, the atmosphere of this tour was fixed most fiercely and emotionally at our final performance in the Lensoviet sports palace, across the Neva in an almost suburban outpost of Leningrad. All our appearances had been sold out; the large trade-union syndicates had been assigned the distribution of tickets; there were none to be had for many young students and older artists. Therefore Balanchine announced an additional free, open performance—first come, first served—for the dancers, musicians, painters, and poets of his city. After the final ballet, a delegation from these workers of mind, fancy, and heart marched onto the stage, their leader bearing an ivory-handled silver samovar filled with red roses. I sat with a conservator from the Hermitage who spoke excellent French and English and had often traveled West. The delegation's captain, dancers clustered around him, began a speech to Balanchine. The Cuban crisis had passed, but its menace hung in the air like a faint scent of sulphur. The audience was charged with inchoate emotion, a mixture of warmth, regret, and that vague hope in delinquent brotherhood which men feel when mutual terror fuses common anxieties for a brief thrilling moment.

The speech in Russian went on, emotionally and at length. The audience grew impatient; it was late and rainy; the evening should have ended more aptly. Finally Balanchine was presented with the silver and ivory urn. He handed it to one of our girls. For a long half minute he stared at the floor, his silence covered by a solid burst of applause. After he'd raised his hand to stop it, he spoke, very clearly, one sentence in Russian which I could not follow. It caused an absolute blanketing of every cough and breath. Nervously I asked my friend from the Hermitage what Balanchine had said. *"C'était assez triste,"* she said. "It was simply, Thank you: in troubling times which we may share in time to come, try to think of us as we are tonight; we'll try to think of you as you are tonight!"

There had been lighter moments. At a cocktail party given by Ambassador Foy Kohler on our departure, the guest of honor was Madame Ekaterina Furtseva, the cultural commissar. Mr. Kohler, who had been a rock for us and his country, complimented our company on their exemplary behavior over their weeks in the Soviet Union, during which cultural exchange and even diplomacy had trembled on the brink of what one dared not risk. He raised his glass: "To the dancers of the New York City Ballet who, through thick and thin, on good stages or bad, made no false step."

MAY, 1963: *New York*
STRAVINSKY ON BALANCHINE'S ARRANGEMENT OF
Movements for Piano and Orchestra:

To see Balanchine's choreography of the *Movements* is to hear the music with one's eyes; and this visual hearing has been a greater revelation to me, I think, than to anyone else. The choreography emphasizes relationships of which I had hardly been aware—in the same way—and the performance was like a tour of a building for which I had drawn the plans but never explored the result. Balanchine approached the music by identifying some of the more familiar marks of my style, and as I heard him fastening on my tiniest repeated rhythm or sustaining group, I knew he had joined the work to the corpus of my music, at the same time probably reducing the time lag of its general acceptability by as much as a decade. I owe him even more for another aspect of the revelation: his discovery of the music's essential lyricism. I gather that his dramatic point is a love parable—in which ballet is it not?—but the coda had a suggestion of myth that reminded me of the ending of *Apollo.*

The ballet, which might also have been called *Electric Currents,* is a double concerto for male and female solo dancers, both identified with the piano solo. The choric group is spare—none of Balanchine's usual attendant caryatids this time but only a hexachord of those beelike little girls (big thighs, nipped-in waists, pin-heads) who seem to be bred to the eminent choreographer's specifications. The full dancing sextet is identified as a unit only in the Interludes, an idea which projects the shape of the entire piece with great clarity.*

In November, 1960, Balanchine introduced Stravinsky's *Monumentum pro Gesualdo,* which had had its orchestral premiere in Venice two months before. Accompanying the atmosphere of this earlier piece, Balanchine evoked the deliberate, almost sinister gravity and fatality shadowing court dances performed in the lifetime of this prince of madrigalists and murderers. *Movements for Piano and Orchestra,* with which it would come to be paired in repertory, was first played in New York in April, 1963. Choreographically it is even more compact, relentless, spare—a comment on one of the most complex of Stravinsky's later statements. The special quality of a "late" manner, the terminal florescence of an old artist's expression, has often been analyzed relative to Beethoven, Titian, or Rembrandt. Edgar Wind, a provocative historian lecturing on the "old age" of Raphael, who died at thirty-seven, produced an ingenious exposition of this painter's metaphysical and even biological maturation, considering the age and perfection of his early work and the expansion of its sequence. Stravinsky made sharp distinctions between ordinary clock time and other dimensions of encapsulated or concentrated temporal metrics through an imploded intensity of musical ideas which permitted no fat or rhetoric upon the fluid structure of his motor process. His constant shift in interests, musical or worldly, kept him lean, active, and full of youthful thought as he progressed through calendar time during nine decades.

It was our great fortune that Stravinsky honored us as a virtual partner in many important orchestrations from 1937 through 1972. He enforced the unique responsibility or opportunity of making our ears, minds, and bodies stretch to the limits of his elastic achievement. While it was obvious that Balanchine benefited directly and immediately from successive analyses of his scores, it is often overlooked that our dancers also learned new means of think-

* Igor Stravinsky and Robert Craft, *Themes and Episodes,* 1966, pp. 24–5.

ing and counting, and thereby moved to measures that were physically and theatrically unprecedented. A synthesized syncopation of sound and silence, the torque and break of symmetrical or asymmetrical balance and imbalance, the ability to follow and encompass modalities in motion as if they were tonally dictated—these contributed to the kinetic sophistication of performers whose apparatus would not be limited by a past academy or middlebrow music of dubious quality.

Stravinsky also educated our audience and our orchestra, for Robert Irving, who had cast his lot with us after our first Covent Garden season, embraced this strange and wonderful repertory as a true *maître d'orchestre*, as comrade in arms and legs of *maîtres de ballet*. Stravinsky wrote ruefully of his *Movements* that Balanchine "has joined the score to the body of my music far faster than it could ever get there by way of the concert hall—where in fact it has not yet arrived." Ten years later this was still true. Irving built an orchestral group into a coherent instrument which would become recognized, before and during the Stravinsky Festival of 1972, as unequaled anywhere. It was accustomed to play difficult orchestrations, and whether a novelty was by Toshiro Mayuzumi, Iannis Xenakis, Morton Feldman, Morton Gould, or Robert Russell Bennett (for Richard Rodgers), it was given the preparation and performance of full symphonic exposition. Part of this came from the knowledge that Balanchine, as musician, knew exactly what he was doing when making dances for music. Having himself extracted piano versions of new pieces for himself and rehearsalists, he showed little fumbling, waste, or indecision. He could start composition and his orchestra could start reading, with ingredients already laid out, prepared in order and quantity, and waiting, like fresh uncooked food on a kitchen table, to be combined into an appetizing dish.

NOVEMBER, 1963: *New York*

Conference with W. McNeil Lowry, Marcia Thompson, his deputy, and Eugenie Ouroussow, director, School of American Ballet, at the Ford Foundation concerning survey made and submitted by Ballet Society, Inc., relative to a national program for the support of ballet, its education and production. A ten-year schedule is blocked out, encouraging general regional growth as well as aid to specific companies across the country.

The concept of an American national ballet institution on the model of the French, British, Canadian, or Russian systems would appear to be logical, but local conditions in the United States make such parallels impractical. The Comédie Française, the Royal Shakespeare Company, the Bolshoi Ballet, the Scala Opera have been formed to suit local social, political, and artistic climates which have little resemblance to those on this side of the Atlantic. After we had made a year-long study, backed by testimony from a majority of the interested teachers and producers, the Ford Foundation granted the School of American Ballet funds to support itself on a stricter and more secure basis—and to aid tax-exempt schools all over the continent both through subsidies and through scholarship grants. But profit-making schools were perforce excluded. Grants-in-aid to individual regional companies for production and development were handled directly by the foundation, not through us.

The program, a pioneering effort in the United States, was neither easy to organize nor simple to administer. Its very announcement provoked a wild storm of waspish protest, presupposing that Balanchine had been granted hegemony over world dance. While he had been only indirectly involved, since he was managing our company and continually composing new works (and not for us alone), it was natural that his advice would be followed. Persons in whom he had confidence would implement the planning, since the program was focused entirely on classic academic traditional ballet, of which he had been undisputed leader for half a century. A famous figure in the "modern dance" called me at home one night around midnight, furious at what she felt was our takeover, and said, "You're nothing but a common thief." Journalists reacted virulently on the part of those who were not included in the Ford Foundation's program—those who by definition had rejected any contact with the classic discipline as an infringement on their inviolate and fractional idiosyncrasy.

But in this scheme, individuals were not being promoted,

whatever their individual talent. The program was designed to support regional education—schools and civic companies that shared a common idiom and in many cases had the same repertory works as well as dancers with identical training. For all its presumably regressive structure, the academic dance possessed a popular legible language and was taught from about the same syllabus all over the world, while the "modernists," from whom most of the indignation sprang, had in half a century never armored themselves with a coherent or collective expression. They had no more than a dozen self-canonizing idioms, whose energetic and aggressive characteristics prevented them from making any impact as a group with a common agreement for joint preparation or performance, and they had been unable to cooperate in the practical economy of repertory performance. Also, with the inevitable disappearance of first-generation founding figures, any succession was fragmentary. Works once framing these individuals were of necessity abandoned, although many were of historical interest. The Ford Foundation, the School of American Ballet, and various beneficiaries weathered the storm of disapproval. It was ill-tempered, ill-founded, but bearable, dissipating itself soon enough.

But in the aim to raise the national level of practice and performance, there were inherent problems which can never be solved by subsidy, direct or indirect, however generous. For example, suppose that an ambitious and talented girl or boy, educated on the Pacific Coast and given good basic training there, joins a local company. How much does the dancer owe to the company which grants him a start or even an early reputation? Is he condemned by loyalty to remain forever where he commenced by circumstance? What are the feelings of directors of regional companies who find their best dancers dazzled and seduced by the concentrated glamour of the Atlantic Seaboard? As for the New York City Ballet, we can satisfy conscience that we never approach any individual who is under contract to another company, nor do we discuss contracts with dancers who have not already terminated a previous association. Dancers who come East and join us often return to their parent group for guest appearances. Local teachers, however loath they may be to let their most hopeful students leave, can boast of their future development.

But while it is true that New York is not America it is equally obvious that ambitious kids know where the action is. Since Hollywood is no longer much of a focus or magnet, Manhattan has more to offer than less noisy, anarchic, or chaotic capitals. Along the East Coast, in the South and Southwest, and on the Pacific Coast, we enjoyed excellent relations with both teachers and companies and gratefully accepted scholarship students sent us with the highest qualifications. Balanchine has always been generous in giving ballets without charge to regional groups who desired them. Levels of local training and performance were certainly raised, as had been the intention of the Ford program. In the most populous area of the Middle West, however, it had no effect. Chicago remained in splendid isolation, despite the long and consistent pioneering of Ruth Page over half a century. Unlike Boston, Philadelphia, Washington, and San Francisco (to say nothing of Vancouver, Toronto, Winnipeg, and Montreal, which had their own excellent Arts Council program), Chicago was the single American metropolis which, after innumerable tentative efforts, would build no representative company, despite the continuous local vitality of its opera, symphony, museums, and libraries.

APRIL, 1964: *New York*

Checking the almost completed State Theater with Philip Johnson. Central chandelier still not winched to rise and lower with the curtain. The gilt-bronze proscenium frame, pierced for lights, will not be lit—yet. Installation of sculptures by Lipchitz, Reuben Nakian, Jasper Johns, etc. Tastefully placed, not one was intended for its present location. Brass stair rails delayed. Dressing rooms comfortable; practice room as big as the stage floor. We have to be thankful for the best theater for dance in America (the world?).

The State Theater at Lincoln Center opened on schedule, with few gross overages, disasters, or corrections necessary. At the opening Governor Rockefeller, through whom it had come into being, said cheerfully to Balanchine: "It's all yours, George. Take it from here." Such continuing largesse was not within the capacity of any donor, however grateful we may have been for his generosity or initiative. The battle for the control of a popularly priced house under our autonomy was by no means over; in fact, the worst of the war was still to be fought. It would end only in 1968 with a truly Pyrrhic victory. Through thick and thin Morton Baum fought the brutally high-handed attempts to contravene the rights of City Center. Finally, with the aid of Betty Cage's powerful legal and extralegal intelligence, he did indeed gain control, for our city and the City Center of Music and Drama, as well as for the New York City Opera and New York City Ballet. Then at a tragically early age, he died.

The transfer from Mecca Temple on West 55th Street to the State Theater at Lincoln Center Plaza was inevitably awkward and costly. What scenery we had hardly fitted the much higher, larger, and deeper new stage. We had commissioned no novelty to serve as an appropriate launching of the occasion, but Stravinsky sent us a delightful surprise—a twelve-tone fractured fanfare, which trumpets sounded from the top balcony of the promenade to send people from the foyer into the auditorium. The City Center in such palatial premises would no longer be able to present itself uniquely as a poor man's facility. Our format was now irrevocably on a grand scale; in some eyes, it was the Big Time. Among those rendered nostalgically disconsolate by our change of venue was Wystan Auden, who, allowing *Es muss sein,* was unreconciled to rose marble and gilt bronze, regretting a comfy shabbiness and familial warmth at Mecca Temple, with its cozy Italian bar across the street. Such regrets were shared by few singers or dancers, who could now be sure of hot showers and decent dressing rooms, to say nothing of breadth and possibility in expanded performing space. The State Theater magnetized new audiences. At first they came from curiosity to judge the bright building, but they soon returned to see performances they had ignored in the gloomy old one. At the prompting of the Ford Foundation, we introduced a subscription system which guaranteed moderate security from advance payments so that we could plan rather than, as so often before, merely improvise. There were, of course, complaints that those who had not taken the trouble to subscribe were "never" able to buy seats. This was rarely true, but absolved people whose interest was only cursory.

Our big full-length *Midsummer Night's Dream* was revised for the new frame. Balanchine continued to alter details, and never seemed satisfied with the processional based on Mendelssohn's "Wedding March." However, its narrative exposition was clear as could be, and Arthur Mitchell as a dusky Puck, Edward Villella as a bouncy, bejeweled Emperor of Faery, seemed even more magical in a far taller forest. *The Nutcracker*, aided by Lincoln Center's production fund, was given its present embellishment by Rouben Ter-Arutunian, who also redesigned *Swan Lake* and *Ballet Imperial* (now called *Tchaikovsky Concerto No. 2*). From memories of his youth at the Maryinsky, Balanchine now animated Petipa's *Harlequinade* (called *The Millions of Harlequin* in 1900). From the New York City Opera company we borrowed Ter-Arutunian's settings for Rossini's *La Cenerentola* with its "penny-plain, tuppence-colored" enlargement of a Pollock Victorian toy theater. In this Villella disported himself like a true jumping jack in the multicolored patches of Bergamo, while Patricia McBride danced an angelic Columbine. Antony Tudor introduced his wistful and passionate *Dim Lustre* from 1943, with new watercolor-and-ink cloths by Beni Montresor. Sir Frederick Ashton now saw an accurate revival of Britten's *Illuminations*, which had been out of repertory for many years, performed to his satisfaction with a younger cast.

Our sensitive and skillful ballet master, John Taras, set Aaron Copland's *Dance Panels* (1962) as *Shadow'd Ground*. He had wished for the collaboration of a young poet, and at his behest, Scott Burton invented a series of rhymed epitaphs as inscriptions on stones slanted in a burying ground. It took its tone from rural New England, a boating party ending in disaster, the fateful adventure of a volunteer who joined the Lafayette Escadrille—the ordinary individual mortality defined in a country graveyard. John Braden's surround was an ingenious series of interlocking overhead panels on which were projected Kodachrome landscapes, unpeopled but suggesting sites where action took place below on the plane of the stage floor. It was a conscious attempt to explore our new facilities. Richard Buckle, who had flown from London to see Taras's charming work, said: "A big company in a big house has a right to a big failure." Failure, or the accusation of it, always rankles. For me, *Shadow'd Ground* did not fail; what was attempted succeeded on its own terms. However, its quiet discretion in so large a frame seemed discrepant. Its failure was in the assertion of so somber and elusive an ambience at a moment that seemed to call for brighter colors, louder noises, and more jovial action.

JANUARY, 1965: *New York*

Looking at Gustave Doré's illustrations in his *Spain* and *Don Quixote* for ideas and style. Nicolas Nabokov's historical analysis of *Hispanidad*, the concept of grandee and hidalgo. Balanchine's memories of Petipa-Minkus version of 1869, which he danced at the Maryinsky in 1916. Unanimous decision to avoid folkloristic dance forms. Esteban Francés—palette for the piece: grays, brown, black-and-gold armor of El Greco's *Burial of Count Orgaz*; the Escorial, not the bullring or *feria*.

Some artists with innate energy beyond the strict realms of their profession at times utilize an acute political instinct, an exemplary general education, and a worldly experience to pursue extramusical careers. This tends to remove them from serious consideration by colleagues and critics as legitimate participants in a puritanical advance guard. Apart from his acute intelligence and devotion to the promulgation of the arts through international festivals and conferences, Nicolas Nabokov is one of the few current composers who possess a melodic gift in an epoch when melody is condemned as the resort of the ostentatious lowbrow or reactionary coward. As a protégé of Diaghilev's he began his career in 1928 by collaborating with Tchelitchev and Massine on *Ode*. He has since pursued a lonely path on which persistence in harmonious, tonal expression has caused his more perfunctory contemporaries to ignore his work.

Twenty years ago, Nabokov had written an orchestral suite portraying Dulcinea's attachment to the Knight of the Doleful Countenance. Balanchine had admired it, and they spoke of an expanded dance-drama. It was Nabokov's special lyric gift, not his comic, grotesque, or ironic commentary on Don Quixote's character, that appealed to Balanchine. The notion of this subject resurfaced over the years. Tchelitchev in 1937 had proposed the Don as the first in his projected *Episodes* balancing Hamlet and Don Juan. Morton Baum had even asked Balanchine to choreograph Richard Strauss's tone poem *Don Quixote* of 1897, but the scale of the orchestration was too large for our pits.

Balanchine and Nabokov, with considerable aid from Esteban Francés, painter and Catalan, not from La Mancha, fashioned a skeletal structure which offered the atmosphere of Cervantes' Spain as the source of the Don's character, which would display his overwrought fantasy as more real, logical, and appealing. Even in a three-act ballet there is opportunity to suggest only a fraction of the novel's incidents, and even less of the preposterous delusions which Gustave Doré so precisely delineated.

Cervantes transcends nationalism, and it is vain for a non-Spanish company to aim at much indication of "authentic" Iberian folk forms. As far as local color went, however, we had in Francés a powerful partner. Trained as an architect, he is a master of illusory perspective and an easel painter of merit. After Tchelitchev, Eugene Berman, and Noguchi, he has been our most satisfactory collaborator in the line of Diaghilev's use of artists whose preoccupations are not primarily theatrical. In his textured impasto, illusionism, and rich chromatics, he had absorbed and would re-create the mineral climate of a barren landscape relieved by spatters of crimson, gold, and bronze. His elegantly detailed costume designs, executed by Karinska, were visions prompted by Zurbarán and El Greco, combining the chivalric rigidity of velvet on armor, starched lace against satin with sackcloth and rags, which clothed court, church, and countryside in the late medieval sunset just before Velázquez.

However, in many ways the ballet never had a chance to be completed. Since we could not afford to shut the theater, it was prepared, in spite of a multitude of technical problems, within the ordinary schedules of one repertory season. We should have had extended rehearsals, with the auditorium closed to the public. The premiere was a gala benefit to help pay for the production. Mechanically it was more or less viable, but the complexity of the spectacle and its governing ideas had no time for maturation. Over the next half-dozen years Balanchine made numerous piecemeal changes, retaining the obvious high points, eliminating what seemed less efficient, transposing the order of whole scenes. In the process he cut many precious fragments. But the strength of the concept, the haunting opulence of Nabokov's melodies, the splendor of Francés's decorations, the nightmare of storm-blown windmills, giants, and monsters have always interested audiences, no matter what changes were interposed. At the start, but less frequently now, Balanchine himself took over the role of the Don. When he performed, as in the first seasons, with Suzanne Farrell as Dulcinea, it was the most compelling realization since Chaliapin's filmed version. In various revisions the synthetic folk dances gave trouble, and secondary incidents were replaced by new music and more formal dances in the style of Petipa and Ivanov. Nevertheless, the Iberian Catholicism of the basic concept—Dulcinea as Ideal Woman, Repentant Magdalen, Innocent Shepherdess, Virgin of Seven Dolors, paired with the Don as Man of Sorrows, Fool of God, Idealist, and Tragic Hero, were powerful metaphors, touchingly visualized in performance.

As for "success," again, the word taunts; the achievement is intangible. The magic and scale of the scenic devices, the handling of children as Moors and Crusaders in the puppet show, the imperious pageantry and ritual sadism of the court ball, above all, Balanchine's extended classic dances at the commencement of the third act—these never failed to delight. The expansive serenity of the ending in its grisaille sobriety, against which passes a parade of ecclesiastical princes, religious orders, cross-bearing flagellants, is strongly supported by Nabokov's cathedral bourdons. But we always hoped for concentrated weeks of undivided study and rehearsal which would have welded a dispersed spectacle into the compactness, intensity, and wholeness it deserved.

JANUARY, 1966: *New York*

Bob Craft, with Balanchine, discussing unplayed music suitable for dancing. Schubert's incidental music? Scriabin—present unpopularity, inevitable revival? Boulez, *Le Marteau sans maître*? Carlos Chávez's Toccata for Percussion? Chamber music?

Brahms's *Liebeslieder Walzer* transferred well from City Center to State Theater's big stage. Bob suggested Schoenberg's orchestration of Brahms's Piano Quartet in G minor (Opus 25, 1861), which sounds, he says, like a "fifth" Brahms symphony.

Balanchine's *Brahms-Schoenberg Quartet* was first danced in April, 1966. It was the initial "abstract" work designed for a new space and the larger scope of a considerably enlarged company. None of the dancers in any of its four movements appeared twice. Balanchine had often said that chamber music (particularly string quartets) is not suitable for supporting big ballets, since chamber music pieces are "too long, with too many repeats and are meant for small rooms." Schoenberg himself was reproved for his elaborate orchestration of this particular piece. He wrote his reasons to Dr. Alfred Frankenstein, the distinguished critic, when it was first played in California: "1. I love the music. 2. It is seldom played. 3. It is always very badly played, as the better the pianist, the louder he plays and one hears nothing of the strings. I wanted for once to hear everything and this I have achieved."

Karinska's ball dresses, court uniforms, and gypsy regalia are in a range of autumnal reds and browns, dusty rose, silvery pink, maroon. The dances seem steeped in the apprehension and change permeating the sunset of the Austro-Hungarian monarchy. They suggest a world drunk on "wine and roses" which consoles itself with the anxious gallantry of hussars on palace duty and the intrusion of gypsies in a Hofburg ballroom. A dusky vision, the ballet has a texture that is acid and sweet, serene, noble, and violent. Certainly its music may not have been planned for theater, but its use corroborates suspicion or hope that a vast unread literature hides innumerable possibilities which only require suspension of prejudice, the flouting of fashion, and relentless curiosity to uncover and utilize.

JULY, 1966: *Saratoga Springs, New York*

Preparation for opening new Performing Arts Center. Despite 17-week construction strike, the theater is complete, landscaping

laid out, parking lot lit. Eugene Ormandy, conductor, the Philadelphia Orchestra, objects to noise from adjacent waterfall, which
will be tunneled for silence. Enormous acoustical reflector above
the proscenium mouth, like a Medusa's mask. The acoustical engineers consider it a sculptural masterpiece and insist that muting its
light color will kill the sound projection.

Diaghilev had been granted Charles Garnier's beautiful miniature opera house in Monte Carlo by the hereditary prince of
Monaco, as an adjunct to roulette, *chemin de fer*, and baccarat
tables. There, new seasons of the Ballets Russes were prepared
following the company's return to France after the First World
War. We had long hoped for a similar facility, half vacation spot,
half workshop, where in unhurried calm we might test future
dances without the customary urban pressure. We had played
previous summer engagements in Ellenville (New York), Los
Angeles, Washington, Red Rocks (Colorado), Ravinia (Chicago),
and St. Louis, but never over an extended period or with much
continuity. Richard Leach had managed summer festivals at
Aspen, Colorado, before leaving the direction of planning for
Lincoln Center to plan Saratoga's ambitious July and August programs. He invited us to play there every July, while the Philadelphia Orchestra would play every August. In the thirties, Franklin
Roosevelt's Works Progress Administration aided the depressed
economy of the "Capital Area" around Albany by erecting an
elaborate complex of neocolonial brick-and-limestone buildings in
a dense pine woods. There were halls for mineral-water fountains, a
hotel, a bottling plant, restaurants, and a small, intimate theater.
Attached to this state reservation was an enormous public swimming pool and a vast plant nursery which stocked the state park
systems. In the sixties the community was again suffering from bad
business. In an imaginative pump-priming operation, Governor
Rockefeller and his Park Commission authorized the design and
construction of an auditorium seating some five thousand persons
under cover, while as many more could be accommodated on the
graded grass lawns beyond.

John MacFadyen, architect of the open-air theater, in collaboration with engineers, acousticians, and landscape gardeners, devised an ingenious solution for access to a very large free-hanging

balcony. Three walkways lead directly from the top of a natural amphitheater into the hall, with no need to climb stairs. A sound-proofed roof protects the public from mountain weather, which the Adirondack foothills sometimes breed, while the sides are left open to spectacular sunsets and starry skies. There are stage facilities based on the scale and proportions of our State Theater, practice and rehearsal rooms, a generous orchestra pit, and good dressing rooms.

The dancers at first took over an unfinished motel, consisting of cottages in a settlement beyond the town, commonly known as The Dustbowl, or Kibbutz. But it soon became clear that there would be little time available for preparation of new ballets, although Jerome Robbins's *Goldberg Variations* received its roughing out in the summer of 1970. Current repertory was maintained with efficiency, but swimming pools, horse racing, and Lake George were relaxations too powerful to resist. Our workweeks had much increased over the years; the dancers needed rest. In the exuberance of enjoyment there were hazards—broken toes from soccer games played recklessly in bare feet; ferocious sunburn; too much dosing with mineral water.

I had known Saratoga in the early thirties with Walker Evans, the photographer who made brilliant and valuable records of the vast mid-nineteenth-century wooden resort hotels. Now the Grand Union and the United States had been torn down for parking lot or supermarket. Skidmore College was building a handsome new campus on the outskirts of town, and the new dormitories provided housing for our musicians. While the prime month for horse racing is August (when seasonal rentals triple), we associated ourselves in July with the American Dressage Institute, which enjoyed the instruction of principal riders from the Viennese *Spanische Hofreitschule*—in 1972 celebrating its four-hundredth anniversary. This unique performing-arts institution has made a true ballet company out of generations of white Lipizzaner stallions. It is a living exemplar of baroque equestrian art, as perfect in its archaeological purity as Gagaku or Noh. Balanchine spent two weeks learning to ride a retired veteran Lipizzaner. Demonstrations of *haute école* equestrian disciplines by Austrian and American riders were held before the ballet performances, to the music of Handel, Haydn, Mozart, and Lanner.

In alternate years, we opened Saratoga with a week of A *Midsummer Night's Dream*, in which painted scenery blended imperceptibly into the surrounding woodland, or *The Nutcracker*, when July heat magically produced a snowstorm. Dozens of children from local dancing teachers replaced the small students from our New York school. A number of our dancers bought summer cottages of their own and identified themselves with the Saratoga community. However agreeable the atmosphere, the net result as far as our institutional existence went was merely four weeks of steady work; not one new ballet would be introduced for its world premiere. It became only too clear that a semivacation engagement is not a situation that lends itself to experiments or to a true "festival," in the European meaning of Salzburg, Spoleto, Aldeburgh, or Edinburgh. While any progressive company depends on novelty for existence, and while money is often available for costumes and scenery, the element of time is at once the most costly and least available ingredient of a new production. And time is unappealing as a focus of patronage; a closed theater "loses" money. In countries with standard subsidies from arts councils or propaganda ministries, this is considered money spent, not "lost." In America, hospitals, museums, libraries, and schools are necessities in which loss is basic, however grudgingly recognized. But in theater, particularly in lyric theater, of which ballet and opera are the main categories, deficits are so large that a proposal to shut an auditorium for preparatory experiment seems to be the straw that breaks the camel's back.

DECEMBER, 1966: *New York*

In our costume shop, Madame Karinska's first models and samples of appliquéd plastic gems lighter than glass, glued or sewn to supple bases on velvet and brocade. Problem of creating glitter without wiping out face and form. Choice of "jewels." Pearls also? No; too close to flesh color, and nonreflective.

As a demi-oriental boy from the Caucasus, Balanchine had always been fascinated by the irreducible mineral treasure of mine and mountain. Some of the most impressive artifacts in

Leningrad's Hermitage are huge vases turned from great hunks of Ural semiprecious stones, porphyry, malachite, sardonyx, and basalt. His friend the violinist Nathan Milstein had introduced him to the jeweler Claude Arpels, who allowed Balanchine to fondle a splendid collection of gems. A metaphor to demonstrate perfection, emeralds, rubies, diamonds are the residual matter of aeons, consummately shaped and faceted as an incarnate mathematical paradigm of price, preciousness, luxury; hence of luck or fortune. They are lavish paradoxes of high cost and small size, unbreakable durability against soft mortal flesh, cool fire flashing from some self-generating eternal source. In 1947 for Balanchine's original Paris choreography to Bizet's long-lost and recently recovered Symphony in C (which Stravinsky first told him about), then entitled *Le Palais de Cristal*, he assigned jewel colors to the four movements. When our *Symphony in C* (the identical dances) was introduced in New York the next year, it held no gemlike connotation. However, the notion stuck in Balanchine's memory.

Jewels is a "full-length" ballet without a plot. Karinska's taste and ingenuity robed it in a sightly cohesion appropriate to its flashing pretexts. Dresses and tailoring were fitted and blazoned with lapidary skill. Some cost-conscious carpers questioned the need for consummate attention to needlework which is so delicate between the fingers that the detail is bound to be lost on the far side of the footlights. But Karinska declared: "I sew for girls and boys who make my costumes dance; their bodies deserve my clothes." Karinska's attitude toward thread, needle, and tissue is different in kind from the commercial costumier, as *cordon bleu* cooking differs from home fries in a hash house. Her insistence on an absolute criterion is not reckless extravagance but a practical approach based on the chemistry of the human lymphatic system. Dancers sweat; sweat is as corrosive an acid as exists this side of hydrochloric. Karinska's underpinnings are built like a bridge, cost hours to construct, and endure for many seasons. The caution in her craft inspires a like pride in the wearing by, and bearing of, dancers. As partner to music and choreography, her stitchery of galloon, rhinestone, sequin, and tinsel contributes to the general dazzle.

Balanchine had considered some orchestral music of Schoenberg's for a sapphire section, but blues command an awkward range of gelatins for stage illumination. And in combination with rubies and diamonds, the blue stones take on a patriotic tinge already accommodated in *Stars and Stripes*.

Contrast of musical coloration was considerable. The translucent serenity and transparent shimmer of Gabriel Fauré's pieces from his *Pelléas et Mélisande* suite (1898) and his incidental music for *Shylock* (1889) suggested a submarine summer-green garden of moss, lime, and—Emeralds. Rubies—Stravinsky's Capriccio for Piano and Orchestra (1929)—dictated an ironic speed and lyric humor for dashing variations by Edward Villella and Patricia McBride. A platoon of pony jockeys and filly ballerinas danced in oxblood or crimson epaulettes and belts. Diamonds used Tchaikovsky's Third Symphony (the *Polish*, 1875, less its first movement)—two scherzi, a grand adagio, and a big polonaise, seeming to employ the entire company of ninety and fill the stage to surfeit, although only thirty-four dancers are used. This is one of the best examples of Balanchine's applause-machines, different in style but similar in effect to the finales to the other Tchaikovsky scores for *Suite No. 3* and *Concerto No. 2*, the Gounod and Bizet symphonies in stimulating climactic excitement and response. Minutes before the end, the fluid collective organism drives toward a sumptuous peak. The audience's empathy and instinctive appetite for block-busting muscular effects devour a big crescendo, gulping at a stage crammed with uniform, symmetrical, head-on movement, and firm primary gesture while the big orchestra builds to a smashing curtain tableau. *Jewels* has been an unequivocal and rapturous "success" since its introduction; the very title sounds expensive before a step is seen. But some who watch it frequently find that Emeralds rather than the bouncier Rubies or the panache of Diamonds are indeed the most exquisitely set gems in this particular *parure*.

APRIL, 1969: *New York*

Listening to pianos onstage and off for Jerome Robbins's new Chopin. Neither Gordon Boelzner, our solo pianist, nor Balanchine wishes the piano amplified, but its presence onstage is limiting and has been used before in Jerry's comic ballet *The*

Concert (1956), which is to be revived. Balanchine suggested a platform over an end of the orchestra pit, unless the balcony's overhang smothers sound.

Robbins had turned his energy to Hollywood films and Broadway musicals, notably *West Side Story* and *Fiddler on the Roof*, after his earlier *On the Town*, which he derived from his ballet *Fancy Free* of 1944. Possessing an analytical method and choreographic authority second only to Balanchine's, he naturally wished to exercise personal possibilities unhampered by conditions which our schedule imposed. He proceeded to an impressive and fruitful career with his own troupe and later, through aid from the National Endowment, experimented with dancers of his choosing, on his own time, with no need to produce a definite piece by a given date. His quasi-religious treatment of Stravinsky's *Les Noces* for Ballet Theatre, while diametrically opposite to Bronislava Nijinska's masterpiece of 1923 for Diaghilev (now admirably danced by the Royal Ballet), had its own massive if wrongheaded integrity. However, he admitted afterward that he preferred Nijinska's version, which was characteristic of his basic objectivity and clear eye. After years of independent labor, he gave evidence of interest in our enterprise.

Balanchine has always wished for someone, almost anyone besides himself, to share the pressure of continuous composition and production. Out of any three novelties, only one has much chance of remaining in repertory after two seasons. His own work dominates almost by default. This is naturally irritating to everyone who chooses to believe that Balanchine tyrannizes over other ballet masters and that they are prevented from working with him only by his jealous fear of some potential competitor. Alas, one hunts in vain for so lucky a find, although journalists have kept themselves busy and proud year after year discovering dozens. Balanchine had long acknowledged Robbins as the native-born choreographer with the strongest structural and musical sense.

We had attempted many times to broaden our base. Frederick Ashton, working with Cecil Beaton, had given us two successes: *Illuminations* of 1950 and *Picnic at Tintagel* (Sir Arnold Bax's *Garden of Fand*) of 1952. However, with Ninette de Valois's retirement as director of the Royal Ballet and Fred's logical succession, he had his own big garden to cultivate, and he was by temperament happiest on the far side of the Atlantic. As for Antony Tudor, perhaps we failed to find him a comfortable frame. Of our five ballets from him, only a revival of *Dim Lustre* (1964) was retained, although our *Lilac Garden* (1951), in the lush shrubbery which Horace Armistead took from Fragonard's panels in the Frick Collection, had one of its strongest presentations anywhere, with an exceptional cast (Nora Kaye, Tanaquil LeClercq, Hugh Laing, Tudor himself). It is not simple for choreographers schooled in climates other than our own to arrive cold, as it were, and warm up impassive if not faintly hostile dancers who are slow to change habits of acceptance or resistance.

In rehearsal Robbins drives, and displays himself as driven. He appears more instinctive, less analytical than Balanchine, at least in the immediacy of composition. When he returned to us, Balanchine assigned him most of his own rehearsal time for some four seasons, from 1969 through 1972, during the preparation of *Dances at a Gathering* and *The Goldberg Variations*. There was no reluctance in this temporary abdication, either in New York's winter or Saratoga's summer. A painter aims at perfection far more easily than a choreographer, for the painter works at his own pace. Although external compulsions of one-man shows or private commissions may prod him, time is his own. But ballet masters must reckon by the union scale, union conditions, and time-and-a-half for overtime, to say nothing of allowing for daily rehearsals to maintain a current repertory and adjusting to the injuries and replacements inevitable for any company that dances hard eight times a week. Nor is it easy for a tightly bonded family of performers accustomed to one type of domination or obedience to embrace or even submit to another entirely different personal method. Our dancers were developed on Balanchine's systems, which are fantastically rapid, whatever their immediate form or subsequent alterations.

Robbins's choice of Chopin's piano pieces was dictated by affection and at the risk of self-repetition. His *Concert* amounted to a comic masterpiece in its parodies of the classic academic idiom. While it often used identical musical material, italicized by sections of a thumping orchestration, within its format, the figure of the solo pianist is as important as any of the dancers. After

Fokine's *Les Sylphides*, which we would revive as *Chopiniana* (without costumes or decor), complacent critics might consider that nothing further should hack at the already eroded monument of Chopin. Robbins worked against, and overcame, varieties of doubt, since his instinct for an intrinsic quality in pianistic vocalism, the haunting echoes of folk sources in their lyric tenderness, enabled him to evoke a vision that was without precedent, one which he magically extracted from the resonance of a grand piano.

Dances at a Gathering places five girls and five young men on some ambiguously native earth, far, yet not too far, from Chopin's own ground. Minimal costumes suggest, mainly through blouse and boot, that the men are neither princes nor peasants, although gently born. The girls wear filmy shifts and are clearly dancing out-of-doors, but as neither countesses nor shepherdesses. They are charming, well-bred young women. The time is possibly past midsummer, fading into autumn, the year perhaps closer to today than to any "romantic" past. The tone of movement proposes mutations of national dancing which, a century ago, adapted themselves to big ballrooms, but which still are infused with earthy vigor and informal courtesy. The men belong to some confraternity; the girls might be cousins; their contacts are more familial or tribal than passionate. Robbins empowered his dancers with so strong a personal flavor of homage to Chopin's spirit that the sequence of duets, trios, quartets, quintets, and their combination expanded into a kind of formal drama, although there was an almost total absence of personalizing characterization, except in the exquisite palette of Joe Eula's costumes. There is no narrative except in a contrast of musical mood, no marked climax, but rather a series of crescendi or diminuendi, which fill metaphorical incident with suave fun, sweet games, and the hint or threat of violence. As a finale, there's an elegiac, offbeat processional, a progressive thanksgiving or hymn to native soil. No exact reference is ever given, however; the processional may apply to the ages of man rather than the map of a nation.

Robbins and Balanchine work as a duet in tandem. Both are too secure in endowment and practice to compete where there is no need for competition. They are separated by nearly twenty years, yet their joint respect for music as a floor for dancing can forge no firmer bond. For thirty years Robbins has watched Balanchine more closely, with more benefit, than any other ballet master. While it is impossible to imagine *The Cage* without a double image of the bacchantes' final fury in *Orpheus*, the metrical division which Robbins gave his hive of horrid creatures is due as much to Stravinsky's syncopation as to Balanchine's structure. Similarly, the lovely finale of *Dances at a Gathering* derives from the last three minutes of *Night Shadow*, but now with the dancers turned to the front to face the audience. It is so astutely adapted that few audiences are conscious of the conversion.

It is not alone from Balanchine that Robbins has borrowed or digested, just as Balanchine himself has rifled the whole range of gesture and movement from well-known repertory "classics," circus, music-hall, film, and memories of which only he can identify the original source. However, digestion, assimilation, absorption amount to much more than "being influenced by." Stravinsky said that no artist is more himself than when he imitates somebody else, for it is personal choice or taste that counts. Think of Rimski-Korsakov in *Firebird*, Pergolesi in *Pulcinella*, Delibes in *Apollo*, Handel in *Oedipus Rex*, Gesualdo in *Monumentum*. Robbins wanders far, works hard in many companies, is not attached to any for long, has seen and read a multitude of pictures and books. What he notes and hears continually strikes sparks in his mind's tinder, which is always ready to take fire. What he possesses to a surpassing degree is the gift for shock, for conscious eruption, for an attack by novelty in broad, legible statements.

SEPTEMBER, 1969: *New York*

To the Juilliard School, Claremont Avenue. Peter Mennin, the director, invited me to meet Norman Singer, in charge of musical attractions at Hunter College. Discussed the Platonic Ideal of an executive manager for City Center. Memories of Morton Baum; the good old, bad old days, beyond recall. Nervousness about a musicians' strike.

Morton Baum's death in February, 1968, was a paralyzing blow. It removed an anchor on reality. For some anxious months we carried on as we might, acting more or less autonomously if automatically, although token control naturally remained with our central authority. The City Center on 55th Street, the State Theater at Lincoln Center, each had its problems. The State Theater was an added burden to Baum; we were only beginning to make a new facility function. We managed to stumble on as if there were no possible replacement for Baum, while realizing that eventually we'd be forced to find one. However, the battle with Lincoln Center, Inc., had been won by Baum, assisted by the intransigent strategy of Betty Cage, the resolute support of the New York City Opera, and unyielding loyalty from Baum's associates. Control of the State Theater would rest in our hands, with no latent threat of exploitation by any high-bidding impresario or agency that could charge whatever prices "special" attractions might be made to justify. The house we had jointly conceived and fought for would remain a permanent, populist home for singing and dancing. This was Baum's victory and legacy.

Without Baum's political sense, honesty, empirical method, and courage, we were confused and in shock. No one else could run the City Center the way he did. His procedure and attitude were attached to a definite historical epoch—from Fiorello La Guardia through Robert Moses to John Lindsay. With his passing, a chapter was over. Our scale of operation was completely changed; City Center was now the arena of a multitude of added activities. It needed direction for increasingly broad and varied programs and service on an international as well as a national basis. Its program would continue to compete with commercial concert-managements, manipulated directly or indirectly by television or the subsidiaries of banks. City Center would continue to provide interesting foreign and native attractions at low prices. Performing-arts agencies in America have always been greedy and monopolistic. Now a number of hopelessly unprofitable adventures, from home and abroad, found a haven in the nooks and crannies of Mecca Temple. Meanwhile, even the larger managements needed to book houses smaller than Madison Square Garden, in those months when the Metropolitan Opera operated its own subscription series.

Providentially, circumstances brought us Norman Singer, who then controlled concerts at Hunter College, whose philosophy of programs complemented and supplemented the City Center's.

There he had managed a large hall and smaller theater (where both American Ballet Caravan and Ballet Society, Inc., had danced). His programs were no less distinguished, the artists he presented no less renowned, than those appearing at Carnegie Hall at twice the price. He was both an educator and an impresario familiar with world markets. He had also worked at summer festivals in Aspen, Colorado, and possessed a general experience and catholic taste which recommended him on every level.

Nor was he naïve. The necessary intransigence of opera and ballet, our prickliness, irritability, or independence, had lit a couple of candles which were not hidden under any bushel. On our first meeting, he asked what would be the gravest fears relative to our autonomy. Apart from the fact that Baum had always recognized Balanchine and Rudel as laws unto themselves, we pictured ourselves as rational brigands whose motto was: "A little too much is just enough for us." This did not daunt Singer. We told him we feared "efficiency" in any form. On any board of directors like Lincoln Center's, overwhelming sorrow came over finance committees at each manifestation of rising costs (less of materials than of labor; less of construction than of performers or performances). The affluent realtors, lawyers, brokers who charge themselves with the promulgation of art in performance naturally turn to efficiency experts to propose how costs can be cut. They crave the impervious wisdom of computers, time clocks, cost accountancy, and personal reformation. The efficiency experts are presumably hired because they have no knowledge of the special climate of theater and will be properly horrified at the looseness, changeability, fantasy, and hysteria of professional behavior. They know how a corporation should be run, profit or no profit, whether it be a bank, hospital, museum, or library. Losses should be modestly predicted, with every inch of planning spelled out, and no further problems. As for isolated personalities and their pretensions to unique service, isn't everyone replaceable and expendable?

Singer knew exactly what we were trying to tell him. What few realize who have not survived in theatrical wonderlands is that there is an elixir without which no performance has a chance of persuading the public (for long) that what is performed is worth the price of admission. This magic has little to do with good taste, intrinsic aesthetic values, advertising, an honest box office, a pretty theater, and a fair reputation. It is hysteria. Distinctions can, of course, be made. Hysteria in the performing arts is not (necessarily) neurotic, although it may show itself in the more spectacular masks of schizophrenia, paranoia, or other poisonous egocentric manias. Freud, faced with the genius or pathology of Dostoevski, said that when confronted with the artist, psychoanalysis must lay down its tools. Not all performers are hysterics, although all are continually under psychic stress, since they risk what they may make from their private psyches for public judgment. Unless they possess that excess of electrical energy which is easily confused with aberration, it is unlikely that they will overcome the essential shyness of every rational self-doubter to project themselves past the footlights. Offstage, except in transient lucid moments, the conduct of many theatrical artists can be read as irrational, untidy, wasteful, unjustifiable, and exasperating. Why can't these folk behave like other folk? Because they are not like other folk.

Norman Singer was accustomed to the climate of hysteria, which breeds many viruses of treachery, loyalty, excitement, and brilliance; but this was exactly what fascinated him. In our stews and swamps, his job was to clear a place where artists in their best minds and moments could use onstage what might be dismay, high spirits, self-indulgence, or practical joking offstage.

OCTOBER, 1969: *New York*

With Balanchine and Hershy Kay leafing through George and Ira Gershwin's collected songs: " 's wonderful! 's marvelous (That you should care for me!)." "Do, do, do what you've done, done, done, before—(Baby!)." "I'm bidin' my time, 'cause that's the kinda guy I'm." "Who cares? (If the sky cares to fall in the sea?)." Hershy knows of a tape recording of George Gershwin playing his own arrangements; it can be inserted as a cadenza in a suite of dances which he'll arrange for large orchestra.

When George Gershwin died of a brain tumor in Hollywood on July 11, 1937, the master of dodecaphony, Arnold Schoenberg, said the next day in a radio broadcast of the memorial service: "Music was to George Gershwin not a matter of ability. It was the air he breathed, the dream he dreamed. I grieve over the deplorable loss of music, for there is no doubt that he was a great composer."

Music written for light opera or social dancing provides a wealth of diverting scores which corroborate our nostalgia for a not too remote past. Stephen Foster, Offenbach, Gilbert and Sullivan, Irving Berlin, Cole Porter all wrote very singable songs which make danceable tunes, and these tickle aural and visual reminders of our parents' youth or our own. But when Balanchine, after three decades, took Gershwin's songs, he had no thought of basing a ballet on a synthetic revival of the taste of the twenties or thirties, no intention of presenting an affectionate pastiche of Fred and Adele Astaire or Ginger Rogers. He had no interest in musical-comedy hoofing or tap dancing as such. What he wished to demonstrate was the intrinsic wit, polyrhythmic genius, and melodic beauty of Gershwin as a propellant of motor metric, impelling the use of his tempi and tunes toward the classic dance. There would be side glances at Broadway musicals, while Jo Mielziner's metamorphic skyscraper and Central Park South–scape might have served well as an early *New Yorker* cover.

Balanchine had been set to work with Gershwin on *The Goldwyn Follies* in his last summer. I had met him through Eddie Warburg's friendship with Kay Swift, whom Gershwin had proposed for *Alma Mater*, our first "American" ballet. Gershwin and I once had a talk when during a penthouse party we took refuge in the pantry. He'd been hunting for a subject for an opera, not at all like *Porgy and Bess*, but something with a chance to use black singers, not alone in solo voices but for massed choral effects. He rejected *Uncle Tom's Cabin*, although, as he said, there were the canonical roles: Little Eva (soprano), Simon Legree (basso), St. Clare (baritone), Topsy (falsetto!). He could not imagine an audience—half of which having been brought up seeing the local "Tom-shows"—accepting the pretext as much beyond parody. Our hope for e. e. cummings's *Tom* had proved impossible or implausible for the opposite reason: it was overheroicized.

I suggested the figure of Toussaint l'Ouverture or Christophe and later gave Gershwin John Vandercook's *Black Majesty*, a sketch of the rebellion in Haiti against the French. Orson Welles and John Houseman had recently had a triumph in Harlem with the Federal Theater project, transposing *Macbeth* from Dunsinane to somewhere near Port-au-Prince. Gershwin seemed bemused by the proposal, but hesitated at the demands of a piece attached to a past epoch, the need to pay some attention to minuets, waltzes, polkas. Did I think William Faulkner could write a libretto? He wrote films, after all. The perfect librettist for him, he had in his pocket: Ira! Yes, for songs; none better; but to construct three acts . . . like Da Ponte, Ghislanzoni, Boito, Illica, or Giacosa. The pictorial possibilities appealed to him: uniforms, the Duke of Marmalade, the Duchess of Orangeade, jungle, voodoo.

Gershwin was also a painter, like Schoenberg and cummings, but rather more professional than either. His was a translucently sunny spirit; so natural a cheerfulness, such impersonal good humor in so powerful and focused a talent are rare. None of it was saccharine or affected; he had none of the "famous personality's" compulsive self-framed mannerism. The quality of light irony, sage humor, sweetness, and delight radiated from George's presence and saturates the lyrics and music of the brothers Gershwin.

Balanchine has always been preoccupied with popular idioms, the argot of every language, popular musical theater, and films. The first work of his I ever saw was a *pas de deux* in an American tour of Nikita Baliev's Chauve-Souris in 1925. This talented troupe of White Russian singers and dancers gathered from Paris nightclubs, where they earned a living in exile by their wits and skills. They had as impresario or emcee a big apple of a man. Baliev bore an astonishing resemblance to my father, who much admired him; by some chance symbiosis they became friends. My father, as master of ceremonies, would give fairly convincing imitations of Baliev for amateur nights at his country club; the Russian visited us in Boston when he came through on tour. Balanchine as a young boy had married Tamara Gevergeva, a student in the Leningrad Academy. They left Russia together, and later they both joined Diaghilev. Balanchivadze turned into "Balanchine," she into "Geva." Tamara quit the Ballets Russes to join the Chauve-Souris, and for her Balanchine made an "Etruscan" *pas de deux* which seemed to me, in Boston's old Wilbur Theater, perverse, pornographic, and passionately interesting.

Before the curtain, Baliev appeared to describe the next

number. He poked snide fun at Balanchine's choreography before anyone had a chance to see it. I had the nerve to ask him why, if he included it on his program, did he run it down? He said he was, like my father, a merchant and not a crusader ("like your fraynd, Meestaire Dee-awg-ee-leff"); that he depended on no patronage save his public; that he introduced such *avant-gardisme* as the "Etruscan" duet just as he would offer a novel soap or perfume. The Ballets Russes had begun to have a certain trans-Atlantic chic. Also, he thought the duet funny and sexy and even rather liked it. However, one must consider saving the public's face if it is not smart enough to accept novelty on first sight. Before this, I'd not considered that theater might possess a pragmatic or commercial side. I had thought that all works passing within a proscenium must perforce be "art"—some possibly better than others, but as much "art" as architecture, sculpture, or painting, in whose holy provinces commerce need never intrude. Baliev was a stateless exile, the first of many I would meet. From him I discovered that performing artists were also declassed gypsies who not only, in his words, sang "sahd sonks" but who had nothing to protect them but a scrap of paper labeled a Nansen passport. This a few immigration officials might accept while others would not, just as some audiences would be pleased enough to enable the artists to eat better, or even oftener, than others.

When Balanchine landed in New York he was paid a pittance. He never asked us for a binding contract, nor was he given one. Within a year, however, he was approached to make dances for the "final" edition of a Ziegfeld Follies, and soon afterward he began his partnership with Lorenz Hart and Richard Rodgers. After Gershwin died, he worked with Vernon Duke, who in 1924, under his own name of Vladimir Dukelsky, composed *Zéphire et Flore* (Massine–Georges Braque) for Diaghilev. Balanchine was the first to insist on the word "choreography" as applied to invention of dances on programs and posters for Broadway musicals. His extended sequences in *Babes in Arms, I Married an Angel, On Your Toes, Cabin in the Sky, Louisiana Purchase*, and other commercial successes raised the level of dancing in the eyes of both performers and public. In 1968, after we moved into the State Theater, he revived *Slaughter on Tenth Avenue*, Richard Rodgers's number originally invented for Tamara Geva and Ray Bolger, while Jo

Mielziner enlarged his cerise-and-maroon honky-tonk bar from *I Married an Angel* of 1938. But now, restudying George Gershwin's songs, which he prized for their great residual value, Balanchine anthologized the most compelling and seductive songs as a symphonic suite.

Like many of our new ballets at their first appearance, it was presented with simple dresses and rudimentary scenery—projected blowups of skyscrapers at night. But *Who Cares?* found favor, at home and abroad, and nowhere more warmly than throughout the Soviet Union in 1972 on our second tour.

JUNE, 1970: *New York*

Annual stage performance by students of the School of American Ballet at the State Theater, for subscribers and Friends of the City Center. Program, *Konservatoriet* (Act II, 1849), by August Bournonville, staged by Stanley Williams, and *Coppélia* selections (1870), arranged by Alexandra Danilova, after Arthur Saint-Léon. The Friends filled the theater twice.

Our School of American Ballet was newly installed in handsome quarters on the third floor of the splendid complex of theaters, concert halls, studios, and classrooms which constitutes the Juilliard School, only a long block from the State Theater at Lincoln Center. Designed to our specifications by the architects and engineers Belluschi, Catalano, and Westermann, the space assigned was the result of years of consideration and negotiation. While our school has no legal connection with Juilliard's corporation, we were enabled through the patronage of the Ford Foundation to lease space for our perpetual use.

Studios were as large as the performing area of the State Theater's stage, well lit by high windows of uninterrupted glass. (We had, with considerable difficulty, managed to perforate the back and side walls of our State Theater offices with mean slits, inserted almost as an afterthought. Air conditioning supposedly obviates any need for daylight, since windows must be sealed, but the psychological effect of hermetically sealed rooms is depressing.) Balanchine now restudied the systems of the studio floors to provide more spring than those in the theater. An interlace of pine slats, thinner, but laid in more depth, covered with battleship linoleum, provides what might seem to measure as a minuscule lift. But it spares knees and ankles in the skeletons of bipeds who were not structured to compete with birds or kangaroos. The school's foyers were hung with a pictorial history of the development of stage dancing, old color prints of Petersburg's palaces, and George Platt Lynes's photographic record of our early years.

The conveniences for teachers and students that are needed in a ballet school do not sound glamorous, but a generous supply of brightly tiled showers and commodious lockers is more welcome than any luxury. Anyone inspecting the recently erected buildings in Kiev, Leningrad, or Moscow must be deeply impressed by the Soviet's concern for its patrimony of aspirants to its ballet companies. While no American school, however fortunate, can compete with such massive subvention, we now enjoyed vast improvements over anything obtainable on the corner of 59th Street and Madison, or later at Broadway and 83rd. There are separate dressing rooms for both young and more advanced children; teachers have their own space for robing and relaxation; there is even room for a Ping-Pong table. The administrative offices are bright and comfortable, overlooking a panorama of Broadway traffic. Considering the prevailing conditions in this country, and our desperate absence of dormitory space with the supervision required for young students from outside New York, the situation at Juilliard is realistic and efficient.

While our first generation of masters continued with the lively instruction of Felia Doubrovska and Muriel Stuart, our early stalwarts Pierre Vladimirov and Anatole Oboukhoff were gone. From the Royal Danish Ballet, Stanley Williams, dancer, ballet master, and teacher with a world reputation, brought us his experience of tradition, teaching, and performance that are parallel to but quite different from our predominantly Russian academy. He taught the style and steps of August Bournonville, Scandinavia's contemporary of Petipa and Ivanov, who put the emphasis on strength in male soloists. Madame Alexandra Danilova, who was trained with Balanchine and Doubrovska in the old imperial and state schools and who danced with them under Diaghilev, provided her arcana of stage behavior and technique to our students. Dancers who had been in our school and company for years, and who now no longer performed, also joined the faculty—among them Elise Reiman, Richard Rapp, and Suki Schorer. Dancers who are continuing to perform, yet who have a definite predilection for teaching, also began to master the difficult skills of instruction. These represent a new generation, with a philosophy of performance gained from Balanchine's repertory. We were fortunate in finding two teachers who continued the traditions of instruction formulated in Russia. Helene Dudin, who graduated from the Kiev Choreographic Academy and danced in Leningrad and Moscow, left during the Second World War. Antonina Tumkovsky, who had similar training and experience and studied under Vaganova in Leningrad, came to New York in 1949.

Ballet schools are little vineyards with aging racks and bottling plants. Some years provide prime vintages; others are less generous with the juice of the grape. While we have always attracted long-legged, promising girls in quantity, more boys with more promise have now begun to come. From 1963, two separate grants from the Ford Foundation Division of Humanities enabled us to expand and develop. Because of the cautious interest and courageous wisdom of W. McNeil Lowry and Marcia Thompson, his deputy, we now stood in a fair way to become a service school on a national scale, although scarcely on the Soviet level comparable to a West Point or Annapolis. Our Ford program presupposed a highly selective policy in which we cooperated with affiliated regional schools. Continental tours of inspection by members of our faculty corroborated the opinions of those teaching at the grass roots and enabled local schools to send talented students for advanced study and later employment past local possibilities. Scholarships for training by hometown teachers are awarded gifted teen-agers for whom the extended cost of serious instruction is often impossible. Beginner groups are sponsored in regional schools as testing grounds and additional sources of talent for eight- to fourteen-year-olds who (for economic or environmental reasons) would not ordinarily enroll in a ballet school. These young people receive free instruction from one to three years; then the more promising may continue on local scholarships. Such students may find employment in the community, or go on to advanced schools of their own choice in

some of the larger centers. They may also be awarded full scholarships and modest maintenance at our own school, with the prospect of eventually joining our company.

In addition, Balanchine conducted advanced seminars for
teachers who came from all over the Americas, while our instructors visit widely scattered schools for repeated periods of concentrated teaching. Several of our former dancers have become responsible for schools and companies of their own. Balanchine's
repertory is extensively performed by regional companies. It is also
taught all over the globe by ballet masters and mistresses trained in
it, as well as by the dancers who continue to appear in these works.
While our school has no civic, state, or federal support, and while
our company is far more representative of a metropolis than of a
nation, the School of American Ballet has indeed set a standard for
the country, and is recognized internationally for doing so. Not
only are our dancers increasingly called to perform or teach in
Germany, Holland, Switzerland, and Japan, but the school attracts
foreign soloists and teachers to New York. The rationale of its
leadership and instruction under the long-term guidance of
Eugenie Ouroussow, Natasha Molostwoff, and Natasha Gleboff is
recognized throughout the world, as it was recently in the London *Times*, as a "star factory."

OCTOBER, 1971: *New York*

With Balanchine to see Richard Clurman, Time-Life Building, with budget of Stravinsky Festival. Tried to persuade Balanchine to insert one ballet a week into repertory, during twelve
weeks of spring season. He refused, insisted on one concentrated
week. However, if all thirty ballets are produced at once, the
State Theater must be shut in midseason for one week, adding
$100,000 to costs. Clurman "sympathetic," which Balanchine took
for assent.

Stravinsky's death the previous April meant both the end of an
epoch and the entrance of a number of new ballets to his music,
sparked by a mammoth celebration of his achievement in June,

1972. Counting by sundial or clock time, he was surely an ancient. By the metric of art and spirit, he was much in the running and would remain so as long as our dancers could count. Even before his mortality was fact, Balanchine had proposed a lively homage, not so much in praise as in gratitude for his gifts, which could best be expressed by their public demonstration. The expense involved in money, mind, and muscle would be considerable. We were prepared to commit production capital for three years to budget the single week, assuming the likelihood that we could gain as many additions to repertory at once as over the longer period. However, this meant an outright involvement of money that we did not, or in all probability would not, have to spend.

Norman Singer had already assumed the day-to-day business of ensuring our survival, but he was scarcely permitted to plan ahead on such a scale against the pressure of imminent schedules. Long-range programming deep into the seventies was necessary. With its two permanent theaters and rental of others, City Center's civic and national programs had so expanded that it was now the largest public performing-arts service in the world. Annual expenditures were some ten million dollars, of which a third was deficit. Fresh sources of support would have to be found from state and federal agencies, while big business corporations showed more interest in committing themselves for further tax-exempt contributions. Educational and charitable foundations had been generous, but with their fixed policy of terminal grants, their support was always limited in duration. The problem was to find a successor to Morton Baum.

The solution seemed strange. A man was chosen who, while recognized in the confines of his profession, had even less of a public face than Baum had had. Unlike Baum, however, his successor did not even have the reputation of an amateur in the performing arts. For some decades Richard Clurman had been an executive in the publishing empire of Henry Luce; he had been charged most recently with coordinating the worldwide bureaus of Time-Life's national and international news gatherers. He was at home equally in Saigon or Seattle; his continual physical contact with global action gave him access to any office and to most persons who could possibly be useful in collecting world information. He had no special interest in opera or ballet; opera was something of a blank book; ballet, he might guess, was about dancing. He liked games, however—those performed publicly and others conducted otherwise. He had an expert's understanding of the personal performance of men in power, and of the people they manipulated. To him as a journalist, life in the raw and *Life* in print, time as history and *Time* the weekly news capsule, were spectator sports, whether in Moscow, Miami, Madrid, or Manhattan. More important, he was accustomed to star performers, although a proscenium did not frame their stage. He had experience in judging the unique value of reckless reporters, intrepid and passionate foreign correspondents, and prima donna photographers. Stress and extremity were familiar in his world; emergency, accident, replacement, and catastrophe were normal.

When Clurman explained to Julius Rudel, John White, Betty Cage, Balanchine, and me his doubts about being responsible for opera singers and ballet dancers, he hardly had to be told that, on a human level, there would be no surprises. One way or another, he'd heard it all before, with a different cast of characters, on a broader scale. However, principles of excellence in performance, and in breadth and quality of service, amounted to a similar expenditure of energy. What doubts we had concerning inroads on our autonomy, such as the chance interjection of Time-Life efficiency experts, reorganization, or office reform, were quickly dispelled. Dick Clurman said firmly, and meant it, that he was incapable of accepting the job unless we continued as if Morton Baum still sat at the desk where the buck stopped. He agreed to hold the handle of the umbrella over City Center, and we were to proceed much as before.

Our proposal for the Stravinsky Festival was a first big test. In our eagerness to make the complexity of the operation absolutely clear, it was not necessary to exaggerate the costs or difficulties. Nothing had ever been attempted on such a scale in this country before. When Diaghilev proposed his invasion of Western Europe in 1909, he had the advantages of a czar's privy purse, Russian Foreign Office propaganda for the Entente Cordiale, and later, an international committee of patrons—Polignacs, Murats, Rothschilds, the Aga Khan—implemented as much by cash as by a coherence of class. In New York there was none of this. Clurman estimated the challenge rather like a pianist strumming chords or a painter laying out a palette. It was not that some sounds or colors were preferable, but that each had its own tones in combination. Had we offered him only custodial supervision of our maintenance or survival, then other theaters of war or peace would have been more attractive to him. Nevertheless, to embrace huge deficit financing with open eyes as a virtual introduction into an enchanted jungle, whatever the attraction or justification, may be taken as foolhardy. Anyone seeking ease or comfort in the vicinity of theaters is ill-advised—something Clurman did not need to be told. So the ballet and opera were licensed to proceed. But now we viewed in a different light our lists of the works we wanted to produce to demonstrate Stravinsky's long career from Opus 1 through his last years. Previously, we had thought that anything, everything, or nothing might be possible. Now with tangible proposals and a budget accepted, we could figure realistically what might be produced at the State Theater in the months, weeks, days, hours, and minutes until 7:30 P.M., June 18, 1972.

JANUARY, 1972: *New York*

Ronnie Bates has received and hung the "moon" for Jerry Robbins's new *Watermill*. It is not a film projection but half a plastic globe, lit from within, with a shutter that changes it from thinnest sickle to full moon. Teiji Ito's small band of musicians rehearses onstage—a Bugaku-gamelan combo. Barking dogs, sea-gull cries, wind and jet plane noises, over-and-under, on tape.

After *Dances at a Gathering*, Robbins felt compelled to design still another work to Chopin's piano pieces. *In the Night* was a nocturnal encounter, its ambience more of ballroom than of open field. There was little repetition of motive or movement from the earlier *Dances*; while shorter and less expansive, it satisfied. He had also been considering the entire series of thirty variations composed in 1736 by Johann Sebastian Bach for the harpsichordist Johann Goldberg. In 1938, during a third and final tour of Ballet Caravan, William Dollar had set a third of the series to attractive choreography. His dancers wore costumes having no bearing on any historic epoch; their tights were marbleized in veins of black, white, and gold, under the influence of Tchelitchev's then-current fascination with the striations in marble. Robbins used the complete suite of variations originally composed for Count Kayserling, a sleepless nobleman, so that Goldberg, his court musician, might alleviate his insomnia.

Experiments were made with an actual harpsichord, but its sound did not carry in Saratoga's huge auditorium, while amplification altered its timbre. An unamplified concert grand was preferable. *Goldberg Variations* lasts considerably over an hour, and was originally performed with no intermission. Its demands on both dancers and audience are not light. Our subscribers in New York and our captive audience in Saratoga have, over the years, accustomed themselves to our insistence on making them listen hard at the same moments when they look with attention. A minimum of visual adornment and emphasis on unfamiliar rhythms and sonorities demand a concentration which is willing to accept a certain didactic tyranny. This has been taken as arbitrary or even tiring. While our decorative or cosmetic style has been visually meager or underprivileged, it has had compensations in the aural element. Close listening is different from loose hearing; hard looking is not the same as easy viewing. In *Goldberg Variations* there is little adornment to distract from a density of formal structure. Drama and decor are inherent in contrasts of tempi or accentual movement, made kinetically plastic by metric and melody rather than painted color. In such a context it has a deliberate intensity unique in our repertory.

Its "theme" is gravely declared by two dancers uniformed in an adaptation of court dress worn in Bach's day. Having stated this as a basis for subsequent deployment, the pair disappear while their companions appear in contemporary classroom practice dress. During a complex progress through thirty variations, bits and pieces of costumes are acquired, so that by the complicated combinations of the final *quodlibet*, the entire large cast is clad in the discreet festive apparel of some provincial baroque court. To reaffirm the entire musical exposition, the two figures of the introduction now reappear alone on an empty stage, in the resumed simplicity but equal formality of their own practice uniforms. The ballet has turned itself inside out, like a superbly fashioned glove, embroidered on both sides in changeable silk. *Goldberg Variations* concerns dancing in "time," Bach's as well as ours, as well as the time it takes dancers to measure and encapsulate a historical past within a historical present. Robbins's demonstration of the composer's formal patterns is exhaustive instruction in hearing and seeing, relieved by memorable vignettes of abrupt action, acrobatic amusement, generous invention, and fine dancing. His was a daring intellectual concept and, in its own terms of taste and format, well risked.

When Robbins was pondering yet another novelty, he remained reluctant to use the weighty sonorities of a symphonic orchestra. However, he had now achieved four works based on an unaccompanied piano, and they all stayed in repertory. Still fascinated by the exploitation of altered, expanded, or mutated elements in unsuspected temporal duration, the extension of possible measurings beyond clock time, he dispensed with a fixed or concrete timetable in *Watermill*. It is laid out as metrically unstructured, except by impositions of mood through visual short circuits and atmospheric poetics. The musical partnering by Teiji Ito and his group of exotic instrumentalists sounds as quaintly appropriate interjection, punctuation, or aural italics. What Robbins now proposed was tantamount to repudiating Bach's insistent arithmetical beat—and abandoning all classical geometric movement and gesture such as have been prompted by occidental music inherited from dance suite through the sonata form to the symphony and beyond. Music for *Watermill* was reduced to the service of a superexistential sound track, fragmented, spiky, wispy—the cursive trilling of birds or insects through rasping reeds on some imperturbable inland sea.

Measurement or expansion of ordinary passing time and division of space are two factors upon which our most characteristic and enduring works have been based. Most of these works are densely compacted of movement, attached by invisible sewing-machined stitches to a musical lining or substructure. *Watermill*, on the other hand, is a loosely woven translucent tapestry within which passes a linear three-dimensional procession. Time stands still; it does not pass; but figures proceed through its element circuitously without progress, like fish in a bowl. The units are bipeds who are also numbers on a planetary moondial. The work can be taken both as timepiece and space clock. The visual surround, suggesting a monochrome brush-and-ink scroll, is lightly fondled by barely perceptible breezes which rub dry sheaves of grass, rustle fallen leaves, toss about a few early flakes of snow. In it a single male human enjoys, endures, combats time of day, seasons of years, asleep or awake, meditating and remembering, acting or dreaming. He recalls childhood, adolescence, and in present manhood foresees senility. The moon-lamp waxes and wanes, from cuticle to pale celadon fullness, fixing its mean or noble scale against the reflection of some sister planet. Added piquancy was gained by casting Edward Villella, whose phenomenal acrobacy, speed, and muscular power are famous, in the role of a monumentally static Hamlet-like protagonist. His physical control makes him capable of sustaining such relentless slow motion. The tempo of the ballet is, in all truth, fiendishly slow. At first it seems slower than a normal heartbeat, than systole or diastole. One intelligent critic confessed that she began to feel as if she might go mad from a dislocation in her ordinary habits of sensing a passage of what we commonly take to be "time." *Watermill* is also a race against anxiety which endurance temporarily wins.

JUNE, 1972: *New York*

Stravinsky Festival. Dress rehearsal for *Pulcinella*; singers and orchestra; tons of scenery, trick effects; dozens of children, incomplete choreography, lumped together in organized chaos. Not enough spaghetti; masks don't fit; however, as with other rehearsals in this effort, no tempers lost; cheerfulness, no forebodings of disaster.

Our ambition was to display a panoply of Stravinsky's representative scores, some without staging; from first to last recognizing his entire range in one compact, monumental week. Some of us had hoped, for ease, economy, and a lighter load on performances, to distribute it all over three months, our twelve weeks of a normal spring season. However, Balanchine insisted on the imploded fusion of one big bang. The point of a feast was to gorge, not nibble; this was no simple *zakuska* but a state banquet in a State

Theater. If each new ballet was scheduled with a week between, the whole impression would be diluted. Subscribers might pick only works which by chance, in advance, they considered amusing. He was, of course, correct; the festival as planned and produced had the air of a holiday, with crowds embarked on a luxurious cruise, crossing an ocean for a gala vacation. Over the one crammed week, from Sunday to Sunday, unfamiliar faces grew friendlier in the climate of a common excursion. The concentration of premieres and music unheard before generated its own enthusiasm. Yet all passed so quickly that at the end one wondered how, or indeed if, it had really taken place. There was scarcely a sense of daylight spent outside the theater; everyone seemed constantly congregating at an al fresco picnic or birthday party. As for the procession of performances onstage, they tended to blur in their current immediacy. Their memory was revived later when they took their places, revised and refined past the first festival occasion, in our permanent programs. Then great peaks of sound, sight-and-sound, or sights alone could be savored anew.

Although some thirty works were performed in the seven days, many pieces that had musical importance were omitted after due deliberation. Balanchine always considered the tremendous orchestration of *Le Sacre du Printemps* beyond a choreographer's capacity to compete with, although this by no means deterred the Royal Ballet, La Scala, the Paris Opéra, or other companies from attempting it. *Les Noces* is visible in Madame Nijinska's original version of 1923, beautifully performed in London, as well as on tour, by the Royal Ballet. Jerome Robbins's recension is active with Ballet Theatre. *Oedipus Rex*, although intentionally static, has received impressive presentations, notably by Michel Saint-Denis for the Sadler's Wells Company; it is in repertory with the New York City Opera. Balanchine wished to stage *The Flood* again, since its initial presentation had been a disaster because of a television corruption rather than any shortcomings of the piece itself or its production. This was too costly for the festival; in time it must be done. *Renard* and *Mavra* were too small in format for revival on a big stage. *Perséphone* is declamatory, although this beautiful score is grateful for a visual frame; but we reserved the fullest choral effect for the benediction of *Symphony of Psalms*, which only angels should dare to dance. Our final choices were a matter of agreement among Balanchine, Madame Stravinsky, Nicolas Nabokov, Goddard Lieberson, Robert Irving, and Robert Craft— friends, associates, historians, and preservers of his music in memorials, recordings, or continual performance.

Planning for the many onstage rehearsals was in the hands of Ronald Bates, our executive stage manager, and his capable staff. Ronnie came to us after the Army from apprenticeship at the American Shakespeare Festival. Over the years he joined our family by marrying into it. He and the lovely dancer Diana Adams would have a daughter named, inevitably, Georgina. Part master electrician, part master sergeant, he is also a poet and inventor of stage illumination. His sleight of hand in making time when there was no time, of inserting extra rehearsals when there were overwhelming demands from equally justifiable calls, the drain on tact, nerves, and intelligence with no sleep for three weeks except snatched naps on an offstage cot—these accomplished the Stravinsky Festival. His taciturnity, lack of waste motion, appreciation and achievement of the preposterous or impossible are too often taken for granted.

Ronnie's ordinary climate is emergency—replacement, improvisation, quick choice of substitutes. His daily duties require him to maintain high operating averages despite inevitable if unforeseeable accidents arising from the nature of a hydra-headed beast: dancers' injuries; failures of fingers on levers, ropes, or buttons; fatigue in electronic circuits; Jerry Robbins's indecision; Balanchine's caprice; mutual changes of mind; drastic alterations needed when costumes and scenery are viewed under stage lights for the first time. For the Stravinsky week, Bates laid out scheduling a month before as if he were a junior Eisenhower preparing mini–Operation Overlord. He captained his own general staff, but also under his single command were Balanchine, Robbins, John Taras, the younger ballet masters, the dancers, and a large crew of stagehands who were as sensitive to their conductor as Robert Irving's musicians were to him. Far above the auditorium, in the light booth topping the highest balcony, were the highly strung quartet operating two dyna-beams and twin xenon special-throw lamps, which vignetted individual soloists as they moved across the stage. In such carefully modulated movement as that to be framed in Balanchine's *Duo Concertant*, their pinpointing of isolated arms, hands, fingers would participate in the choreography itself.

Over the years before and after we moved into the State Theater, Robert Irving, our musical director, forged a band of instrumentalists which by now is recognized as the peer of the major symphonic orchestras. He could have become permanent conductor to half a dozen civic orchestras in Britain or the United States, but his temperament and talents were suited to work with dancers. When he returned to New York with us after an engagement at Covent Garden, there were plaintive protests at his seduction and loss to the Royal Ballet. But he turned into a New Yorker, and later in Saratoga, he was as passionate a racer of horses as before he had been an ardent mountain climber. In variety and quality, the repertory he could offer his orchestra was superior to any other in the same category. It was he who was responsible for the choice of soloists, singers, and chorus for the vocal parts in Britten, Brahms, Kurt Weill, and Stravinsky.

As for the public's reception of our Stravinsky Festival, it was everything we had hoped. All critical judgment apart, the *New York Times* covered the event as news on its front page, as well as in special features and editorials. The weeklies followed suit, and a flock of foreign correspondents flew across the Atlantic to spread the word throughout Britain and the Continent, and as far as Japan. While some of the new works would be more complete later, and although the percentage of anticipated casualties met its quota, the event, both in immediacy and increment, justified itself.

From the souvenir program published for the Stravinsky Festival, June 18, 1972:

> I must leave it to others, better professionally qualified than I, to estimate Stravinsky's achievement as a composer. I can, however, I think, speak with some authority about Stravinsky as a paradigm of the creative artist, a model and example from whom younger men, be they composers, painters, or writers, can derive counsel and courage in an age when the threats to their integrity seem to be greater than ever before.
>
> First, let them pay attention to his conception of artistic fabrication. "I am not," he said, "a mirror struck by my mental functions. My interest passes entirely to the object, the thing made." An artist, that is to say, should think of himself pri-

marily as a craftsman, a "maker," not as an "inspired" genius. When we call a work "inspired," all we mean is that it is better, more beautiful, than we could have possibly hoped for.   —*W. H. Auden*

Of course, *Petrushka, Sacre, Oedipus,* were and are great beauties, but for Stravinsky, they were his past, well beloved and well remembered. It was his fantastic output of new ideas at a period of his life which many would have considered a time for consolidation, rest, and (alas, with many artists) repetition, which made him, right up to the end, the most contemporaneous of men. Yet, it was this quality that irritated so many. Just as a child wants his parents or grandparents to look and act their age, so Stravinsky was expected to act the respectable old master in his carpet slippers, rewriting all of his now famous music. This, of course, didn't suit him. And he entered new worlds.   —*Goddard Lieberson*

In cleaving to free-will he refused to frame his self as a romantic agonist—self-serving, self-indulgent, self-slaying, a role adored by flashier tragedians of the era. Unfashionable except for a few ferocious friends after his initial notoriety, he was firm in a faith towards formal wholeness. Abstraction, fragmentation, self-expressionism was the order of the day, canny hysteria canonized as idiosyncratic revelation. He credited concreteness, stricture and structure, inherited objective disciplines, for responsible collaboration with dozens of patrons and publishers, hundreds of performers serving a multitude of audiences in an elevated social context. He never let fractional means, sound as sound, color as color, artifice for artifice's sake with their inflated partialities satisfy him as interesting or worthy ends. Stylization is formula, not method. Personalism is a nosegay of accidental cullings, freezing talent at one lone repetitive peak. The person of sure practice proceeds by an ever-developing potential. His whole work, over seventy years, came to command a world of witnesses.   —*L. K.*

The festival opened formally with the fanfare which Stravinsky had written for the State Theater's inauguration April 19, 1964. It was sounded from the top ring of the promenade. When the audience was seated within, Bob Irving's fine orchestra played the "Greeting Prelude," an arrangement of "Happy Birthday (to *You*, dear 'Eager')." This was composed in 1955 as a singing telegram to Pierre Monteux, conductor of the tempestuous premiere of *Le Sacre du Printemps* in 1913, on his eightieth birthday. It was described by its composer as "a half-minute primer of canonic art." Then Balanchine appeared before the curtain to welcome assembled guests and to present them with an unannounced miniature gift in the form of a single movement, the scherzo (all that was recoverable) of Stravinsky's Opus 1, which Madeleine Malraux, the pianist, had been able to transcribe from the manuscript of a lost Sonata in F sharp minor written in 1902 at the age of twenty, even before Stravinsky sought advice from Rimski-Korsakov. Madame Malraux's continuous exquisite performances were one of the week's chief delights. This fragment was followed by the orchestra alone presenting *Feu d'Artifice* (*Fireworks*, 1909), the morsel that magnetized Diaghilev's first curiosity. Then Jerry Robbins tossed across the stage a stylish, delicate, and witty version of *Scherzo Fantastique* (1908), made more vivid by the kaleidoscopic dancing of four young boys, all quite new to the company, with Gelsey Kirkland, a recent and electrifying soloist.

The opening pieces were followed by two Balanchine blockbusters: *Symphony in Three Movements* (1946) and *Violin Concerto* (1931), magnificently rendered by Joseph Silverstein, first violin of the Boston Symphony. These novelties could have been enough to distinguish two ordinary seasons. Coming as they did, head-on at the very start of the celebration, they served as vindication not alone of the festival's pretensions, but of the powers of its progenitor. Balanchine had achieved an age and status when it had become profitable, and in a sense mandatory, to proclaim his talent desiccated, his authority dubious. The attention paid to, and deserved by, Jerome Robbins's four recent triumphs, three on a big scale, gave credence to hopes that his senior might now be discounted, and someone (anyone) introduced to crack the monotony of hearing Balanchine spoken of as being on the same level as Picasso or Stravinsky. However, the present breathless constructs of fresh rhythmic response and gestural complexity in two large ballets were a devastating demonstration of augmented capacity. They were startling innovations—as far ahead of *Agon* as

Agon had been of *Orpheus* or *Apollon* at the midpoint and debut of Balanchine's career. Thus abruptly were introduced the most startling results of a partnership that had begun nearly half a century before. This astonishing evening concluded with Marc Chagall's de luxe illustrations of *Firebird* which, perhaps more transparently than any choreography by Balanchine or Robbins, made visible its famous orchestral iridescence.

In the ensuing six performances some pieces were obviously less captivating or convincing than others. Opportunities given to younger choreographers were possibly daunting, since it put them on the line with their elders and betters. From the musical aspect, however, all the scores chosen were of the same quality as the "major" works. John Taras's handsome pageant of *The Song of the Nightingale* (1919) was particularly pleasing. Balanchine had re-staged it for Diaghilev in 1925 with decor by Henri Matisse. Taras did without scenery, but Rouben Ter-Arutunian transformed his stage space into a black velour jewel box. There a begemmed night-ingale and her sweet-songed but sadder-vested sister scintillated against the mandarin parade of a slipper-satined court and its gorgeous embassy from the Japanese emperor. Taras's *Scènes de Ballet* (1944), which had been set by Frederick Ashton for the Royal Ballet in 1948, provided beautiful performances by Patricia McBride and Jean-Pierre Bonnefous, with a large and skillfully manipulated corps. Bonnefous as Orpheus, Francisco Moncion as the Dark Angel, and Melissa Hayden as Eurydice restored *Orpheus* (1948) to something above its initial beauty, for Isamu Noguchi had now enlarged and refined his elegantly sculptured objects and crocheted costumes to the scale of the State Theater's proscenium. *Orpheus* had been preceded by *Apollon* (1928) and followed by *Agon* (1957). Arthur Mitchell, now director of his autonomous Dance Theatre of Harlem and its school, danced his original part in *Agon*, superbly partnering Allegra Kent in her exceptional clarity and strength. These three masterpieces of the Balanchine-Stravinsky collaboration, bridging four decades, were thus seen and heard as often intended for the first time.

Robbins and Balanchine together worked out the raffish pantomime of *Pulcinella* (1920), with Eugene Berman's stu-pendous evocation of a townscape for Neapolitan *commedia dell'arte* spectacle. There was not nearly enough time to present it with the finesse it merited, but Edward Villella's ithyphallic monster father-figure of all the world's Punches was a merrily ironic and acrobatic impersonation. Violette Verdy was perfectly tailored as a soubrette of surpassing elegance. With her Gallic savor, precision, waifish regret, and neat musicality, she served as his good fairy, mistress, partner. As a final fillip, Balanchine and Robbins appeared briefly as raggle-taggle beggars lambasting each other in a rub-a-dub duello. The stage was packed with the huge company, augmented by one dozen small Pulcinelli from our school. For once no one said we had stinted on the visual, for Genia Berman's monumentally rackety frame and masterfully delineated curtains were architectural delights. To be sure, there were those able to take pleasure in displeasure by lamenting the abandonment of our usual stripped and stoic format for such an unseemly burst of decorative extravagance. Stravinsky was used to this clan of critics; he had written:

> *Pulcinella* was my discovery of the past, the epiphany through which the whole of my late work became possible. It was a backward look, of course—the first of many love affairs in that direction—but it was a look in the mirror, too. No critic understood this at the time, and I was therefore attacked for being a *pasticheur*, chided for composing "simple" music, blamed for deserting "modernism," accused of renouncing my "true Russian heritage." People who had never heard of, or cared about, the originals cried "sacrilege": "The classics are ours. Leave the classics alone." To them all my answer was and is the same: You "respect," but I love.*

Circus Polka (1942) involved fifty-four baby ballerinas from our school, organized into waves of *entrées* under a ringmaster in riding breeches, tailcoat, and top hat. This was the marshal of the rout, Jerome Robbins himself, snapping a whip, dragooning the children into enormous cursive initials signed on the stage floor: I.S., with two tots crouched into two dots. Robbins's *Requiem Canticles* (1966) was an austere abstraction of ritual lamentation, impersonally eccentric, but in an elevated range of invention in negative accents of inversion and fluttering deformation. It was a

* Igor Stravinsky and Robert Craft, *Expositions and Developments*, Doubleday & Co., Garden City, N.Y., 1962, pp. 128–9.

metaphor of the aberration or alienation from ordinary behavior which grief unlocks. Robbins's skill and experience in theatrical organization were a prime factor throughout the festival. He was aided by Tommy Abbott, once a student in our school, later Robbins's assistant in transferring his musicals from one company to another and from stage to film. For us Abbott facilitated the deployment of very young children in swift but deliberate regimentation, without which their presence would have been useless.

The finale of the festival began on a clear, early evening, an unsmogged azure June Sunday, with Balanchine's *grand défilé* of the entire company and the children, for Stravinsky's *Choral Variations on Johann Sebastian Bach's "Vom Himmel hoch da komm' ich her"* (1956). The original theme piece was written in 1747 as a "test" which would admit Bach (aged sixty-two) into a "Society for Musical Knowledge." Balanchine took these canonic variations, with a choir (but without organ), and wove a processional tapestry in which orderly ranks of soloists and subordinate dancers were infiltrated by the youngest and smallest, shuttling through the cat's cradle of its web. First dancers, corps, young and more advanced students were paraded as if they were guardsmen changing their sentinel duty in dress (un-dress) uniform before a Palace of Music. This served as prelude, summation, and homage to the life work of a master of temporal dimension. In asymmetry and its resolution, balance and its upset, it was a didactic illustration of Stravinsky's dictum: "Music is the best means we have of digesting time."

The festival finished with an exalting and exalted offering of *Symphony of Psalms* (1930). It was not danced; our dancers, staff, ballet masters sat to listen on the stage floor encircling the orchestra, now set within the proscenium. Above them Rouben Ter-Arutunian had hung a glowing suggestion of silver and ivory organ pipes. Observed from the balconies, the dancers' bodies in hushed repose might have served Edgar Degas for a monument to the service which plastic stasis owes music. Robert Craft conducted *con amore*; sound seemed channeled toward Vera Stravinsky, seated serene and lovely in the first ring. The ultimate iteration of "Laudate" always makes a cathedral of whatever hall in which these psalms are sung. Stravinsky said that he had been impelled by a vision of Elijah's chariot of fire ascending to the Godhead:

Never before had I written anything quite so literal as the trip-
lets for horns and piano to suggest the horses and chariot [yet
at the same time not literal at all. As for the] final hymn of
praise . . . I can say [that] one hopes to worship God with a
little art if one has any, and if one hasn't, . . . then one can
at least burn a little incense.*

From the first evening, Balanchine had insisted there should be no
hint of mourning for a man whose absence was only physical. He
recalled the custom of his native Georgian province, where raisins
and grain are distributed at a graveside as evidence of the continual
sowing and harvest of the human and the divine. So, after the
swelling conclusion of the *Symphony*, a silent audience left the
theater at the close of the grand affirmation of one enormous word.
Its trisyllabic structure echoes the trinity of body, mind, and spirit
which Stravinsky's genius praised. With the still resonant final
DOM-I-NUM vibrating in ears and heart, every looker-and-listener
was handed a slug of vodka to speed him on his way.

FROM THE *Evening Gazette* (YURI SLONIMSKY),
Leningrad, SEPTEMBER, 1972:

In Stravinsky's *Violin Concerto* (1931), Balanchine dons the
full armor of "visible music" which, incidentally, the composer considered to be his partner's highest achievement.
Balanchine consciously and wholeheartedly devotes himself
and his performers to the fulfillment of this task which he considers the most important. In his devotion to it he occasionally
transforms people onstage into graphically outlined symbols
(could this account for the dancers' black outfits?), performing every zigzag of Stravinsky's thought, irony, joke, etc. No
matter how unexpected, artful and complex the combinations
of sound, Balanchine immediately responds by corresponding
combinations of arms, legs, torso and head. There is food
for thought here—occasionally dance becomes servant to

* Igor Stravinsky and Robert Craft, *Dialogues and a Diary*, Doubleday & Co.,
Garden City, N.Y., 1963, pp. 78–9.

music, and the human quality to the dancing. And at such times, it seems to me that the performers are like marionettes operated by an experienced puppeteer. Only in the two duets do the soloists, and in the *capriccio*, the corps de ballet, cease being the slaves of the interpretation of sound, acquire flesh and blood and indulge in human emotions.

The official Marxist aesthetic evoked by the New York City Ballet's second Soviet tour was somewhat less strident than that precipitated by our visit ten years before. Now Balanchine's style was more familiar, and the political climate of Nixon's *détente* was far less ferocious than Kennedy's crisis over Khrushchev and Cuba. With the exception of Baku, we revisited the same towns—Kiev, Leningrad, Tbilisi, Moscow. Every performance was sold out before the company arrived. The previous summer Madame Ekaterina Furtseva, Soviet Minister of Education and Culture, had dispatched Konstantin Sergeyev, her eminent ballet master, to Saratoga to choose from our repertory works which might meet with official approval. Sergeyev had known Balanchine from early days in the Leningrad school; they had remained in contact over the years. Now he spent ten days familiarizing himself with our repertory, dancers, and methods. He gave the company a class of his own, which vividly demonstrated differences in technique between the systems Balanchine had developed in the United States and those currently taught in the Russian state schools. Sergeyev viewed the new Stravinsky works, which were performed on a weekly basis in Saratoga. For the Russian season he chose ballets with music by three native composers—Tchaikovsky, Stravinsky, and George Gershwin (whose parents, at least, had been born in Russia).

On the tour the musical-comedy tone and style of *Who Cares?* found particular favor. So did Robbins's two recent works to Chopin's and Bach's piano music, firmly executed by Gordon Boelzner, our indispensable staff soloist, who now was becoming an orchestral conductor as well. *Dances at a Gathering* and *Goldberg Variations* were also happily received in Poland, where, in handsomely restored theaters in Lodz and Warsaw, the tour ended.

The dancers had been performing without interruption for

nearly a year. Following Saratoga, they had flown to Munich to represent the United States in the cultural division of the Olympic Games. Without respite they launched the fall-winter season of 1972–73, in which several ballets culled from the Stravinsky Festival would, after changes and revisions, enter permanent repertory. *Pulcinella* received special attention. Eight white mice were added to the entourage of the Mouse King in *Nutcracker*. From the unused sections of Riccardo Drigo's charming score, considerable additions were made to *Harlequinade* to show off the dazzling antics of Edward Villella, born to be both Arlechino and Pulcinella. Late in November the audience included a delegation of Peking diplomats from the United Nations. In January the magnificent Chinese acrobats attended performances and came backstage to meet the company. There were ripples of rumors which put our company dancing on the Great Wall in jig time. However, negotiations with the State Department over the second Russian tour had consumed months of triangulated maneuvering between Moscow, New York, and Washington, and by now we knew the difference between oriental and occidental estimates of time and money.

JANUARY, 1973: *New York*

Conference with Madame Karinska, Rouben Ter-Arutunian, and Balanchine over *The Birds of America*, anticipating bicentennial celebrations of 1975–76. Karinska's sketches for apple festival, emceed by Johnny Appleseed, with entrées of pippins, Winesaps, Gravensteins. Audubon's birds, as painted by the "lost dauphin"; Indian sources in Catlin, Kane, and Buffalo Bill's Wild West Shows.

The proposal for a three-act heroic ballet based on an "American" subject had preoccupied us intermittently for three decades. The novelists Louis Bromfield and Glenway Wescott (and even Céline) had written extended libretti. But as with e.e. cummings's *Tom*, their narratives, while perhaps excellent for film or lyric biography, offered few pretexts for classic dancing. From 1965

Balanchine had discussed his requirements seriously and precisely with Morton Gould, who understood the demands of academic dancing transformed into a popular musical idiom with taste, celerity, and brilliance. His score for Jerome Robbins's *Interplay* (1952) proved his capacity for stimulating dance steps. He now composed portions of a large score which suited Balanchine to perfection.

The demi-myth of John James Audubon, sensitively adumbrated by Constance Rourke, placed the great naturalist in the role of son to Louis XVI, come from the Antilles, where he had been somehow spirited after the execution of his parents. In a quasi-Virginian forest, he met the birds whom he would later depict. We identified him with Johnny Appleseed, who strode across the Middle West sowing orchards and continued westward to the Golden Gate, where he married the daughter of Chief Thunderbird. At his wedding the various native strains which compose America would receive embassies from the rest of the world, in a setting recalling Audubon's legendary origin, and as well, the sources of classic dancing at the court of Versailles. The expense of such a work on the scale necessary would be high; hence from year to year we postponed any serious thought of scheduling it. But the approach of the two-hundredth anniversary of our nation's founding seemed to indicate that, with the possible support of the National Endowment under the adroit manipulation of Miss Nancy Hanks, some federal funds might be forthcoming.

As for the constant proposals for new works, there would be a perennial oscillation of gain and loss. Robbins planned a dramatic abstraction of the tale of the Dybbuk, with a score by Leonard Bernstein. But his long-time collaborator accepted the Charles Eliot Norton chair of poetry at Harvard, where he would follow Stravinsky, T. S. Eliot, and his own master, Aaron Copland. From Iannis Xenakis, Balanchine commissioned a nonelectronic score, for we have an orchestra eager to embark on any next step forward or backward from recent advance-guard sonorities. *Anti-Earth* is projected as a big science-fiction black joke, set for the spring of 1976. The bicentennial celebrations will doubtless precipitate other works on native themes.

The first "American" ballet I ever saw was on the stage of the Boston Opera House (built by Eben Jordan of Jordan Marsh, my father's rival in the department store business). It was Henry Gilbert's *Dance in Place Congo*, performed in the season of 1919. Gilbert, a musicological pioneer in the material just preceding jazz, had been fascinated by the songs of descendants of African slaves. Of this work I recall only an enormous stage crammed with dancers in striped bandana kerchiefs. Whether they were in blackface or were indeed black I can't remember, but there was a knife fight, tides of motion, and a blackout finale. Dancers whirled madly; I was twelve years old.

Every so often Robert Irving, our musical director, leafs through stacks in the music library at Lincoln Center, researching an increasingly remote possibility of reviving forgotten American scores of the pre-Stravinsky epoch which made use of "Indian" or "Negro" or "folk" motifs. Most of Cadman, Chadwick, Converse, Hadley, Parker, or even Griffes sounds wanly naïve beside Charles Ives, who handled his indigenous material with a quirkier, more mordant touch. There were many other projects lying in abeyance for the right circumstances to launch or resurrect. We thought of a ballet based on the lost glory of Saratoga's Grand Union colonnade and Colonel Canfield's gaming pavilion. We had spoken to Frederick Ashton about the notion of Newport as a surround for the sale of an American heiress to a British viscount, in the climate of Henry James. Balanchine dreamed of a *Salome* to a score of Alban Berg, and of a non-Spanish set of dances to harpsichord music by Padre Antonio Soler, Scarlatti's pupil. There were Kurt Weill's powerful miniature Noh play, *Jasager* (plus *"Neinsager"*), and Reynaldo Hahn's *Fête Chez Thérèse*. As for expressly advance-guard music, there have been few recent scores suitable for an orchestra of our quality and equipment which also serve for more than flashy *pièces d'occasion*. In 1960, Stravinsky met with a group of aleatory and electronic "young" composers in Buenos Aires. One of the disadvantages of a provincial situation is that it provokes in artists an eagerness to outdo the rest of the world in "experiment" or "creativity" at one remove, perhaps to compensate for their distance from world centers of international exchange. As Robert Craft has reported in *Dialogues and a Diary*, among the questions discussed were "the problems of trying to teach an 'integrated-traditional' as well as a 'mathematical-experimental' study of musical composition (no conclusions)," and the faults of *avant-*

gardisme, which are "its dependence upon a superficial aspect of competition—the need to outdo the other at all costs—and its ignorance of music in the pre-electronic era (no remedy)."

There are, of course, complaints that the New York City Ballet has become conservative, "establishment." Since being established means having a chance to plan rather than improvise, to enjoy continuity and stability approaching the level of foreign state-supported institutions, we welcome the epithet. We have always been conservative, in the sense of preserving a traditional dance language, based on the music which most adroitly or capaciously subsumes it. With Stravinsky's disappearance, the self-appointed obligatory advance guard which he announced, led, and commanded for nearly sixty years assumes the taint of a disjunct, not very useful, self-serving closed fraternity, more interested in competitive shock in an area of sociopolitical happenings or put-ons than in servicing any ongoing repertories. The most for which one can hope from composers are useful scores of any source or coloration—ebony, bronze, or pinko-gray. What remains certain is that there are dancers capable of exposing both the virtues and the shortcomings of novel measurings of time and space. Over the last thirty-five years, where has the exposure of new or unfamiliar music been most transparently effective through the lens of classic dancing? In Paris? Moscow? Milan? London?

In New York!

POSTSCRIPT
1973-1978

For ROBERT GOTTLIEB,

inspirer of this and many other ballet books

When Robert Gottlieb thought it might be useful and possible to reprint the text of the large illustrated monograph of 1973, in both paperback and hardcover editions without photographs, updating the story to celebrate the thirtieth anniversary of our company as now constituted (although under various names it actually existed for another decade), I gathered together files of book and press notices over the years, lingering particularly over those which were inimical or negative. This made a considerable handful; there were few mentions which could be considered ecstatic or even highly favorable. In no way could these have been compared with those enjoyed by the Ballet Russe de Monte Carlo, which had declared itself the sole legitimate heir of Diaghilev's policies and repertories. Our American Ballet and Ballet Caravan collected a few A's for effort; perhaps they deserved no more. Any clear results of the work of our school were not quickly in evidence, nor would they be plain for some twenty years; then, mainly by inference or knowledgeable deduction. Balanchine was recognized as a professional, however unorthodox; also as separatist or defector. For today's audience of ballet-lovers under thirty-five it is difficult to recapture the reaction of audiences of the late thirties and early forties, which were the formative years of a company that went on to build itself logically on the philosophy and practice of that time.

Our company was consistently downgraded for its lack of scenic backcloths by important painters of the School of New York, by Jackson Pollock, Franz Kline, Adolph Gottlieb, or Willem de Kooning, since it was presumed that had Diaghilev been around, he would have continued a formula of discovery which gave Picasso, Derain, and Matisse their first one-man shows, in the scenery for ballets after 1917. We endured our share of failures, financial as well as artistic. We lacked both support and prestige of patronage by international or local high society and steady tours by Sol Hurok's high-powered booking organization. This and other factors combined to frame an image which hardly spelled the kind of "success" which is gratifying to a big paying public or the working press.

Bad notices are no harder to swallow than medicine; you meet those who tell you they never read (bad) notices, and hence never mind how unfriendly voices sound. I have always read every review or gossip column that a press-clipping service can send. I don't pretend I have not been both jealous and vindictive; there are only half a dozen critics who I have ever thought were qualified to disagree with me. Finally, my opinion has made small difference; dancing gets itself done and, fatally, either survives in repertory or doesn't, despite what I or anyone else thinks about it. When one is as close as I have been to scenes of action, knowing much about the needs and conditions of performance, it is patently impossible to be remotely "fair." Certain ballets have been dogged by bad notices from their debuts, yet still persist in repertory. A case in point is Balanchine's *Don Quixote*, which has been performed annually since 1965. Not a year has passed without serious changes altering the "original" version. One would be hard put to find a really favorable notice, yet in 1978 all six showings were almost sold out, and in it Suzanne Farrell received one of the greatest ovations of her career.

There are varieties of journalistic attention with different impact which can be graded from zero to whatever plus percent. Critics can instruct those interested in what to buy or see, but the instruction rarely extends past the footlights, no matter how ambitious some influential critics have become. The first critics I read for their learning were Carl Van Vechten, Cyril Beaumont, and John Martin, in the thirties. They taught me how to search in depth for what was being done. They had been looking for decades longer than I had had the chance; they seemed qualified to speak. So later did Edwin Denby, who had himself been a dancer. Until the arrival in 1973 of Arlene Croce on *The New Yorker*, the weeklies were occupied only in cursory reportage. The temptation of journalism is always to say something for the way words sound, rather than analyzing what actually happens. The specialist magazines, the academic quarterlies, contain the most "serious" (lengthy), reverently observed notices; their effect on audiences is zero. Too often they are directed to colleagues writing similar notices for other quarterlies. Yet in all of this one detects little rancor comparable to that which covers films, books, or pictures; the intention manifestly is to help—dancer and dance designer.

However, one does chance across a few pieces which, written some years back, might now make their authors uneasy. Just before the Stravinsky Festival (1972), there appeared in close succession a handful of articles intended to serve as prophetic and admonitory epitaphs for Balanchine. He was finished as an imaginative artist; his work was limited and repetitious; he was approaching seventy; he had been around too long. Among professional opinion-makers there is always a latent impulse of negative energy which could be called the Aristides principle. Aristides, a long-time public servant of irreproachable integrity, was exiled by the Athenians mainly because, as one citizen wrote on his potsherd, he'd become tired of hearing him called "The Just."

Balanchine's omnipresence, his virtual omnipotence in classic traditional dance, his maintenance of silence in which he steadfastly refused to explain or justify his quiddities, naturally provoked antagonism. A generation of putative "young choreographers" with no endowment save muscular energy resented his impalpable stronghold, which seemed to repel or reject outsiders from his criteria and achievement. While they improvised, took shortcuts, counted on fashion, he continued to brandish the whetstone of tradition. A number of ballet teachers, some with no vast qualifications either as experienced dancers or as analytical specialists, were scarcely enchanted by his own technical preferences. His style proclaimed a rugged efficiency that could break the backs and hearts of students and instructors who were less completely committed to the historical process of pedagogy and performance, of which he remained servant and master. A straw man was conceived and labeled "the Balanchine Dancer," generally speaking a lanky girl with a pinhead, a zombie, computerized past "soul." Since alternatives to classic ballet usually invoke "self-expression" as salvation, and since the "self" of most aspirants is dubious as to both maturity and information, and since Balanchine's work depends on architectural pattern and musical structure demanding abnegation of the self in favor of the mosaic of design, opposition to his direction was only logical. He has been described as a kind of Ivan the Terrible of ballet; an article in the *Village Voice* told the sad tale of a lady who claimed to have been destroyed in her psyche by exposure to his ruthless, inhuman schematization in the corps de ballet. She was driven to marriage, babies, and kitchen, and not a minute too soon.

Theatrical dancing is not a diversion; dedication necessary to perform with increased virtuosity does not depend on impulse, desire, or will alone. American students are taught or allowed to believe that they can or could (ideally) have the chance to accomplish whatever they wish, provided they wish enough. Degrees of desire ensure the success of ambition. This philosophy, licensing improvisation as an end rather than a means, has legitimized three or four generations of "modern" dancers. It has proliferated a demi-science of dilettante practice disguised as dance education all over the nation. Very few persons are suited to play the piano professionally; to paint, write poetry, sing, or "dance." In dancing, primary physical limitations or capacities are a first hurdle. These include the implacable presence of a restricted instep, an inadequate turn-out, heavy hips, large breasts, short neck, short legs, long trunk. Even presupposing a "perfect" body (which objectively hardly exists), sensitivity to musical phrasing, ears that measure music, also come into account. Most important of all is a moral acceptance of and allegiance to the rocky road of approximate perfection, full of ruts and potholes, which requires submission of the partial self, toward development, attention, and direction, enforcing the abandonment of easier and more idiosyncratic paths.

Balanchine's insistence over the years on a dancer's instrument rather than on flashy individual bipeds, a corps de ballet plus soloists of top efficiency according to his criteria, is hard policy, exclusive and excluding. It has a quasi-military stringency; indeed, his company has survived only as an infrequently compassionate dictatorship. This can be cruel, devious, blunt, impersonal, indeed "unjust." Policy, in any powerful institution or agency, reflects *Realpolitik*. It is not charitable; its educational aspects are intended to benefit the organism, although individuals greatly profit from contact with it if they are capable of surrendering primary self-interest and have the endurance to utilize steady tempering. It does not propel toward immediate self-expressiveness although many have found fulfillment in the work.

The drastic permissiveness of American behaviorist morality has corrupted generations of dance students who, through self-indulgence, mendacity, or convenience, have imagined themselves professional dancers. Few very young children have any clear idea as to what they want to be or do. To some mothers the apparent rigidity of the classic dance class imposes hours of pure discipline and keeps kids off the streets. Some children without any focused ambition compensate for their mother's frustration; others, magicked by footlights, fancy themselves instant ballerinas. Against such superstition, Balanchine, his training, and repertory have been a steady, minatory voice, rarely verbalized but constantly visible in the testimony of his school and company. So firmly held, so supremely arrogant a position, such positive energy, must arouse its negative opposite. From talking to dozens of parents over the years, one finds a couple of ferocious catchwords which terminate sticky conversations in which there's no use in further talk. To a child, neither happy, energetic, nor well favored: "Do you want to dance, or does your mother want you to?" (Remember J. M. Barrie's *Sentimental Tommy*: "My mother says I'm not hungry.") Explaining to a student why he or she has not been chosen for a desired situation: "Rule number one: there's no Justice."

A dancer's career, like a pianist's, a soldier's, or a scientist's, is a serious enterprise, involving the entire corps and psyche in a way and to a degree different from ordinary business affairs. First, it is rarely about money, or if money is involved it is of less than secondary importance. One can hope dancers may eat and sleep properly, that they may soon enjoy a parity of salary with other performing artists, but few who dance expect to have a large scale of luxury for their lives. Money is not why they dance. Dancers are members of an aristocratic civil service which continuously performs for the pleasure of a public. This special public recognizes their serving according to their competence at a particular historical moment. Balanchine's repertory of forty years has also educated an audience, and by his insistence on a corps, indeed a semi-demi-military corps, has augmented the prestige of the profession, far past the glamorous aura of two or three highly paid world stars.

And he has recognized hard truths in his calling. Quite apart from technique, he has made these glaringly legible. This has not promoted charm or flattery; in some cases it has saved time and money. It enforces self-knowledge, clears paths, makes possible excellent performance. In a time of debased aesthetic qualifications, it has established criteria. But the force and authority to raise and defend such principles are taken less as a public obligation than personal accusation or damaging judgment.

From the beginning, Balanchine's education and early performance were supported by central authoritarian governments, first by a czarist regime, briefly by the Soviets, followed by a private reduction of more or less identical principles by Diaghilev from 1924 to 1929, although this last governance was penurious in its decline. In the United States, beginning in 1934, we managed to find private patronage; later the bounty of Rockefeller and Ford Foundations; more recently New York City itself, the New York State Council on the Arts, and the National Endowment for the Arts. In addition to friendly foundations and corporations there have been individuals who wished to see our work carried on. However lean a season, we have never exactly starved, despite our history of early bankruptcies and reorganizations. We came to gain stability; with it a modest freedom or independence, in part by financial luck or logic. This was done in the face of long-accepted recipes for theatrical success—the *salade russe* of eclectic popular programs, the inflation of star names, exploitation by commercial management. What has been difficult for a half-interested public to realize or admit is that, under the captaincy of Balanchine, our company and school are different *in kind* from other companies and schools. We refused, from the start, a repertory of the nineteenth century as a staple or mandatory basis, yet we used the classic idiom as a flexible springboard. Balanchine rejected a tidy or specious appeal to precedent. He hammered out his own concept of feasible repertory. Even when small in format, we aspired to the grand scale of a large state-supported troupe. While, as far as gross numbers go, we may never approach the regimental force of the present Russian corps de ballet, we have become the largest dance company in the United States. This impedes easy touring but offers our production and presentation high potential.

It becomes clearer, as time goes on, what Balanchine has done with his promulgation of a doctrine, curriculum, and policy. It could by no means suit everyone. We are a company serving a megalopolis; our frame is metropolitan. To penetrate the precincts of Balanchine's precision, a dancer must depend upon special factors of character and temperament, a willingness to trust a credo of self-denial at the moment when egos are inclined to feel their first selfhood; to admit the prescience and power of a regimen based on achievement which even in fairly close proximity to its source holds itself mysterious. This mystery is hardly self-assertive; it is simply the evidence of a body of logic based on a large and varied accomplishment which manifests itself only after a considerable time. There is nothing about Balanchine's composing or teaching that resembles those lightning flashes of revelation through improvisation which have been the luck of certain individuals, particularly in the "modern dance." What he imparts takes time to receive and absorb. For some, indeed for many, it takes too long. But for some dancers who prize dancing above rapidly accelerating self-exposure, there has been hearty satisfaction. Such may seem small at the start, and must be accepted in a stoic light; little is ever promised. Praise is given less than reassurance. However, increasing strength arrives, a security based on analysis in rehearsal, an almost privately transmitted information of concrete craft supporting quality. If one has to find parallels for the nature of training which Balanchine's ballets require when rehearsed by himself, one would of course recall the instruction of piano, violin, or voice by great masters, but also the discipline of the humane sciences, behavior, and morality by masters of the Society of Jesus.

It is not yet the moment to define the precise nature of service that Balanchine offers in the large perspective of the development of classic theatrical dancing, but his repertory, danced by his company, prepared by his school, and familiar in theaters all over East and West, is an indication of more than half a century of thought and labor. In an epoch encompassing two world wars, which has seen lethal attacks on every tradition of organized metric in verse, design, and plastic art, an age that canonized and commercialized negotiable personalities, broadcast dilettantism and amateurism in the name of freedom or self-expression, the traditional ballet almost alone has survived and indeed very much strengthened itself. In a large sense this is due to one man.

JANUARY 2, 1974: *New York*

Ronald Bates clearing lines to hang massive yardage of black flame-proofed silk for *Variations pour une Porte et un Soupir*. Testing for effective sonorities for the sound of a creaking door and an asthmatic lung. Despite criticism of our auditorium's acoustics by certain singers, sounds that the ballet needs come across loud and clear, including the squeak of toe shoes heard plainly in the back of the top balcony.

The French composer Pierre Henri, experimenting with "non-musical" sonorities, used an amplified creaking door swinging on ungreased hinges paired against the breathing of a body in love, anxiety, or agony. The stage was draped in the enormous skirts of a dancer drenched in blackness, menace, or death as she struggled to come to some sort of companionship—erotic, maternal, mortal (?), with a gray-skinned biped, insectile, infantile, neuter but not exactly inhuman. One might read tokens and metaphors of drowning, frustration, suffocation. The theatrical scale was gigantic; the light-struck flood of black silk rippled and ballooned in an orgy of peristaltic motion. Fatally the duet, heroically performed by Karin von Aroldingen and John Clifford, assumed something of the aroma of a high-grade nightclub number. Technical arrangements were no easier for stage crew than for dancers. The action of the silk drapery had to be synchronized with music and the metrical play of the choreography. The effect was by no means unimpressive, although the enormous yardage tended to smother much personal anguish in the *pas de deux*.

Balanchine had been engaged in both the manipulation of silks and the dominance of a *femme fatale* before. In 1933, in Paris, with *Errante* (to Schubert's "Wanderer Fantasy"), magically designed by the painter Pavel Tchelitchev, there was no painted scenery, only long strips of translucent vellum upon which lights were thrown from behind. At the end, the abandoned muse was drowned in a vast cloud of white China silk, within which she battled less and less frantically as the curtain fell. In the television production of Stravinsky's ballet-cantata *The Flood*, the designer Rouben Ter-Arutunian used an inchoate blob of slimy black-primed silk to suggest uncreated matter before God touched the waters.

In the undifferentiated, unshaped, threatening mass without margin, definition, or form, dancers inside this skin moved it with every suggestion of creeping unlimited possibility. They writhed, uncoiled, merged their bodies, as the inverse of definite silhouettes or chiseled profiles. The motion of light on luminous woven stuffs is a most absolute contrast to the sharpness and plasticity of stripped human bodies.

Ballets like *Errante, The Flood,* and *Une Porte et un Soupir* were never candidates for "success." They may depend on a certain shock value in their difference from what might be expected from the rest of the repertory. They also have their incidental function of exercising or even extending the often passive visual capacity of an audience. Comparatively few viewers make much effort to search the stage; instead, accustomed to television, they only scan it. Many of Balanchine's ballets hide bones under a surface skin uncovered only by constant sightings. The ancient boast of "I don't know much about art, but I know what I like" is often prompt judgment of work fresh in repertory. Many settle for what they "like," or rather, what is accidentally coincidental with their preference. "Taste," or habits of seeing, is quickly corroborated, accommodated, and rejected. Habits are not too difficult to upset, and there is genuine delight in the instinctive negative of refusals. Failure, or unsuccess on an immediate level, may not arouse as much animal pleasure as success, but there is satisfaction in rejection. On whatever basis, one exercises a personal aesthetic judgment, often retaliating against the self-assertive tyranny of artist-makers. This is hardly to say, however, that there are never some works that are better than others. In a progressive repertory such as ours, there have been a number of works, now lost, which if done today might receive a quite different reception than was accorded them at their premieres.

It's time wasted to lament the brief life of *Une Porte et un Soupir.* It will not be revived; perhaps it doesn't deserve revival. Pierre Henri's mechanized noises have the common failing of scores using mechanical apparatus distinct from the traditional orchestra. Since Stravinsky's death, the "advance-guard" seems generally to compose for academic audiences or token "world premieres" that seldom survive in repertory. However, Balanchine's loyalty or stubbornness to the sighs and a door resulted in a strangeness, irritation, beauty even, which sticks provocatively in the memory. It offered no virtuoso role. It presented a visual poem in a big frame. It was thin but not empty. From a philosophical position defining repertory policy, it posits the problem of novelties and alternatives. Balanchine is always searching for new music—old and unfamiliar as much as recently written. He had kept Pierre Henri's tapes for some seasons, waiting for the proper moment to fit a ballet based on them into a season's schedule. Perhaps he waited too long; finally, he felt a commitment to the composer to produce his work. The classic dance, as he has extended it, is such a strong, legible, and elastic language that it can accept and even benefit from inversion, another range of plasticity, a different tone of voice. These alternatives may do little by way of providing sudden cash, or enhancing or enlarging subsequent programs, but they forcibly cause reconsideration, enlarge both positive and negative vision, and pull received ideas into hard question. Balanchine's role in the forging of repertory has also been didactic. Many works have been ploughed under in the process, and while it might have been well to have revived those which somehow stayed sharply in memory (*Roma, Gounod Symphony, Tyl Ulenspiegel, Metamorphoses*), to say nothing of his many lost Diaghilev ballets, he has preferred to use surprising music. "Failures" often pave the way for later "successes." Ballets that have lived longest are not necessarily those which were first warmly welcomed. Part of the craft of repertory is judgment which prods an audience by stubborn insistence or by long experience of laws of fluctuation in public acceptance.

Increasingly, owing to Balanchine's instruction, our public has become participant with our company. At least a determining section of it has begun to feel it has a right, even an obligation, to respond by love or hate. This warmth, pro or con, is ultimately passionately supportive. Certainly we wouldn't want it any other way, nor will Balanchine stop his whimsical, reckless, capricious, or knowing adventures into the dubious realms of alternatives.

FEBRUARY 14, 1974: *New York*

Reading Bernhard Pick's *The Cabala* and other related books on Jewish medieval alchemy and magic; a massive bibliography, homework for Jerry Robbins's ballet based on the legend of the Dybbuk. Fascinated by gematria, the system of alphabetical letters according to their numerological value; romantic cosmology of Eastern European Jewish tradition. Can such material be made legible as dance?

It is easier to write after the fact about the malfunction of a balletic proposal from its first notion than to explain its success. Success wipes out all intermediate steps, including false ones. In repertory, success is simply defined: it is work that, at first sight, promises a certain permanence in repertory, which can be retired and revived after initial exposure. Failures may be putative successes that for good or bad reasons don't make it. When we learned that Jerome Robbins had the idea to use as germ the concept of the Dybbuk, it seemed logical and appropriate. When he asked us to commission Leonard Bernstein to compose a new score, it felt right. *Dybbuk* came into broad theatrical consciousness with the drama by S. Ansky, initially presented by the Russian Yiddish Art Theater after the First World War. In New York I saw the first American production in English, at the Neighborhood Playhouse on Grand Street in 1920, with Aline Bernstein's scenery and costumes inspired by the original Russian expressionist version. It was my first sight of highly stylized ritual theater and made a tremendous impression from the cohesiveness and intensity of every element on the stage.

The play concerns a young dedicated theologian, apprentice to the mysteries of the cabala, pledged by his parents to a young girl. Her father breaks their engagement, deeding her to a richer suitor. Her lover consults his magic books; at the crucial moment of self-illumination he is consumed by the cosmic forces his learning has released. He dies, but returns to possess her body. Elders of their village in the pale of settlement, invoking the same powers against negative energies, attempt to exorcise his demon, but her lover, in death, claims her.

Robbins made it clear from the start that his ballet would not be a melodramatic pantomime following the story, but instead a series of "related dances concerning rituals and hallucinations which are present in the dark magico-religious ambience of the play and in the obsessions of its characters." Both Robbins and Leonard

Bernstein, his long-time collaborator, were thoroughly familiar with such an ambience. The East European tradition of Jewish music and dance, sacred and secular, is rich. Ever since the Russian art theaters of the twenties and thirties had utilized this lyric vein in productions by Evgenii Vakhtangov, Alexander Tairov, and others, a body of fictive material assembled itself, comparable to the mythological territories of Western folklore nourished on magic and mystery, from druids to witchcraft. While the Yiddish material could hardly have penetrated popular imagination to the degree of King Arthur, Robin Hood, or Macbeth, nevertheless to some part of the knowledgeable theatrical public, Ansky's *Dybbuk* enjoyed its considerable reputation. Robbins had enjoyed a huge popular success with his Broadway musical *Fiddler on the Roof*, which borrowed lighter, less mystical veins from a similar background. Bernstein was expert in his use of similar melodic material; his orchestral score for our *Dybbuk* is, and not alone from its purely theatrical aspect, one of his most powerful. It is authoritative, convincing, massively sonorous, strong rhythmically, and eminently suggestive of movement. What went awry?

Robbins seemed tortured by specifics. Somehow he felt it was no longer interesting, or possible, to state the original story as narrative. The plot was too definite, commanding, hence banal. He agonized over his conviction that the ballet should be "abstract" or *abstracted* from the source. It is hard to say what prompted such conviction, or what he intended, except that narrative pantomime was to be excluded and the dances, in their residual movement alone, would express the quality and character of the legend. It was almost as if he were attempting to exorcise the familiar ambiance of *Fiddler on the Roof*, which might be imagined as the other side of the same coin. The sequence of his new dances tended to presuppose that the audience had either read or seen Ansky's play, or was familiar with Jewish folklore, a presumption not always justified.

Rouben Ter-Arutunian's decor was starkly handsome. A huge parchment manuscript page framed the ritual movements of People of the Book, upon whose venerable waxen surface was projected the magical cabalistic Tree of Life, together with other sacred symbols. Black-and-white prayer shawls with their long fringes bordered the parchment.

At the first performance, voices of two cantors intoned a stately invocation, but these were soon eliminated. The first performance passed well enough and seemed to promise more use than other smaller works. The score made a strong impression; it seemed as if Bernstein, after many years conducting the New York Philharmonic Orchestra and others all over the world, had recovered his earlier career as a formidable theatrical musician. But soon after, instead of building onto present elements, Robbins commenced cutting—first, characteristic details of the men's costumes, then their dances, eventually other key aspects of the production. It was as if he were unable to make the work "abstract" enough; as if some dybbuk were pursuing him, to prevent him from revealing secrets that should not be shown to a profane public. Thus differentiations of character and contrasts of persons were sheared away. Finally, after more surgery and disagreement with the composer, Robbins withdrew this ballet—at least for the present. Perhaps his large and flexible talents will be drawn back to it at another time and will repair it to his satisfaction.

In considering what went wrong (in the event of a "success" one hardly questions what went right), I admit I never saw need for abstraction. Perhaps Robbins felt that Ansky's dramatic plot was too elementary, overpicturesque, too specifically ethnic, that the source material must be transformed, pared down to give it relevance or surprised into a new life of its own. There may be a case for essentializing narrative structure, clearing away inessential characters and subplots in order to canonize capital characters or situations. But here, while the music was drawn powerfully from ethnic material, and dance steps could hardly resist following Bernstein's domineering pulse, there was a constant if almost haphazard effort to strip the action of any shred of literal legibility. There were remote echoes that might be identified with the drama, had one seen or read it. Beyond Robbins's instinctive urgency in movement, the progress of individual variations seemed demonstrations of individual skill rather than any exposition of tragic lyricism. When characteristic decorative details were removed, furthering "abstract" intention, the dancing effectively removed itself from the initial springboard of dybbuk or cabala.

Insistence on "abstraction" brings up serious problems attached to the history of taste in our time, the philosophy of "modernism," and a permanent doctrinaire advance-guard. Abstraction has been the indispensable formula for visual art over the last half century. Before the First World War, Cubism provided a quasi-mathematical skeleton of vaguely geometrical architecture, exhausting itself as a progressive movement in its first few years. However, a Cubist rationale or academy has been useful as a teaching aid ever since. Abstract expressionism seemed to promise the best of two worlds, self-purification welded to self-expression; a presupposed, root essentializing plus personal, individual declaration. It was a puritanical style that eschewed figurative representation with a puritanical strictness which seemed to invoke at once Hebraic and Moslem inhibitions against daring to reflect the image of a Creator. Historically, one can understand the presumed necessities that called such practice into being, but like most tendentious movements, it turned into an academy preserving its doctrine while exhausting its earlier, fresher impulses. In dance, particularly "modern dance," abstraction eliminated some amount of rhetorical pantomime, decorative padding, and useless parades, the automatic perpetuation of the nineteenth-century "full-length" ballet. But with Nijinsky, Stravinsky, and Balanchine, a spirit of concrete motor expansion demonstrated the stylistic potential of the traditional classic dance in a freedom of choice. Ballets became shorter in clock-time with more and faster movement. Dance design itself replaced mimicry. In many but by no means all cases with Balanchine's own repertory, need for overt sequential narrative is gone. Movement itself suggested whatever ambiance was proposed. This could hardly be called an "abstracting," since dance was a very concrete physical expression of proposals that music stimulated. With *Dybbuk*, a core of instigation was removed. What was left was the ornamentation of a void.

Those who insist on a strict accountability for such disappointments know nothing of the hazards of progressive repertory. Any ballet company that refuses to insure itself by a repetition of withered four-act works from the nineteenth century has to undergo the constant birth agonies of new compositions. These are forced into being out of a spectrum of needs: to provide novel and flattering roles for dancers worthy of them; to present novelty as a shot in the arm (often a shot in the dark); the obligation to signal special occasions, social or political. And above all this, there is the purest mandate to afford choreographers of promise or proven ability the chance to achieve new work increasingly prompting their imagination, work that urgently commands itself to risk the light of day.

MARCH 3, 1974: *New York*

Rouben Ter-Arutunian's models for three acts of *Coppélia*. Although a large-scale production, it is designed to be hung in repertory; unlike *Nutcracker*, it can be struck in one stagehands' call without overtime, to be hung for a single performance. Balanchine felt Act II (Dr. Coppélius's workshop) was overcharged with alchemical instruments, retorts, dolls, spare limbs, and magical paraphernalia. For Act III (Dedication of the New Carillon), Rouben inscribed the bells with all the collaborators' initials from the composer Léo Delibes (1870) to Shoura Danilova and himself.

I was taken to Paris first in 1923. Effects of the First World War were hardly apparent; the city appeared as if it had been painted by Impressionists of the eighties. The nineteenth century remained visible in many conserved aspects and conservative institutions. The Grand Opéra, Charles Garnier's marvelous fairy palace, had survived the stabling of German troops in 1870 and the zeppelin raids of 1916. Big Bertha, the Kaiser's long-range Krupp siege-gun, hit a full church but spared the Opéra. Ballet was still in the hands of the academic Franco-Italian tradition, led by Albert Aveline and Carlotta Zambelli. It had managed almost completely to evade the influence of Diaghilev's innovations. Principles of a strict hierarchical tenure system grading the dancers and rigid academic conservatory standards of musical taste obtained. This corresponded to the sumptuous frame of the opera-house architecture with its stupendous mineral splendor, its grand staircase waiting to be manned on gala evenings by the Garde Républicaine in their cuirasses and horsehair-plumed helmets.

There was a brand-new ballet, *Cydalise et le Chèvre-pied*, music by Gabriel Pierné, choreography by Léo Staats. Zambelli danced Cydalise, and Aveline was her faun. An excellent dancer, nevertheless he was not even a remote cousin of Nijinsky's heroic scandalous biped. When the curtain rises, Styrax, a young faun, is being given a lesson on panpipes; he is naughty; an older satyr ties him to a tree. A nymph (who has at the same time been taking a ballet lesson) unties him, but, still naughty, he refuses to escape and hitches a ride on a (real) passing coach (with horses) to Versailles. There the king's company is rehearsing *La Sultane des Indes* (a pastiche of Rameau). The faun provokes Mlle. Cydalise (La Pompadour?) with his flirtatious *entrechats* and *cabriolets*; he manages to get into her bedroom, etc., etc. The huge stage was filled with dancers and children from the ballet school; scenery was changed with dispatch; execution was elaborate and obviously well prepared. There was an air of stuffy luxury, or cushioned irrelevance. This was "ballet" indeed, and at the very Grand Opéra, but even to an inexperienced if eager eye, the spectacle seemed mean and wan. Whatever its richness, or massive forces deployed, attention given to its design was impressive and, in a negative way, exhilarating, like too much candy. Had I known enough to analyze this in historical perspective, here was a capital example of high bourgeois French taste at its most plump and plush, a manifestation that Diaghilev at the same time and in comparative poverty was making mock of with new productions by Matisse and Nijinska, Braque and Stravinsky, on a far lesser scale of visceral opulence. While I was left questioning the rich and silly parade of nymphs, fauns, satyrs, and courtiers, the actual mechanics of a working opera house were very exciting. Not until some thirty years later, when we were given the use of the State Theater in Lincoln Center, was I able to satisfy myself with the manipulation of a similar instrument.

Whatever disappointment at *Cydalise et le Chèvre-pied,* a real enthusiasm was redeemed by a performance of *Coppélia,* Léo Delibes's venerable score first heard in Paris in 1870, on the eve of war, through whose premiere Napoleon III, his last night at the Opéra, managed to keep awake. Over decades it had become "signature" ballet for its own house and, as well, had gone around the world. Petipa made his own arrangement for Petersburg; ten years later, in 1894, it was revised by Enrico Cecchetti. It was this version, danced in their youth, that Madame Alexandra Danilova and Balanchine followed when *Coppélia* was set for our dancers.

From Paris in 1923 what I most remember was the thumping

music for the czardas, mazurkas, and other national dances. Physical energy absent in *Cydalise* found itself plentifully here, not in the finicky correctness or diminished scale of broad movement then characterizing the French classic school, but in stylized spontaneity which while like the classic acting of the Comèdie Française was wholly professional yet not entirely artificial. Here was neither the plastic posing of the diluters of Isadora nor the mawkish frailty or "soul" of the followers of Anna Pavlova and Fokine. To be sure, what I myself had tasted of ballet was at best thin wine, but even with so little strength one gets a hint of the real thing. I bought Victor recordings of Delibes's czardas and for a long time hummed over the memories of the Paris production, its massive movement and smashing rhythms. But, because of its universal popularity in a number of revivals by other companies, it was something we were hesitant to undertake.

Nevertheless, among numerous possibilities which over three decades have been intermittently proposed to Balanchine—quite apart from revivals of all-but-forgotten ballets from his own or Diaghilev's repertories—there was always *Coppélia*. Whenever there were one or two gathered together in any way close to decision-making, there were also suggestions toward a *Sleeping Beauty*, as if a ballet company can be considered to come of age only after having surrendered to the magic of that monument. And, of course, there might be a full-length *Swan Lake*. It was this length, exactly, that Balanchine minded. His second act of *Swan Lake* with use of unfamiliar and rejected music, his elimination of the four cygnets and acceleration of the finale, presented the essence of what is best in the ballet (choreography by Lev Ivanov), which the perfunctory national dances of the tiresome third act only serve to dim. We already had a number of works to Tchaikovsky music. Balanchine had also used fragments of Delibes over the years, but he felt that until now he never had dancers who could be suitably cast.

In the original Paris production of *Coppélia* Franz was danced by a girl, following an extant French tradition of *travesti*. Girls cast as boys are in less ancient lineage than boys playing girls. The cult of the ballerina fostered by private impresarios who held the lease of the Paris Opéra in the 1830's and 40's became a cult to be exploited as commercial necessity. This developed into a national preference and effectively destroyed the importance of the male dancer, except as *porteur* or support, for more than half a century. When questions are raised as to the authenticity of a given revival, these stop short as to the wisdom of casting a contemporary ballerina as a boy. It would possibly have its own antiquarian charm, but would require an insistence and acceptance of history pointless to burden a public with. Nevertheless, the problem of a male dancer suitable to the role of Franz as Balanchine imagined it certainly was, for a long time, an impediment to our ultimate revival. With Patricia McBride an ideal soubrette as Swanilda, Helgi Tomasson as Franz, her boyish bumpkin hero with his strong self-effacing elegance, and Shaun O'Brien as a masterful crotchety old Dr. Coppélius, the moment seemed ripe.

As usual, there were also political considerations. *Coppélia* is a large work that did not exist on a similar scale in many rival productions. As newly staged and freshly designed, it would be useful for that portion of the public which longed for broad narrative mimicry, often feeling starved on our repertory's meager diet of pantomime. The music was familiar and popular. In Balanchine's recension of the third act (which is usually fragmentarily staged or even omitted in many revivals), he employed a couple of dozen small children from our School of American Ballet as "Golden Hours." Three teams of these very young students actually danced, not on pointe, but using a considerable range of steps. For many of them, except those who had already appeared in *Harlequinade* or *Nutcracker*, this *Coppélia* would be their long-remembered debut on the professional stage. They transformed what is often an ordinary finale into a rousing gallop which brings the curtain down with thunder.

Also and importantly, Madame Alexandra Danilova, a senior instructor at our school, danced a triumphant Swanilda through the 1930's and 40's. Her photographic memory made Act II the climax of the ballet. Her choreography for the mimed scenes given to McBride, Tomasson, and O'Brien is a gem of expressive use of hands, arms, eyes—the virtuosic capacity of the whole body in dumb show. Often enough we have been slighted for a lack of emphasis on pantomime. We do not teach it in our school; Balanchine does not believe it can be taught as a useful separate language, apart from gestural passages in specific ballets. Traditional pantomime, relics of what obtained in the nineteenth century as canonical for operatic or dramatic gesture, appears rigid or quaint stylization today, but hardly comparable to the fly-in-amber crystallization of the vitality in the Noh or Kabuki. Classical traditional mimicry is indeed alive in Danilova's second act of *Coppélia*, but it is intimately connected to the dancing and its highly stylized action is both legible as narrative and appropriate to the origins of the ballet's original context.

Patty McBride's performance in Act II of *Coppélia* is not only an occasion for delight but a criterion of professionalism. Mimicry and difficult dancing are almost equally involved; welding the two in a tight relation is the unerring authority of a mistress of classic dancing. As Swanilda she plays at playing roles—virginal village maiden, rustic hoyden, and, in her "Scottish" and "Spanish" variations, the mature ballerina of tradition. Hers are not realistic but lyric, stylized impersonations. There is no attempt (or need) to pretend she has fewer years than she owns, but her strength, attack, and energy demonstrate spirit and craft only years of experience accumulate. Patty peppers her impersonations with piquancy, a smartly italicized petulance, naughtiness, jealousy. She dances the soubrette of *Coppélia*'s original epoch, part picture-postcard, part opera-house poster. She steps out as a four-color lithograph of verve and mastery. She learned the role from that other mistress of this manner, Danilova. Now students watch Patty's performance as their particular model. A product of our school, she came up through the ranks of our company. In good times and bad she has never failed to use steps as sparks that have kept us bright; there have been times when she could properly be thanked for having kept our entire ensemble in focus.

Coppélia's third act offered problems. In Paris it was dropped permanently after 1872. Balanchine restored it, retaining three classical variations and adding an extended classical duet for McBride and Tomasson. I particularly liked the "War" entrance. In *Coppélia*'s original libretto by Nuitter and Saint-Léon, the *prétexte* suggested the several occasions for which bells of the new town carillon might peal, including "Prayer," "Peace," and "War." Hot on a thunderstorm, Balanchine brought in a troupe of male and female Valkyrs in full armor and glistening spears. The orchestra suggests a Wagnerian corps de ballet had strayed into the Grand

Opéra from the Folies Bergères or Les Bouffes Parisiennes. This gave offense to some, but considering that the birth of this ballet was almost a fanfare for the outbreak of the Franco-Prussian War (in which, against all odds, France declared war against Germany), the choice of costumes was by no means inappropriate, while the pyrotechnical dancing of Colleen Neary and Robert Weiss was as brilliant as the music.

APRIL 15, 1975: *New York*

Auditions at the School of American Ballet. Around seventy applicants present themselves for the summer course, out of some 1,600 who applied, from whom are chosen full-time winter students. More than half from outside New York City, taking advantage of Easter vacations. Many more boys than before; those accepted between twelve and sixteen. Others are already formed by previous training and impossible to develop for either school or company.

When Balanchine first came to New York in 1933, he insisted on establishing a school as basis for an eventual producing company. As time passed, and our School of American Ballet strengthened itself, its purpose and presence sometimes tended to become taken for granted. Its function, often presupposed, was underestimated. Through the sixties, a grant-in-aid from the Ford Foundation ensured its existence, and it had found a permanent home in the Juilliard School building contiguous to Lincoln Center and across the plaza from the State Theater. The school continued to offer training for a majority of dancers in our company but also began providing dancers in considerable numbers for many other companies here and abroad.

No foundation subvention lasts forever; the Ford Foundation grant would terminate in 1978. Initially it included scholarships on a national basis for students over a widely distributed geographical coverage. This had been abandoned and replaced by regional auditions conducted by members of our school's staff. It became necessary to seek wider funding. During the years of Ford support, it was generally imagined that we needed nothing else, but while, as a rule of thumb, our school budget is one-tenth that of the New York City Ballet, it remains about ten times harder to raise. There is little attractive glamour in a teaching institution. Occasionally, scholarships may be found for promising or talented students, but these can turn out less well than was originally hoped and implicit risk tempers a donor's enthusiasm. Visible magic, glowing from the stage, makes excitement and unlooses purse strings; daily classes, with their imperceptible improvement, can be a dull diet, yet without them we would find no apprentices, no revivified corps de ballet, no new soloists.

In the professional world of performing artists, our school became well known, its facility recognized as without peer in the United States. It is impressive to watch, working here among the ordinary students, such preeminent artists as Nureyev and Baryshnikov. Unless one recognizes their faces, there is little to distinguish them from other bodies, for they come to work, to sharpen their already princely instruments, dressed as they may be in patched tights and worn slippers. That they never seem to outshine less advanced students shows superior courtesy. Their friendliness and complete lack of pretension afford another sort of instruction, one modest, mannerly, and as valuable as academic exercises.

Balanchine continues to supervise the faculty of the school, although he no longer teaches there. He commands his own company class every morning; this is scarcely elementary instruction. He shows what he needs for dancers working in his own ballets Training in our school, which gains admittance to our company, has primarily prepared dancers for Balanchine to take over. They have already learned enough to be perfected by him. His classes have become something of a legend. They are accompanied not by piano alone, but by a continuous running patter, poetical, metaphorical, gnomic utterances which make direct or oblique commentary on the kind and quality of movement he is striving to demonstrate and obtain. His explanations of how and what he wants, a specific manner of motion, are cherished like jewels by those who have the interest and energy to listen; further, to absorb. This is not given to all—while exercising their bodies also to make equivalent effort with their minds. It is not easy to appreciate the residual value of what Balanchine seems easily to toss away in every casual morning's demonstration. But a cadre of dancers who manage it always exists. It is these who hold the legacy of our repertory.

Unlike government service-schools in England, Canada, France, and the Soviet Union, no American dance school enjoys overall support from our federal government. Our school still has no residence for students young or old, which deprives us of the cream of future corps. Parents will not risk the jungle-pavements of Manhattan. Recently, the National Endowment for the Arts made a historic award to the School of American Ballet, toward the establishment of an endowment, which must be matched by our school three to one. It has been difficult to attract public monies, since we consistently refuse to award diplomas. Forty years ago Balanchine determined we would never award a meaningless piece of paper which in essence could signify merely that a student had spent a certain number of hours in class, without reference to the quality of work such training had achieved. The uses of a diploma are few; it can help get teaching jobs in institutions which have dubious professional levels. A dancer's performance is the best and only diploma that is realistic testimony, but studios and students all over the world prize a framed "diploma," as if it were an obligatory credential equivalent to that legitimizing a surgeon, dentist, or lawyer. Accreditation is a thorny political problem; any board or committee that has the right or obligation to declare individuals qualified or not must have criteria that are, in its field at least, expertly recognized. In the United States, anyone claiming to be an "artist" is an artist; anyone wishing to dance can "dance," and by no very inflated extension, "teach." Any infringement of the right to "teach" constitutes an attack on one's right to earn a living. A great number of children who have auditioned at our school write on their applications that they have been "studying" from five to ten years. When analyzed, this means that they may have, off and on, for ten years, taken a ballet class every other Saturday.

Increasingly, the School of American Ballet becomes my preoccupation. It is not that I felt I had less function with the company, but Balanchine's time and attention are focused on it, almost to the exclusion of everything else. It has grown into the largest dance organization in the nation. It now requires a greatly augmented staff of specialists with in-house agencies for Special Events,

Group Sales, Public Relations, Audit, and Touring. In the old days, half a dozen hands managed everything; today it takes a platoon of experts. What I might have contributed by the way of occasional suggestions in producing new works, as formerly, has become limited, since, increasingly, new ballets depend on music and dancing alone.

Nor is it, as far as the school goes, that I have any overwhelming interest in "education" as such. I saw, and see, the school as a forcing bed for talent, talent that I hope can be developed for the increased strength of the company. The school has assumed new importance with the recent astonishing growth of interest in ballet all over the country. This is reflected by the large numbers applying for admittance: between January and June, 1978, more than sixteen hundred young people applied for entrance to the year's summer course, during which students are chosen for the full school year opening in September. There were places for only two hundred and twenty. There is a big increase in the number and quality of boys who are able to study, and in students sent by their governments—from Europe, Latin America, and Japan.

Eugenie Ouroussow, who came to us as a very young girl when we opened in 1934, died. For four decades she served as the operative backbone of the school. Now our two Natashas (Molostwoff and Gleboff) continue her work as administrators, with no lack of Slavic expertness or American energy. While Balanchine has always claimed to have been spiritually an American (via Harriet Beecher Stowe, Mark Twain, Jack London, and ragtime) before leaving Petersburg fifty-five years ago, there is little question but that our school and company have had their Russian tinge, in the faculty of one and the philosophy of the other. It has been crucial that our Natashas are rooted in an old-fashioned Russian ambiance. Balanchine has always exercised his brand of benevolent dictatorship. This has also been extended, if at one remove, to our school. It has provided an important degree of discipline in the schedules of scholastic life. The regime is strict if fairly flexible; advancement has always been by merit rather than by time spent in school. Maintenance of order is loose, unobtrusive, but enough to enable work to proceed in orderly progression and—as Balanchine wishes—in silence.

We find that, over the years, parents discover this silence, if at first mysterious, ultimately attractive. They have accepted it as a useful corrective, or even therapy. It is antithetic to progressive (permissive) education. Our standards of correctness approach the military, while encouraging individual capacity. Some children, if or when they discover they have minds of their own, may not wish to dance. Exercise at the *barre* is agreeable enough up to the age when the big world blossoms into alternatives; then, other possibilities present themselves. There is the human temptation of accepting pupils who can pay, whatever else their qualifications may or may not be. We do not have enough money for minimal maintenance, let alone for sufficient scholarships. In the Soviet Union students are wholly subsidized; their parents are paid an amount equivalent to what their children might have gained from other work. It costs some seven thousand dollars a year to house, feed, and school a child from twelve to seventeen in New York City, including secondary academic education at the Professional Children's School, where our children can obtain their high school certificates. We are beginning to receive donation of scholarships for gifted children from several regional centers.

With the energetic aid of Nancy Norman Lassalle, a former student of our school, a National Council has been organized. Its members assume responsibility for supporting activities of the school all over the country, supplying aid locally to promising students with an ultimate eye on New York, meeting annually in New York for our school's Workshop performances. One may hope that, by the new century, the School of American Ballet, like the Soviet academies, will approach the prestige and security of other national service schools. A "West Point" of the classic dance has been an anxious expectation for nearly fifty years; in the next twenty-five perhaps it may become reality.

MAY 13, 1975: *New York City, St. Luke's Hospital*

As Mayor Fiorello La Guardia said, "A hospital is no place for a sick man." Double cardiac by-pass. A team of oriental anesthetists—Japanese, Chinese, Korean. I assume their sense of time (and patience) is slower, or more metrical (?) than ours. I shall have to miss four programs, sixteen new works in three successive weeks of the Ravel Festival, the first time since 1934 I have not seen our repertory premieres.

Balanchine has always had special affection for the city of Paris, or at least its Grand Opéra and musical life in the town. Here it was that Diaghilev established a home in exile for the Ballets Russes. After Petersburg, Paris was the school of Balanchine's youth. French music, painting, cooking, wine, *haute couture*, and dancing came first. He worked on several widely separated occasions on the stage of the Grand Opéra. In 1930 he was nominated its *maître de ballet*; illness intervened. Instead, he went to Copenhagen and three years later to New York. Maurice Ravel embodied the spirit of Paris's lyric impulse that came into definition shortly before the outbreak of the 1914 war. Following Debussy, he was not vastly admired by Diaghilev, Cocteau, or the militant Cubists and Dadaists. To them he seemed an academician who aspired to the advance-guard by disclaiming the official academy to which he essentially belonged. Although Diaghilev commissioned *Daphnis et Chloé* in 1911, it had not triumphed as a stage piece. Some years later he refused *La Valse*. Nevertheless, except for Stravinsky, Ravel left the most considerable body of Western music suitable for theater (apart from opera). The Stravinsky Festival of 1972 served as precedent. Balanchine had worked with Ravel in 1924, producing the debut of *L'Enfant et les Sortilèges* in Monte Carlo, and we had revived it in 1947 on the very first program of our Ballet Society. In 1951 he successfully arranged Ravel's *La Valse* (preceded by *Les Valses Nobles et Sentimentales*, which has been in our repertory ever since).

The Ravel Festival was scheduled to spread itself over three weeks so as to avoid the logistical problems of the one-week Stravinsky Festival. Comparative qualities of the two composers predetermined the impact of the effort. No one imagined Stravinsky could be surpassed. The two celebrations, although prone to be so treated, were not in the nature of competition. There were questions, to be sure, as to why Balanchine engaged himself to spend time, money, and energy on Ravel. Answers were simple enough: primarily he liked Ravel's orchestration and felt there was material here for exposure in dancing. After Stravinsky, there was no other contemporary composer available whose body of work, as a whole, could serve as a possible source for repertory. And political motives were always present: a need for novelty, gimmicks that attract the press and sell expensive tickets for annual galas which do their best to diminish inevitable deficits.

The opening was graced by Madame Giscard d'Estaing, wife of the president of the French Republic; Balanchine received his Légion d'Honneur in an intermission. Violette Verdy and Jean-Pierre Bonnefous, our two French principal dancers, accompanied by Madame Madeleine Malraux, danced Ravel's pretty *Sonatine*. The diplomatic aspects of the occasion were appropriately fulfilled. As for the artistic elements, I can give only hearsay, since later I was to see only those few ballets which remained in repertory. *L'Enfant et les Sortilèges (The Spellbound Child)*, with its charming libretto by Colette, was again presented, but since it was essentially an opera with singers in the pit, expensive to rehearse and perform, it promptly vanished. One wished it could have been adopted by the New York City Opera company, with whom we share the State Theater, but over the years there has been almost no connection between our two companies, although Balanchine has brilliantly produced opera in Paris, Hamburg, Chicago, and at the Metropolitan. There would have been much to say for a policy employing advanced student apprentices from our school in their last years as members of a corps de ballet for an opera company, as is normal all over Europe, but neither singers nor their management are wildly enthusiastic about dancing; our experience with the Metropolitan Opera in the thirties gave us a taste of what may be involved in attempts to mix ballet and opera. Equally, it may have seemed normal to support a single orchestra for both opera and ballet, or at the least an orchestra and a half. This has proved equally impossible, because respective musical directors can never decide on which instrumentalists to retain; finally there has been no agreement. This situation will never be easy to resolve, since labor union negotiations are much involved. However, when one accuses the United States of being a meager supporter of performing art, one must recognize the sizable area of comparative luxury which our often wasteful affluence permits.

Jerome Robbins's treatment of *Ma Mère l'Oye* followed Ravel's own libretto to the letter. This was a portmanteau anthology of

Mother Goose children's stories, done with Robbins's colloquial mastery of dancing and action à l'improviste. Ever since his *Pied Piper* (1951), he has proved himself a wizard in the virtues of necessity, the surprising richness of poverty. When we had little money he inverted bits, pieces, and scraps into a genial mockery of lavish production values by their very denial. Using fragments of scenery from repertory that would be easily recognized by audiences which had seen them time and time again, he now constructed a ballet that was partly an in-joke and entirely a delight. He used a large company of dancers, among them very young children from our school, in a succinct narration of each fairy tale, the names of which were elegantly inscribed on ribbons pulled out of a wicker costume hamper. The work had skill and charm; it enchanted a public both new to its music and ignorant of this aspect of Robbins's professionalism. The music, in its porcelain, tautly metallic sonorities, served perfectly to italicize the action. Individual vignettes stand out: tiny Hop o' My Thumb, a midget far cleverer and braver than his seven cowardly brothers; the apotheosis, an affectionate caricature of the marriage of a Princess Aurora, staged with grandeur on a scene-shifter's ladder amidst the waving streamers of a beggar's triumph.

There were those who felt that the exquisite texture of the music's orchestration deserved a more full and exotic furnishing, but, lacking a genius for costume (the presence of a carefully careless Matisse or Derain—artists who could be placed alongside Ravel in the quality of their gifts), it would seem hard to justify a decorative elaboration that might have enhanced the canny innocence of Robbins's choreography. The Ravel Festival, like the Stravinsky Festival, was short on visual attributes; it is no secret that our repertory, unlike Diaghilev's, has made its way on dancing rather than on decor.

Suzanne Farrell left the New York City Ballet in 1969, and joined the Ballet of the Twentieth Century, Maurice Béjart's company based in Brussels. There can be no denying that her absence was mourned, not alone by Balanchine but by her partners, colleagues, and public. It is unprofitable to speculate whether such a departure should be interpreted as courage, treason, or a refusal to submit any longer to conditions that seemed at the moment confining, as well as a desire to explore alternatives in new capacities and possibilities. Such separation is sometimes necessary for one or both parties and it can become irreversible. Farrell returned in the winter before the Ravel Festival to dance with an extraordinary freshness and greatly increased technical brilliance. The years spent with Béjart, a talent and energy far more loose or instinctive than Balanchine's, seemed not only to have heightened her physical proficiency, which had always been large, but to have increased her emotional projection, which had heretofore seemed smoldering.

The first new work Balanchine composed for her was Ravel's *Tzigane*. Essentially a "gypsy number," it commenced with a five-minute solo of surpassing physical demands and emotional intensity. The music is not exactly a Hungarian cousin to the composer's *Boléro*, but its nightclub overtones cannot be ignored. Supremely well crafted, expertly scored, confidently played by Lamar Alsop, our first violinist, this music gave Balanchine, with his ever-ready tact, the opportunity to invent a star turn for Farrell. It framed her extremities of abrupt angularity and off-centered plastic posturing in all their fiery contrast to her natural "classic" grace and ease, her steely fragility and chill authority. In a perverse pattern of steps, Balanchine turned the familiar *hungarisch* idiom of opera-house Lisztian divertissements inside out. Its positioning was so odd, the sequences in their reversal so unexpected, that what might have been rejected as parody was transformed into assertive rehabilitation. Farrell did not impersonate a "gypsy"; her body played with theatricalized elements of wildness, caprice, longing, and arrant independence which could be read as intensely secret and personal. Was part of this an echo of her own wandering, of the fact she had at last returned to her tribe's encampment, while proclaiming her own increased identity and independence?

In any event, Farrell's reappearance marked a rise in the company's spirits, another chapter of growth. At the same time there arrived a new generation of young dancers from our school. The histories of ballet companies, like other institutions, can't be read as steady progress from strength to strength. Viewed from a positive period, the path seems always up, but history insists on times that must be endured as well as enjoyed. And there is no doubt that a powerful personage throws off an aura, sometimes of positive, less often of negative, energy. Farrell's peculiar qualities, the impression these have made in a variety of ballets, have contributed something unique to our repertory. Like other powerful artists she invests her own mystery, an enclosed alchemy of power, vulnerability, the control and conscious manipulation of tension. When she dances it is not only a body in motion but an apparatus analyzed and directed by operating intelligence. It is as if some sort of radium slumbers but is always present and ready in her corporal center; when ignited, it glows to white heat. It enables her to transcend occasions, patterns, appearances. It commands recognition but is not always easy to read. Balanchine has been able to provide a habitation in which this core is fired, or can activate itself. The long opening and the finale of *Tzigane*, with the entrance of Peter Martins and six boys, is such a vivid frame.

The other Balanchine work that seems to have salvaged itself from the Ravel Festival to persist in repertory is *Le Tombeau de Couperin*. Ravel had composed this not only as homage to a great predecessor of the *ancien régime*, but to the spirit of eighteenth-century *mesure*, the rational and metrical, while its gravity and haunting melancholy reflected the composer's memory of a handful of friends lost in the First World War. Whereas *Tzigane* was a piece focused on a solo dancer, *Le Tombeau* canonized the corps de ballet, a company of dancers. There are no soloists, only a double quadrille of girls and boys echoing, balancing, mirroring one another.

The atmosphere of *Le Tombeau* derives from a theatrical court manner, a style that appropriated country dances, distilling them into a discreet yet severe elegance. The floor patterns, viewed hastily, seem to be primary squares or diamonds, but these melt into one another like angular fragments of glass in a kaleidoscope. The whole suite of dances is suffused by an air of mutual consideration from single pairs to quartets, to their doublings and resolution back into original quadrilles. Sixteen dancers, costumed in practice clothes, were chosen for parity of height and proportion; they looked like a company of cousins. Their uniformity was not military; while they performed with precision they maintained a flexible, impersonal intimacy. The manners of courtiers, the high style of the eighteenth century, depend on consideration—a sense of status and obligation. The classic metaphor is the minuet, a dance designed to be gravely achieved indoors. The *Tombeau* suite might be dances done on grass in the open air; tempi are quicker; the design is not a minuet's duet but a *contredanse* quadrille. The swift accomplishment of devious figures, the sweetness of humane encounters, the delicacy of footwork, made the ballet an instant success, perhaps the single work to emerge from the Ravel Festival as an unqualified enrichment of repertory.

Since the dancers are uniformed in ordinary practice clothes and there is no distinction of individuality in the twin quadrilles, the ballet might have appeared icily impersonal, with that *ésprit frigidaire* about which Parisians complained when we first danced in France twenty-five years ago. But here, though the structure is tight, the manner is loose, as if the performers were giving themselves a party, footing measures to which they had long been accustomed. Balanchine had proven his intimacy with this genre in *Square Dance* (1957), in which he had brought a champion professional dance caller to accompany the metronomic insistence of Vivaldi and Corelli. Recently Balanchine had revived it, without the spoken calls, with a new and complex solo, brilliantly designed for and danced by Bart Cook. But there are worlds of difference separating Vivaldi and Ravel, between the optimistic urgency and driving impetus of the eighteenth century and the melancholy ripeness of Ravel's twentieth-century fragmented recension of the rococo. *Le Tombeau* has its own deliberation, but its split diagonals and fractured quarterings are imbued with a courtesy and mutual attention for which the headlong insistence and high spirits of *Square Dance* had no time.

SEPTEMBER 5, 1975: *New York*

Meeting at 25 Broadway with John Samuels III, new president of the City Center of Music and Drama, Inc. Discussion of the legal status of the New York City Ballet, its lack of autonomy, its vagueness in financing. Problems of stability, continuity, succession, possible increase of public and private support. The monstrous increase of our annual budget; the need for corporate entity.

Projections of funds needed into the 1980's, and the means to raise them.

It had taken me some months to recover from surgery. When I was well enough to work I found that a number of changes had been made in our particular world of which I was scarcely aware. The most important was the arrival of John Samuels III as chief of the legal body that controlled the rights, properties, contracts, and leases which were the concrete physical basis for the existence of the New York City Ballet. The only thing I could discover about Samuels was that there was no one who could tell me anything about him; from where he had come; indeed why or how he had become involved with our company. At the start this was puzzling and disturbing. I respected Samuels's passion for privacy, but on the other hand, one does want to learn something about the man who is charged with one's future. As an irreducible minimum, it was a matter of record that he derived from Galveston, Texas; that he had gone to college at Texas A & M; that he had graduated from the Harvard Law School, had briefly practiced law in New York, and was now seriously engaged in the coal business, specializing in industrial coal.

His office was once the boardroom of the old Cunard steamship line. It was set inside Benjamin Wistar Morris's palace, which today has suffered the ignominy of having its magnificent lobby turned into an improvised post office. The Cunard boardroom is not quite as large as Mussolini's headquarters in the Palazzo Venezia, but Mr. Samuels's office somehow suggested it. Paneled in rich Elizabethan oak, a carved ceiling rises some forty feet high. Leaded-glass windows still show ships famous in the story of trans-Atlantic navigation. A foyer holds vitrines with splendidly mounted hunks of various types of coal, polished and spotlit. This was the locus of a tycoon and bespoke a scale and background with which one was familiar from films, if not from life. I stared at an enormous unframed canvas of a Provençal landscape (by Vuilliard? Yes. By Vuilliard). All this gave me pause; by no means antagonized, I was rather bemused. Where was I? Where in a world which adorned itself like this was the New York City Ballet, whose operations, to put it at its best, were ingeniously improvised from week to week? Must I steel myself for a flying squadron of efficiency experts about to tidy up our comfortable domestic anarchy?

However, all the surrounding decor was mightily in contrast with the presence and manner of its master. This room was saturated in personality: the Cunard Line or its relics with museum-scale contemporary art; an industrial philosophy with a sense of the visual as present history. Yet Samuels himself seemed all but anonymous; his profile was so low as to be almost assertive. There would be no immediate self-betrayals. But I began to realize that there was one element here which was startling and consistent: the theatrical. There were also some big, highly polished, black African wood sculptures. Who had been responsible for the set-decorations? I felt more comfortable; we both preferred to inhabit theater. John Samuels had cast himself as a tycoon. It soon appeared he had a clear idea of what the New York City Ballet was about.

For a long time it had bothered Betty Cage and me that the title "New York City Ballet" had no legal force. It was a historical, pragmatic fiction. Our company, of itself, did not own one stick of scenery or one shred of costume. Its name was on no contract; cash given or collected for its use was deposited in no bank account which could be released by any of our signatures. The reasons for such confusion were clear enough. Ever since the death of Morton Baum at the time we entered the State Theater, preparations for which he had arranged (from our side) single-handedly, we had soldiered along on lines of procedure he had improvised before 1947. However disorderly or extralegal, these were the only ones by which he could have managed. It was his genius for improvisation, his fantastic skill in pulling rabbits out of battered silk hats, which permitted growth and survival for the New York City Opera and Ballet companies.

From 1943 through 1963 Baum had his own marvelous and mysterious ways of conducting business with the help of Edna Bauman, his single selfless secretary, and Ralph Falcone, a wizard accountant capable of keeping the entire Internal Revenue Service at bay. Throughout that time, considerable sums of money had to be manipulated. The intricacies of the Baum-Falcone methods of accountability were such, and the apparent poverty of any physical manifestations so great, that few questions resulted in punitive action. Baum conducted business as a paternalistic amateur patron-director. He assigned us our seasons and budgets. He could endure and absorb differences of opinion, often because there was seldom enough cash to permit alternatives, while Balanchine's energy and ingenuity in producing repertory compensated for any inadequacy or untidiness. We might question Mr. Baum's allocations, even his taste (which ran to the Germanic), but never his belief in our right to exist, to persist on our terms, and, through his insistence, persist we did. There was a kind of freedom or euphoria in this mode of management. It suited our needs then, but it would come to be an irrational and expensive way to conduct what had become, fatally, big business, employing about three times as many dancers, staff, and stagehands as when we had given ourselves the name of New York City Ballet in 1948, and had moved into the State Theater in 1964.

John Samuels had not entered into a connection with us without preparation, but it took me some time to discover how and why this had been effected. At first sight, contrary to the lavish surround of his office, he revealed only the manner and appearance of a classically discreet mask, that of a London banker. Meeting him was much as if I had come to ask his advice about the disposition of a fortune, which, in its way, was poetically true. To start with, we both had considerable attachment to Britain, its painters, draftsmen, horses, furniture, traditions, and tailors. This was symbolic of a discipline and taste that was not difficult to translate into terms of those principles which subsumed our ballet. I found I did not have to test his preference or question his interest in any kind of physical mastery over recalcitrant materials, animal or mineral. If he did not understand the minutiae of what went into the production and maintenance of a repertory, he understood very well its general elements. He liked fine craftsmanship; he knew this did not come cheap or quickly.

John Samuels is not given to extensive declarations or sanguine promises. While he remained something of a mystery as a man (essentially all I would ever learn of his public manifestations was from a *Fortune* article which only he could have promoted), we did discover he had adopted our company in a serious way, and that soon we were to benefit greatly from this adoption. When he was in New York he became as accessible as Morton Baum; when he was in London, he could easily be reached. What was more important, he could be found at the State Theater three or four nights a week. He never interfered with production plans or made a suggestion relative to dancers, whom he entertained generously at his several princely homes, with real talent for fun and friendliness. Gradually it became clear he identified himself with our fortunes. He precipitated the formation of an independent corporation and our individual bank account. At the end of two years he had made himself an important member of our family, one to whom we could talk about the serious, nontheatrical problems which burden and support a productive if nonprofit institution. He had come to us, almost accidentally, through the good offices of Lincoln Center for the Performing Arts, which holds and administers buildings and real estate, including the State Theater. He could have remained a nominal, token, custodial authority, but instead, through interest and use, he has been Lincoln Center's single greatest contribution to our continued existence.

NOVEMBER 15, 1975: *New York*

Balanchine seems weary; the pressure of a sixty-fourth season up and coming. Need and problem for revivals. Counting lost ballets since 1933—only these best known: *Cotillon, Errante, Gounod Symphony, Roma, Figure in the Carpet.* All forgotten, each would have to be entirely recomposed; more difficult than starting fresh with new music as with *Divertimento No. 15.* No films extant; even if there were, it would not be much help. One most regrets the marvelous dances Balanchine made for Glinka's *Russlan and Ludmila* for Hamburg in 1969; the Strauss-Lully *Bourgeois Gentilhomme* for the Ballets Russes de Monte Carlo, 1944.

Few realize that Balanchine has not only been principal choreographer of our company, but also its prime teacher and rehearsalist. When he has seemed capable of it, which has meant most mornings over three decades, Balanchine teaches "company class," a study period and seminar as much as a warmup. He says that the main thing students learn at our school is how to be useful to our company; once therein, how to *begin* to learn the way he wants them to dance. They already know how to "dance"; otherwise they would never have been selected. But what he wants is something very much in addition to what they have already learned. In the school, combinations and exercises are dictated by a dozen individual teachers without reference to any specific repertory. When dancers work with Balanchine in his "class," they are being tempered for his particular use. His classes for his company are intense, packed, concentrated with his particular kind of analysis and information. Some dancers find them exhausting; excuses have been made that they are indeed insupportable. That is, some dancers cannot support the energy, physical or mental, such exercise demands. All manner of psychosomatic aches and pains can come to the rescue of those who do not feel up to them. However, it is rare that soloists or first dancers beg off, and it is a testimony of quality for those who stick.

Balanchine's twin gifts to American dancing have been high speed and knife-edge sharpness. He has pushed acceleration of the idiom of the classic dance past what had formerly been considered limits of the physically possible or visually gracious. Before Dr. Roger Bannister smashed the psychological barrier of the four-minute mile, this was judged a physiological impossibility. Less than twenty-five years later, more than twenty seconds have been knocked off his record. There is naturally an eventual limit to be reached when lungs and legs can work no harder, but this limit scarcely seems reached. The corps de ballet in our company dance faster, more brilliantly, than the majority of secondary soloists in the various "Russian" companies (not based in the Soviet Union) danced through the 1940's. Balanchine's teaching, as he says, is toward providing "something to look at." It is not enough to look at correctly executed figures in ordinary academic display. Acrobacy is the prime stimulant for dancer and audience. Underlying everything ballet dancers do is the design of legible constructs which are visually provocative in plastic depth. Celerity is the surest spark to ignite attention in the public—along with mastery of the province of air, a disdain of gravity disguised by apparent ease.

Balanchine insists on razorlike sharpness and clarity in profile. The human silhouette must not be papery but solid, to be read as three-dimensional. Also, he has fostered an extreme athleticism, together with speed, surpassing former norms and averages. Over the years, the majority of his dancers have learned to move faster and faster, mastering more steps, motion, and changes of pace than were conceivable forty years ago. Then, a few first dancers alone could be counted on to move quickly without losing their sharp profile. By now this capacity has come to be the property of our corps de ballet as a whole. Candidates for the company from our school have had a technical training from three or four to eight years in preparation for what Balanchine ultimately requires of them. But when in the company, they find the nature of his "teaching" quite another matter, for now his instruction proposes a double tension. He hits at the very basis of the traditional dance language and at the same time proposes combinations of movement which become a novel extremity in its development. This double action is at once advanced instruction and rehearsal for repertory.

As far as rehearsing goes, here Rosemary Dunleavy, herself an experienced artist, operates with consummate efficiency, sparing Balanchine much onerous but necessary labor, because of her extraordinary memory and long familiarity with what she has herself danced and knows he needs. Among our dancers there are always replacements, for injury, absence, change; Balanchine is notorious for constant changes. These shifts reflect the emergence of new dancers, alone or in combination; personal dissatisfaction, but rarely loss of memory. Some dance critics have been continually irritated by his alterations. On the one hand it gives them a chance to prove circumspection by pinpointing the difference; on the other it enables them to diagnose a fancied weakness in the original structure. Something of the same was for a while in evidence when we moved from the City Center Mecca Temple on West 55th Street. Guardians of the old flame felt that *Gemütlichkeit* in all its dust and inconvenience had initiated something sacred, and the new State Theater was a betrayal of precious poverty, or shabby innocence. Initial experiences are sacred, not to be violated.

Balanchine has always had a certain perverse joy in changes unobtrusively made, like those in *Swan Lake*. And there have been more important emendations, alterations, elisions, and additions to a large number of his ballets, dictated less by caprice than by circumstance. The first finale for Hindemith's *Four Temperaments* appeared to resemble either a fountain, a volcano in eruption, or an atom bomb. It was designed for the stage of a high-school auditorium; when we danced on the City Center stage it was altered to its present formation. Sometimes changes are obvious to the audience; often they are apparent only to the dancers themselves. Whether they are "better" or "worse" than the "original" (chronologically first) version is a matter of taste. Any change is only one of many alternatives, of which there may be an infinite series. With an imagination as vigorous and flexible as Balanchine's, difference endlessly suggests itself. When one is continually faced with the entrance of new, fresh, unused bodies, the impulse toward change is very suggestive. His readiness to change is a combination of energy, modesty, and authority; the sense to improve or make more appropriate, a feeling of continual responsibility to new dancers and perfectible design.

Chaconne was a case in point. It had been created in 1963 for a large production of Gluck's Orfeo ed Euridice at the State Opera in Hamburg. Balanchine devised the entire production, which was imagined archaeologically somewhat in the manner of its original debut. Rouben Ter-Arutunian conceived its four acts in the visual frame of the epoch in which Gluck composed the music. It was an extremely careful, elaborate, and beautiful production, quite different in scope and spirit from that Orfeo which we presented in 1936 at the Metropolitan Opera in New York, whose radical stylization and poetic allusions to the past and present precipitated our departure from the Met. That particular production was imagined in terms of the most advanced lyric and pictorial ideas then current, through the hands and eyes of Pavel Tchelitchev, one of our epoch's most able painters and stage designers. For Hamburg, Balanchine used nothing of what he had done before at the Metropolitan. In 1936 we were working for the first time in the format of a large opera house and half-knew we were foredoomed to failure. Hence our effort was recklessly in the nature of a manifesto. In Hamburg, Balanchine was producing for a house famous for an advance-guard policy under the guidance of an astute musician and politician, Rolf Liebermann, with whom Balanchine produced Eugene Onegin, Russlan and Ludmila, and many of his Stravinsky ballets. Orfeo had been in the standard repertory ever since it was first given, just two hundred years before. No "modern" or "modernistic" commentary was called for by

Hamburg; merely close attention to the intention of the composer.

The finale of *Orfeo*, often known as "The Dance of the Happy Spirits," is a chaconne, a dance form perhaps of Spanish origin, originally a slow dance, three beats to a measure, set on a ground bass. However, the form was interpreted or adapted widely. Gluck made a set of contrasting pieces which was obligatory to terminate opera in a festive spirit in the style of the princely courts of the time. *Chaconne*, like the *Tombeau de Couperin*, is a sequence of dances in the taste of Versailles. *Tombeau* is a piece of master cabinetwork for an anonymous double quadrille; *Chaconne*, after a brief introduction in contrast to what follows, is a series of five pieces for soloists and principal dancers, individually characterized and designed as a theatrical divertissement. The costumes, white silk with accents of blue and silver, cut on an ingenious bias, were the ultimate inventions of Madame Barbara Karinska, who had enriched our wardrobe gloriously ever since we could afford decent dress. In Hamburg, singers and dancers were sumptuously clad from designs that took their spirit from the magnificent album of original watercolors by Jean Bérain in the Pierpont Morgan Library. Karinska's clothes, with their spiral twist piped in silver, looked simple. The boys' tabards, the girls' décolletage, seemed plain at first sight, with barely a difference in detail, due to the pervasive white of silk and their discretion of decoration. But, as with the choreography itself, simplicity and uniformity were deceptive; there were layers of complexity which would be revealed only on several sightings. In Hamburg the chaconne came, as normal, at the end of the opera, danced with adequate aplomb but no great bravura. It had rather a perfunctory air as the finish of an evening distinguished mostly by song. The elaboration of investiture, the visual apotheosis which the eighteenth century considered necessary, did little to draw attention to dancing or emphasize its particular quality, which here was by no means archaeological revival but rather a neoclassical ballet in Balanchine's personal patterns. He did not count on his own memory from 1963 for our New York revival in 1976; fortunately, Brigitte Thom, a gifted ballet mistress from the Hamburg Opera, had kept her own notes and memories, and reset the work in ten days.

I had flown to Hamburg for the premiere of *Orfeo*, and it was the glorious visual part of the music-drama which held me the most. I did not retain much clear notion of any dancing, except the massed choirs in the hell scene, with their marvelous sonority and the pantomime of the questions and answers accompanying Orpheus' search for his wife. When I saw *Chaconne* as costumed by Karinska and reset by Balanchine, with a wholly new introduction, it was a new ballet, in great part because of the verve and transparent style of our dancers, particularly the two beautiful duets danced by Suzanne Farrell and Peter Martins. The Hamburg Opera fifteen years ago had a corps de ballet of only comparative efficiency. With Farrell and Martins, there were incomparable performances. Ethereal serenity and floating support from Gluck's celestial melodies evoked monumental tranquillity, a buoyant peacefulness accentuated by muted nervous tension, rapid motion, and solemn strength, which lent a new depth and plasticity to Balanchine's balanced and off-balanced continuum. The abrupt acceleration, often impassive against throbbing strings, found these partners steady at dead center. While *Le Tombeau de Couperin* belongs to landscapes by Watteau or Fragonard, *Chaconne* could be imagined proceeding in some invisible throne room. The dancers were not lords and ladies playing at being happy peasants, but courtiers bringing birthday gifts to their sovereigns, who in the present drama were also first dancers.

OCTOBER, 1975: *London*

Royal Ballet School (White Lodge), Richmond Park. A class of small boys conducted by Robert Parker and Ronald Smedley, in a group of north-country work-dances. The "swords" that make the "knot" brandished at the end of the dance are not weapons but blades of whatever agricultural tools are used locally and can be hand-held. Smart style and vivid presentation of very well-trained kids under fifteen years old. The richness of the British forms of folk dance still extant.

Madame Ninette de Valois, heroic founder of the Royal Ballet, has always been interested in the traditions of folk dancing. Due to her attention, its study and practice was introduced into the curriculum of the junior division of the Royal Ballet School. Their handsome home is a transformed sixteenth-century royal hunting lodge in a great wooded park. Parker and Smedley, the first an instructor in athletics and body movement, the other a well-known BBC television producer, had been chosen as key instructors by the British Folk Dance Society, founded in 1911 by Cecil Sharp to preserve the patrimony of dance and music of the British Isles, which descends uninterruptedly from five centuries of performing, collecting, and remembering. One is surprised at both the variety and the spectacular quality of pattern and movement in a genre of dancing which is often put down as more fun to do than to watch. Arrangements were made to invite Smedley and Parker to teach at our School of American Ballet, as additive and alternative to classic ballet. Years before we had tried to find other alternatives by way of national dances of Spain, Poland, or Russia, as well as the so-called modern dance. There was always something specious in our students attempting Spanish heeltaps and castanets. Actually, preparing them might have served toward opera-dances, but had little point in our particular repertory. As for "modern" dance, it soon became clear that Balanchine's invention in his heterodox design was more extreme than exercises proposed by followers of the principal American "modernists."

The group folk-dances that Parker and Smedley arranged for our annual Workshop performances were extremely successful. As for alternative movement and gesture, there was a free-ranging freedom within elastic limits which our students greatly enjoyed, together with a chance for adding bits of mimetic social comment. Morris, country, and sword dances were taught and presented with gusto. Later programs were expanded to include ballroom dances of late Victorian and Edwardian vintages—Boston, bunny-hug, turkey trot, and tango. When Balanchine came to mount the "Royal Navy" episode of *Union Jack*, Smedley and Parker were on hand to supply a touch of expert information on the sailors' hornpipe.

As for the birth and development of *Union Jack* itself: events marking the two-hundredth anniversary of the founding of our republic were not celebrated with much energy, emphasis, or panache. Unlike 1876, there was no great international exhibition such as the one held in Fairmount Park, Philadelphia. Nor was there any Walt Whitman to recite a centennial ode, as he had for disrespectful Dartmouth undergraduates. The observance of our bicentennial was tepid and perfunctory. This was perhaps wisdom; self-propelled patriotism was scarcely in fashion; the brave panoply of glorious war was muted in the aftermath of Vietnam. As for the New York City Ballet, we had contributed our patriotic due in 1958, with *Stars and Stripes*. *The Birds of America* still remained on a low back-burner, but as time went on and this big ballet didn't get itself done, projections toward it expanded to a gigantic format and scale that seemed only to doom any immediate production.

Nevertheless, an occasion celebrating two centuries of the nation's history could scarcely be ignored, even if the external promptings of journalistic and political pressures were both strained and pallid. How to avoid a smell of self-serving chauvinism, when many if not most of us felt, with Wystan Auden: "I'm not an American; I'm a New Yorker." In fact, where *did* our country first come from? The Vikings, Spain, France. Importantly, Britain, the United Kingdom: England, Scotland, and Wales. Here was something that meant much to me personally. Since a small child I had had the sharpest and most romantic feelings about Britain. My father was a passionate Anglophile; he raised me on King Arthur, Robin Hood, David Balfour, David Copperfield, and Kim. Balanchine had served not only Diaghilev in London but also Charles Cochran, whose musicals then dominated the West End popular theater. From 1924 through 1930, Balanchine also worked in revues and films. In 1926, for Diaghilev, he mounted *The Triumph of Neptune*, a ballet-spectacle the libretto of which Sacheverell Sitwell pasted together from the Pollock "penny plain, tuppence-colored" toy theaters of early Victorian childhood. The British music hall was then very much alive with its highly stylized mimicry, song, and dancing.

Some years before, Balanchine had started thinking about an evening of ballet to be called *Entente Cordiale*. It would open with *Stars and Stripes*, continue with *Union Jack*, and finish with *Tricolore*. *Entente Cordiale* wasn't a bad handle as a catchword, although it didn't mean much literally. As a matter of strict fact—which certainly in our world of ballet deters no one—there exists a specific political significance. From about 1904 to 1906, maneuvers were in hand to maintain the balance of power in Europe (and

Asia). Initiatives taken by the government of Edward VII forged an alliance among Britain, France, and Russia, anticipating Germany's increasing sea power, which eventually led to the First World War. In this, the United States played no part, but the title *Entente Cordiale*—a "cordial agreement or hearty understanding" —somehow stuck. I remonstrated that from neither dictionary nor history book did the Edwardian title have any application to what we were doing. But Balanchine believed *entente cordiale* had an appetizing ring to it; it vibrated with some vague echo in his mind, and accuracy was not in question. For the French portion, Georges Auric, a composer with whom Balanchine had worked with Diaghilev through the twenties, was commissioned to write the score for 1978's *Tricolore*.

Union Jack celebrated America's bicentennial by canonizing ceremonial Britain. It seized rituals of army, navy, and popular theater as a basis for massive spectacle. It was one of the most carefully considered, prepared, designed, and produced works for which we have been responsible; it emerged as one of the most successful as well. To start with, there was a certain piquancy in the idea of observing a national birthday by an affectionate tribute to an ancient ancestor and onetime enemy. The scale of design in Rouben Ter-Arutunian's sets was as large as the number of dancers deployed by Balanchine. The music, chosen and orchestrated from traditional folk, Victorian, and Edwardian popular sources, was by Hershy Kay, who had done similar service for *Western Symphony* (1954), which could be listed as our first "American" ballet, and *Stars and Stripes* (1958), a repertory stalwart which would become the introduction to *Entente Cordiale*. The first part of *Union Jack*, a parade of seven Scottish Guards' regiments, had been anticipated in *Scotch Symphony* (1952), in which Balanchine's use of Scottish dancing in kilts was inspired by the company's first visit to the Edinburgh Festival.

Any strictly "authentic" folk- or national dancing is limited as captivating spectacle as soon as its social charm or open-air freshness wears off. Folk-dancing may have some acrobatic elements, but it is designed for the general "folk," not for professional performers. Steps and figures tend to repeat, for it has a primarily societal function; it is only incidentally theatrical. Hence, faced with the problem of inventing a large and expansive dance work, Balanchine composed a series of classical variations on the Highland fling, reels, and other patterns that bore little resemblance, except in spirit, to what a kilted regiment of enlisted soldiers might manage, but which brilliantly suited male ballet dancers and their unisexed partners on pointe. Choreographic interest was as much in the strategy, shuttle, and shift of blocks of seven "regiments" as in the characteristic movements which they performed. The dance design opposed these blocks in off-beat, mirrored, and contrapuntal motion of unraveling massed and individual groups. Seventy dancers in teams of ten wove across the stage as a metaphorical reflection of the warp and woof of seven sets of tartans in the dancers' costumes, provided by a Canadian firm which specialized in tailoring traditional military kilts and sporrans.

The opening of *Union Jack* is set against a child's shiny paper cutout of a great arch, the towers of which could be a twin Big Ben, or Tower Bridge. Balanchine never before had used so many dancers who actually performed; here were no spear-carriers or extras. We could now assemble a strong cast, among whom the girls' regiment wearing the tartan of MacDonald of Sleat, led by Karin von Aroldingen, was outstanding. It was as if there was an abrupt burst of rapid machine-gun fire from her toe shoes. What Balanchine accomplished in orchestrating his regiments seemed managed as much by mathematics, by some non-Euclidean geometry, as by the idiom of ballet. *Union Jack* is a lyric military panorama, a parade of symmetrical and asymmetrical action, suffused in an atmosphere of orderly service and ritual observance. Also, there is a sober overtone of nostalgic, sunset sadness, an echo of other times when indeed the sun never set on a world empire. At the end of the Scottish section, light fades; the regiments disappear into blackness framed by the tall toy towers.

Instead of trying to cap this extended overture, which could be more than enough in itself for an entire single ballet, Balanchine chose to follow it with what might have seemed the wildest contrast. Patricia McBride and Jean-Pierre Bonnefous dash in, a costermonger king and queen, in the glorious uniform of pearl buttons, the traditional regalia of their street-peddler tribe. Costermongers, traditional apple sellers, were for long familiar figures in the English music halls, using popular tunes and traditional kicks and bumps that American vaudeville would later borrow. Balanchine adapted the style of McBride's balletic elegance, framing it in the sweetly sentimental mimicry of a husband-and-wife "misunderstanding." The proffered property-flower, the fake gin bottle, the property-umbrella were formal as the guardsman's dirk, baton, or sword. Bonnefous, who danced like a combination of Maurice Chevalier and young Charlie Chaplin, and McBride, combining regal flirtatiousness with Irish lace-curtain wit, were joined by two small girls from our ballet school in a costermonger's cart, filled with the (property) apples of their trade. Bets were taken as to whether or not the very mild-mannered donkey drawing the cart would be naughty or not. Only at the premiere did he misbehave.

The third section celebrated the Royal Navy. Ter-Arutunian made a cutout of sails and waves, as if clipped by giant nail-scissors —Portsmouth Harbor, with ships-of-the-line at anchor seen from shore. Balanchine's hornpipes set two boys and a girl, then two girls and a boy; then a ship's company of fifty boys and girls in blue and white, white and blue. Peter Martins transformed his stance and dress from stiffly bearing his tall black bonnet of clan Menzies to a raunchy bosun's summer whites. Suzanne Farrell as a most angelic WREN (Woman's Royal Naval Service) pranced in to the "Colonel Bogie" march, which everyone has whistled since *The Bridge on the River Kwai*. She accented a change of mood and pace from action which up to then had seemed merely jolly or frolicsome. "Colonel Bogie" in the orchestra abruptly brought dancing into our own period. Everything before it was a reference to some past time, however persistent as echoes in the present. Farrell's shameless musical-comedy stylization, her marvelously delivered hard-sell and smashing execution, could be rooted only in today. Just as abruptly, the mood changed again. As the entire depth of the stage was filled successively by enormous silk crosses of St. Andrew of Scotland, St. Patrick of Ireland, and St. George of England, the dancers stood at attention, dwarfed by the gigantic, completed Union Jack. And then, to "Rule Britannia," red-and-yellow semaphore flags were pushed to the dancers from the wings and (having been instructed by a British naval attaché) the entire company wigwagged GOD SAVE THE QUEEN. As the curtain fell, cannon thundered the royal fleet's salute (over the loud-speaker system set in the State Theater's balconies).

Union Jack, despite light-heartedness and comic allusions, had its more pensive aspects. It commenced with a martial review and ended with a stately naval salute to the Throne. In the middle, homage was paid to the hardihood and fantasy of the Anglo-Saxon balladeer's loyalty. There is, of course, something personal that artistic management contributes to every production—however mysterious or invisible it may be to an audience. With *Union Jack* there were elements of personal memory that may have lent bits of color and gesture to the whole. Balanchine's five years with Diaghilev's London seasons made him familiar not alone with the Savoy and Savile Row, the Sitwells, Covent Garden, the variety halls, certain great country houses, and press lords, but the persistence and use of British pageantry as a vivid visual celebration.

My father had been a colleague of Gordon Selfridge, founder of the huge Oxford Street emporium. Both merchants had employed Daniel Burnham, the great Chicago architect and city planner, to design their respective shops. My father held Anderson & Shepherd as the kings of custom tailoring. He dressed me at the age of five in a naval rating's uniform, with a miniature silver bosun's pipe, from Rowe of Gosport. Twenty-five years later I would stand at the corner of Piccadilly and St. James's Street, watching George V, seated in an open landau, accompanied by the Household Cavalry, driving back from St. Paul's. There had been a national thanksgiving service for his recovery from serious illness. His face was as gray as his hair and beard; he looked as if carved for some royal tomb. He was my king, too.

In 1950, after our rather calamitous debut at the Royal Opera House, Covent Garden, Richard Buckle, the critic and ballet historian who almost alone in London had enthusiastically welcomed us, took my wife and me for a late drink to St. James's Palace, where the Earl of Harewood was camping out in tall white bare rooms amidst heaps of crates and stuffed hampers. He was just about to move into a home of his own. Champagne was broken out; he liked American music and American dancers; over the years we became friends. A cousin of the Queen, he is also in his own right a considerable personage. Son of the Princess Royal and Viscount Lascelles, he had been a prisoner of war in Germany, later directed the Edinburgh Festival, and more recently has led the English National Opera Company into an extraordinary position of imaginative efficiency, due to his professional musicality and gift for command. So it seemed a happy notion to ask Lord and Lady Harewood to be guests of honor at the official bicentennial occasion marked by the premiere of *Union Jack*. To observe the formalities, the Vice President of the United States, who had given us our State Theater, commemorating the three-hundredth anniversary of the founding of New York City, in 1964, forwarded his and our invitation. It was accepted. The British ambassador, with a large diplomatic assistance, helped us celebrate the brilliant premiere of one of our most popular ballets.

Stars and Stripes had been a good-natured parody of a patriotic number from some musical of the thirties, something the British call a "send-up." I was slightly nervous that *Union Jack* would strike true Britons as a joke in poor taste, since Americans are rarely licensed to treat alien traditional material lightly. But my friend Paul Findlay, who works in a responsible position at Covent Garden, was also present. I was anxious for his expert opinion which would rather key our inclusion of the ballet in programs at the Royal Opera House, if and when we could accept its long-standing invitation to return to Covent Garden for the first time since 1965. Paul said, "It makes me proud to be an Englishman."

JUNE, 1976: *New York*

Lincoln Center Council meeting. I was called to defend the New York City Ballet in refusing to be televised for "Live from Lincoln Center" programs. Since money involved is derisory and artistic increment nil, I was something less than polite. Other constituents feel not only that this purely negative attitude is damaging to the notion of a cultural center, but also that conditions may improve if there is present participation.

I've never owned a television set; the few times I've watched local programs in hospital, in the houses of friends, or in bars, I've been amply confirmed in my distaste. I know British TV is better and BBC programs on "educational" networks appear as the best that can be shown. Balanchine has a rooted dislike of being dictated to by TV directors, but he *has* telecast our *Nutcracker* on several occasions; in 1958 for CBS he himself played Drosselmeyer. Even in those prehistoric days emission wasn't much to boast about. Commercial TV directors and their staffs always start by admitting they know nothing about ballet, but are experts in TV, which means they know next to nothing about any visual aspect important to choreographers. What they know about are the conditions imposed by advertising, which is the sole reason and support for any cash one can earn by the medium, except token prestige occasionally thrown in to sweeten a smelly pot.

In a brilliant essay in the *Times Literary Supplement* (London), in June, 1976, Professor Edward Mendelson of Yale gave an extended surgical analysis of the conditions of television. I sent copies of the article to a dozen titans of the media. It obviously stuck in their throats, for I never received an answer, even in defense. Mendelson's thesis was simply that nothing on commercial television, even by way of "creative" shows, can afford to compete with the advertising that pays for the program. Nothing produced by way of entertainment can consciously attempt to obliterate the drumbeat of the market message. Naturally, for the aim of TV is neither art nor education, unless it is thought that either as pretexts may sell more gas, beer, soap, or cars. This policy infiltrates the lowest member of a camera crew and makes the lens itself enemy to any essential integrity. Photography of dancing is a special problem, apart from any possible commercial exploitation, because of the built-in limitations of the very size of the TV box. Three-dimensional plasticity is always deformed through the lens, color falsified, and the angles and editing, promising to make ballet "more interesting," are usually an irrelevant betrayal.

Also, since the nature of merchandising is to buy cheap and sell dear, there's little money left for the likes of dancers, as opposed to the exorbitant rewards to popular singers or actors. The networks now occasionally propose an exposure of ballet, as enlargement of our audience, a popular or populist expansion. Ballet companies should feel lucky to be exploited by the wonderful people who give us murder, mayhem, discreet incest, divorce, brain damage, etc. The dreadful facts of life which corroborate trash, waste, and boredom have, hidden in their fat plastic garbage bags, a few shards of residual political truth. Even ballet's continued existence is political; to survive one cannot be intransigent as a saint, and choose a suicidal canonization. Along with the need for cash, of which politics is a paramount condition, compromise is hardly absent from popular art (like ballet). But we are not lucky in being able to call it truly "popular" even at this point.

The New York City Ballet travels little. Its scale is now too large for any but the larger cities to cover touring costs; then only for at least a two-week engagement, or, under unusual circumstances in an unusual place like West Palm Beach. We are funded in part by the National Endowment for the Arts, and by the New York State Council on the Arts. We were and are grateful to Nancy Hanks and Kitty Carlisle Hart, with their staffs and committees, for enlightened and continuing support. But what was Nancy Hanks to say to Republican congressmen who could ask questions about the *New York City* Ballet, which gave more performances in Russia (twice), Britain (three times), Israel, Japan, Australia, Greece, Poland, Germany, France (four times), and Italy than in America outside New York. "New York is not America." We haven't been west of the Mississippi in years, although we will go to Chicago and tour upper New York State in 1979. So—what's our exculpatory answer? TV, natch.

The practice and craft of politics is unavoidable for any institution that touches public monies, and this can also be extended to those that beg from private or semipublic sources. But there is a difference between beggars, who need funds to sustain themselves, and competitors for the manipulation of large fiscal power. Cultural beggars are more politely termed courtiers, although their struggle for money frequently occurs in arenas more like the office of a headmaster in a parochial school or a police precinct than Florence or Versailles. Wallace Stevens, for years officer of an insurance company in Hartford, Connecticut, and at the same time one of the important poets of his epoch, said: "The imagination that is satisfied by politics . . . has not the same value as the imagination that seeks to . . . compose a fundamental poetry."

There are government and foundation handouts to poets. Otto Kahn, after J. P. Morgan one of the most discerning of our music and art patrons, indeed supported the fundamental poetry of Hart Crane. But the distinction between "fundamental" and every other quality of lyric-making is too complex a question to leave to popular politics. Despite the populist politician, certain

crafts must live by elitist criteria, and it is this standard of fundamental superiority which television touches at its peril.

As for Lincoln Center, I have about as much sympathy for
its need to find an eleemosynary face as for the beauties of TV
itself. Someday I may wish to detail the tale of Lincoln Center as
I saw it built, and while normal political accommodations have
been made, and gentlemanly courtesies obtain, it is a fact of life
that one scarcely loves one's landlord. Lincoln Center is a real-
estate holding company which aspires to some positive social role.
It acts no worse or better than any other landlord; for the charitable cash it collects annually is something of a convenience. One
would hate to be dependent upon its tender mercies if one were
in danger of bankruptcy. There was little in the philanthropy of its
overall umbrella to make me soften to its insistence on televising
us "Live from Lincoln Center." It was emphasized that previous
telecasts were wildly successful, that the Nielsen ratings were
astronomical; fan letters flowed in like a grateful avalanche. Maybe
it even attracted new subscribers or ticket buyers. It was a fact
that millions saw something or other on the tube which reflected
something or other that was happening in the flesh around the
fountain of Lincoln Center Plaza.

So—for political reasons, exterior and interior—we let them
televise *Coppélia*, "live." It passed well enough, that is, not much
worse than static duets or trios of grand opera or uninteresting
photography of string sections of orchestras sawing away while the
ecstatic conductor contributes an act that resembles torture by
laser beams or preparation for his crucifixion. Despite Balanchine's
earnest pleas, "experts" involved determinedly set their camera in
the top balcony of the State Theater so that dancers shot from
there looked as if they were wriggling on the stage through the
wrong end of an opera glass. This was to prove that the event was
indeed veritably "live," and had not been previously taped. Which
seemed only to prove that if one buys a cheap seat at the State
Theater, one can't see anything. This struck me as miserable advertising, but I'm no expert.

Several months before this, Balanchine was persuaded to go
to Nashville, Tennessee, to produce some portions of his ballets
for NET. I didn't go. He liked Merrill Brockway, the director,
our dancers were fairly paid, the studio was large, conditions were

excellent; the twin resultant programs were well received, and there will be more of them. One should not, I suppose, deprive people all over the country who have never seen our repertory of the experience or even pleasure of acquaintanceship with our company, however remote.

There are, however, films of dancers which when translated to a big screen are beautiful. The few minutes of Baryshnikov dancing in *The Turning Point*, an otherwise preposterous camp, were magical. Nureyev's version of *Don Quixote*, produced in Australia with an excellent local cast, was very well done. The best filmed sequence I have ever seen was the opening of Ken Russell's marvelous *Valentino*, which, like many other first-rate works, at first showing gained no success. It not only revealed a great dancer as an equally great actor, but in the climactic boxing match, it photographed one of the most astonishing *pas de deux* ever filmed. What was virtual perfection in setting, speech, music, and dancing was Nureyev as Valentino teaching Anthony Dowell as Nijinsky the tango, in a vast hotel ballroom, circa 1914. Nureyev's concentration ignites Dowell into a dazzling sequence of virtuoso acrobatics, which Russell's camera caught to perfection. Reduced to the dimensions of the TV screen, it would have seemed miniaturized puppetry. Films in theater still hold reflections of human breath, blood, and muscle. They may be tailored to cash for the producer, but often enough they are admirable or even heroic. Commercial TV is a parasitic infection in which mendacity competes with irrelevance. "Educational" side effects may offer some palliation; war has always improved the practice of surgery.

OCTOBER, 1976: *New York*

Inevitability of a strike by musicians of our orchestra. I have neither the energy nor the experience to negotiate a new contract. General depression and gloom, despite knowledge that every strike ends some time; that we have survived more or less the same thing every three years for twelve years.

The worst thing that ever happened to the New York City Ballet was the musicians' strike of 1976. It seemed worse than other strikes which, as far as contributing factors go, were almost identical, because elements of the rational were almost completely absent. It is significant that in all our history, we have never been threatened by a strike of our stagehands or (except in 1973, when they decided to anticipate an orchestra strike) our dancers. Stagehands make a good living; they are often older men accustomed to rough work, but with us, in constant contact with young people and children, they always behave in a paternal or fraternal manner, as if they were senior members of the same tribe, or uncles in the same family. They practice a craft; their handling of schedules and scenery in our complex repertory has been a model of professional efficiency and goodwill. Their response to the light-handed control of our production-stage manager, Ronald Bates, and his loyal staff members, Kevin Tyler, Roland Vasquez (an ex-dancer from our company), and Perry Silvey, has always been prompt, uncomplaining, and silent. Our stage, and what transpires there when inhabited by dancers, has to be controlled and maneuvered like a logistical operation. Balanchine radiates calm characterized by nonverbal communication. I've also known the atmosphere of theatrical enterprise which indulged itself in hysteria, disorder; the euphoria of egotistical desperation. But not with us. Ronnie Bates learned his unflappability in the Army. I'm on record as admiring martial art; my ambition has always been for the United States to support a service school, in the style of a West Point, for the dance. Balanchine was brought up in the quasi-seminarian discipline of the Russian Imperial School. Stagehands, dancers, and stage staff are silent servers of order and display.

With musicians of our orchestra, the situation is entirely different. In attempting to explain the basis of their contention in past, present, or future strikes, it is naturally hard for me to be "fair," since my credo always starts with the belief that there is no absolute justice. I won't list minutiae of our strike, attempt to indicate the fever chart of negotiation or the politics and by-play of frustration, rage, hate, and fatigue which are common to much labor action. It is only fair to record that our side had a strong team led by staff members—Betty Cage, Barbara Horgan, Eddie Bigelow—who were supported past the extremes of responsibility or duty by our board members, John Samuels III, Frederick Beinecke II, and Robert Gottlieb. A strike such as ours, indeed possibly the majority of other strikes, is a combination of nervous breakdown, fierce internecine skirmishes, and tragedies of errors caused by accidental, political, conscious, and helpless motivation. The hours and hours of numbing negotiation, goodwill and ill will, cross-questioning and cross-examining, were to a great degree smoothed and mitigated by the expert handling of Vincent Mc-Donnell, chairman of the State Board of Labor Arbitration.

The musicians' strike was not about nothing. What that something amounted to is easy to locate but difficult to diagnose. The musicians acted from a profound sense of dissatisfaction which aimed itself at New York City Ballet, but which was itself essentially rooted in history. What is a ballet orchestra? A band of instrumentalists engaged to play music. What sort of music? Scores that impel dancing. Where do the dancers perform? On the stage. Where do the musicians perform? In the pit. As far as quality goes, the orchestra of the New York City Ballet led by Robert Irving is perhaps the best ballet orchestra in the world. It is certainly comparable with the orchestra of the Metropolitan Opera Association (which also has had its quota of labor trouble). Ballet orchestras and opera orchestras play in orchestra pits, not on the stage of symphony halls. Their repertory is not the symphonic repertory; it is a limited list of repeated scores. Unseen and infrequently recognized by audiences, musicians have gone through training as long and onerous as dancers who, by and large, are younger, and who receive individual appreciation if not adulation. Musicians enter their training with as much expectation as dancers. At first, it is perhaps youth which permits them to be content as a collective and semi-anonymous body.

Strikes are protests, and in their early stages contain a fluid euphoria for the strikers which amounts to an invigorating release. Strike funds are still unspent; a sense of autonomous freedom from ordinary routine makes any quick compromise unreal and undesirable. Unless strikes are settled early on, euphoria changes to firm negations of all rational possibility, and as excitement leaks away, negotiation solidifies into stubborn leaden reiteration. As our strike continued, serious consequences arose. Balanchine's impatience was manifest; he spoke of leaving for Europe, where every capital opera house beckoned him. Dancers were released to find work, and many found it. Ultimately the season was canceled (and only a few weeks restored at the end). Our loss was in the neigh-borhood of a million dollars. This marked the lowest point of thirty years endured by our company. Press and public, generally speaking, supported dancers as against musicians. When the strike was at last settled, the orchestra was roundly booed. For a time our conductor Robert Irving would not bring them to their feet to receive their well-earned applause before the final ballet of the evening. Today, all this is half-forgotten—except by those (I sus-pect on both sides) who suffered wounds in the war, for it was indeed a battle, a battle that threatened the existence and con-tinuity of our company.

However, six months after the strike, our recovery was almost complete and a mysterious resurrection asserted itself. From the worst of worlds, almost abruptly began an ascension onto a plateau we had never reached before, as if great nature were compensating for one of history's wasteful, absurd, and painful seizures.

FEBRUARY 3, 1977: *New York*

A series of divertissements by August Bournonville set by Stanley Williams, senior male teacher at the School of American Ballet. Balanchine's comments on Danish style distinguished from Russian academic dance of the nineteenth century; the pedagogi-cal uses of Bournonville's choreography as a strong alternative to Petipa and Ivanov.

Despite his British birth and name, Stanley was trained in the Royal Danish Academy for a career in Copenhagen, where, in 1930 and 1931, Balanchine served as ballet master. Stanley first came to our school as guest teacher in 1960 and has taught with us ever since. His arrangements of dances he knew from his youth for our annual Workshops impressed us not only for the technical address of his students, but for genuine interest of the choreography by August Bournonville (1805–79), a gifted and prolific ballet master who, single-handed, created a style and repertory which have hardly a parallel in character or quality. He inherited strains of Franco-Italian classicism formed in the eighteenth century. His dance designs were quite different from although parallel to the more famous French, Russian, and Italian choreographers of his time. The Royal Danish Ballet showed his revived work in repertory to American audiences, while Danish dancers introduced several of his ballets into the repertory of American companies. The criterion, or standard of authenticity, for these reproductions was, of course, their current Danish recension. When we asked Stanley Williams, who had performed in these works throughout his career as dancer, he made it clear he would strive toward the spirit rather than any extant letter of Bournonville's original intention.

The Royal Opera House in Copenhagen is not a large house. Its stage is comparatively small, judged by dimensions of our own State Theater. Bournonville's ballets, by and large, were narrative pantomimes interspersed with brilliant dances, but also employing crowds of supernumeraries, children, and spectacular theatrical elements. Stanley sent to Copenhagen for the original costume designs of the portions to be staged, but we would have no scenery, crowds, supers, or children. He presented an essential sampling of Bournonville's attitude and ambience in a space perhaps twice that of the original. Bournonville's patterns were severely delimited by the theatrical conditions that obtained in his time. His range of bodily movement was by no means as wide as developments since. His scale, set against our physical extensions, was small. His idiom was circumscribed and, although much of it required brilliance and control, would seem to our audiences comparatively simple contrasted with contemporary acrobatics. However, the manner of execution, a certain deliberateness, an impending suspension in the boys' leaps, a rigid frontality which was not exactly static but seemed set, posed, almost fixed, lent a curious, attractive, and piquant air to sharp movement and gesture.

From the moment the curtain rose on a corps de ballet of black-jacketed fishermen and peasant girls, there was an air of strangeness, or difference from classicism bred by Russian teachers. Our dancers performed with a kind of cool joy reflecting northern skies and harbors. There was little of the expansive grand manner of an imperial court, yet folk elements, such as one might detect, were transformed by an exuberant elegance which could only have come from a noble theater. In the set of dances taken from contrasting ballets, we had the advantage of a strong native

Danish contingent, Peter Martins, Adam Lüders, Ulrik Trojaborg, and the ever impressive Helgi Tomasson, an Icelander but one as familiar with Copenhagen as with Reykjavik.

Stanley Williams had not aimed at satisfying Danish nationalism nor the logical objections of dance historians who had known the choreography surviving in its native habitat. He reconstructed a ballet of interest, using an unfamiliar vocabulary, adapted to conditions of our times and company. Well received at its first performances, it seemed to have only a single failing, lack of a finale. Later, the familiar tarantella from *Napoli* (1842) was put into rehearsal. Its original eight couples were increased to ten to fill our stage; the mimicry of the individual couples was carefully traced and danced with abandon. Balanchine was enthusiastic, and the piece took permanency in our repertory.

It was perhaps odd that Balanchine was so happy about Bournonville. Possibly he sensed a source, not alone in the carved profiling and odd reversals of steps, but also in the clarity and dispatch of patterned sequences. Also, there was the weight of apostolic succession, an unbroken line of breeding, bits of which contributed to his own mastery. Balanchine's favored teacher was Pavel Gerdt, instructor of the senior class of the Imperial School, master also of Fokine, Nijinsky, and Karsavina. Gerdt's teacher had been Christian Johansson, a famous Swedish dancer, who died in Petersburg in 1903; he was partner to Taglioni, teacher of Pavlova, Preobrajenska, and Kschessinska. Johansson's master was Auguste Bournonville, who visited Petipa at the Maryinsky Theater and heard him complain that Russian court audiences suffered from divertissementitis and had no interest in serious ballet.

APRIL, 1977: *New York*

Balanchine proposes an "Austrian Evening": Mozart *Divertimento No. 15*, which now has the best all-around cast since its premiere in 1956; a ballet on Salome with music by Alban Berg; and a big waltz number. What can Balanchine do different from, or superior to, *La Valse* or *Liebeslieder Walzer*? Are we being pushed toward future Scandinavian, Iberian, or Polish evenings?

I remember *Panamerica* (1960), when we offered eight ballets from Latin America, as not the happiest of gimmicks.

Requirements of showmanship for filling a big theater by appealing to a large (and, it is hoped, growing) popular audience may not seem one of the prime preoccupations of a ballet company frequently chided for its elitism and disdain for the commercial star system. That we have been able to survive as an institution based on an almost monolithic repertory of a minimum of well-worn pieces is due to choices Balanchine and Jerry Robbins have risked their power to make, and make work. Balanchine has never played his piano in an ivory tower; he's drummed and thumped it just above sounds from the street. Time and again he has cannily estimated appetites of the public at a particular moment. Instead of corroborating taste or catering to the already convinced, he has offered pieces ahead of the easiest consumption.

Also he has made harsh judgments for those who remember ballets we wish he might revive. Revivals are almost more doubtful to make work than novelties; the original circumstances can never be repeated. The first roster of dancers can never be duplicated. I have always felt that both the Schubert-Tchelitchev *Errante* (1935) and the Kurt Weill–Ter-Arutunian *Seven Deadly Sins* (1958) with Wystan Auden's ingenious English translation would be welcome additions. But Balanchine feared that *Errante* with its Loie Fuller veils and rainbow lights might seem old-fashioned, while *The Seven Deadlies* would be lost without a singer of the caliber of Lotte Lenya (for a while, in 1977, it looked as if Bette Midler might be available). It is neither simple nor easy to plan, and then score, a "hit." However, the apotropaic superstition that warns against assumptions of success is indeed a superstition. The possibility of failure can be diminished, to a degree, by analytical process. Hits, on a level of median or lower taste, are not hard to strike, but a hit on uncompromising terms of taste, surprise, and excellence demands the attention which only long experience plus intelligence brings. It was at once safe and daring to risk the parade of large forces of time, music, and money on a subject that has already been treated repeatedly and even exhaustively. But now, as usual, Balanchine took his impetus from the orchestra.

Although he had designed waltz-ballets for decades to scores by Beethoven, Brahms, Johann Strauss, and Vittorio Rieti, there remained masterpieces in dance literature he had not touched. *Vienna Waltzes* would be neither a history of a dance form nor a mimed drama. It would use Viennese popular music in the atmosphere of the place in which and for which it was written. This was the spirit and personification of the myth of a town which made the waltz its own, whether in band music in public parks, music hall, or light opera; ultimately, in great palaces and public ballrooms. Following Balanchine, Ter-Arutunian—the designer who had come to be our collaborator in much the same way that Diaghilev employed Alexandre Benois and Léon Bakst—naturally took his key from the music. Scenically, *Vienna Waltzes* is among the most richly appropriate and stylish suggestions of site and situation we have ever been given.

An orchestral prelude dissolves its brief brilliance into the penetrating tinkle of a Hungarian cymbalom; the curtain rises on a large tree-filled parkscape of "The Vienna Woods." Karin von Aroldingen, in a ball gown of slipper-satin flesh-pink, strolls in among the trees on the arm of Sean Lavery, an ash-blond hussar in black and gold. This very young man, quite new to our company, had not been trained in our school but had his apprenticeship in several European companies. He combined excellent technical efficiency with an understated, stylized, but very appealing elegance which manfully suited von Aroldingen's strong, ravishing languor. Balanchine's choreography fed couples into the forest one by one; finally the stage was filled with a regiment of green-uniformed officers with their full satin-skirted partners in shades of blush rose.

During rehearsals, five chairs placed in depth had stood for five very tall plane tree trunks, serving to guide the dancers in an obstacle course of avoidance. The waltz threaded around the trees, but so as not to lose the visual flow of movement, Ter-Arutunian's trees were constructed of transparent netting stretched on steel armatures, so that the shifting waltzers were never wholly invisible. The end of "Tales from the Vienna Woods" reversed its beginning, with the slow disappearance, arm in arm, of the black-uniformed cavalier and his partner; the cymbalom echoed the opening; then the orchestra swelled into its final chord.

"Tales" was followed by "Voices of Spring," a purely balletic interlude, enchantingly danced by Patricia McBride and Helgi Tomasson, with eight girls on pointe costumed in woodland pinks, browns, and greens, under a canopy of filtered light and green leaves. "Voices of Spring" was abruptly capped by Johann Strauss's "Explosion Polka," in which eight dancers led by Sally Leland and Bart Cook, preposterously dressed as *incroyables, merveilleuses,* and music-hall girls, seemed to have strayed into the forest from a popular ball. This was by no means a waltz; it served as a flagrant contrast to what had been and would be revealed. It was as if one were given a sip of strong liqueur or iced sherbet to clear the palate of too rich a mouthful of chocolate and whipped cream. Balanchine was not allowing cloying familiar melody to diminish the freshness of new dances. Then the forest slowly disappeared; the scene changed to a sumptuous evocation of a restaurant-nightclub in the manner of 1900. Ter-Arutunian used highly reflective copper and silver surfaces with a backdrop of stretched and stiffened Mylar to build an enormous mirror. All through the first part of the ballet, the mirror had glinted intermittently through forest leaves. Now more shone through rococo swirls of the nightclub's decor, framing the magical waltz from Lehár's *Merry Widow.* Although steadfastly performed by Kay Mazzo as the Widow and Peter Martins as the Danilo figure, in imperial Austrian uniform, this was not the strongest portion of the ballet. There were not enough people on the stage—the other dancers were changing costume for the final waltz—yet the large-scaled scene demanded a more massive body of motion. Almost at once Balanchine started altering details of costume; sooner or later a means for adding more dancers would be found. Then he decided on a complete change in choreography and clothes, but as usual, exterior pressures, a new season coming up, and overwhelming success of the remainder of the piece prevented the assigning of time, money, or concentrated effort to repairs that were required.

The diminished, almost domestic scale of the "Merry Widow" was proportional to the grandeur of the final "Rosenkavalier" waltzes. The restaurant-nightclub of the "Merry Widow" vanished into the night. The stage was stripped, leaving the gigantic Mylar mirror, while a flight of chandeliers composed of deer horns descended. An architectural frame inspired by the Vienna *sezession,* particularly the checkerboard sophistication of Gustav Klimt, gave a huge scale to the ballroom. Everything transpired in a mirror world of black, white, and silver. The mirror was seamless, reflecting dancers as undeformed images. At the opening, on an empty stage, one saw only the conductor, Robert Irving, facing himself from the orchestra pit. The proscenium of the State Theater had never seemed so high, nor its stage space so wide. Strauss had rescored his wonderful waltz adapted from the second act of *Der Rosenkavalier* as a concert piece, which gave climactic support for Balanchine's ballet. The company was in full evening dress, not in the epoch of Franz Joseph's Hofburg, but rather as for the annual New Year's civic ball when the entire floor of the Staatsoper is covered over to stage level. It was a recollection of Vienna between the great wars, post-Hapsburg, but still in the sunset realm of Hugo von Hofmannstahl and Richard Strauss.

After a brief introduction of paired figures, recapitulating the commencement of "Tales from the Vienna Woods," a solitary girl, in the décolletage of a full-trained ballgown, with long white gloves, sparkling in diamonds, makes her solitary entrance. Her apparition, projecting an aura almost as strong as some marvelous scent, develops into a strange discontinuous solo, broken by almost chance intrusions of a man, her shadow partner, or lover. Suzanne Farrell had never before glittered with the dusky radiance and ironic pathos of the first night of *Vienna Waltzes*. Among all the seventy dancers, appearing and disappearing with her spectral companion, she danced with intensity of mood and motion as if lit by some interior spotlight. Balanchine had composed a sequence of *ports de bras*, in which her supplicating or inviting arms made a whole dance by and for themselves. Now he introduced all the principals of the previous action in short brilliant solos and combinations. At first, Karin von Aroldingen, Sean Lavery, Patricia McBride, Helgi Tomasson, Sally Leland, and Bart Cook, in the uniform strictness of their black-and-white dress, were all but unnoticed among other waltzers, but the choreography ingeniously wove itself into a separation and canonization of each pair in the recapitulation of the coda. The final surge of "The Rosenkavalier" waltzes seemed a massive motion in which the company was depersonalized in a musical expression of movement. At the climax, the dancers broke their chain of steps, facing front, wheeling into a symmetrical group portrait. There were those who considered this a perfunctory finish; something more "unusual" might have been imagined. It would be hard to know what. The music ends with a smashing final chord; applause generates as soon as the orchestra signals the drop of the curtain. There is satisfaction in the frank declaration of a finish, which is also a static apotheosis.

Vienna Waltzes was by no means the "greatest" of our ballets. Its "classicism" as representative of a generally "classic" repertory was rudimentary. Only one scene used toe shoes. It hardly compared in ingenuity or depth to the grand series of Stravinsky works. Elements in it had been often used by Balanchine before. But, in answer to some egregious questionnaire as to what has been our "most successful" attraction, *Vienna Waltzes* would probably be cited. For four seasons every performance scheduled was sold out; it brought into the theater a new public, many of whom had certainly never been in the State Theater before. Whether or not they would return to look at our more characteristic dancing on other evenings might be questionable. As sometimes happens, word of mouth, the nature of a work about which there seemed to be unanimous acceptance even before its first gala performance, the photogenic quality of its vision (reproduced immediately in the press) combined to make a "hit" of dimensions which one may have hoped for but hardly expected.

Such success prompts meditation on fortune and misfortune. We had been at work for nearly forty years. There had been a considerable body of ballets with valuable elements which failed to become "hits"; the effort, energy, and courage that brought these into being were all ploughed under. It might be philosophical to claim that nothing is lost, that what is of true value emerges in some other, later, or alternative form. Nevertheless, there are genuine losses and sometimes we have been chronologically in luck. This last was the case with *Vienna Waltzes*. We didn't necessarily prepare for it by consulting horoscopes, current events, or the daily press, but both exterior and interior factors were in favorable conjunction; it was generally, publicly in agreement to find this ballet smashing. Its reception was sometimes couched in terms of discovery, as if the whole affair was some sort of extraordinary novelty, as if we had suddenly emerged into the legitimized approbation of Broadway taste. This didn't hurt; our *Waltzes* also coincided with a broad heralding of "dance" (ballet) via television and film (and live performance) all over the country. At no time in the last fifty years had dance been taken more seriously; for this one might be grateful while wondering whether the *Waltzes* in its recapitulation was a beginning of something on a larger scale of possibility, or a demonstration of what could succeed within social or political conditions. We had reached a point in our process when we certainly needed large-scale works to support an operation involving about a hundred dancers, plus staff, orchestra, stagehands, a fund-raising department, and a costume shop. In our old days, we could fail with "experimentation" because our format was small; if all was lost, that all was, in sum, little enough. Today scale is of first importance, and while our big ballets are carefully prepared, budgets studied, and schedule analyzed, there is no certain security. The generosity of private patrons and their foundations (notably Fan Fox and Leslie R. Samuels for *Vienna Waltzes* and *Union Jack*) remove some menace of risk, but who likes to have his name attached to a flop?

In administering a repertory organization, taste different in kind from a museum is involved. In a museum, the director is responsible for the conservation, acquisition, and display of objects, which includes publication, loans, and exchange. This is so complex that now it is becoming more convenient to have a business-and-money director who ostensibly works with (?), below (?), or above (?) an artistic director. This brand of teamwork is too new to be judged clearly. In a ballet company, and I speak only of ours, Balanchine has always had a watchful eye on money; he has hardly ever been accused of extravagance, except in ideas. His professional authority has always controlled choices of expenditure. On a number of occasions there have been sharp disagreements on timing. He has had promising ideas that were hot and exciting scheduled for a next season, but money was not available at that particular moment. So possibility was delayed and sometimes lost; some other project offers itself or is seized. He makes do with what can be done at the particular moment. Here is where chronological luck comes in. Improvisation has always been the name of our game: a seizure of elements lying at hand, ready if not exactly eager to be taken up.

It is money that keeps us open. There are auxiliary groups and committees who, under professional direction, support the company's existence. Their contact with the dancers on a friendly basis is often close, but Balanchine keeps a polite distance. Arts management has now become a kind of science for which the universities offer pieces of paper calculated to get the recipients jobs—among others, managing the performing arts. Seminars in accounting, handling the media, approaches to foundations, can't do much harm; may even be useful. Some students will gain internships; some may even find work, but the only training for someone interested in running a ballet company is in association with dance production. This presupposes an instinct of respect for the veins of imagination which are at the heart of any progressive institution, but the worst part of academic courses in management is the logical emphasis on money, while the nature of quality in work is considered irrelevant, too mercurial, or too explosive to touch upon. I have watched some refugees from Wall Street, bored with brokerage business, who offer themselves as managers, believing they can bring the (more or less) rational methods of the bond market to sell ballet tickets irrespective of the quality of repertory. And I have seen some lawyers, fascinated by the untidiness of backstage, who have felt if only it could be packaged (or given a tidy "image") all would be well. This is not to disdain bankers or lawyers. Wholly different types of both have kept us healthy, but these particular collaborators have understood that our world is not governed by mass media, hard-sell marketing, demographic surveys, or computerization.

APRIL, 1977: *New York*

Working at School of American Ballet. I rarely get over to the State Theater to see what Balanchine is preparing. One hears through the grapevine that, contrary to everything planned or promised, he has taken completely unsuspected scores—by Verdi and Hindemith. I hoped it would have been a revival, or restructuring, of *Metamorphoses* (1952), with its wonderful huge beetle-

bug out of Kafka. But no; it is *Kammermusik No. 2*. The Verdi is
ballet music from *Don Carlos*.

Balanchine always has a number of ideas in percolation, a few
of which magnetize enough concrete impulse to trigger the start
of positive composition. He constantly collects piano scores, and
some unlikely orchestral ones as well, which he reduces to two-
hand adaptations for rehearsal purposes if he likes them well
enough to start thinking of a ballet. His music is usually surprising, whether familiar or unfamiliar. Sometimes he uncovers a useful piece from remote and unfashionable sources. During the
epoch of High Modernism, captained by Stravinsky's seasonal
menu of novelties which prompted recipes for other useful mor-
sels dished up mainly by French or Russian contemporaries, there
was small need to hunt but only to choose. But "modernism" ran
its course as a crusade; by the end of the Second World War, it
had fixed itself as a historic chapter. "Modernism" could begin
to equate itself as Fin de Siècle, although the century was hardly
ended chronologically, but its initial impetus seemed strained
toward innovation, particularly in music, as it did also in painting,
architecture, and literature. "Modernism" became an epoch like
L'Art Nouveau, which instead of remaining permanently novel,
like the permanent revolution of Marxism, joined itself in the
historical index to Futurism, Cubism, and Art Deco.

Sometimes it was regretted, mainly by practicing composers,
that Balanchine was not open to the seductions of *musique con-
crète*. However, he had tried a purely electronic piece as early as
1961 (*Electronics*, by Remi Gassmann), as well as Iannis Xenakis's
Metastaseis and Pithoprakta (1968). Among possibilities he might
have chosen were Ligeti, Hans Werner Henze, Olivier Messiaen,
Karlheinz Stockhausen, Luciano Berio, Roger Sessions, and a
dozen others. What attracted Balanchine to scores that were determinedly atonal or lacking in memorable melody was their unfamiliar but commanding sonority; in many cases the requirements
of composers called for orchestras double the size of ours, with a
need for rehearsal hours far greater than we could justify.

The morning after the U.S. astronauts accomplished their
moon landing, I said to Balanchine I hoped they would bring back

a new color, or that they would find a new palette which they could photograph and we could reproduce. He had been doing some homework on the sun and its potential. The spectrum giving us our rainbow was a refraction governing our solar system; we could not expect any variation past the sun's effect simply by traveling a comparatively short astronomical distance to the moon. Similarly, one might have hoped for a new sound, yet the most electronic ingenuity has resulted in is a range of noise no greater in variety than the limits of echo chambers. Neither John Cage's "prepared" pianos nor Harry Partch's charming toys nor the Moog or other synthesizers have offered much to enrich ballet repertory. In fact "experiment" with sonority has every aspect of an academic game, fascinating for players of a multidimensional chess. One cannot doubt the seriousness of the research, and an affluent society may hardly question foundation grants that have funded the hunt for an extension of auditory experience or possibility. However, it is only fair to repeat that the sounds so far forthcoming have done nothing to support dancing, although this would hardly disqualify the effort among obsessed specialists at Columbia or Princeton. What classic ballet needs, whether the music be melodic or atonal, is a strong beat. Deliquescence may be provocative or useful, as an alternative, but only as a counterbalance giving spice to a rhythmic repertory. Most marginal "experiment" is inevitably doomed to retirement when novelty or shock has faded. When Modernart petrified into a period, the shock quotient of the permanent advance-guard disappeared as well. The next shock was, as usual in the history of taste, the reassertion of those values which Modernart claimed to have destroyed—figurative painting, eclectic architecture, rhymed verse, classic ballet. Currently, the Museum of Modern Art lives off recapitulation—a specialized exhibition of "The *Late* Cezanne." And useful this is, but no less a revival than *Coppélia* or *Swan Lake*.

Pierre Boulez, the leading French composer and conductor of his day, served a not entirely happy series of seasons as musical director of the New York Philharmonic Society. We never saw him in our theater. Balanchine knew his discs and went to Avery Fisher Hall to hear him conduct his personal compositions. A principal dancer in our company, a friend of both Boulez and Balanchine, urged that they meet. Balanchine asked why: "Because both our names start with B?" "No, no; because one is a great conductor-composer; the other a great etc. etc." They met. Next morning I asked our great etc. etc. what the evening was like. "Marvelous; you know her mother is a very great cook: her *quiche.* . . ." "Yes: but what about Boulez?" "Ah," said Balanchine, "he's a physicist and I'm a gardener."

Among other oddities Balanchine had already borrowed was a bouquet from Vincenzo Bellini, themes mostly from his opera *La Somnambula,* which Vittorio Rieti had charmingly orchestrated as *Night Shadow* in 1946, for the Ballet Russe de Monte Carlo, before we existed as the New York City Ballet. It came into our roster in 1960, danced memorably by Erik Bruhn. When we called ourselves the American Ballet Caravan, on our way to a tour of Latin America we asked Benjamin Britten, then living in Amityville, Long Island, to score a series of Rossini piano pieces from his *Soirées musicales* (1941). This we furnished with costumes by the painter André Derain, left over from Balanchine's Ballets 1933 for *Les Songes* (Darius Milhaud). In 1960, Balanchine took Donizetti's ballet music from his little-known opera *Don Sebastian.*

It was not that there was lacking a great deal more viable music in the enormous operatic treasury of Bellini, Rossini, and Donizetti, but Balanchine had already explored each for rhythmic possibilities, or at least had sampled them. The three ballets he confected from their sugar and spice were more or less substantial hors d'oeuvre, or desserts. Now he would reserve for his gourmet's appetite a novel savor. The dominant school of European opera-house dancing in the last third of the nineteenth century was Italian. This had even superseded French influence in St. Petersburg. Sharp attack, accentuation of small brisk steps, speed, sharpness, brilliance gave a fresh infusion of acrobatic virtuosity to the Slavic vein, which was further strengthened by the advanced specialist teaching of Enrico Cecchetti, master of Anna Pavlova and Vaslav Nijinsky. Later he taught for Diaghilev's company in Western Europe, which included Balanchine as dancer as well as ballet master. A musical phenomenon of recent decades has been an extraordinary revival of *bel canto* operas, sparked by the late Maria Callas. Balanchine might be said to have adapted this operatic style, without any archaeological accuracy but with considerable musical equivalence. Now he found in Verdi's *Don Carlos* eighteen minutes of ballet music that, so far as records show, had not before been performed in New York.

For his *Ballo della Regina*, Balanchine had developed the ideal high-soprano dancer in Merrill Ashley, who had commanded attention in a number of different roles over the past few seasons. To the music of Verdi she was now revealed as a fantastic mistress of *allegro*, moving with more speed, cutting her profiles with greater diamond-edged sharpness, intensity, precision, and strength than almost any dancer within memory. Her absolute mastery of the physical demands of Balanchine's brief solo apparitions was never in doubt. What was more remarkable was her absence of strain, a smoothness that never smothered accents but which cleared from her movement all taint of gross athletics. The ballet itself could not be considered a "major" work, but it occasioned a number of major performances by Merrill Ashley, to which audiences responded with self-satisfied delight.

At the first performance of *Don Carlos* in Paris in 1867, the last act lasted too long. Then it was less a problem of time-and-a-half overtime extra pay for the stage crew than a need for music patrons to catch the last suburban trains departing at midnight. Hence cuts were made which were by no means uniform in subsequent productions variously given all over the world. These have been recently restored piecemeal, the ballet rarely included. It had been introduced into the opera's action by the professionally ingenious pretexts of its liberettists. The dancing ostensibly takes place "in a grotto"; Ben Benson's simple dresses and Ronnie Bates's clean lighting reflected pearly echoes of Capri's Blue Grotto. Balanchine's arrangement is a series of classical variations brusque and difficult. At the end, the intrusion of a fragmented processional or noble march struck some as being out of keeping with the chain of steps which linked most of the score. The music itself had connection, if only atmospherically, with the operative narrative involving Don Carlos and the Princess of Eboli. Although in the ballet visual sumptuousness was stripped away and there were neither singers as soloists nor chorus on stage, its musical inheritance from the world of opera was clear enough. Operatic dancing and balletic song are the strengths of opera-house ambience. Ballet has been and can be danced in the open air, in Roman amphitheaters, under tents, in arenas or convention halls; its true home is the opera house, its twin sister, the operatic repertory. In *Ballo della Regina,* the dancers were in the service of some silent opera company.

Although Balanchine has utilized a considerable number of symphonic French scores, he has not particularly favored French ballet music, except for *Coppélia,* and when he was obliged to mount *Carmen* and *Faust* while he was working at the Metropolitan, Paris, or Monte Carlo. Italians invented the genre of *bel canto* and, as well, its balletic equivalent, which Madame Marie Rambert calls *la danza bella.*

Before I had time to watch any rehearsals, I heard rumors of a new work Balanchine had commenced to music by Paul Hindemith. We had gone to visit him in 1951, when he was teaching at Yale. His *Symphonic Metamorphoses on Themes of Carl Maria von Weber* Balanchine set as *Metamorphoses,* with an unforgettable performance by Tanaquil LeClercq as The Dragonfly. Hindemith was an eminent teacher and theorist; he had written *The Four Temperaments* at Balanchine's suggestion in 1940, and over the years he had felt, as an exile, he seemed to have lost contact with theater, in which he commenced his career. The costume designs for *Metamorphoses,* which were among Madame Karinska's masterpieces, were based on butterflies and fireflies, and included a monstrous beetle straight out of Kafka's horrifying fable. All were later destroyed in a warehouse fire, so our ballet was abandoned. Except for *The Four Temperaments,* we had no other composition by this master of twentieth-century tonal structure. Now Balanchine decided to take his *Kammermusik No. 2.* It was prepared almost in secret and emerged largely as a surprise.

About anyone as powerful as Balanchine there usually coagulates an infectious body of gossip which after sufficient repetition gets itself dignified as myth, if hardly ever as truth. One of the more vulgar fallacies is the idiocy encapsulating "the Balanchine Dancer"—inevitably and simplistically: a girl. This gainsays the years with Diaghilev, when he composed *La Chatte* (1927), *Apollo* (1928), and *Prodigal Son* (1929), to say nothing of a series of later works in which the male dancer dominates or is equal in importance to the ballerina. However, among other dicta, he is loosely quoted for saying "Ballet is a woman," or something approximating this, as if he were discounting the capital accomplishment of Nijinsky, Fred Astaire, Nureyev, Baryshnikov, and Peter Martins—and platoons of other excellent men who grace American dancing. Nevertheless, ballerinas, from Taglioni and Anna Pavlova to their lineal descendants, continue to serve as convenient ciphers for the "romantic" classic dance; men seem more often fixed in classic roles which are antiromantic.

For Hindemith's *Kammermusik* Balanchine chose a team of eight males as a kind of collective soloist, with two solo pairs, Colleen Neary and Adam Lüders, Karin von Aroldingen and Sean Lavery: four tall, rapid, and confident performers. However, the burden of the ballet fell on the squad of eight boys selected for their uniformity of height, precision, and musicality. They seemed indeed a band of brothers. What Balanchine ultimately arranged for them beggars verbal analysis, although Arlene Croce, in her brilliant review in *The New Yorker*, came as near to managing a reduction into words of a fiendishly difficult composition as is possible to construct. Those familiar with *Agon* (1957) at its first performance may recall the blinding effect of a density of motion which was at once labeled "computerization." *Kammermusik* was a considerable geometrical progression past *Agon* in its packed amalgam of evocative gesture and movement. It was as if a current of electricity had galvanized the asymmetrical male choir into impersonal, jagged, abrasive whiplash energy. Gradually, *Agon*, which at first seemed raw, jerky, and charmless, acquired the handy acceptance of a well-worn artifact. But the new Hindemith appeared, however fascinating, slightly repellent, inhuman, desperate, insistent, harshly deliberate; even cruel. Its ingenuity was not to be gainsaid. Balanchine had found a novel plasticity in depth, an unsuspected dimension of negative power. The ballet is so crammed with action that the eye almost cries for arrest, so that its structure may be absorbed in the fullness of its visual logic. It seems a three-cornered race among soloists, the men, and the orchestra whose triple play keeps each in harness if not in a troika, competing for the public's attention.

Snow blindness is an occupational disease of polar explorer

and mountaineer. If conscientious observers peel their eyeballs to keep up with *Kammermusik* they could suffer a temporary loss of focus. Some English poetry defeats a first reading; one thinks of Father Hopkins, T. S. Eliot, W. H. Auden, and David Jones. It is not their shared religious conviction which removes them from facile comprehension. It is the charged density of intention, their shocking penetration. If their verses are beautiful, it seems almost incidental, for their relentless exploration of intellectual material meant far more to them than elementary pictorial color or sonorous felicity.

Kammermusik, for me, is the most extreme and extended exercise which Balanchine has made. Perhaps it partakes unrelievedly of the dryness, graininess, uncompromising charmlessness of Hindemith's metallic score. It is pitiless yet not entirely joyless. It has the questionable gaiety, or even pure efficiency, of a very odd job supremely well done, although the aims or end use of the applied mechanism is seldom brought into question. It is possible that this mechanism is benign. If so, the better for all of us. It is also possible that it's blind; that the uses to which it may be put have not entirely outlawed a mindless if mechanic malevolence. Yet the octet of boys, clad and moving as some sort of olympic athletic team, exude a metallic grace by virtue of the means and manner by which they are joined and a style in which they've been long accustomed to match each other's bodies and serpentine or spastic motion. The eight boys unquestionably have minor differences in height if mathematical measurements were taken, while major differences in facial structure would photograph individually. However, Balanchine's choreography tends to weld them into one, even while they may divide as do chromosomes in cell division. They fuse, and then become simply eight young men with brilliant technique, pleasant faces and personalities surrendering themselves to a miniature ritual for which they are happy to be schooled and skilled. Their games, drama, or mechanical functioning are interrupted by Neary, Lüders, von Aroldingen, and Lavery, taller even than the corps of eight men, moving against them, alone, in competition, and together. The two couples represent individuals as units, independent of machine parts. At least they propose that there exists personalism to some degree which survives the dense domination of a mechanism that, collectively, has more will or life of its own than even human bipeds as spare parts.

DECEMBER, 1977: *New York*

A number of young Danish dancers here at our school to work with Stanley Williams. In the same class, George de la Pena, soloist from American Ballet Theatre (trained by us), Paul Russell from the Dance Theatre of Harlem, Rudolph Nureyev, and Peter Martins, from our company. Forty-two men, too many for individual criticism, but shows the present state of interest in male dancing.

When we opened our school in 1934 there were few well-trained boys or men who had been schooled in the United States. Apart from scattered teaching by czarist exiles, refugees from Diaghilev or the touring troupe of Anna Pavlova, the Albee-Keith-Orpheum circuit of vaudeville and, later, movie "presentation houses" were the main sources of male dancers. There were always excellent hoofers, tap dancers, specialist "eccentric" and "novelty" performers: James Cagney, a superb dancer (as in his film biography of George H. Cohan), Fred Astaire, Buddy Ebsen, Bojangles Robinson, Ray Bolger. Cagney has been a particular admiration of ours; I saw him first at the Neighborhood Playhouse, then in his Broadway debut (*Little Ole Boy*), and in every film he made. Because of a piece I wrote about him in *Hound & Horn*, a critical quarterly I once edited, he visited our school on Madison Avenue and 59th Street to watch classes. Through the years we kept in touch; he always supported the principle of the male dancer as an exemplar of performing skill, of which he was so capital a criterion.

In a revue number called "Dancing in the Dark," the music for which is still heard on radio programs, Fred Astaire, in the early thirties, actually impersonated a male ballet dancer, and with some authority. It was the moment when the Ballet Russe de Monte Carlo first played the United States, and while an enthusiastic reception was then almost limited to New York City, Broadway was not slow to pick up a little luster from "Russian Ballet."

George Gershwin, John Alden Carpenter, and a number of other American composers were familiar with Diaghilev's seasons through the twenties in Monaco and Paris, and it was in this atmosphere of an elite coterie and limited acceptance that Balanchine came first—to hunt for American male dancers.

I've written before of our enormous admiration for Lew Christensen, who, with his brothers Harold and William and the dancers they were later to marry, had been experienced from the vaudeville circuits. Anyone looking at photographs which George Platt Lynes took of Lew in the first edition of this book must agree that such golden grace of person, and extraordinary physical endowment, is rare. If it had not been for the presence of Lew, I don't think I would have continued with ballet, during and after our worst trials of the thirties, the initial bankruptcy of the American Ballet Company, our withdrawal from the Metropolitan Opera, and lesser disasters which appeared then to amount to the fact that I personally had no further function. My role had, until then, been secondary. Balanchine, naturally, was free to pursue whatever course he might have cared to follow. However, it was how Lew danced on stage and behaved off that signified to me a future, and within it a potential for American male dancers. Christensen is a Mormon; as the name indicates, ancestry is Scandinavian. He was taught by a well-known Italian classicist, Luigi Albertieri. Balanchine said, early on, that Lew's multiple pirouettes were the cleanest he ever saw, and years later that, as a teacher, he produced the best male aspirants on the continent. In the thirties, he danced the best *Apollon Musagète* both Balanchine and I have ever seen. His luminous clarity in life, and on stage his apparent separation from mundane consideration—indeed his sober naïveté—gave a luster to his performance which was, in the lost accuracy of the word, "divine." His brother Harold had for a time (like James McNeill Whistler and Edgar Allan Poe) been a cadet at West Point, before quitting to dance and teach. A vestigial military bearing attached to all three Christensens; in Lew, with us, it assumed a focus in his talent for command. He combined, in one body, beauty, perfect physical endowment, musicality of a high professional level, a developed acrobatic technique, and an elegance of stage manners which was an exact reflection of his inherent morality. Also, he would prove to be a dance designer of taste, ingenuity, and humor.

Long before I met him, Balanchine was a known quantity on a level of prestige and achievement that removed me from any collaborative contact useful to him. I couldn't speak Russian; we talked in French for twenty years, but our private lives were worlds apart, and while we worked together in harmony, apart from theater we knew each other hardly at all. Rather, we know each other's uses well enough, but what the other does in his spare time has never occupied either of us. This is as it should be. My father had a business partner for thirty years; neither had ever been invited to the other's house, yet they were exactly as good "friends" as it proved useful to be. The same is true of Christensen and myself. He was raised in the West; his West remained a magnet. After the war, I had hoped he would stay in our orbit, implement our company, if there was one, teach in our school when a succession proved necessary. All this might have been possible—except for the Hitler war. We won the war; the West won Lew. If the San Francisco Ballet Company is today as strong as it is, it is largely due to the Christensens' massive contribution to its company and school.

Through the years, as Balanchine has discovered ballerinas who have corresponded to his fantasy as embodiment of a lyric feminine ideal, I have watched for male dancers incarnating native qualities of candor, a sense of time and place, the area of masculine ability and possibility. James Cagney's broad portrait-gallery—racing driver, naval officer, vaudevillian, con man, cowboy, and, of course, gangster—carried a photographic conviction poetically rooted in social class, locale, and national history. Lew Christensen danced Virgil Thomson's filling-station attendant; years later, Jacques d'Amboise performed the same role. Jacques was no replica of Lew, but he bore similar bloodlines, less heroic, more bumptious, happy, elegant, and younger. So it came to happen that Jacques' best roles, for me, also fulfilled my imagined "American" archetype. The Great American Dancer was invoked in the same voice used by those who prayed for the Great American Novel. It has been assumed, not without reason, that the Great American Dancer must be Russian, just as the Great American Soprano must have been Italian (or Greek, born in Brooklyn). This is changing.

It was neither a baked-fresh-daily American quality which attracted me, nor individual characters in themselves, although in the course of our working together, Lew, Jacques, and I continue to exchange confidences about dancers and dancing which amounts to intimacy. What magics me, what I've looked for longer than I've been involved in theater, is the personification of archetypes, which embody the essence of metaphysical possibility in varieties of forms legible to an audience. Ballet dancing is always a paradigm of potential, a frame that presents facets of the extreme possible. Included also are difficult and dangerous aims toward symbolic perfection, immediate as in *Filling Station*, ideal as in *Apollo*. It can also be antitraditional, eccentric, stripped yet sumptuous, as was Edward Villella's naked self-revelation in Jerome Robbins's timeless *Watermill*. Every fall when new boys enroll for the first time in our school, I notice shapes and sizes attaching to the herd of candidates who, one day, may even become first dancers. They cannot be classified, for faces or bodies even in late adolescence are deceptive; maturation plays odd tricks. But behavior in class—in men's class, or particularly in adagio, where boys support the girls —gradually reveals basic factors which determine the quality of a dancer's service. Every year there seem to be three or four boys who connect, in my mind, with an apostolic succession in our history which I date from Lew Christensen through Jacques d'Amboise.

In moments of doubt, or troughs of depression which can be identified clinically as disease or religiously as despair, those who are sensitive or susceptible await miracles as signals that they are blessed, graced, or forgiven. Certainly enough signs exist to confirm those who wish proof that God doesn't exist. As for myself, I've never doubted His existence. If proof has been needed for me, it has been to have had everything I've ever needed or wanted— Balanchine, his company, our school, dancers, a theater. I require no other. But the glory of these gifts reads as if I thought God's giving was by neat bundles, rewards for a good boy who tried to do his best. Thinking of all the good boys I've known in whom God, alas, seems to have been too busy to have shown much interest, I can't take much credit for personal identification or the awards of divine providence. It is not modesty that makes one reiterate that dance has a life of its own, that God seems to be interested, since it continues without interruption, whether in the State Theater at Lincoln Center or elsewhere. Bankruptcies, failures, wars, interruptions, shrink in the sequence and consequence of history. Certain bodies, those of dancers, dance designers, teachers, administrators, are the receptacle of a graced service, which is also helped by mind and metric.

One remembers individual dancers, no longer with us or alive, who not only gave pleasure but personified perfection. The names of some of them are scarcely known to a present generation of ballet-goers, but a few may be listed out of gratitude; good photographs of all of them exist. They helped form my taste or preference; sometimes they coincided with and corroborated an already half-formed predilection. It is not too long a list; there are many others whose practice and bearing I admired; some were famous performers sufficiently honored without one more bouquet. Leon Woizikovsky and Yurek Shabelevsky—both powerful character-dancers, the first with Diaghilev, then later, with the first years of the Ballet Russe de Monte Carlo, where Shabelevsky, another Pole of urgent energy and charm, filled important parts. I particularly recall Frederic Franklin as "The Wolf of Gubbio," in the Massine-Hindemith *Nobilissima Visione* with Tchelitchev's marvelous evocation of the Italy of St. Francis of Assisi and Piero della Francesca; Jean Babilée, epitome of Cocteau's snub-nosed *voyou* in his fierce acrobatic rage of *Le Jeune Homme et la Mort*. Herbert Bliss could not by the widest hyperbole be named a great dancer, but in several roles he projected his transparent mother-of-pearl angelic clarity, which, for me, was stronger even than talent or technique. Subjective judgment is more confessional than historical, but when he died, far too soon, I was not surprised to receive letters of condolence, since somehow we seemed to share a bloodless brotherhood. I was reminded of the *Greek Anthology* epitaph which begged earth to lie lightly on a dead dancer whose steps had been so light on it.

It is well known that Balanchine has not encouraged the star category, yet he has always prized powerful dancers. Once I was in the office of the director of an important art gallery; on the walls were a pair of extremely beautiful, fairly large miniature portraits by Corneille de Lyon, an excellent sixteenth-century French painter. We agreed as to their exceptional quality—the acuteness of psychological observation, the beauty of the restricted palette, their exquisite condition, all of which amounted to appetizing rarity. They were waiting to be offered to an acquisitions committee, and I congratulated the director on the wisdom of his choice. "Oh no," he said, "they're not of museum importance, they're too small to be noticed." Fortunately, we have never been a national museum of ballet. Some have striven to be just that. The key nature of museums is their static, frozen accumulation of past treasure. Balanchine has depended on tradition, but never on the defense of indefensible authenticity. We conserve tradition as a vein to be mined, refined, recast, extended. Alchemical process serves the jeweler's craft; pearls, diamonds, and garnets are not to be disdained, nor other gems of less price. The setting of opals or emeralds is enhanced by other stones of contrasting glory, whatever their size, shape, or cost. It's easy for audiences to settle on stars, and for managements to sell the single glittering object, but this is not how new repertories are assembled or an institutional company maintained.

Nevertheless, whatever nomination or assigned category, one never denies the existence of exceptional gifts. Performers shining on stage have their heavy duty. They are always in hazard; their physical energy consumes them and is consumed in muscular expenditure. Usually there is little excess left over to supply contributions to artistic invention or company management. We have had the fantastic luck to have lately such a dancer in Peter Martins. He was entirely trained at the Royal Ballet School in Copenhagen. When Jacques d'Amboise was injured, Martins was asked to dance Balanchine's *Apollo*. Although his future in Denmark was open and promising, he risked coming to us. Emigration to New York, in his first years, was not entirely happy. Translocation was awkward, uncomfortable; he thought seriously of returning home. There were several difficult conversations. It is all but impossible to persuade someone against his firm will; occasionally it's possible to question the volition. In Peter's case one feels it was less a desire to go back to Copenhagen and ultimately a possible directorship of the Royal Danish Ballet than to find himself a position in our company and accustom himself to the special mandates and conditions of its artistic director. Discussion prefacing the resignation or departure of a valued dancer is more disheartening and emotionally exhausting even than labor-union negotiation. Committees representing labor are collective bodies; the unhappy dancer is an individual. Usually our blessing at all threats of desires to depart has been: "Go in peace." When a gifted ballerina announced to Balanchine she wished to leave, he said just that, in those three words. Whereupon she came to me in tears, complaining that he didn't seem to care whether she stayed or not.

I cared very much whether Peter Martins stayed. His value to us was hardly unrecognized, but Denmark offered him honor and power. There, he could do as he pleased; his financial situation would be more stable. If he used Copenhagen as a base there were many European companies eager for his services. As for myself, I had a personal interest. Apart from his arresting physical presence, technical mastery, and capacities as a hugely pleasing professional artist, he holds the elixir of authority that comes only with God-given gifts. To me he appeared as the fulfillment of an ideal of heroic male dancer that, in my youth, had been lodged with Lew Christensen. Of approximately the same size, both were fair-haired, both Scandinavian, both admirably trained, both carriers of training traditions alternative to the Russian (Bournonville, Cecchetti), both favored also with a rare natural fund of analytical intelligence, which placed their own private careers in the broader perspective of a permanent institution. Both were Northern; coarsely considered, this may be imagined as the possession of cold nature or thin blood. But native restraint, detachment, coolness, hardly negates their sense of fun, the absurd, or of craft.

Now Peter has begun to choreograph. His early essays, to diverse music by Ives, Auric, and Rossini, gave evidence of a talent for the linkage, invention, or assemblage of closely related steps. A most familiar fault in many "young choreographers" is eagerness to use as much of the classic academic vocabulary as they can, as if a parade of movement somehow amounts to ingenuity or, at the least, competent facility. Peter's individual talent lay in an economy of reversals. Instead of attempting to cap one effect by another even more startling, he reiterated the accents in an initial statement or combination by altering it slightly, by turning it on its head, as it were; by ringing changes that, inside out, strengthened the impression of devices already demonstrated.

Suffice it to say that like few others of his generation, Peter has the gift of enchaining steps. When Balanchine assigned him composition, he used a large amount of concentration learning to invent, or at least determining whether or not he could. One noticed a slight withdrawal in his stage performance—not that he danced with less energy, but there was an air of withholding, a kind of mental abstraction that was unfamiliar. I spoke of this to a dancer close to Peter; he said, "Yes—but remember, choreography is a full-time occupation that demands as much if not more concentration than performance does, particularly for an artist who has only just begun trying to add to an awesome repertory." Inventing dances is as hazardous as acrobatics; one can fail, no matter what the previous experience. Peter Martins commenced composing as a kind of test service, a game, but with the same confidence he shows when he fulfills the patterns of choreographers his senior. There is still more need for his dancing than for his dance design, but it is a comfort to have been given the suggestion that a considerable capacity is latent.

FEBRUARY, 1978: *New Haven, Connecticut*

Fourth in a series of eight seminars given at the Yale Drama School on "Arts Management." Twenty graduate students of capacity and perspicacity, about to graduate and hunt for jobs with a piece of paper furnished by the university at an estimated cost of $25,000 (for three years). Where can they find work they want, in institutional theater?

I agreed to teach at Yale for two reasons. I was interested in a recruitment of educated and intelligent young men and women who might be equipped to continue our work. And my schedule in New Haven allowed me to spend a couple of hours a month at Paul Mellon's beautiful English Art Center, with its dazzling permanent collection of pictures, its brilliant series of changing exhibitions drawn from permanent holdings.

I've never wished to teach in the formal sense, although I've been asked, since the kind of information I've accumulated is best transmitted on a one-to-one basis. What most young people wish to hear in seminars about theater is the personal opinions of the teacher, which is gossip, or the addresses of directors or managers who might give them jobs. Most graduate students have had experience in more or less professional summer theaters or regional drama facilities. What interests them is the politics of production, the condition of commercial theater (Broadway), and whatever chances there may be to survive in a chancy profession. Many will end up teaching; to young, hopeful students this amounts to exile and a second-best. What I tried to do briefly at Yale was to give as naked a map of repertory practice as I know it, but since my knowledge applied to a unique situation, and has no general application to any other enterprise, it couldn't have done the students much good, although we may have found each other bright, sad, or funny.

"Arts Management," stripped to its bone, means money-raising and money manipulation, which includes the art of wheedle, the craft of begging, the metaphysic of moral energy. It adds up to mathematical chances of survival. It cannot be taught, any more than choreography can be taught. There are no such animals as instant choreographers, any more than there are instant dancers. Arts managers can't expect to "make" money; they are doomed to try to find it. What this has to do with the "arts" depends on specific situations. While managing a regional drama company has some problems that overlap on management of a symphony orchestra, the crux is in the quality of direction, which means the character of the artistic *director*. The artistic director is only incidentally a *manager*. It is true he often has to manage to survive, and in this must depend on a supporting staff. The director of a drama company is different in kind from the conductor of a symphony orchestra. The promise and behavior of these beasts cannot be projected from three years of postgraduate study at Yale or any other school.

With the New York City Ballet, a self-enclosed conglomeration of energies and capacities, there is little to propose that would be of use to any other ballet company, since no other ballet company is controlled by Balanchine. One becomes accustomed to negative criticism of the management of our "arts," and not from the press alone. People within the organization who are entirely devoted, people on its fringes who are passionately loyal, at certain stages of development diagnose imminent doom, interior collapse due to inefficiency, lack of communication, individual insecurity, rival threats, defections, and, of course, fiscal apocalypse. One of the oddest aspects of this phenomenon, which is no more unnatural or unreal than the effect of sunspots on our weather, is that it often surfaces when the audit of box office is at a relatively high level, when the number of subscribers touches a new peak. It is as if the gods of chance may be placated by doomsday prophecy. When Napoleon's mother was told to be proud of the fact that she had given birth to kings of France, Spain, Italy, etc., she said: *"Pourvu que ça dure"* (O.K.; may it last).

There is no doubt that factors giving rise to such fears are real and present. Tension, competition, fear of failure, etc., exist always and everywhere; that one might imagine them either absent or unlikely in arts management is innocence indeed. Idealism in the service of art, a beggar's pleasure, resembles the stock market except in smallness of ciphers. What an arts manager learns from experience of such warnings, which are never in the same tension or condition, is to watch the product as shown or performed. Kindly folk have, on occasion, not been slow to tell us, entirely for our own good, that, alas, they have "learned" the morale of our company was very low. Morale is not easy to judge; if one taped dressing-room talk, apart from shrewd technical analysis of performance or choreography, one could be hardly surprised at expressions of personal sentiment which were not wholly "positive." Again, I refer to my obsession with military metaphor. Griping is useful as a general release; from the ranks it doesn't rise very far. In extreme physical situations it scarcely exists. Long ago I found there was only one barometer of morale: performance. I have never seen dancers in our company, or any other, throw a show, no matter what personal griefs or irritations may have existed. Dancers are not overpaid, although they will soon approach parity with the older trade unions.

It is perfectly true there are strains and elements in our organization and its practice which might give well-schooled arts-management graduates a bad abrupt nervous breakdown. Once I had a notion that, as a change, I'd like a male secretary. The person who had been with me for twelve years, and who had salvaged my affairs while I was in the service, was getting married. I thought that, resuming management, I might now depend on a simulacrum of a master-sergeant. I hired one. He lasted exactly one day, even though he needed a job. He happened to arrive at a difficult moment, when we were starting a new venture; everything seemed in confusion and disorder preceding a dress rehearsal. But the truth was, he lacked the temperament to estimate and endure disorder, emergency, hysteria. Also he had no interest in dancing. However ragged the atmosphere, or secretive the individuals, or foolish the behavior of artists, it is our rule number one that any serving supporter must be magnetized by theater, in the theater by dance, in dance by Balanchine. He has always drawn on the virtues of silence. Those attracted to his service serve in silence, or quickly learn to keep their mouths shut and their bodies busy.

It would be normal to suggest that the prime problem of continuity for our company is the management of Balanchine. It is almost true, but one must be precise as to what this means. Does this imply he can be manipulated; or, on the other hand, does he control? This is a semantic, artistic, and political crux. It can best be compared to the structure of governance under which he was born and educated. The following comparisons are, of course, inexact, but certain connections are difficult to discount. Parallels are more in the nature of comparable categories than equivalent individual personalities. Georgei Melitonovitch Balanchivadze resembles Nikolai Aleksandrovich Romanov as an individual chiefly in his personal autocracy, spiritual orthodoxy, and political conservatism. In Barcelona (1936), Stravinsky, Balanchine's greatest partner, said in an interview:

> . . . I do not work with subjective elements. . . . my artistic goal is to make an object. . . . I create the object because God makes me create, just as he created me. . . . I cannot accept surrealism or communism, despite my conviction that both are right on many points. The bourgeois is the one who is not right. . . . Aesthetically I am unable to accept materialism. . . . My religion makes me a dualist. . . .*

The imperial principle depends on absolute pyramidal authority. Absoluteness depends upon the historical situation. The autocracy of Peter the Great was more absolute than that of Nicholas II, for under Nicholas, serfdom had been revoked. A Duma existed, and while the dynasty was moving to its end faster than it knew, there was token democratization. The Russia of Peter was primitive, dubious, but full of promise; of Nicholas, established, sophisticated,

---

* *La Noche* (Barcelona), March 12, 1936. Copyright owner: Trapezoid, Inc.

and decadent. Ballet was nourished as part of court panoply comparable to the mineral baubles of Fabergé. As far as art appreciation goes, one recalls that the only words Czar Alexander found to praise the composer for *The Sleeping Beauty* at its premiere were: "Very nice." Diaghilev hoped for and confidently expected imperial diplomatic support for his first season of Russian Ballet in the West. It was withdrawn at the last moment. In Europe, for twenty years, Diaghilev heroically maintained a sort of court in exile; he became a czar without a realm—except of Western dancing, music, and painting. Europe, between the wars, had no focus of patronage, no base to which Diaghilev could attach himself. He survived painfully between Paris, London, and Monte Carlo as best he could. In London he was not above appearing in small theaters, or in music halls between animal acts and popular comedians.

After forty years, Balanchine has established a company that bears the name of what has long been known as the virtual capital of the Empire State; it reflects a social democracy rather than an empire. However, with us an imperial principle maintains. By virtue of authority gained by the assembly of a repertory Shakespearean in its range and variety, scope and intensity, he has come to show the classic dance as perhaps the most invigorating traditional imaginative expression of the last quarter of the twentieth century. His autocracy expresses itself not alone for his own dancers, but in the repertory of every ballet company that aspires to a progressive position in his epoch. The odd feature of his almost universal present acceptance seems to be in a combination of the slowness with which this authority came to be recognized as absolute with the lack of any change in quality over the four decades framing his prolific energy. One can point to *Prodigal Son* of 1929 or to *Serenade* of 1934. Neither shows "immaturity" or "promise"; they may be works by a young man of twenty-four or thirty, but their shape and invention are as secure as his most recent ballets. It is hard to divide his "early" work from a "middle" or "late" one. It was as if he'd been born ready to go. Naturally his years in a Russian ambiance, where he had danced the entire repertory of Petipa plus what was then available of Fokine, was an advanced apprenticeship. His close observation of Diaghilev's method of direction, his enlistment of allies, his improvisation in survival, gave him clear advantages. He learned as much as he needed to about managing a company.

While there have been many individuals constituting a loyal, practical, patient, long-suffering, and able staff at each period in our company's growth, it is Balanchine who has ultimately managed or chosen—according to his principles, impressive and imperial.

Authority derives from belief in one's self—in the intensity of one's chosen service. For whoever comes after us, for those who will be given the task of maintaining our repertory or building new works onto it, there will be the guidelines of Balanchine's philosophy. This comes to be shared by students in our school who may not be able to put it into words, and dancers in our company who have in awe and silence observed its effect. *Service* in the military sense, to serve in silence, without spoken question, is the key. Not everyone is intended to be a virtuoso classic dancer, nor may everyone subscribe to the mask of anonymity which members of our company have learned to wear as a shining badge. Their anonymity is no more a disguise than their fingerprints, their height, the color of their hair or eyes, but the initial token embrace of a collective semi-demi-namelessness admits them to a band where the dance outshines the dancer yet where the dancer finally can come to proclaim an essential self.

Since I have played roles in this story, and a fair amount of half-truth has referred to my part in it, perhaps it is only proper to claim what I think I've done. An article on the choice of a new director for the Metropolitan Museum of Art pointed to the presumably positive tandem relationship of Balanchine and myself. The Metropolitan Museum, the greatest collection of art objects in the Americas, following the precedent of Chicago and other of our large museums, has appointed a director charged with "business" activities, who is superior in authority to an "artistic" director, supposedly in charge of the curatorial staff, the choice of exhibitions, and the organization of objects. This article proposed that such an arrangement worked well in the development of comparable or parallel institutions, as in, for one, the New York City Ballet. I was evidently cast as "business"; Balanchine as "art." No greater nonsense was ever promulgated.

Time will tell whether or not the subsequent choice of the Metropolitan's formula may work well. For a ballet company such as ours, this arrangement, realistically, is nonsense. I have reiterated that my father thought me a financial idiot; my personal fortune has always been handled by my brother. Monies coming to our company, which have kept us alive, would have come whether I was around or not. Authoritative magnetism attracts support; Balanchine would have had a like career whether he had remained in Denmark or returned to Paris. He was destined for the United States before he left Leningrad. After 1933 he was sick of Europe. The timetable might have been different; results would have been much the same. He has worked for himself, Diaghilev, de Guinzbourg, de Basil, Broadway, and Hollywood. The quality of his product has never suffered in a shift of management.

What is implied by this pretentious excess of modesty is that an artistic director has to *direct* the "art" of the institution, particularly if that art is alive, not an inert, however glorious, residue of nostalgia. I've never once in forty-five years suggested to Balanchine either a morsel of music, or the casting of a particular dancer in a ballet, new or old. I have never attempted to arrange scheduling of repertory or tried to project or limit the cost of any new work. I've had nothing to do with price policy in subscription or box-office sales. I've never voiced disagreement over individual dancers, their arrival, presence, or departure. While I have admired a few contemporary painters and sculptors, I have never proposed any as collaborators after Pavel Tchelitchev's abdication from theater. I knew it was hopeless; Balanchine's imagination is less visual than plastic. He likes flowers, in their place (gardens, not cut), but "paintings" don't get to him. He says Diaghilev took him to a museum (The Louvre): once. I have not been a "business" manager. It has been suggested I was a kind of public-relations something-or-other. It is true that I've written down what Balanchine suggested or what I've understood him to have said. There may have been occasions when he has put a severe strain on one's patience, through what seems to have been indecision or caprice—for example, his refusal to revive *Apollon Musagète*. His refusal to revive *Liebeslieder Walzer* is justified by the cost of four singers of the quality of Fischer-Dieskau or Rita Hunter; he feels less fine voices are derisory compared to the quality of our dancers. It is hard to schedule new works according to his fluctuating interest and energy, whim or idiosyncrasy. But in our "business," any "business managers" who decided to wield a whip hand would have found themselves minus an "artistic director" in about five minutes.

So—after all this hedging—what can an author claim to have done, and if as little as he cares to count, why does he think it proper to confess all this? I take credit for the choice of design of the State Theater with Nelson Rockefeller's subvention from Albany, and for contriving that Philip Johnson design it. He should have planned all of Lincoln Center, following his magnificent original precast-concrete proposal. I have been backstage and out front many nights and have developed a thermometric eye for what is being seen. Our staff contains cautious and energetic characters who have stuck with us and who, after many years, keep the show going, providing floor and frame for those who dance.

Finally, as for "management" of a ballet company, choreographers don't grow on trees. However, the dance has a life of its own, and one need not worry about our future managements. Boards of directors, apart from raising their ever-growing quota of cash, have only one irreplaceable function: the selection, appointment, and support of a succession. Such boards of such companies must remember that cash is secondary; audits must be kept, sensitive corporations and agencies courted and satisfied. But unless the repertory continues to be piquant and provocative, the potential apostolic artistic director will secede and take with him the best elements of an insurgency—as Diaghilev did in 1914, and as Balanchine did in 1932.

APRIL, 1978: *New York*

Balanchine called me to come over to his home. He was cooking, preparing pascha, babka, koolich, etc., for Russian Easter. I was not prepared for what he had to tell me. Mikhail Baryshnikov wishes to join the New York City Ballet, on our ordinary terms. Four years ago this would have been unthinkable, for him and for us. Now, everyone concerned seems delighted.

The moral stance of our company has depended on Balanchine's philosophy of relative self-abnegation approaching anonymity, but with a latitude of contractual arrangements for artists to take other work (except in New York, where we may be playing against other troupes). This attitude is virtually unique. It's been no secret that, in the past, several well-known dancers might have welcomed the chance to work with, or under, Balanchine and Robbins, but on their terms, not ours. Artists who achieve eminence measured by the weekly amount of money they earn naturally wish the freedom of an open market, elastic schedules with few restrictions as to long-term commitments which do not take into consideration the fair thrusts of fortune—new jobs, chances, partners. Such demands we have always refused to accommodate, for both practical reasons anticipating seasonal programs and cost in preparatory time and money. It is impossible to judge the value or quality of performance by cash alone, but it is elementary justice to recognize the discrepancy between the amount a "star" gets per performance and what any of our first dancers is paid by the week. In the case of Baryshnikov, he understood perfectly well what he would be sacrificing, as far as dollars go, if he came to us. He would, however, be free to accept guest appearances outside New York and in Europe. But when he joined us he voluntarily bound himself to abide by our reckoning. What he would lose materially only he could estimate. Certainly he would not starve, but as a notoriously generous man, he probably could no longer give a great deal away. So why had he given up possibly the most lucrative career of any dancer in the twentieth century to come for as little as he knew was our absolute?

Let us assume that at the age of thirty, four years of dancing experience in the West since his defection from Russia had taught him much both of American standards and of his own identity. In Russia, he had been incarcerated in a political system and a theatrical repertory which was ultimate suffocation. While there are still fine male dancers in the Soviet Union, with all the energy and money spent on ballet training and their enormous pool of manpower, it is remarkable that there are not many more. One thinks of Vasiliev and the greatly regretted Soloviev; but are there more than half a dozen others of the capacity of Baryshnikov or Nureyev? These last two chose to risk their great break; it cost both of them more than is easily estimated in spiritual anguish, the amputation of youth and family; exile, silence, anxiety, or lurking doubt as to family and friends who have been left behind; possible rewards abandoned.

Baryshnikov, in America, had taken every opportunity to diversify his roles. In his long quest for alternatives to the limited classic nineteenth-century repertory, he embraced a spectrum of whatever choreographic invention was widely available, and this with loyal attention and full devotion to whatever he was given to perform. He did not stint himself on material offered, whatever its chances for survival, either as repertory work or as a flattering vehicle for his person. In fact, he would hardly have chalked up against any of these experiments any notable failures; several had been signal successes, at least at their first performances and if one believes rave notices. However, few of them seem to have given him a role that took advantage of his extraordinary capacities and set him in a fresh frame or definitive character; neither did most of them provide him with steps that much more than dutifully absorbed his attention or capacity. Several of the roles exploited him inversely by cheapening his allure into a popular luminary; others were incapable of enhancing his enormous range and gave him unlikely steps and patterns which he mastered with facility but with little gusto. But then always he could return to *Giselle* and the predictable if awesomely thunderous reception his unique appearance was guaranteed to ignite.

During his American years, he always kept an eye on Balanchine; he had danced *Theme and Variations* and had commented publicly on the extraordinary difficulty of its leading male role. He had managed to find ways to dance *Prodigal Son* and *Apollo* in Europe (and the former in Chicago), but these performances were not prepared by Balanchine. During the 1977–78 winter season he had watched our company three or four times a week, when he was himself not dancing next door at the Met. He had taken class for a long time at our school with Stanley Williams. A number of members of our company had seen him dance in Leningrad on our last trip to the Soviet Union in 1970; a few had become his friends. But he had as yet no direct contact with Balanchine. I watched him in class, much struck by his simplicity of manner, his absorption in instruction without ever showing off, his helpfulness and modesty in contact with our own boys. He throws off a sunny air, in life as on the stage. It is easy to see why he was magnetized by Balanchine. We could offer him the greatest variety of repertory with the most progressive language of the classic dance. Jerome Robbins had already worked with him on *Other Dances;* there is no gainsaying that Robbins and Balanchine offer a combined repertory which, as far as contemporary works go, is unrivaled. To immerse himself in this repertory, with no question of terms, what roles he might get, what acceptance he might expect, was an index of his selflessness.

There was, of course, the normal flurry in the press when the official notice of Baryshnikov's "defection" appeared. Balanchine left the burden of the news release to the dancer; there was an excellent, complete, and just analysis by Anna Kisselgoff in the *New York Times.* This should have allayed questions and doubts, but these persisted. Were we forsaking our philosophy of thirty years? Were the members of the company happy or unhappy about this extraordinary development? When Balanchine finally gave a statement, he simply said that both he and Mischa were trained in the same school (Petersburg-Leningrad), and that it was good to have another healthy boy around.

As for reaction by our dancers, Peter Martins embraced me, as if the whole company was to be congratulated. I happened to meet Jacques d'Amboise in our school; he spoke to me about his son Christopher, who had just been taken into the company, along with three other extremely gifted boys. Jacques said that when he started twenty-five years ago, he had lacked style; he needed a model. He found one—in André Eglevsky. "Chris can't find one in his father; but now he has Baryshnikov." For me, Jacques' statement and attitude showed a peak of impersonal professionalism, a selflessness in judgment that makes it possible to penetrate to the inner moral core of our art. It is this attitude that makes the academic classic dance the most fruitful of expanding theatrical traditions, and shows the spirit which the noblest dancers incarnate.

The burden of male roles in our repertory as far as first dancers goes had fallen more and more on the immensely capable shoulders of Peter Martins and on the elegant Helgi Tomasson. Among senior members, Jacques was dancing less; he had undertaken the promising task of becoming Dean of Dance at the State University of New York in Purchase. Jean-Pierre Bonnefous, tormented by surgical problems, was encouraged by Balanchine to prepare a second company for touring where our big one could not venture. Edward Villella, suffering his own physical incapacities, was appointed Cultural Commissioner of the City of New York in the new

Edward Koch administration. Still, we have a dozen or more capable young soloists of increasing capacity, and Baryshnikov would certainly be welcome not as a relief dancer but as a criterion of what the male body can achieve when implemented by school, heart, and mind.

SPRING, 1978: *New York*

Money-raising and marketing tickets. Technical testimony based on demographic analysis of audiences. Acquisition of new mailing lists. I usually get four copies of the same brochure announcing a new season, due to expense and difficulty of cleaning accumulations of names. I know it's important, but the effort to be interested is worse than pulling teeth.

Until a few years ago, preponderance of effort in our organization was spent on the physical production of ballets, their commissioning and maintenance, getting them onstage. Owing to expansion of the scale of public interest, the increased size of our theater and company, selling approached the importance of staging. The strict and organized techniques of production were reflected in the composition of music and dance, the painting of scenery, the construction of costumes. It may have been irresponsible not to have bothered much whether people came to watch what we did; this was a limitation of my energy. One can't do everything; my habit was formed in days when our audiences were not large and our deficit, compared to what it would grow to be, more or less manageable. I knew techniques for selling existed. My father was a merchant with innovative notions and a progressive professional philosophy. When I was about fifteen, it was considered possible I might go into the department-store business—or at least serve an apprenticeship to see whether or not I might be fitted for it. I would not have been; instead, I served a year's training in a stained-glass factory, and knowledge of its craft later proved useful. I admired my father's tastes and listened with fascination to his and Gordon Selfridge's proposals for a department-store-of-the-future, which, if I described it today, would sound like Jules Verne or Ignatius Donnelly designed by the firm of Buckminster Fuller and Morris Lapidus. It was not entirely megalomaniacal; both Selfridge and Father were canny marketeers. Selfridge had written a plump book, *The Romance of Business*, which I read without finding much that was romantic, although the Fuggers, the Medici, and Marshall Field had their advantages as shrewd art patrons. I recognized that department stores were not arranged or maintained by improvisation, that there were complex skills in pleasing a public, and if the public was not pleased one way or another, the likelihood of permanence in any institution, financial or artistic, was short-lived.

Hence, in the back of my mind, even though I was never hungry, I worried about money. There have been others who have largely assumed the burdens of our menacing bankruptcy. Betty Cage, among the multiplicity of her other services, has always been our company's cushion. As a rich boy, I found it hard to ask others for help, although this was cowardice and laziness. I was always comfortable, but this hardly excused me from making an effort, particularly since everyone knows the approximate income of everyone else, and I was certainly not in a class with Marshall Field, Fuggers, or Medici. Before we moved into the State Theater our operations, as one might view them now, were haphazard and, while not exactly random, scarcely corresponded to the pattern of efficiency-expert desiderata.

In our beginnings it was convenient for me to formulate ideal constructs as targets to shoot at—the Ideal American Dancer, the Great American Ballet, and the Enemy. The Enemy was an amorphous monster, a multiheaded hydra, one of whose brains serviced the Efficiency Expert. It or he was conceived in my mind long before the age of computers. He was frightening because he appeared to be a person of drastic expertise; later he would become a mindless residue of numerical data. When all else fails, summon Efficiency Experts. One grants their political use when owners or responsible managers want to clean up, or clean out, lists or staffs. When one is too shy or scared to dismiss someone, it pays to find a plausible dollar reason for so doing. We have had and kept a staff from which hardly anyone was fired and few left. But there were those who considered that our perpetual poverty was not only inefficient but naughty. This evil might easily be washed away by installing procedures which had proved both effective and lucrative in packaging cereals.

Tidiness has a place, even in theater. It's important to keep toe shoes in neat heaps, labeled with sizes which individual dancers need. Tidiness in storage, wardrobe, the library of musical scores, and company payrolls is not destructive. Tidiness in the manipulation of theatrical performance, in attempts to maneuver the lyric imagination, is fatal to the process that assembles repertory. Strict schedules may be projected for political or public-relations reasons, but, as far as the promise or introduction of new works goes, these are broken as often as they're kept. There is one trustworthy enemy to tidiness: hysteria. Webster says that *hysteresis* is, among other things, "in a magnetic material, as iron, a lagging in the values of resulting magnetization due to a changing magnetizing force." Dancers' bodies are not metal, but the best have wills and muscles of elastic iron. Magnetization draws them to concentrations of free force or energy. The process is explosive, electric, and may often appear to outsiders as hysterical. Also, it's often untidy. The intensity of currents racing through theatrical process is similar to that which implements other arts. Spectacular demonstrations of apparent waste or untidiness in formative stages of invention seldom bother scientists, but one has seen bankers approach psycho-neurosis when supposedly fixed schedules gang a-gley.

One is told it is wicked to be untidy, and one learns to be grateful to those who, against all odds, impose profitable order on theatrical operations. For there has been a positive side to considerations of our potential profitability, or lack of it. The publisher of this book, having adopted our ballet company, has deployed a considerable fund of experiential common sense and a fresh eye on scheduling, advertising, and exploitation. Since he too spends his work days with more or less mercurial artists, his process with us has not only been profitable but painless. In 1978, after working with the schedules and selling of several seasons, Robert Gottlieb shares our satisfaction at counting box-office receipts of about the largest audiences we've ever attracted, among whom is the largest continuing group of seasonal subscribers who has ever supported the New York City Ballet. This result has elevated us into a situation that removes us, if perhaps temporarily, from the threat of efficiency experts.

Another hydra-head of the Enemy is the Demographic Survey. It might not seem like a bad idea to know where your audiences come from, how they get to and from your theater, how much they are willing to pay—even what sort of ballets they wish to see. It is reassuring for generous patrons, foundations, and corporations to know effort is being made to secure basic data which might eliminate waste or prophesy futures. This is rational; certainly only a hysterical paranoid would question such questioning. We have suffered a variety of demographic surveys. The same questions are always asked: identical responses given. As for the average answers:

Our particular audience comes mainly from the island of Manhattan, north of Canal Street, south of 125th Street, between the East River and the Hudson, with weekend additions from Brooklyn, Long Island, northern New Jersey, and southern Westchester. They reach our State Theater from remoter areas by shared or self-owned automobile, or mass transport consisting of train, bus, or subway. They are willing to pay, by rule of thumb, about half what a ticket costs at the Metropolitan Opera Association, across Lincoln Center Plaza. The types of ballet our audiences will pay for are not computed by averaging past hits, nor can they be assembled in committee. Ballets our audiences pay for are those of which our repertory continues to consist. It might be granted that answers to such demographic surveys could be found in unclassified material of public sources, in addition to the testimony of any reasonably intelligent fifth-grade child.

Those whose pleasure or business it is to specialize in efficiency systems, marketability, or demographic surveys are fascinated by blind process rather than precise prescription, except when success crowns their predictable prognosis. The question of quality, especially when it involves intangibles such as the loose play of poetic fantasy, is difficult if not impossible to quantify according to ciphers that may apply to antiques, pictures, jewelry, or foreign automobiles. What a ballet company like ours needs is not *more* money, or more performances, but what is far more dear—*enough* money to maintain the stability of an elastic maximum operation, in terms of both dancing bipeds and the intelligent analysis of our operation's mathematics.

Our audience, which has been developed over three decades, has been partly self-educated by continued observation. By no means everyone cares for the classic dance, or even the neoclassic idiom of Balanchine and Robbins. Less than a third of the audience of the New York City Opera company crosses over to subscribe to the New York City Ballet. Each separate ballet company playing in New York has its enthusiastic, loyal, and partial public. Our audience could be characterized as a family audience; that is, it takes our company as a familial entity. It watches its members emerge from the chrysalis of the school, sprout new wings, and develop less as stars than as individual soloists in a symphonic ensemble. The response it grants us is, one might say without much exaggeration, an analytical, patient, appreciative, deeply interested one. Since our public demands an intellectual response similar to that of the art-gallery-goer or music-lover rather than that of a stargazer or groupie, it has followed our repertory's choreographic explorations with adventurous satisfaction. No marketeer need ask it what kind of a new work it requires. Its expectations have been formulated by an established aesthetic of renovated tradition, musical surprise, and the continual promise and fulfillment of talented new performers.

MAY, 1978: *New York*

Dress rehearsal for School of American Ballet's annual Workshop performances. Shoura Danilova's *Scènes de Ballet* (Glazounov); Jean-Pierre Bonnefous's *Quadrille* (Johann Strauss), and Jerome Robbins's *Interplay* (Morton Gould). The triumph of the occasion was Suki Schorer's production of Balanchine's *Divertimento No. 15* (Mozart).

In our school, the annual Workshop, started thirteen years ago, not only sums up a year's work; it also heralds a new generation of dancers. There are good years, poor years, and indifferent years; the same applies to grapes of vintage: 1978 produced a bumper crop. The actual two performances of each demonstration are now held in the beautiful wood-paneled opera-theater of the Juilliard School, practically under professional performance conditions. There is a large and excellent orchestra of undergraduate players led by a graduate-student conductor. The stage is ample, the lighting clear, the occasion festive and inviting. It is no secret that scouts from

many companies have hawks' eyes on our dancers, and since the
school always has more than we can quickly place in the New York
City Ballet, a number of other companies are the beneficiaries of
the event.

In the past, Madame Alexandra Danilova has resorted to her
fantastic memory for portions of older ballets she recalls from her
youth at the Maryinsky Theater. This year she composed herself,
in the spirit of the later Petipa, an elaborate series of dances for a
large company of girls and boys, of which the adagio sections were
particularly appealing. Suki Schorer, for many years a brilliant virtuoso in our company and now a commanding teacher in our
school, took almost a year to prepare Balanchine's beautiful but
fiendishly complex masterpiece *Divertimento No. 15*. There were
those who said, and perhaps even thought, that this performance
was better danced than our company did it on the stage of the
State Theater. If the hours of rehearsal spent on its preparation
could have been added up, and the dancers paid by union contract,
we might have been bankrupted. It was indeed splendidly performed with sharpness and accent which would rival, although
scarcely surpass, artists who had lived through it for many seasons.
The euphoria aroused by watching unknown or unnamed ado-
lescents move into the roles of ballerinas and first dancers tends to
dismantle objective analysis. I watched Mikhail Baryshnikov during this performance. He held a surgical eye on the proceedings;
after all, how many times had he been through this himself? Amid
the polite, the perfunctory, and the enthusiastic applause, I saw
him applaud—once.

This was for *Quadrille*, a series of dances to Viennese waltzes
arranged by Jean-Pierre Bonnefous, for children from our youngest
division. Costumes were borrowed from the party scene of *Nutcracker*. Jean-Pierre has a particular affinity for small boys, recalling
his own youth at the Paris Opéra. A suave and beautiful performer,
he has an instinct for traditional but ever-living elegance which
shines in his personal manner and in the historic style he transmits.
I had seen a ballet of his to a piano concerto of Camille Saint-
Saëns, a ballet which, to me, seemed a perfection in miniature. It
might have been called, after Watteau, *L'Embarcation pour Cy-
thère*. I was eager for Balanchine to see it, with the chance of including it in repertory. But Balanchine became ill; schedules were

filled, the chance shunted itself off, and as sometimes happens, the occasion appears to have been lost. However, Jean-Pierre knows steps, and how to put them together with character. His homage to Degas in *Tricolore* shows how he has absorbed the classic amplitude and theatricality of the Palais Garnier.

Jerome Robbins's jocose *Interplay* entered our company's repertory in 1952. It was a work for a young company of young dancers. A quarter of a century ago, its jazzy score corresponded to the then familiar pulse of popular music which our dancers relaxed by dancing to, after hours. As we matured and dancers grew older, jazz turned into rock, which slid into other mutations. It was impossible to stay steadily in balance with the latest fad in syncopation and improvisatory variations. But Robbins's choreography held a basic hardihood of charm and structure, while its mannerisms, which in older performers might seem affection, in young ones appeared as a period revival. Wilma Curley, who had danced the original version, rehearsed eight striking kids, four boys and four girls. The girls were already apprentices, rehearsing with our company. Christopher d'Amboise, Jacques' son, had just been taken; when Balanchine saw the other boys, he took the lot. *Interplay* is designed in the vernacular of the early fifties. We have developed a genius for instant nostalgia, and this choreography, offered as a revival without any apology, surpassed every expectation by its vitality and sweetness of humor.

There is always a danger in trying to force novelty by attaching it to a current fashion, either of painting or of music. Ballets that date due to chic decor, their immediate reference of sentiment or dress, must be strong enough in the structure of intrinsic dancing to survive the exhaustion in taste. *Interplay*, thanks here to the skill and exuberant muscle of advanced virtuoso students, came out fresh as a daisy. The following Sunday night, it was presented integrally as part of the program for one of four "Robbins Nights" on the stage of the State Theater. The eight fledgling dancers may not at first have been entirely happy about the spacing, on an area approximately twice the floor of Juilliard's opera-theater. Ronnie Bates skillfully zeroed the lights down so that the movement took place within a footage that was more domestic than operatic; everything worked well. The audience at Juilliard comprised well-wishers, parents, friends, fellow students. At the State Theater it was a regular subscription audience, sympathetic but by no means individually partisan. The ovation at the end of the performance was deserved; a sheet added to the house program stated that *Interplay* was danced by students of the School of American Ballet. What neither dancers nor audience knew at the curtain calls was that all the boys were now members of the New York City Ballet.

While Balanchine himself has not taught at the School of American Ballet for many years, he takes a lively interest in its activities, exerting a strong repressive or encouraging hand. Recently, its board of directors, among efforts to augment income to meet challenge grants offered by the Ford Foundation and National Endowment for the Arts, proposed instituting a small fee for students wishing an audition which might admit them to the school. Such a fee, assumed as universally practical in private educational institutions all over the country, hardly covers the costs of handling applications and of the paperwork necessary to maintain files. Balanchine curtly vetoed the proposal, phoning back: "Absolutely not; we don't need this—yet." Assuming we had charged five dollars to cover each application, it might have gained us ten thousand dollars a year. Assuming an annual budget of some seven hundred thousand, surely such an amount will not be a vast hardship, but it expressed his attitude about open enrollment with a symbolic ease of invitation, welcoming, possibility; a political philosophy of modest populism in a ferociously elitist profession. But he also had said, "We don't need this—yet," realizing full well what a general economic inflation has done, that classes of thirty or more students limit individual attention awarded promising students, and that there is always a drift, unconscious or not, toward students who can pay. Yet on the other hand, Balanchine's educational philosophy may be interpreted as financially imperial or self-indulgent. When our youngest students appear in *Coppélia, Harlequinade, Nutcracker*, and *Don Quixote*, they are just as beautifully dressed from the shop founded by Karinska (now sensitively continued by Ben Benson) as all our elder ballerinas. The costumes are very expensive; since bodies they clothe are small, material and detail might be skimped. Balanchine wants the children to recognize perfection in workmanship, the beauty and choice of silks and satins, the craftsmanship of jewelry, the care taken to present dancers as important artists. This all amounts to education in taste, theatrical elegance, the richness of theatrical illusion, the importance of precious attention as a normal commodity. The corps of devoted women, under Madame Sophie Pourmel, attend our fledgling ballerinas as ladies-in-waiting. Madame Pourmel also teaches good manners when children wait to be dressed and undressed. Life in our theater starts at nine or ten; youngsters learn the habit of order and silence necessary for precision, entering the stage on cue, following the conductor's baton, marking the correctness of positions onstage, considering colleagues and partners. So it is small wonder that some parents push their offspring into ballet with more urgency than is perhaps prompted by their victims, as a sort of correctional facility, a gilded, cushioned prison. It is hardly cruel, but possibly unusual, punishment, yet watching dozens of kids in three or four teams, trained for our full-length works, one considers dandelions in full head, and how many of their thousand seeds germinate to make one other dandelion.

MAY 8, 1978: *New York*

Dress rehearsal of Jerry Robbins's *Sketch Book*. Balanchine in the country for a holiday. Robbins tells Ronnie Bates to level lights along the blades of the foils so their metal glints. Costumes from *Goldberg Variations* brought down to try on, but there is no point in more than suggesting the eighteenth century for this first essay for *The Arts of the Gentleman*.

Robbins had planned a large-scaled full-length three-act ballet for at least three years. *The Arts of the Gentleman* was a manual of arms, equitation, and dance which taught manners, defense, and attack to young men whose training in fencing, horsemanship, and court ballroom manners equipped them for noble duty. The first part was sketched in the fall of 1977. Robbins enlisted the aid of a Hungarian master-swordsman who was also armorer to the Metropolitan Opera Association. The profiled vocabulary of fencing has certain spectacular elements which recall ballet, but it is a science dedicated to the extremely economical geometry of offense and defense within restricted silhouettes. The single dimension, as in high-relief, reduces the area of body which can be hit; fencing, accurately or academically demonstrated, is an exercise for combat survival to be executed rather than watched. Robbins with extraordinary ingenuity took this body-language and invented a formal dance from the sequence of its canonical movements. He stylized it ever so slightly by the suggestion of white guard gloves and cocked hats, which were ceremoniously doffed in the ritual preceding mock encounter. It was a tour de force of brilliance; of considerable interest was the fact that the ensemble of a dozen boys included several who only a fortnight before had danced in Robbins's *Interplay*.

Robbins had been seriously ill, nor had his recovery been quick. He had apparently abandoned *The Arts of the Gentleman*, only the introduction of which he had been able to sketch. Balanchine also had been ill. We usually promise subscribers and patrons two novelties a season although scheduling has become increasingly so indeterminate that now we announce them only as "New Ballet Number 1" and "New Ballet Number 2." At Balanchine's insistence, Robbins again took up the fencing episode which he had commenced, elaborated it, and prepared it for presentation. He called it a sketch toward the large three-act work, if and when we should find time and money to complete it. Time was, or had become, almost more of a consideration than money. In May, 1978, we could foresee a very full schedule through 1981. Repertory has to be maintained; we had engagements outside of New York, both here and abroad, more demanding than in ten years, and yet the presentations of new works ensure the vitality of the company. *Sketch Book* was at once a forecast and fulfillment. Besides the dominant contribution of Jerome Robbins, it also reinforced the strong impression Peter Martins had already made as a potential choreographer.

Whether it was Robbins's enforced rest that induced reconsideration, his absence from the theater, or his return to it fired by enthusiasm for a thrilling new wave of strong young dancers, *Sketch Book* displayed the full spectrum of his unique professionalism. The portions intended for his proposed *Arts of the Gentleman* showed one aspect of his talents—mastery of given or received material, its transformation from raw data into an artificed construct. But one was hardly prepared for quite another considerable ballet in the same series of "sketches." Jerry took some three-quar-

ters of his music from Verdi's extremely beautiful ballet-music for
I Vespri Siciliani and invented a purely classical ballet, without
the slightest inversion or idiosyncratic comment. Here was indeed
a new Robbins. If his name had not been attached, one might have
thought it had been composed by some consummate master of the
canonical academic dance. There was nothing hinting of an individual comment, nor any suggestion of Jerome Robbins himself—
except fleetingly (the abrupt cameo comparable to the apparition
of Alfred Hitchcock in every one of his films), when his four boys
almost imperceptibly bow and nod to one another. Verdi's music
quite surpassed the ordinary necessities of opera-ballet, and under
Bob Irving's baton assumed a symphonic fullness which propelled
the clarity of steps Robbins had found and combined. The ballet
commences with a fanfare of four high-flying boys; they really fly.
On top of various surprises, there was, in the *pas de deux*, a debut
of no ordinary interest. Kyra Nichols, beautifully supported by
Sean Lavery, was revealed as a ballerina of considerable potential
—noble, steady, assured, with a serenity and holding power much
past her eighteen years. This year marked the insurgence of a group
of young women of exceptional proficiency: Merrill Ashley, now
a principal dancer with large responsibilities; Heather Watts, newly
promoted to soloist rank; and Kyra Nichols, still officially in the
corps.

Daniel and Joseph Duell were given very flashy dancing by
Robbins. The elder of these brothers from Dayton, Ohio, was
already a firm, agile, gracious, and expert classic technician. Jerry
gave him an extended variation (solo violin, by Telemann) even
more difficult and taxing than anything in Balanchine's *The Four
Temperaments*, with which it had kinship. For the two brothers
together, there was a *pas de deux* by the baroque composer Heinrich von Biber for which the pit piano had been "prepared" by
papering the strings. Sounds from it, a grand piano transformed
into a bellicose harpsichord, accompanied a series of ferocious athletics utilizing sword play, accented by musical silences filled with
the swishing noise of steel striking air as the boys spun through
space.

The *Sketch Book* might have been called "Work-in-Progress," a
fashionable appellation frequently used by "advance-guard" practitioners. There were some complaints that the sections of dances

shown were too "finished" in performance, and yet none was seen in full or proper context. This last was true. Indeed when Balanchine saw Madame Danilova's ballet to Glazounov's *Scènes de Ballet* for our 1978 school Workshop, he commented that it was "too professional." I gather he felt the style of a school should be roughly academic with no need for extreme polish, and that of an opera house absolutely proficient. It may be possible that an opera house is no place to show work-in-progress, but if circumstances enforce the necessity of pinch-hitting—which *Sketch Book* certainly was—why should even its fragments be less well performed than they could be?

JULY 2, 1978: *New York*

Finale of sixty-eighth New York City season. Program: *Entente Cordiale* in its entirety. Packed house, screaming standing room. Brilliant *Stars and Stripes*. Somewhat improved (tinkered-with) *Tricolore*. Smashing *Union Jack*. Standing ovation. Balanchine, in a pale-green linen suit and yellow kerchief, takes six curtain calls. Stage crew working till 4 A.M. dismantling scenery and lights, packing for Saratoga.

Every now and then Balanchine becomes enchanted, mesmerized, magnetized by chance notions deriving from some aural fragment, and danced steps result which mean more to him than to other less fascinated viewers. He fell in love with the rhythm and succinctness of sound in radio and TV commercials, jingles endlessly used to sell breakfast food or airplane tickets. Behold: *PAMTGG*.

This ballet, alas, with no benefit of commercial support whatsoever from the company advertised, has been taken as the nadir of our "creative" career. It was easy to hate, so that, even in this aspect, it fulfilled a useful function. More positively, I felt (and I was not alone) that it held interesting, even beautiful images, borrowed from Balanchine's innumerable arrivals and departures from the world's airports. There was a broad vision of a landing field at night, the semaphore of hand signals from electric torches held by safety stewards, and some wonderful adagio combinations from floating and flying. The fact that it was launched by advertising slogans, that it was an anthology of procedures suggested by airports and flight, was enough to sink it before it could have become airborne. Music was not much help, and since Balanchine is musically determined, a bet on the failure or success of a new work, for those who have heard the proposed score, reduces critical risk. As for *PAMTGG*, the attempt to weave a symphonic treatment based on fragmentary jazzy jingles was doubtless doomed.

In considering "success" and/or "failure," if one took a relatively objective view of our achievement over the last thirty years, it would have to be conceded that "success" (smash hits for the daily press) has never had an edge. We always skirt and often approach (temporarily) "failure." As for example with the *New York Times* on *Union Jack.* Yet the greater part of surviving repertory which had coolish or warmish receptions (rarely hot) has continued to accumulate attention which increases in heat and intensity (*The Four Temperaments, Agon,* more recently the Hindemith *Kammermusik*).

Entente Cordiale, like *Jewels,* consists of three disparate ballets, by three different composers, but on a single theme or pretext. Predictably, *Stars and Stripes* was an instant triumph, and so was *Union Jack,* despite the *Times. Tricolore,* inserted between them, was at first exposure a fair bid to join *PAMTGG* in ignominy. Placed between two blockbusters—a patriotic summons to regard Radio City Music Hall as Fort McHenry, or the Fourth of July as a family outing hosted by Mamie and Ike, with an homage to all that exists of the divinity that doth hedge a king, even in Buckingham Palace today—their French cousin seemed born underprivileged. Part of this was due to the extraordinary dancing of the company as a whole in the two other displays, the bravura of the ballerinas, the strength of our younger male dancers. But part was also due to the lack of sharp focus on France as a popular lyric source. Peter Martins's realization of a Basque folk dance had ingenuity and mastery of a large corps, but there was little to speak for the Basque spirit of independence except handsome scenery and costumes. Jean-Pierre Bonnefous's evocation of Degas used the painter's race track, jockeys, and stage of the Grand Opéra. Here at least the public could make contact with a predigested vision, while Ter-

Arutunian's scenery and costumes paid touching homage to great painting. It was hardly Jerome Robbins's fault that the finale didn't work. *Tricolore* even at its fifth performance, now incorporated into *Entente Cordiale*, could not by the wildest stretch of the imagination be compared to *Stars and Stripes* or *Union Jack*, but it had taken on some interest as a parade and was as well received by its audiences as many other ballets once in need of drastic repair.

Balanchine's seminal idea, linking a trio as spectacles made out of populist lyric expression of the United States, Great Britain, and France, owing to the luck of the first two, indicated a happy crown for the whole. After all, France had the cancan, the Grand Opéra, the "Marscillaise." Only an inevitable intrusion of hubris imposed its horrid issue. From his hospital bed Balanchine indicated to Martins, Bonnefous, and Robbins what he would have done had he been able, even down to names and numbers of dancers. His behests were loyally followed; Jerry Robbins manfully took on the finale as a duty and executed it with as much panache as could be mustered. Rouben Ter-Arutunian, with inventiveness and taste far exceeding a purely professional exercise, designed a sumptuous frame which revealed itself as costly as it was. Indeed, cost was a reason, if there was to be no other, for salvaging the work.

Balanchine had frequently worked with Georges Auric, the composer, during the Diaghilev seasons of the late twenties. He recalled him as an amiable and professional collaborator, master of *musiquette*, an heir to Erik Satie in the popularization, or repudiation, of conventional French *conservatoire* symphonism. A member of Les Six, a vanguard of the advance-guard of the period, with Poulenc and Cocteau, he was now its sole survivor. Cocteau, after the First World War, had made polemic and practice of "the rehabilitation of the commonplace." This was a powerful policy; Les Six condemned Ravel, not for his refusing official academic recognition, but "for having deserved it." The score Balanchine commissioned from Auric in his and the century's seventies, while it benefited from the orchestration of an expert, turned out to be not exactly what was either hoped or expected. Times change. In the twenties, Auric as a young man had admired but not as yet felt the rhythmic and tonic thrust of Stravinsky, who then was still considered, for his most acceptable work, as the exiled monster voice of barbaric Russia. Auric, Poulenc, Cocteau, Braque, Picasso, whatever their hereditary provenance, were Parisians. Paris was the city of Coco Chanel, capital of *haute couture* and Modernart. It was this remembered Paris that Balanchine evidently thought to memorialize, even though it had not existed since the Second World War. Stravinsky had set his implacable imprint on music that launches ballet steps, robbing conventional musical accompaniments of much of their rhythmic innocence or melodic charm. Auric had developed according to his own individual capacity and conviction; he was no longer a man of the twenties.

Had Balanchine himself been present to handle the given musical material, possibly something more attractive might have come of the score. It may still come. A critic wrote after listening to *Agon* (once) that Balanchine could compose combinations from a telephone book. Needless to say, this is untrue. I remember when we received the piano score of *Agon* and it sounded like nothing of which my ears could make any logic, I asked him, myself a tonal ignoramus, what it would sound like from a pit band. He said that he found it entirely "appetizing." It is true that his experience and superior skill can more often than not find devices transforming seemingly intransigent music into something weirdly magical. At the moment, however, due to his illness, he could not enforce this power, except at one remove. There were those who joked that he had succumbed as an evasion. But of course this was not at all true. He became unwell because he had undertaken nonstop, uninterrupted composition for five decades with nothing resembling any prolonged vacation other than weekends between duties. As for his basic general health, his rapid recovery and the fact that he was rehearsing and actively correcting dancers within a month after his hospitalization gave the lie to a rumored gravity of his condition. Illness survived strengthens—as rest, meditation, warning, and the sense of survival against odds and ill luck.

The reason for the unsuccess of *Tricolore* lay also in the condition that France has no internationally legible popular dance-step tradition corresponding to what was easily recognized in English folk-dancing or British music halls. The Garde Républicaine, the civil national guard, to us, is not equatable with the Brigade of Guards. The cancan has become a universal nightclub number, but fluffy ruffles are too familiar a stereotype to be acceptable straight on. Balanchine thought to transform it by costuming cancan dancers as hybrid drum-majorettes. It didn't exactly work. The martial finale which must sustain comparison with those of *Stars and Stripes* and *Union Jack* was superbly costumed in an adaptation of the Garde authentic uniform, magnificent casques with long horse-hair plumes, the model of which was sent us from Paris by Violette Verdy, now mistress of the ballet of the Grand Opéra. Auric perhaps could not have rung variations on "La Marseillaise"; previously we had used no national anthems, but the French have the most rousing of any. Avoiding it for reasons of taste or decorum, Auric might have used some of the splendid marches, "Sambre et Meuse" or "Le Chant du Départ." Instead, he provided a synthetic march which might have suited a patriotic film but which was little help as a balletic rabble-rouser, which was what the doctor called for. Balanchine returned, quite recovered, determined to reconstruct the ballet in spite of everything, and began at once to make changes, if only in details. His willfulness is exceeded only by his surgical expertise. The last of *Tricolore* has not been seen or heard.

SUMMER, 1978: *New York*

Meetings to make plans for celebration of the thirtieth anniversary of the company. An idea to revive a series of repertory works not presently danced as a conspectus of the development of the repertory. Practical considerations render this impractical. I prefer to place all time and money on one big new ballet, preferably *The Birds of America*, of which Morton Gould's new score is finished, Ter-Arutunian's designs are sketched.

Ten years of activity preceding the actual formation of the New York City Ballet stand as a preparatory prelude rather than part of our consecutive chronicle. These early years can count as tentative experiment with a very few solid additions to repertory, as well as training valuable dancers and a solidification of the basis for our school. The Second World War marked the end of our beginnings; by 1947 we were in a position of being able to think of ourselves as an entity approaching an official institution bearing the name and seal of the municipality of Greater New York, which we were licensed to use in tours abroad. Looking back over three decades or glancing at the summary narrative included in these pages only fills one with regret at the inadequacy of one's report, the inevitable omission of names and incidents which might have been mentioned; the confirmation that theatrical history resolves itself into gossip or anecdotes which are seldom vivid or finally significant. The principal services by which our thirty years may be considered memorable in the widespread theatrical activity of the United States during this time are those dancers trained in our school, repertory created for our company, the audience magnetized by the direction, spirit, and quality of both. This has been achieved by the invocation of old and honorable traditions, maintained with singleness of purpose, rigor in discipline, and domination of criteria in which a certain morality governed. Without an inheritance from Russian roots of our faculty and its system, Balanchine could not have built company or ballets, while Robbins would have had no instrument to manipulate. Factors contributing to build school and company are embedded in the context of our times—New York in the fifties, sixties, and seventies. When the cultural chronicle of the epoch comes to be written, signs will emerge of shift and change which now are too close for location or estimate. As we approach 1980 there are some notable indications of developments which thirty years ago were hardly predictable, and now, even when they have been more or less realized, are not easily visible.

Paris ceased to be capital of world culture even before the fall of France. Change was initially noticeable when the School of New York was a catchword identifying a group of abstract expressionist painters who seized priority of prestige from Paris and commenced to command taste and prices for three decades. With the aid of European exiles, architectural design became a virtual American monopoly. As for music, at least the genre of popular bands and vocalists could not be considered without our inheritance from jazz. This was clear decades before the end of the fifties. It had by no means been true of dance. While American dancers were respected, even in Europe, thirty years ago the ground swell toward classic ballet was not much more than a hopeful ripple, except for pioneers who were generally European-trained and for their small but growing audience of enthusiasts. Consider the situation of ballet in the

United States at the end of our seventies. There is more activity in the field than ever before. The mass schooling of young children in the discipline of the classic regimen is unprecedented. The so-called modern dance, formerly an advance-guard of dance activity from the early thirties through the sixties, has retired into the position of senior citizenry without institutional issue, a fourth generation of innovators, or an audience of theatrical density. What life there was in this movement has been compromised by borrowings from ballet. Improvisation as a didactic technique is finally discounted as self-indulgence. It is now generally recognized that no aspirant much past the age of ten is going to amount to much by way of becoming a virtuoso acrobatic performer, upon which all ballet companies depend. Via television, and to some degree film, ballet has entered a considerable area of massive popular recognition. Legitimization of the male dancer as a musical athlete has been largely accomplished. Journalistic coverage of ballet, at least in attention to personalities of important artists, has found a place in dailies and weeklies which, although smaller than that awarded sport, is comparable to that which has long been assigned to the plastic arts. It is too much to say that ballet is accepted or enthusiastically regarded by many as being no less magnetic than some sports—perhaps golf or tennis? There are possibly other reasons for interest in the classic dance which have to do with manners and morals, a subject awkward to approach, since the philosophical or semantic factors involved end either as self-serving defense or polemics of special pleading.

However, I am hardly the first to suggest that roots of theater are religious, or that foundations of religious observance early expressed themselves in dance. In an epoch punctuated by two world wars, a disastrous permissiveness in child-rearing and education, decline in church observance, and anarchic fragmentation in every plastic art, surviving formal disciplines have tended increasingly to become more attractive, not alone for survival as a sign of strength, but for present potential and future service. Ballet is immediately legible, even when its entire sense is not grasped in depth at a single scanning. What can be clearly seen in any well-executed performance is a group of beautiful young people in prime of health, trained for a rigorous profession, working in transparent harmony according to metrical laws superior to their individual wills or accidental preferences. This may well be translated as a paradigm of theological structure and principle—submission to a superior order, consideration of fellow bipeds, pleasure in tracking a sequence of steps which can be described, without excessive exaggeration, as a lay rite.

André Malraux long ago named museums the cathedrals of our present. Opera houses are more lively, although often containing less lovely artifacts than museums, but theaters in which dancing and singing take place can become a frame for festive, quasi-ceremonial occasions. Ballet dancing is patterned possibility and responsibility; by extension, an exemplar of unlimited consideration. The training of a dancer's body toward acrobatic, expressive virtuosity is not entirely remote from the training of a doctor of medicine or other highly specialized scientists. Just as candidates for a priesthood surrender certain aspirations, including worldly goods and the license of personal choice, so dancers in a company have entered a more-or-less conventual body of which the sovereign rule is: Obey.

Popularity of ballet today perhaps needs no further explanation or justification. The numbers of children, talented or not, who wish to dance guarantee a future of the art which is not to be written off as a response to an ephemeral impulse. Dance has always existed, with a life of its own, although sometimes it seems to choose odd or unlikely frames to fill. The question of the future of a single company like ours, focusing on a personal situation, is one which is hardly satisfied by prophecy or prognosis. For a decade now, there has been speculation as to: after Balanchine, what, who, or when? He lived through the death of czarist Russia. The Imperial School was uninterruptedly reborn as the Soviet State Academy. He survived the death of Diaghilev in 1929, eventually to found three companies of his own. He discovered young dancers whom he trained to move according to his requirements and, a quarter of a century later, saw them teach in a school which has now existed ten years longer than the New York City Ballet itself.

In our company there are fiercely strong elements of a cadre which keep its repertory alive. It has also become evident that there are elements in it capable of instruction, composition, and leadership. Our company now enjoys a material stability which, however tenuous or fragile, is a launch for future possibility that Diaghilev himself hardly ever knew. There are, of course, always those who attach themselves to past associations, memories of a former time, to be cherished like personal possessions, which indeed they are. "It wasn't like this at the old City Center" (on 55th Street). "It wasn't like this with the old Ballet Russe de Monte Carlo." "It wasn't like this in the old Diaghilev Company." "It wasn't like this when old Petipa governed the old Maryinsky Ballet." All are absolutely right and true. The way it was is never the way it is, thank God. The way it is will never be what happens next. What happens next will be many things, each and all different from anything before, each needing energy to accommodate, to inspect, to discover, on new terms. A past that is not in use is dead. Present and future have a chance to be alive. What has been chewed, tenderized, or predigested is swallowed easily. Slices of neat fresh rawness in fish or flesh are different. As for proposing continuity in institutions, including one's own, there is the indulgence of betting on sweepstakes for which contenders are still unposted.

Proprietary participation is the due of all fans, music-lover or ballet-buff. Passion for performers is different in kind from appreciation of collective performance; the two tend to be confused. Those who automatically shout *bravo* (or indiscriminately, *brava* or *bravi*) at favored artists add color to curtain calls and do minimal harm. Sol Hurok, shrewd mastodon of *impresariiii*, was wont to stand at the back of the orchestra floor during seasons of the "old" Ballet Russe (de Monte Carlo). His eye was ever more on box office than stage, but he managed to take up his post to bravo like a bull as the curtain went down. In those ancient days, the Italianate fashion of screaming hadn't caught on; there were sensitive patrons who shushed such brash encouragement for its poor taste. Today we've come a long way, baby; fans who yell show not only that they know La Scala well and the ballet better, but Rudi, Mischa, or Peter, best. This is not belittling gross response that sells tickets. However, the quality of such response brings into question the qualifications, rights, power, and seriousness of public attitudes.

Repertory institutions magnetize at least three areas of action, which may be counted on or distilled in serious discussion of continuity or succession. There is some consequence in a public that attends performances with regularity and considers a company something of a family, having marked the entrance of new dancers onstage from their school days. Their opinions can be equated in a rough way to those governing best sellers, popular films or plays, museum exhibitions, and liberal politics. Then there is a tightly bonded core of semiprofessional observers, ex-dancers, teachers, obsessed observers whose lodged and focused commentary when couched in clear, clever, and concise dicta tends to be echoed in unexpected places, including printed quotations which stick as labels and affect taste. Then there is journalism, which is often more interested in getting a story with a good lead and a good picture than taking much trouble with the presumed subject. This is due to strait-jacketing space and editorial economy as much as lack of focus from the reporter.

In New York City, our quota of daily papers is three; of weeklies (that commonly count for ballet), six. Reportage is more corroborative than analytical or didactic, dwelling more on personalities than on patterns they pursue. There have been times when a journalist, forgetting or forsaking prime functions, ventures into assuming a demi-political role. Commonly this happens at the express invitation of managements who hope to anticipate the favors of the press. Or this may be a quest for a change in policy which indeed has not, as yet, been determined. There is a naïve expectation that a pundit can repair or project what a repertory has thus far failed to manage.

Max Beerbohm and Bernard Shaw read as the best advice for chronicling theatrical management and performance. Each in a characteristic caveat, and indeed at the very entrance of his career as critic of the West End scene, armed himself against usurping a style that might read *ex cathedra*, oracular, or olympian. It was their tailoring of commentaries to an almost domestic intimacy, an attention or solicitation approaching love, an immediacy grasping at snapshot imagery, that makes it still a delight to read of plays and players whose names themselves mean little or nothing save in these precise notations. Nor did they indulge themselves in rushing history at the debut of a new playwright, even a Granville-

Barker, Frederick Lonsdale, or Somerset Maugham, with: "Hats off, gentlemen: a genius."

We have not had cause to worry about the negative power of the press. We've been flattered for our efforts and forgiven for our shortcomings. We have been careful and grateful for care and courtesy, and have not hesitated to acknowledge appreciation, which has been constant. We have not been crippled by annihilating notices, although there have been a few, because an active repertory is hydra-headed—when one new-born ballet is lopped off or no longer rehearsed, another buds up. We have had few "hits," in terms of commercial box office; attention to these might be thought to draw interest away from the rest of our roster. However, induced popularity sells out the theater, and an overflow public that can't buy tickets for a hit settles for other programs which it may learn to like and look at.

The foregoing, which may seem discursive or beside the point, is perhaps not beside, but around it. It attempts to assuage those who are betting or who may soon bet on the endurance, survival, or continuity of what our thirty years have built. Journalism is often projective gossip; what one reads in a columnist's daily stint may not be serious, but this and other suggestions create an atmosphere that has little reference to central or essential promises or planning. Because of advancing age, circumstance, illness, or fate, there is normal speculation as to next steps. These are proposed but hardly charted in the press.

If there is a single element that both Balanchine and I have shared since birth, it is a sense of survival. He derives from Georgian bloodlines, which not only are among the oldest of classic Graeco-Armenian strains but also bear the longest-lived Ibero-Caucasian genes. My father taught me, at so early an age that I can't remember first when, that the duty, despair, and destiny of Jews was to survive and proceed. Why, or for what, he left for me to discover. The fact that Jews exist to serve, like Christians, Moslems, and Buddhists, was explanation enough. Balanchine, in his avatar as a gardener, has often compared his notion of a ballet to a useless rose garden. It's pretty, but who needs it? It's fun for the gardeners; chance passers-by aren't hurt by the blossoms, unless they're careless about prickles. Maintenance, pruning, grafting, seeding, cutting, and flower arrangement have been our work. This amounts to survival on our terms. As much thought and work over the last seasons has gone into a projection of continuity into the immediate future as has been spent in raising money.

When the time comes, as it must, for our company to make critical choices, there will inevitably be "disappointments," indignation, and alarm. The choices will be, to many in the press and public, "impossible to understand." Alternatives that may have seemed more logical, correct, tasteful, or obvious will have been denied or ignored. However, for those who have been close to the heart of the matter and who have had sober and informed interest in the destiny of our company, those who have followed the directions indicated over three decades and who are not much swayed by casual judgments or picturesque futures, there are simple factors which will have been taken as determinants. Our company has depended, depends, and will depend on our school; both have come to be funded to an important degree by the National Endowment for the Arts. While this, and the contribution to our company from the New York State Council on the Arts, hardly balances budgets of either school or company, such prestigious funding offers official seals of approval. At the least it proves our audits and accountancy are responsible. This encourages other donations; we have been vetted by objective computers and not found wanting. In addition, we have gained generous patrons, individual persons, foundations, corporations, bequests. In whatever manner one judges the political or economic metabolism of nations, our twin corporations seem no less healthy—or frail—than the preponderance of other institutions with comparable historical life-spans: museums, libraries, opera companies, orchestras. We have become an "establishment" corpus, and while this has been regretted by some few nay-sayers with more nostalgia than we need for those bad old days, at present, we are able to plan rather than improvise. We have supportive boards of directors, like other established institutions, from a broad cross-section of our industrial, financial, and legal communities. "Establishment" is neither as secure nor as pejorative a label as it may seem. However, our present status hardly threatens bankruptcy as an imminent menace as so often it was in the good old days. There is a fiscal structure for continuity. Granted the nature of modest but constant official support of the performing arts in the United States into and through the 1980's, survival in terms of payrolls, union negotiations, a theater, and dancers becomes only an ordinary preoccupation.

On the artistic or metaphysical side—what some enthusiasts call "creativity" and which Balanchine names "assemblage"—there is, naturally, what has long been Question Number One. The replacement of artistic direction is a riddle aching to be brought into the open both by the half-informed, those with something approaching ill will, and by many vigorously concerned. Everyone can be at rest. In our case, there will be no "replacement." Nor was there any such for the Chevalier Noverre, who dominated ballet in the eighteenth century, or for Marius Petipa, who ruled nineteenth-century ballet. Petipa's repertory to a surprising degree survives on every continent, including Africa and Japan. A repertory, a patrimony of ballets, tended as carefully as the collection of six-hundred-year-old bonsai in Tokyo's Imperial Palace conservatory, is not replaced; it is preserved, maintained, refreshed to give rebirth by grafting and seedlings. Noh theater is some three centuries, rather than three decades, old. It exists in the full flower of its formal splendor. Balanchine has not replaced Petipa; nor did Stravinsky replace Tchaikovsky; nor did he, Glinka. The expression of a sensibility is present as a continuum, to be seized upon by important possibilities.

With films, records, and trained memories, preservation—and conservation and continuation—is somewhat easier than before. Ah, yes, but who are the people who will tend to such maintenance? Rest easy. We have them; they perform presently and responsibly on the stage of the State Theater in Lincoln Center some twenty-three weeks every year, plus seasons in Saratoga and Washington, and every few years in either Paris, Berlin, Copenhagen, or London.

This may be all very well—but just who will supply the New Repertory?

Who indeed . . .

One need not bolster gossip by proclaiming whatever personal opinions may contribute to the confusion that will surround all answers to so crucial a question. If one said one knew, or could point toward a single talent, it would be vain and inconclusive boasting. If one said one had no notion, it would not be true. For superstitious reasons, then, let us evade it. Boys and girls who soon enough will join present inventors or assemblers of our repertory in fashioning novelties over the next decade may not now be as conscious of their capacity as I hope I am. However immodestly, I take gross credit for persuading the twenty-eight-year-old Balanchine in 1933 to come here when both Fokine and Massine were far more eminent and, with means I either had or could touch, might have been available. Anybody observing our seasons doesn't need to task Balanchine with whom he might consider "promising." However, there are undoubtedly those also who have not yet had time to show of what they can be capable in terms of constructing interesting steps to magical music. They are present. They will be called.

The field is open. Outside our company and school are those who derive from Balanchine at various removes and have attempted to borrow his taste, which sometimes they misunderstand as a method. For every example of *haute couture* rated by its initial cost as an "original," there is the dilute reduction of the identical garment mass-produced by Seventh Avenue. In contemporary painting, there was for some decades a "School of New York"; before that "Schools" of Paris, Rome, Munich. Balanchine's is the School of American Ballet, its attachment to traditions of the Maryinsky Theater and the Petersburg Imperial School. I shall be surprised if those who are responsible for our artistic succession will have been bred without some knowledge of this milieu. Entrance to Olympic Games, Kentucky Derby, Grand Prix, and Indianapolis 500 are all "open." But to whom? To those whose qualifications, whose quintessential capacity equip them for the possibility of "winning." Machines and the equipment of athletes are more often analyzed than contributors to ballet repertory. The early stages of peak contests may resemble democratic process, but the genes in dogs and horses make champions through handling and aristocratic criteria. Dancers, dance designers, and dance administrators are produced the same way. Natural selection enters early on; later, even irrational luck may intervene and the most unlikely animals take the ribbons. But for what, after the event, can only be called the grace of God, any of half a dozen putative winners might have lost—or won. Relative skills are not hard to master; anyone who plays a piano can improvise. Anyone who dances fairly well can put steps together with a beginning, middle, double tour, final pose. In the so-called creative process, or more accurately, invention or assembly and imaginative construction, it is ultimately analytical intelligence which counts, a combination of organs in head and body taking into consideration multiple factors that not only make new ballets but maintain the flexible institutional frame within which they continue to be produced and visible. Intelligence capable of analysis is also informed by taste, an innate sense of scruple and shrewdness in handling persons and monies, a musical comprehension, a visual curiosity in plastic form, good fortune, and a few of God's other and rarer gifts. Without these last, all others fail.

In this enumeration of talents I am of course describing two master dance designers, tyrants of taste, artistic managers, one of whom I've not known, and one I have: Petipa and Balanchine. I don't doubt that the next half-dozen, still anonymous choreographers who will be working into the twenty-first century will be greatly different in kind, although not in quality, from their predecessors. Nor will the companies these half-dozen will administrate or manipulate be any surprise to them. Nor will the dancers whom they are given greatly differ from those we know today.

For those who are genuinely worried about the future of our company, I recommend that they watch our performers in their performances, and our repertory with its shifting casts. Watch the work of our school; worry less.

Saratoga Springs, New York
JULY, 1978

P.P.S

JULY 4, 1978:

I answer a letter from an academic sociologist, backed by a great corporation, asking for my opinions as to the popularity of ballet in America for a file-and-forget "survey."

The metric of the sociologist is weakly mathematical. Its object and its presumptive objective method can hardly eliminate the bias, individual or collective, of the interrogator. Shepherds watch their sheep, but who watches the shepherds? One of the many blameless ways for corporations and foundations to spend money is to license surveys. Surveys are particularly appropriate if they have neither reason nor effect, will arouse no controversy, and yet may hold some imprecise potential to encourage research when filed and forgotten. Why have ballet audiences grown in the United States?

Latencies of interest and focus correspond to historical necessities. The decline of organized religion in the ancient sense of church observance has by no means decreased metaphysical energy or curiosity. Indeed, as we have seen in the rise of interest in Eastern forms and the many expressions of heterodox Spiritualities, the interest of youth in the otherworldly is on the rise. Rituals well performed were first taken over from classical antiquity by the church fathers: cathedrals were great opera houses *avant la lettre*. The secularization of the church, its fraction and attempts to heal it by ecumenical aims, has, consciously or not, proposed something approaching a general searching or questioning congregation. Since God ceased having His portrait painted as a nude Santa Claus, since nuclear energy with its hopes and fears has permeated the universal imagination, Prime Mover, First Cause, Hollower of Black Holes, Master of Order inspires that type of awe which we once spelled as Yahweh. If these terrible titles could be reduced to one word, perhaps that word, even in the very start, is order. Order is also what is ordained; its pursuit includes those who, in its pursuit, are also ordained.

Ballet is a secular rite; if it is well performed, the congregation applauds; detonations fuse in air; the God has appeared. There has been a transient manifestation of Order—and this despite chaos, anarchy, corruption, pollution, and death and disorder. Order is what ballet is about—just as is music—but with a difference, and this difference is, I think, why its present popularity is not only an ephemeral phenomenon, but as steady and solid as the attraction of museums or symphonic orchestras. In it, order is both visually and aurally legible. Elements of hazard involved in the risk and execution of its acrobatics excite that portion of a public absorbed also by competitive sports. The continual emergence of new dancers in new ballets satisfies that passion for novelty which is a theatrical norm. The sight of exceedingly attractive young persons, highly skilled and moving in an extreme thrust of their physiques' capacities, is a metaphor of chance and gift seized and well used, of potential explored and shown in full capacity. The reason ballet is so popular today is that it frames a bare morality in perfect miniature which, however momentary the vision, is both blazingly evident onstage and equally absent in the exterior public dimension. In those of our theaters where ballet is housed with some continuity or stability, ballet performances represent maps or models of an ideal civil state, The Republic, commonwealth; The City of God. They are communions of experts and enthusiasts, two-hour services celebrating mutuality of credence in something superior to the miserable I or Me. The mosaic anonymity of corps de ballet and the kaleidoscopic assumption of multiple roles and characters by individual dancers are comparable to choirs and hierophants who, in the splendid vestments of their faith, served under high stone vaults. The reason ballet has arrived in its present impermanent permanency of popular acceptance is its transparent demonstration of the principles of service and order. As an increasingly accepted symbol of our society's spiritual preoccupations, it could be hardly less representative of an "Age of Me."

It is not a slight impulse to feel drawn toward such an exposition of service and order. It is by no accident that musicians and scientists are among the most faithful and knowledgeable friends of ballet. Metric is their constant judgment of order and orderings, which also include steps counted and dances metered. While artists measure by fantasy and scientists by mathematics, imagination and counting are shared by both. Great artists, dancers, musicians, and scientists are our only magicians; legible mastery of their several orderings is about as near today as we can come to miracles. Participation in performance, by several supports—applause, money, friendship—is a de-selfed testimony to the magic of methodical process haloed by art. The target of applause, in ballet, is dancers who enter their house of service early on, endure schooling as seminarians and athletes, and touch a source of order comparable to that which moves the sun and other stars.

Over the last half century, the academic classic dance has been in the custody of a single person. Before him, Marius Petipa held the same position for a similar tenure. Others have used the language with ingenuity, wit, and beauty. Few have matched Balanchine in capacities either to extend the idiom or to assemble steps which hold interest, both for dancers and for their audiences, over so extended a period. The classic academic dance is neither a series of styles or fashions which correspond to shifting hemlines or waistlines, nor a packageable product grateful to renovation from ingenious boxing or wrapping. What Balanchine has been able to do is to take the academic skeleton and, without essential repudiation, re-form it by extension, and reclothe it in novel measurings and surprising release. This exercise amounted to reconstitution, a propulsion past the capacities of previous practitioners. It depended on sophisticated equipment, not only in his own mind and body, but in those dancers first schooled in the traditional system upon which his own practice is based, and then further trained by him in class and rehearsal to fulfill the stringency of unique requirements.

He was the child of an epoch in contemporary history in which space and time were awarded new dimensions, in a universal shrinkage of mileage and an acceleration of movement. Two world wars in their holocausts cleared away much romantic rhetoric which was once social amenity and imaginative convenience, but which no longer stands for much except as thin decoration. Ornament became a luxury; the modern dance, born out of a historical inadequacy of training and tradition, made a virtue of necessity and abstracted itself into a position of ethical virtue. For acrobatic virtuosity it substituted starkness, self-pity, and canonization of the ego. Modern dance was only as strong as the personalities which promulgated its particular idiosyncratic accents. Children never took to it.

As for the enigma of Balanchine's mind, its endurance, operative intelligence, or inventive capacity, it would be brave indeed to attempt its anatomy without information which is still incomplete. He has been compared to Petipa, but this is matching muscle more than mind; the complexity of contemporary music reduces the serviceable scores of Minkus and Pugni to parallels with Stravinsky which approach the ridiculous. Strangely enough, there is indeed a fairly accurate prose portrait of a character which does in several ways correspond to our choreographer. He is Monsieur Edmond Teste, and is the subtle invention of the great French poet Paul Valéry.* M. Teste (Mr. Mind, Master Head, Sir Intelligence?) is analyzed in depth by Valéry, and a sampling of this analysis, for those hardy enough to follow its ratiocination, may tell us much of Balanchine's peculiar capacities.

His memory gave me much thought. The signs by which I could judge led me to imagine incomparable intellectual gymnastics. This was not, in him, an excessive trait but rather a trained and transformed faculty. Here are his own words: "I gave up books twenty years ago. I have burned my papers also. I scrape the quick. . . . I keep what I want. But that is not the difficulty. *It is rather to keep what I shall want tomorrow. . . .* I have tried to invent a mechanical sieve. . . ."

After a good deal of thought, I came to believe that Monsieur Teste had managed to discover laws of the mind we know nothing of. Certainly he must have devoted years to this research; even more certainly other years and many more years had been set aside for maturing his inventions, making them his instincts. Finding is nothing. The difficulty is in acquiring what has been found.

The delicate art of duration, time, its distribution and regulation—using it on well-chosen things to give them special nourishment—this was one of Monsieur Teste's great experiments.

* "La Soirée avec M. Teste," 1896, Vol. 6 (edited and translated by Jackson Mathews), Princeton University Press, 1977.

He watched for the repetition of certain ideas; he sprinkled them with numbers. This served to make the application of his conscious studies in the end mechanical. He even sought to summarize this labor. He would often say: "Maturare! . . ." [Become mature!]

. . . This man had known quite early the importance of what might be called human *plasticity*. He had investigated its mechanics and its limits. How deeply he must have reflected on his own malleability!

I had a glimpse of feelings in him that made me shudder, a terrible obstinacy in his delirious experiments. He was a man absorbed in his own variations, one who becomes his own system, who commits himself without reservation to the frightening discipline of the free mind, and sets his pleasures to killing his pleasures, the stronger killing the weaker—the mildest, the transitory, the pleasure of the moment and the hour just begun, destroyed by the fundamental—by hope for the fundamental.

. . . Monsieur Teste had no opinions. I believe he stirred his passions when he willed, and to attain a definite end. What had he done with his personality? What was his view of himself? . . . He never laughed, there was never a look of distress on his face. He hated sadness.

LIST OF PREMIERE PERFORMANCES

Produced by

THE AMERICAN BALLET,

THE BALLET CARAVAN,

AMERICAN BALLET CARAVAN,

BALLET SOCIETY,

and THE NEW YORK CITY BALLET,

From March, 1935, Through June, 1978

THE AMERICAN BALLET

Serenade
CHOREOGRAPHY: George Balanchine
MUSIC: Peter Ilyich Tchaikovsky
(Serenade for Strings in C major)
DECOR: Gaston Longchamp
COSTUMES: Jean Lurçat
PREMIERE: March 1, 1935, Adelphi
Theater, New York. (Prior to the
official premiere, *Serenade* was pre-
sented by the Producing Company
of the School of American Ballet,
June, 1934, at the Warburg estate
in White Plains, New York, and
December 6, 1934, at the Avery
Memorial Theater, Hartford,
Connecticut.)
PRINCIPAL DANCERS: Leda Anchu-
tina, Ruthanna Boris, Gisella Caccia-
lanza, Kathryn Mullowney, William
Dollar, Charles Laskey.

Alma Mater
CHOREOGRAPHY: George Balanchine
MUSIC: Kay Swift
(arrangement by Morton Gould)
DECOR: Eugene Dunkel
COSTUMES: John Held, Jr.
BOOK: Edward M. M. Warburg
PREMIERE: March 1, 1935, Adelphi
Theater, New York. (Prior to the
official premiere, *Alma Mater* was
presented by the Producing Com-
pany of the School of American
Ballet, December 6, 1934, at the

Avery Memorial Theater, Hartford,
Connecticut.)
PRINCIPAL DANCERS: Leda Anchu-
tina, Ruthanna Boris, Gisella Cac-
cialanza, Kathryn Mullowney, Heidi
Vosseler, William Dollar, Charles
Laskey, Eugene Loring.

Errante
CHOREOGRAPHY: George Balanchine
MUSIC: Franz Schubert (*Wanderer
Fantasy* for piano, orchestrated by
Charles Koechlin)
COSTUMES, LIGHTING, AND DRAMATIC
EFFECTS: Pavel Tchelitchev
PREMIERE: March 1, 1935, Adelphi
Theater, New York. (Revival from
the repertoire of Les Ballets 1933.)
PRINCIPAL DANCERS: Tamara Geva,
Charles Laskey, William Dollar.

Reminiscence
CHOREOGRAPHY: George Balanchine
MUSIC: Benjamin Godard
(orchestration by Henry Brant)
DECOR AND COSTUMES: Sergei Soudei-
kine
PREMIERE: March 1, 1935, Adelphi
Theater, New York.
PRINCIPAL DANCERS: Leda Anchu-
tina, Ruthanna Boris, Gisella Cac-
cialanza, Elena de Rivas, Holly How-
ard, Annabelle Lyon, Elise Reiman,
William Dollar, Paul Haakon, Jo-
seph Levinoff.

Mozartiana
CHOREOGRAPHY: George Balanchine
MUSIC: Peter Ilyich Tchaikovsky
(Suite No. 4, *Mozartiana*)
DECOR AND COSTUMES: Christian
Bérard
PREMIERE: March 1, 1935, Adelphi
Theater, New York. (Revival from
Les Ballets 1933. Prior to the official
premiere, *Mozartiana* was presented
by the Producing Company of the
School of American Ballet, June,
1934, at the Warburg estate in
White Plains, New York, and De-
cember 6, 1934, at the Avery Me-
morial Theater, Hartford, Connecti-
cut.)
PRINCIPAL DANCERS: Rabana Has-
burgh, Holly Howard, Helen Leitch,
Daphne Vane, Heidi Vosseler,
Charles Laskey.

Transcendence
CHOREOGRAPHY: George Balanchine
MUSIC: Franz Liszt
(orchestration by George Antheil)
DECOR: Gaston Longchamp
COSTUMES: Franklin Watkins
BOOK: Lincoln Kirstein
PREMIERE: March 5, 1935, Adelphi
Theater, New York. (Prior to the
official premiere, *Transcendence*
was presented by the Producing
Company of the School of American,
Ballet, December 6, 1934, at the
Avery Memorial Theater, Hartford,
Connecticut.)
PRINCIPAL DANCERS: Elise Reiman,
William Dollar.

Dreams
(formerly called *Les Songes*)
CHOREOGRAPHY: George Balanchine
MUSIC: George Antheil
DECOR, COSTUMES, AND BOOK: André
Derain
PREMIERE: March 5, 1935, Adelphi
Theater, New York. (Revival from
Les Ballets 1933. Prior to the official
premiere, *Les Songes* was presented
by the Producing Company of the
School of American Ballet, June,
1934, at the Warburg estate in
White Plains, New York.)
PRINCIPAL DANCERS: Leda Anchu-
tina, Ruthanna Boris, Paul Haakon.

The Bat
CHOREOGRAPHY: George Balanchine
MUSIC: Johann Strauss
(Overture to *Die Fledermaus*)
COSTUMES: Keith Martin
BOOK: Lincoln Kirstein
PREMIERE: May 20, 1936, Metropol-
itan Opera House, New York.
PRINCIPAL DANCERS: Leda Anchu-
tina, Rabana Hasburgh, Annabelle
Lyon, Lew Christensen, Charles
Laskey.

Orpheus and Eurydice
CHOREOGRAPHY: George Balanchine
MUSIC: Christoph Willibald von
Gluck (*Orfeo ed Euridice*, 1762)
DECOR AND COSTUMES: Pavel Tchelit-
chev
PREMIERE: May 22, 1936, Metro-
politan Opera House, New York.
PRINCIPAL DANCERS: Lew Christen-
sen (Orpheus), Daphne Vane
(Eurydice), William Dollar
(Amor).

Apollon Musagète
(Later called *Apollo* and *Apollo,
Leader of the Muses*)
CHOREOGRAPHY: George Balanchine
MUSIC: Igor Stravinsky
DECOR AND COSTUMES: Stewart
Chaney
PREMIERE: April 27, 1937, Metro-
politan Opera House, New York.
(Revival from the Diaghilev Ballets
Russes.)
DANCERS: Lew Christensen, Daphne
Vane, Holly Howard, Elise Reiman,
Kyra Blank, Rabana Hasburgh, Jane
Burkhalter.

The Card Party
(Originally *Jeu de Cartes*; later
called *Card Game*)
CHOREOGRAPHY: George Balanchine
MUSIC: Igor Stravinsky
DECOR AND COSTUMES: Irene Sharaff
BOOK: Igor Stravinsky
in collaboration with M. Malaieff
PREMIERE: April 27, 1937, Metro-
politan Opera House, New York.
PRINCIPAL DANCERS: William Dollar
(The Joker); Ann Campbell, Jane
Burkhalter, Lillian Moore, Vera
Volkenau (Aces); Lew Christensen,
Joseph Lane, Douglas Coudy, Erick
Hawkins (Kings); Annabelle Lyon,
Leda Anchutina, Ariel Lang, Hor-
tense Kahrklin (Queens); Charles
Laskey, Joseph Levinoff, Eugene
Loring, Serge Temoff (Jacks).

Le Baiser de la Fée
(Later called *The Fairy's Kiss*)
CHOREOGRAPHY: George Balanchine
MUSIC: Igor Stravinsky
DECOR AND COSTUMES: Alice Halicka
BOOK: Igor Stravinsky,
based on a story by
Hans Christian Andersen
PREMIERE: April 27, 1937, Metro-
politan Opera House, New York.
PRINCIPAL DANCERS: Kathryn Mul-
lowney (The Fairy), Rabana
Hasburgh (Shadow), Gisella Cac-
cialanza (Bride), Leda Anchutina
(Friend), William Dollar (Bride-
groom), Annabelle Lyon (Mother).

THE BALLET CARAVAN

Encounter
CHOREOGRAPHY: Lew Christensen
MUSIC: Wolfgang Amadeus Mozart
(*Haffner* Serenade)
COSTUMES: Forrest Thayr, Jr.
PREMIERE: July 17, 1936, Benning-
ton College Theater, Bennington,
Vermont.

PRINCIPAL DANCERS: Annabelle
Lyon, Ruby Asquith, Charles
Laskey, Lew Christensen, Harold
Christensen.

Harlequin for President
CHOREOGRAPHY: Eugene Loring
MUSIC: Domenico Scarlatti
(orchestration by Ariadna
Mikeshina)
COSTUMES: Keith Martin
BOOK: Lincoln Kirstein
PREMIERE: July 17, 1936, Benning-
ton College Theater, Bennington,
Vermont.
PRINCIPAL DANCERS: Annabelle
Lyon, Eugene Loring, Charles
Laskey, Harold Christensen, Fred
Danieli.

Folk Dance
CHOREOGRAPHY: Douglas Coudy
MUSIC: Emmanuel Chabrier
COSTUMES: Charles Rain
PREMIERE: July 17, 1936, Benning-
ton College Theater, Bennington,
Vermont.
PRINCIPAL DANCERS: Ruthanna
Boris, Lew Christensen.

Promenade
CHOREOGRAPHY: William Dollar
MUSIC: Maurice Ravel
(*Valses nobles et sentimentales*)
COSTUMES: after Horace Vernet
PREMIERE: July 17, 1936, Benning-
ton College Theater, Bennington,
Vermont.
PRINCIPAL DANCERS: Annabelle
Lyon, Ruthanna Boris, Charles
Laskey, Erick Hawkins.

Pocahontas
CHOREOGRAPHY: Lew Christensen
MUSIC: Elliott Carter, Jr.
COSTUMES: Karl Free
BOOK: Lincoln Kirstein
PREMIERE: August 17, 1936,
Colonial Theater, Keene, New

Pocohontas (*continued*)
Hampshire.
PRINCIPAL DANCERS: Ruthanna
Boris, Lew Christensen, Charles
Laskey, Harold Christensen, Erick
Hawkins.

Yankee Clipper
CHOREOGRAPHY: Eugene Loring
MUSIC: Paul Bowles
COSTUMES: Charles Rain
BOOK: Lincoln Kirstein
PREMIERE: July 12, 1937, Town
Hall, Saybrook, Connecticut.
DANCERS: Eugene Loring and entire
company.

Show Piece
(*Ballet Work-Out in One Act*)
CHOREOGRAPHY: Erick Hawkins
MUSIC: Robert McBride
COSTUMES: Keith Martin
PREMIERE: August, 1937, Bar
Harbor, Maine.
PRINCIPAL DANCERS: Marie-Jeanne,
Annabelle Lyon, Eugene Loring,
Fred Danieli, Erick Hawkins.

Filling Station
CHOREOGRAPHY: Lew Christensen
MUSIC: Virgil Thomson
DECOR AND COSTUMES: Paul Cadmus
BOOK: Lincoln Kirstein
PREMIERE: January 6, 1938, Avery
Memorial Theater, Hartford,
Connecticut.
PRINCIPAL DANCERS: Jane Deering,
Marie-Jeanne, Marjorie Moore,
Todd Bolender, Harold Christensen,
Lew Christensen, Douglas Coudy,
Fred Danieli, Erick Hawkins,
Eugene Loring.

Billy the Kid
CHOREOGRAPHY: Eugene Loring
MUSIC: Aaron Copland
COSTUMES: Jared French
BOOK: Lincoln Kirstein
PREMIERE: October 16, 1938,
Chicago Opera House.

PRINCIPAL DANCERS: Eugene Loring
(Billy), Marie-Jeanne (Mother and
Sweetheart), Lew Christensen (Pat
Garrett), Todd Bolender (Alias).

Air and Variations
CHOREOGRAPHY: William Dollar
MUSIC: Johann Sebastian Bach
(*Goldberg Variations*, arranged for
two pianos by Trude Rittmann)
COSTUMES: Walter Gifford
PREMIERE: November, 1938, Athens,
Georgia.
DANCERS: The entire company.

Charade
(or *The Debutante*)
CHOREOGRAPHY: Lew Christensen
MUSIC: American melodies, arranged
by Trude Rittmann
COSTUMES: Alvin Colt
BOOK: Lincoln Kirstein
PREMIERE: December 26, 1939, St.
James Theater, New York.
PRINCIPAL DANCERS: Gisella
Caccialanza, Lew Christensen,
Harold Christensen.

City Portrait
CHOREOGRAPHY: Eugene Loring
MUSIC: Henry Brant
DECOR: James Stewart Morcom
BOOK: Lincoln Kirstein
PREMIERE: December 28, 1939, St.
James Theater, New York.
DANCERS: Eugene Loring and entire
company.

A Thousand Times Neigh!
CHOREOGRAPHY: William Dollar
MUSIC: Tom Bennett
DECOR: Alvin Colt
BOOK: Edward Mabley
GENERAL DIRECTION: Lincoln
Kirstein
PREMIERE: May 11, 1940, Ford
Pavilion Playhouse, World's Fair,
Flushing Meadow, New York.
DANCERS: Leda Anchutina, Mary
Colbath, Peggy D'Arcy, Jean

Davidson, Vera Bobitcheff, Betty
Gilmore, Babs Heath, Jeanne Isaacs,
Marie-Jeanne, Margit de Kova, Peggy
Noonan, Maria Quarequio, Pearl
Schwarz, Mary Jane Shea, Barbara
Stuart, Charlotte Sumner, Hilda
Wagner, Anne Wiener, Virginia
Wilcox, Anna Deere Wiman, Billie
Wynn, Robert Armstrong, Todd
Bolender, Douglas Coudy, Fred
Danieli, Vladimir Dokoudovsky,
William Dollar, John Duane, John
Paul Dunphy, William Garrett, Kari
Karnakoski, Alexis Kosloff, Nicholas
Magallanes, Jay Martinez, Robert
McVoy, Rem Olmstead, Newcomb
Rice, John Schindehette, Serge
Temoff, Nicholas Vasilieff, Ray
Willams, and Robert Wolff.

AMERICAN BALLET CARAVAN

Juke Box
CHOREOGRAPHY: William Dollar
MUSIC: Alec Wilder
DECOR AND COSTUMES: Tom Lee
BOOK: Lincoln Kirstein
PREMIERE: May 28, 1941, Hunter
College Playhouse, New York.
PRINCIPAL DANCERS: Yvonne
Patterson, Rabana Hasburgh, Lew
Christensen, William Dollar.

Pastorela
CHOREOGRAPHY: Lew Christensen
and José Fernandez
MUSIC: Paul Bowles
DECOR AND COSTUMES: Alvin Colt
BOOK: José Martínez
PREMIERE: May 28, 1941, Hunter
College Playhouse, New York.
PRINCIPAL DANCERS: Gisella
Caccialanza, Beatrice Tompkins,
Lew Christensen, José Fernandez,
Todd Bolender, Nicholas Magallanes,
Charles Dickson, José Martínez.

Concerto Barocco
CHOREOGRAPHY: George Balanchine
MUSIC: Johann Sebastian Bach
(Double Violin Concerto in D
minor)
DECOR AND COSTUMES: Eugene
Berman
PREMIERE: May 28, 1941, Hunter
College Playhouse, New York.
PRINCIPAL DANCERS: Marie-Jeanne,
Mary Jane Shea, William Dollar.

Ballet Imperial (I)
CHOREOGRAPHY: George Balanchine
MUSIC: Peter Ilyich Tchaikovsky
(Piano Concerto in G major)
DECOR AND COSTUMES: Mstislav
Doboujinsky
PREMIERE: May 29, 1941, Hunter
College Playhouse, New York.
PRINCIPAL DANCERS: Marie-Jeanne,
Gisella Caccialanza, William Dollar,
Nicholas Magallanes, Fred Danieli.

Time Table
CHOREOGRAPHY: Antony Tudor
MUSIC: Aaron Copland
(Music for the Theater)
DECOR AND COSTUMES: James Stewart
Morcom
PREMIERE: May 29, 1941, Hunter
College Playhouse, New York.
PRINCIPAL DANCERS: Marie-Jeanne,
Gisella Caccialanza, Mary Jane
Shea, Beatrice Tompkins, Lew
Christensen, John Kriza.

BALLET SOCIETY

The Spellbound Child
CHOREOGRAPHY: George Balanchine
MUSIC: Maurice Ravel
(L'Enfant et les Sortilèges)
DECOR AND COSTUMES: Aline
Bernstein
BOOK: from a poem by Colette
PREMIERE: November 20, 1946,
Central High School of Needle

The Spellbound Child (*continued*)
Trades, New York.
PRINCIPAL DANCERS: Gisella
Caccialanza, Ruth Gilbert, Georgia
Hiden, Tanaquil LeClercq, Elise
Reiman, Beatrice Tompkins, Paul
d'Amboise, William Dollar (title
role sung by Joseph Connoly).

The Four Temperaments
CHOREOGRAPHY: George Balanchine
MUSIC: Paul Hindemith
DECOR AND COSTUMES: Kurt
Seligmann
PREMIERE: November 20, 1946,
Central High School of Needle
Trades, New York.
PRINCIPAL DANCERS: Gisella
Caccialanza, Georgia Hiden, Rita
Karlin, Tanaquil LeClercq, Mary
Ellen Moylan, Elise Reiman,
Beatrice Tompkins, Todd Bolender,
Lew Christensen, Fred Danieli,
William Dollar, José Martínez,
Francisco Moncion.

Renard
(*The Fox*)
CHOREOGRAPHY: George Balanchine
MUSIC: Igor Stravinsky
DECOR AND COSTUMES: Esteban
Francés
BOOK: Igor Stravinsky
(English text by Harvey Officer)
PREMIERE: January 13, 1947, Hunter
College Playhouse, New York.
PRINCIPAL DANCERS: Todd Bolender
(The Fox), Lew Christensen (The
Rooster), Fred Danieli (The Cat),
John Taras (The Ram).

Divertimento
CHOREOGRAPHY: George Balanchine
MUSIC: Alexei Haieff
PREMIERE: January 13, 1947, Hunter
College Playhouse, New York.
DANCERS: Gisella Caccialanza,
Tanaquil LeClercq, Mary Ellen
Moylan, Elise Reiman, Beatrice

Tompkins, Todd Bolender, Lew
Christensen, Fred Danieli, Francisco
Moncion, John Taras.

The Minotaur
CHOREOGRAPHY: John Taras
MUSIC: Elliott Carter, Jr.
DECOR AND COSTUMES: Joan Junyer
BOOK: Lincoln Kirstein and Joan
Junyer
PREMIERE: March 26, 1947, Central
High School of Needle Trades, New
York.
PRINCIPAL DANCERS: Elise Reiman
(Pasiphaë, Queen of Crete),
Edward Bigelow (Minos, King of
Crete), Tanaquil LeClercq
(Ariadne), John Taras (Theseus),
Fred Danieli and Paul d'Amboise
(Bulls).

Zodiac
CHOREOGRAPHY: Todd Bolender
MUSIC: Rudi Revil
DECOR AND COSTUMES: Esteban
Francés
PREMIERE: March 26, 1947, Central
High School of Needle Trades, New
York.
PRINCIPAL DANCERS: Virginia Barnes,
William Dollar, Todd Bolender, Job
Sanders, Pat McBride, Janice
Roman, Ruth Sobotka, Jean Reeves,
Irma Sandré, Joan Djorup, Marc
Beaudet, John Scancarella, Betty
Nichols, Gisella Caccialanza, Edward
Bigelow, Gerard Leavitt.

Highland Fling
CHOREOGRAPHY: William Dollar
MUSIC: Stanley Bate
DECOR AND COSTUMES: David Ffolkes
PREMIERE: March 26, 1947, Central
High School of Needle Trades, New
York.
PRINCIPAL DANCERS: Gisella
Caccialanza (Bride), Todd Bolender
(Groom), Elise Reiman (Sylphide),
Tanaquil LeClercq and Beatrice

Tompkins (Bridesmaids), José Martínez (Minister).

The Seasons
CHOREOGRAPHY: Merce Cunningham
MUSIC: John Cage
DECOR AND COSTUMES: Isamu Noguchi
PREMIERE: May 18, 1947, Ziegfeld Theater, New York.
PRINCIPAL DANCERS: Gisella Caccialanza, Tanaquil LeClercq, Beatrice Tompkins, Merce Cunningham.

Blackface
CHOREOGRAPHY: Lew Christensen
MUSIC: Carter Harman
DECOR AND COSTUMES: Robert Drew
PREMIERE: May 18, 1947, Ziegfeld Theater, New York.
PRINCIPAL DANCERS: Betty Nichols, Beatrice Tompkins, Talley Beatty, Marc Beaudet, Fred Danieli, Paul Godkin.

Punch and the Child
CHOREOGRAPHY: Fred Danieli
MUSIC: Richard Arnell
DECOR AND COSTUMES: Horace Armistead
PREMIERE: November 12, 1947, City Center of Music and Drama, New York.
PRINCIPAL DANCERS: Herbert Bliss (Father and Punch), Beatrice Tompkins (Mother and Judy), Judith Kursch (The Child), Gisella Caccialanza (Fishwife and Polly), Charles Laskey (Peg Leg and Constable), Lew Christensen (Puppeteer and Devil), Edward Bigelow (Musician and Doctor), Victor Duntiere (Street Cleaner and Hangman), Luis López (Professor).

Symphonie Concertante
CHOREOGRAPHY: George Balanchine
MUSIC: Wolfgang Amadeus Mozart (Symphonie Concertante in E flat, K.364)
DECOR AND COSTUMES: James Stewart Morcom
PREMIERE: November 12, 1947, City Center of Music and Drama, New York. (Prior to the official premiere, *Symphonie Concertante* was presented November 5, 1945, at Carnegie Hall, New York, on a program "Adventure in Ballet" by pupils of the School of American Ballet.)
PRINCIPAL DANCERS: Maria Tallchief, Tanaquil LeClercq, Dorothy Dushok, Ruth Gilbert, Georgia Hiden, Rita Karlin, Pat McBride, Irma Sandre, Todd Bolender.

The Triumph of Bacchus and Ariadne
(Ballet Cantata)
CHOREOGRAPHY: George Balanchine
MUSIC: Vittorio Rieti
DECOR AND COSTUMES: Corrado Cagli
PREMIERE: February 9, 1948, City Center of Music and Drama, New York.
PRINCIPAL DANCERS: Lew Christensen (Major-domo), Nicholas Magallanes (Bacchus), Tanaquil LeClercq (Ariadne), Herbert Bliss (First Satyr), Marie Jeanne (First Nymph), Charles Laskey (Silenus), Francisco Moncion (Midas), Claudia Hall (The Little Girl), Pat McBride (The Young Girl).

Capricorn Concerto
CHOREOGRAPHY: Todd Bolender
MUSIC: Samuel Barber
DECOR AND COSTUMES: Esteban Francés
PREMIERE: March 22, 1948, City Center of Music and Drama, New York.
PRINCIPAL DANCERS: Maria Tallchief, Herbert Bliss, Francisco Moncion.

Symphony in C
CHOREOGRAPHY: George Balanchine
MUSIC: Georges Bizet
PREMIERE: March 22, 1948, City
Center of Music and Drama, New
York. (Revival of *Le Palais de
Cristal*, first produced for the Paris
Opéra, July 28, 1947.)
PRINCIPAL DANCERS: *First Move-
ment*, Maria Tallchief, Nicholas
Magallanes; *Second Movement*,
Tanaquil LeClercq, Francisco
Moncion; *Third Movement*, Beatrice
Tompkins, Herbert Bliss; *Fourth
Movement*, Elise Reiman, Lew
Christensen.

Élégie
CHOREOGRAPHY: George Balanchine
MUSIC: Igor Stravinsky
PREMIERE: April 28, 1948, City
Center of Music and Drama, New
York. (Prior to the official premiere,
Élégie was presented November 5,
1945, at Carnegie Hall, New York,
on a program "Adventure in Ballet"
by pupils of the School of American
Ballet.)
DANCERS: Tanaquil LeClercq and
Pat McBride.

Orpheus
CHOREOGRAPHY: George Balanchine
MUSIC: Igor Stravinsky
DECOR AND COSTUMES: Isamu
Noguchi
PREMIERE: April 28, 1948, City
Center of Music and Drama, New
York.
PRINCIPAL DANCERS: Nicholas
Magallanes (Orpheus), Francisco
Moncion (Dark Angel), Maria
Tallchief (Eurydice), Herbert Bliss
(Apollo), Edward Bigelow (Pluto),
Job Sanders (Satyr), Tanaquil
LeClercq (Leader of the Bac-
chantes), Beatrice Tompkins
(Leader of the Furies).

THE NEW YORK CITY BALLET

Mother Goose Suite
CHOREOGRAPHY: Todd Bolender
MUSIC: Maurice Ravel
PREMIERE: November 1, 1948, City
Center of Music and Drama, New
York. (Revival from American
Concert Ballet, 1941.)
PRINCIPAL DANCERS: Beatrice
Tompkins (Spectator), Marie-
Jeanne (Young Girl), Todd
Bolender (Hop o' My Thumb),
Una Kai (Bird), Dick Beard
(Prince), Francisco Moncion
(Beast).

The Guests
CHOREOGRAPHY: Jerome Robbins
MUSIC: Marc Blitzstein
PREMIERE: January 20, 1949, City
Center of Music and Drama, New
York.
PRINCIPAL DANCERS: Maria Tallchief,
Francisco Moncion, Nicholas
Magallanes.

Jinx
CHOREOGRAPHY: Lew Christensen
MUSIC: Benjamin Britten
(*Variations on a Theme by Frank
Bridge*)
DECOR AND COSTUMES: George
Bockman
BOOK: Lew Christensen
PREMIERE: November 24, 1949,
City Center of Music and Drama,
New York. (Revival from Dance
Players, 1942.)
PRINCIPAL DANCERS: Francisco
Moncion (Jinx, a Clown), Janet
Reed, Ruth Sobotka, Frank Hobi
(Wire-Walkers), Herbert Bliss,
Barbara Milberg, Barbara Walczak
(Equestrians), Beatrice Tompkins
(Bearded Lady), George Hiden
(Strong Lady), Dorothy Dushok
(Tattooed Lady), Val Buttignol
(Ringmaster).

Firebird
CHOREOGRAPHY: George Balanchine
MUSIC: Igor Stravinsky
DECOR AND COSTUMES: Marc Chagall
PREMIERE: November 27, 1949, City Center of Music and Drama, New York.
PRINCIPAL DANCERS: Maria Tallchief (Firebird), Francisco Moncion (Prince Ivan), Pat McBride (Prince's Bride), Edward Bigelow (Kastchei).

Bourrée Fantasque
CHOREOGRAPHY: George Balanchine
MUSIC: Emmanuel Chabrier
COSTUMES: Karinska
PREMIERE: December 1, 1949, City Center of Music and Drama, New York.
PRINCIPAL DANCERS: *Bourrée Fantasque*, Tanaquil LeClercq, Jerome Robbins; *Prelude*, Maria Tallchief, Nicholas Magallanes, Edwina Fontaine, Yvonne Mounsey; *Fête Polonaise*, Janet Reed, Herbert Bliss.

Ondine
CHOREOGRAPHY: William Dollar
MUSIC: Antonio Vivaldi (Violin Concertos)
DECOR AND COSTUMES: Horace Armistead
PREMIERE: December 9, 1949, City Center of Music and Drama, New York.
PRINCIPAL DANCERS: Tanaquil LeClercq (Ondine), Francisco Moncion (Matteo), Melissa Hayden (Giannina), Yvonne Mounsey (Hydrola).

The Prodigal Son
CHOREOGRAPHY: George Balanchine
MUSIC: Serge Prokofiev
DECOR AND COSTUMES: Georges Rouault
PREMIERE: February 23, 1950, City Center of Music and Drama, New York. (Revival from the Diaghilev Ballets Russes, 1929.)
PRINCIPAL DANCERS: Jerome Robbins (The Prodigal Son), Maria Tallchief (The Siren), Michael Arshansky (The Father), Frank Hobi, Herbert Bliss (Servants of the Prodigal Son), Jillana, Francesca Mosarra (The Two Sisters).

The Duel
CHOREOGRAPHY: William Dollar
MUSIC: Raffaello de Banfield
COSTUMES: Robert Stevenson
PREMIERE: February 24, 1950, City Center of Music and Drama, New York. (Revision of Dollar's *Le Combat*, which premiered February 24, 1949, London.)
DANCERS: Melissa Hayden, William Dollar, Val Buttignol, Walter Georgov, Shaun O'Brien.

The Age of Anxiety
CHOREOGRAPHY: Jerome Robbins (based on the poem *The Age of Anxiety* by W. H. Auden)
MUSIC: Leonard Bernstein (Symphony No. 2)
DECOR: Oliver Smith
COSTUMES: Irene Sharaff
PREMIERE: February 26, 1950, City Center of Music and Drama, New York.
PRINCIPAL DANCERS: Tanaquil LeClercq, Todd Bolender, Francisco Moncion, Jerome Robbins, Melissa Hayden, Pat McBride, Yvonne Mounsey, Beatrice Tompkins, Edward Bigelow, Herbert Bliss.

Illuminations
CHOREOGRAPHY: Frederick Ashton (based on poems by Arthur Rimbaud)
MUSIC: Benjamin Britten (*Les Illuminations*, ten pieces for tenor or high voice and string orchestra, 1939)
DECOR AND COSTUMES: Cecil Beaton
PREMIERE: March 2, 1950, City

Illuminations (*continued*)
Center of Music and Drama, New York.
PRINCIPAL DANCERS: Nicholas Magallanes (Poet), Tanaquil LeClercq (Sacred Love), Melissa Hayden (Profane Love).

Pas de Deux Romantique
CHOREOGRAPHY: George Balanchine
MUSIC: Carl Maria von Weber (Clarinet Concerto)
COSTUMES: Robert Stevenson
PREMIERE: March 3, 1950, City Center of Music and Drama, New York.
DANCERS: Janet Reed and Herbert Bliss.

Jones Beach
CHOREOGRAPHY: George Balanchine and Jerome Robbins
MUSIC: Juriaan Andriessen (*Berkshire Symphonies*)
PREMIERE: March 9, 1950, City Center of Music and Drama, New York.
PRINCIPAL DANCERS: Melissa Hayden, Tanaquil LeClercq, Yvonne Mounsey, Maria Tallchief, Beatrice Tompkins, Herbert Bliss, Todd Bolender, William Dollar, Frank Hobi, Nicholas Magallanes, Jerome Robbins, Roy Tobias.

The Witch
CHOREOGRAPHY: John Cranko
MUSIC: Maurice Ravel (Piano Concerto No. 2)
DECOR AND COSTUMES: Dorothea Tanning
PREMIERE: August 18, 1950, Royal Opera House, Covent Garden, London.
PRINCIPAL DANCERS: Melissa Hayden, Francisco Moncion.

Mazurka from "A Life for the Tsar"
CHOREOGRAPHY: George Balanchine
MUSIC: Mikhail Glinka

(from his opera *A Life for the Tsar*)
PREMIERE: November 30, 1950, City Center of Music and Drama, New York.
DANCERS: Janet Reed and Yurek Lazowski; Vida Brown and George Balanchine; Barbara Walczak and Harold Lang; Dorothy Dushok and Frank Hobi.

Sylvia: Pas de Deux
CHOREOGRAPHY: George Balanchine
MUSIC: Léo Delibes
COSTUMES: Karinska
PREMIERE: December 1, 1950, City Center of Music and Drama, New York.
DANCERS: Maria Tallchief and Nicholas Magallanes.

Pas de Trois (*I*)
CHOREOGRAPHY: George Balanchine
MUSIC: Leon Minkus
(from his score for the ballet *Don Quixote*, 1869)
COSTUMES: Karinska
PREMIERE: February 18, 1951, City Center of Music and Drama, New York. (Revival from Grand Ballet du Marquis de Cuevas, 1948.)
DANCERS: Maria Tallchief, Nora Kaye, André Eglevsky.

La Valse
CHOREOGRAPHY: George Balanchine
MUSIC: Maurice Ravel
(*Valses nobles et sentimentales* and *La Valse*)
COSTUMES: Karinska
PREMIERE: February 20, 1951, City Center of Music and Drama, New York.
PRINCIPAL DANCERS: Diana Adams, Tanaquil LeClercq, Yvonne Mounsey, Patricia Wilde, Herbert Bliss, Frank Hobi, Nicholas Magallanes, Francisco Moncion.

Lady of the Camellias
CHOREOGRAPHY: Antony Tudor

MUSIC: Giuseppe Verdi
DECOR AND COSTUMES: Cecil Beaton
BOOK: after the novel by Alexandre Dumas *fils*.
PREMIERE: February 28, 1951, City Center of Music and Drama, New York.
PRINCIPAL DANCERS: Vida Brown (Prudence), Diana Adams (Marguerite Gautier), Brooks Jackson (M. le Comte de N.), Hugh Laing (Armand Duval), John Earle (Armand's Father).

Capriccio Brillante
CHOREOGRAPHY: George Balanchine
MUSIC: Felix Mendelssohn
COSTUMES: Karinska
PREMIERE: June 7, 1951, City Center of Music and Drama, New York.
DANCERS: Maria Tallchief and André Eglevsky; Barbara Bocher, Constance Garfield, Jillana, Irene Larsson.

Cakewalk
CHOREOGRAPHY: Ruthanna Boris
MUSIC: Louis Moreau Gottschalk (arrangement and orchestration by Hershy Kay)
DECOR AND COSTUMES: Robert Drew
PREMIERE: June 12, 1951, City Center of Music and Drama, New York.
PRINCIPAL DANCERS: Tanaquil LeClercq, Yvonne Mounsey, Janet Reed, Beatrice Tompkins, Patricia Wilde, Herbert Bliss, Frank Hobi.

The Cage
CHOREOGRAPHY: Jerome Robbins
MUSIC: Igor Stravinsky (String Concerto in D)
COSTUMES: Ruth Sobotka
PREMIERE: June 14, 1951, City Center of Music and Drama, New York.
PRINCIPAL DANCERS: Nora Kaye (The Novice), Yvonne Mounsey

(The Queen), Nicholas Magallanes, Michael Maule (The Intruders).

The Miraculous Mandarin
CHOREOGRAPHY: Todd Bolender
MUSIC: Béla Bartók
DECOR AND COSTUMES: Alvin Colt
BOOK: Melchior Langyel
PREMIERE: September 6, 1951, City Center of Music and Drama, New York.
PRINCIPAL DANCERS: Robert Barnett, Edward Bigelow, Jacques d'Amboise, Walter Georgov, Michael Maule (The Men), Melissa Hayden (The Woman), Frank Hobi (An Old Man), Roy Tobias (A Young Man), Beatrice Tompkins (A Blind Girl), Hugh Laing (The Mandarin).

À la Françaix
CHOREOGRAPHY: George Balanchine
MUSIC: Jean Françaix (Serenade for Small Orchestra)
PREMIERE: September 11, 1951, City Center of Music and Drama, New York.
DANCERS: Janet Reed, Maria Tallchief, André Eglevsky, Frank Hobi, Roy Tobias.

Tyl Ulenspiegel
CHOREOGRAPHY: George Balanchine
MUSIC: Richard Strauss (from *Til Eulenspiegel*)
DECOR AND COSTUMES: Esteban Francés
PREMIERE: November 14, 1951, City Center of Music and Drama, New York.
PRINCIPAL DANCERS: Alberta Grant (Tyl Ulenspiegel as a Child), Susan Kovnat (Philip II as a Child), Jerome Robbins (Tyl Ulenspiegel), Ruth Sobotka (Nell, His Wife), Brooks Jackson (Philip II, King of Spain), Frank Hobi (Duke), Beatrice Tompkins (Duchess), Tomi Wortham (Woman).

Swan Lake
CHOREOGRAPHY: George Balanchine
(after Lev Ivanov)
MUSIC: Peter Ilyich Tchaikovsky
DECOR AND COSTUMES: Cecil Beaton
PREMIERE: November 20, 1951, City
Center of Music and Drama,
New York.
PRINCIPAL DANCERS: Maria Tallchief
(Odette), André Eglevsky (Prince
Siegfried), Frank Hobi (Benno),
Patricia Wilde and Yvonne Mounsey
(Leading Swans), Doris Brecken-
ridge, Kaye Sargent, Ruth Sobotka,
Gloria Vauges (Cygnets), Edward
Bigelow (Rothbart, a Sorcerer).

Lilac Garden
CHOREOGRAPHY: Antony Tudor
MUSIC: Ernest Chausson (*Poème* for
violin and orchestra, Opus 25)
DECOR: Horace Armistead
COSTUMES: Karinska
PREMIERE: November 30, 1951, City
Center of Music and Drama, New
York. (Revival from Ballet Rambert,
1936, when it was presented under
the title *Jardin aux Lilas*.)
PRINCIPAL DANCERS: Nora Kaye
(Caroline), Hugh Laing (Her
Lover), Antony Tudor (The Man
She Must Marry), Tanaquil
LeClercq (The Woman in His
Past).

The Pied Piper
CHOREOGRAPHY: Jerome Robbins
MUSIC: Aaron Copland
(Concerto for Clarinet and String
Orchestra)
PREMIERE: December 4, 1951, City
Center of Music and Drama, New
York.
PRINCIPAL DANCERS: Diana Adams,
Melissa Hayden, Jillana, Tanaquil
LeClercq, Janet Reed, Barbara
Bocher, Herbert Bliss, Todd
Bolender, Nicholas Magallanes,
Jerome Robbins, Roy Tobias.

Ballade
CHOREOGRAPHY: Jerome Robbins
MUSIC: Claude Debussy
(*Six Épigraphes antiques* and *Syrinx*)
DECOR AND COSTUMES: Boris Aronson
PREMIERE: February 14, 1952, City
Center of Music and Drama, New
York.
DANCERS: Nora Kaye, Tanaquil
LeClercq, Janet Reed, Robert
Barnett, Brooks Jackson, Louis
Johnson, John Mandia, Roy Tobias.

Caracole
CHOREOGRAPHY: George Balanchine
MUSIC: Wolfgang Amadeus Mozart
(Divertimento No. 15 in B flat
major, K. 287)
COSTUMES: Christian Bérard
PREMIERE: February 19, 1952, City
Center of Music and Drama,
New York.
PRINCIPAL DANCERS: Diana Adams,
Melissa Hayden, Tanaquil
LeClercq, Maria Tallchief, Patricia
Wilde, André Eglevsky, Nicholas
Magallanes, Jerome Robbins.

Bayou
CHOREOGRAPHY: George Balanchine
MUSIC: Virgil Thomson
(*Acadian Songs and Dances*)
DECOR AND COSTUMES: Dorothea
Tanning
PREMIERE: February 21, 1952, City
Center of Music and Drama, New
York.
PRINCIPAL DANCERS: Francisco
Moncion (Boy of the Bayou), Doris
Breckenridge (Girl of the Bayou),
Melissa Hayden, Hugh Laing, Irene
Larsson, Barbara Walczak, Walter
Georgov, Stanley Zompakos (Leaves
and Flowers), Diana Adams, Herbert
Bliss, Una Kai, Marilyn Poudrier,
Brooks Jackson, Shaun O'Brien
(Starched White People).

La Gloire
CHOREOGRAPHY: Antony Tudor

MUSIC: Ludwig van Beethoven (*Egmont, Coriolanus, Leonora III* overtures)
DECOR: Gaston Longchamp
COSTUMES: Robert Fletcher
PREMIERE: February 26, 1952, City Center of Music and Drama, New York.
PRINCIPAL DANCERS: Nora Kaye (La Gloire), Francisco Moncion (Sextus Tarquinius and Hamlet's Step-father), Hugh Laing (Hippolytus and Laertes), Doris Breckenridge (Ophelia), Beatrice Tompkins (Hamlet's Mother), Diana Adams (The Dancer in Gray).

Picnic at Tintagel
CHOREOGRAPHY: Frederick Ashton
MUSIC: Sir Arnold Bax (*The Garden of Fand*)
DECOR AND COSTUMES: Cecil Beaton
PREMIERE: February 28, 1952, City Center of Music and Drama, New York.
DANCERS: Francisco Moncion (The Husband—King Mark), Diana Adams (The Wife—Iseult), Yvonne Mounsey (Her Maid—Brangaene), Jacques d'Amboise (Her Lover—Tristram), Stanley Zompakos, Brooks Jackson (His Rivals—The False Knights), Alan Baker, John Mandia (Her Chauffeur and Footman—Heralds), Robert Barnett (The Caretaker—Merlin).

Scotch Symphony
CHOREOGRAPHY: George Balanchine
MUSIC: Felix Mendelssohn (Scotch Symphony, 2nd, 3rd, and 4th movements)
DECOR: Horace Armistead
COSTUMES: Karinska and David Ffolkes
PREMIERE: November 11, 1952, City Center of Music and Drama, New York.
PRINCIPAL DANCERS: Maria Tallchief, Patricia Wilde, André Eglevsky, Michael Maule, Frank Hobi.

Metamorphoses
CHOREOGRAPHY: George Balanchine
MUSIC: Paul Hindemith (*Symphonic Metamorphoses on Themes by Carl Maria von Weber,* 1943)
COSTUMES: Karinska
PREMIERE: November 25, 1952, City Center of Music and Drama, New York.
PRINCIPAL DANCERS: Tanaquil LeClercq, Nicholas Magallanes, Todd Bolender.

Harlequinade Pas de Deux
CHOREOGRAPHY: George Balanchine
MUSIC: Riccardo Drigo
COSTUMES: Karinska
PREMIERE: December 16, 1952, City Center of Music and Drama, New York.
DANCERS: Maria Tallchief and André Eglevsky.

Kaleidoscope
CHOREOGRAPHY: Ruthanna Boris
MUSIC: Dimitri Kabalevsky
COSTUMES: Alvin Colt
PREMIERE: December 18, 1952, City Center of Music and Drama, New York.
PRINCIPAL DANCERS: Melissa Hayden, Patricia Wilde, Herbert Bliss, Todd Bolender, Frank Hobi.

Interplay
CHOREOGRAPHY: Jerome Robbins
MUSIC: Morton Gould (*American Concertette*)
DECOR AND COSTUMES: Irene Sharaff
PREMIERE: December 23, 1952, City Center of Music and Drama, New York: (Revival from Ballet Theatre, 1945. First performed in a Billy Rose show, *Concert Varieties,* June, 1945, Ziegfeld Theater, New York.)

Interplay (continued)
DANCERS: Carolyn George, Jillana, Irene Larsson, Janet Reed, Robert Barnett, Todd Bolender, Jacques d'Amboise, Michael Maule.

Concertino
CHOREOGRAPHY: George Balanchine
MUSIC: Jean Françaix
COSTUMES: Karinska
PREMIERE: December 30, 1952, City Center of Music and Drama, New York.
DANCERS: Diana Adams, Tanaquil LeClercq, André Eglevsky.

Valse-Fantaisie
CHOREOGRAPHY: George Balanchine
MUSIC: Mikhail Glinka
COSTUMES: Karinska
PREMIERE: January 6, 1953, City Center of Music and Drama, New York.
DANCERS: Tanaquil LeClercq, Diana Adams, Melissa Hayden, Nicholas Magallanes.

Will o' the Wisp
CHOREOGRAPHY: Ruthanna Boris
MUSIC: Virgil Thomson
DECOR AND COSTUMES: Dorothea Tanning
PREMIERE: January 13, 1953, City Center of Music and Drama, New York.
PRINCIPAL DANCERS: Ruthanna Boris, Frank Hobi.

The Five Gifts
CHOREOGRAPHY: William Dollar
MUSIC: Ernest Dohnanyi
(*Variations on a Nursery Tune*)
COSTUMES: Esteban Francés
BOOK: after a story by Mark Twain
PREMIERE: January 20, 1953, City Center of Music and Drama, New York. (Revival from American Concert Ballet, 1943.)
PRINCIPAL DANCERS: Todd Bolender (The Youth), Melissa Hayden (The

Fairy), Carolyn George (Pleasure), Yvonne Mounsey (Death), Jillana (Fame), Patricia Wilde (Riches), Irene Larsson (Love), Jacques d'Amboise (Another Youth).

Afternoon of a Faun
CHOREOGRAPHY: Jerome Robbins
MUSIC: Claude Debussy
DECOR: Jean Rosenthal
COSTUMES: Irene Sharaff
PREMIERE: May 14, 1953, City Center of Music and Drama, New York.
DANCERS: Tanaquil LeClercq and Francisco Moncion.

The Filly
(or *A Stableboy's Dream*)
CHOREOGRAPHY: Todd Bolender
MUSIC: John Colman
DECOR AND COSTUMES: Peter Larkin
PREMIERE: May 19, 1953, City Center of Music and Drama, New York.
PRINCIPAL DANCERS: Roy Tobias (Stableboy), Diana Adams (The Mare), Nicholas Magallanes (The Stallion), Ellen Gottesman (The Foal), Maria Tallchief (The Filly).

Fanfare
CHOREOGRAPHY: Jerome Robbins
MUSIC: Benjamin Britten
(*The Young Person's Guide to the Orchestra*)
DECOR AND COSTUMES: Irene Sharaff
PREMIERE: June 2, 1953, City Center of Music and Drama, New York.
DANCERS: The entire company.

Con Amore
CHOREOGRAPHY: Lew Christensen
MUSIC: Gioacchino Rossini
(*La Gazza Ladra, Il Signor Bruchino*, and *La Scala di Seta* overtures)
DECOR AND COSTUMES: James Bodrero
BOOK: James Graham-Lujan

PREMIERE: June 9, 1953, City Center of Music and Drama, New York. (Revival from the San Francisco Ballet, 1953.)
PRINCIPAL DANCERS: Sally Bailey, Nancy Johnson, Jacques d'Amboise.

Opus 34

CHOREOGRAPHY: George Balanchine
MUSIC: Arnold Schoenberg (*Begleitmusik*, 1930)
DECOR AND COSTUMES: Esteban Francés
PREMIERE: January 19, 1954, City Center of Music and Drama, New York.
PRINCIPAL DANCERS: Diana Adams, Patricia Wilde, Tanaquil LeClercq, Nicholas Magallanes, Francisco Moncion, Herbert Bliss.

The Nutcracker

CHOREOGRAPHY: George Balanchine (after Lev Ivanov)
MUSIC: Peter Ilyich Tchaikovsky
DECOR: Horace Armistead
COSTUMES: Karinska
PREMIERE: February 2, 1954, City Center of Music and Drama, New York.
PRINCIPAL DANCERS: Maria Tallchief, Tanaquil LeClercq, Yvonne Mounsey, Janet Reed, Jillana, Irene Larsson, Alberta Grant, Nicholas Magallanes, Herbert Bliss, Francisco Moncion, Robert Barnett, Edward Bigelow, George Li, Michael Arshansky, Paul Nickel.

Quartet

CHOREOGRAPHY: Jerome Robbins
MUSIC: Serge Prokofiev (String Quartet No. 2, Opus 92)
COSTUMES: Karinska
PREMIERE: February 18, 1954, City Center of Music and Drama, New York.
PRINCIPAL DANCERS: Patricia Wilde, Jillana, Yvonne Mounsey, Herbert

Bliss, Jacques d'Amboise, Todd Bolender.

Western Symphony

CHOREOGRAPHY: George Balanchine
MUSIC: Hershy Kay
PREMIERE: September 7, 1954, City Center of Music and Drama, New York.
PRINCIPAL DANCERS: *First Movement*, Diana Adams, Herbert Bliss; *Second Movement*, Janet Reed, Nicholas Magallanes; *Third Movement*, Patricia Wilde, André Eglevsky; *Fourth Movement*, Tanaquil LeClercq, Jacques d'Amboise.

Ivesiana

CHOREOGRAPHY: George Balanchine
MUSIC: Charles Ives
PREMIERE: September 14, 1954, City Center of Music and Drama, New York.
PRINCIPAL DANCERS: Janet Reed, Patricia Wilde, Allegra Kent, Diana Adams, Tanaquil LeClercq, Francisco Moncion, Jacques d'Amboise, Todd Bolender, Herbert Bliss.

Roma

CHOREOGRAPHY: George Balanchine
MUSIC: Georges Bizet
DECOR AND COSTUMES: Eugene Berman
PREMIERE: February 23, 1955, City Center of Music and Drama, New York.
PRINCIPAL DANCERS: Tanaquil LeClercq and André Eglevsky; Barbara Milberg, Barbara Walczak, Roy Tobias, John Mandia.

Pas de Trois (II)

CHOREOGRAPHY: George Balanchine
MUSIC: Mikhail Glinka
COSTUMES: Karinska

Pas de Trois (II) (*continued*)
PREMIERE: March 1, 1955, City Center of Music and Drama, New York.
DANCERS: Patricia Wilde, Melissa Hayden, André Eglevsky.

Pas de Dix
CHOREOGRAPHY: George Balanchine
MUSIC: Alexander Glazounov (from *Raymonda*)
COSTUMES: Esteban Francés
PREMIERE: November 9, 1955, City Center of Music and Drama, New York.
DANCERS: Maria Tallchief and André Eglevsky: Barbara Fallis, Constance Garfield, Jane Mason, Barbara Walczak, Shaun O'Brien, Roy Tobias, Roland Vazquez, Jonathan Watts.

Souvenirs
CHOREOGRAPHY: Todd Bolender
MUSIC: Samuel Barber
DECOR AND COSTUMES: Rouben Ter-Arutunian
PREMIERE: November 15, 1955, City Center of Music and Drama, New York.
PRINCIPAL DANCERS: Irene Larsson, Jillana, Carolyn George, Todd Bolender, Roy Tobias, Jonathan Watts, John Mandia, Herbert Bliss.

Jeux d'Enfants
CHOREOGRAPHY: George Balanchine, Barbara Milberg, Francisco Moncion
MUSIC: Georges Bizet
DECOR AND COSTUMES: Esteban Francés
PREMIERE: November 22, 1955, City Center of Music and Drama, New York.
PRINCIPAL DANCERS: Melissa Hayden, Barbara Fallis, Barbara Walczak, Roy Tobias, Robert Barnett, Richard Thomas, Jonathan Watts.

Allegro Brillante
CHOREOGRAPHY: George Balanchine
MUSIC: Peter Ilyich Tchaikovsky (Third Piano Concerto)
PREMIERE: March 1, 1956, City Center of Music and Drama, New York.
DANCERS: Maria Tallchief and Nicholas Magallanes; with Barbara Fallis, Carolyn George, Barbara Milberg, Barbara Walczak, Arthur Mitchell, Richard Rapp, Roland Vazquez, Jonathan Watts.

The Concert
(or *The Perils of Everybody*)
CHOREOGRAPHY: Jerome Robbins
MUSIC: Frédéric Chopin
DECOR: Jean Rosenthal
COSTUMES: Irene Sharaff
PREMIERE: March 6, 1956, City Center of Music and Drama, New York.
PRINCIPAL DANCERS: Tanaquil LeClercq, Yvonne Mounsey, Wilma Curley, Patricia Savoia, Todd Bolender, Robert Barnett, John Mandia, Richard Thomas.

The Still Point
CHOREOGRAPHY: Todd Bolender
MUSIC: Claude Debussy. (transcription for orchestra by Frank Black)
PREMIERE: March 13, 1956, City Center of Music and Drama, New York. (Originally arranged for the Emily Frankel–Frank Ryder modern dance group.)
DANCERS: Melissa Hayden, Irene Larsson, Jillana, Jacques d'Amboise, Roy Tobias, John Mandia.

Divertimento No. 15 (I)
CHOREOGRAPHY: George Balanchine
MUSIC: Wolfgang Amadeus Mozart (Divertimento No. 15 in B flat major, K. 287)
DECOR: James Stewart Morcom
COSTUMES: Karinska

PREMIERE: December 19, 1956, City Center of Music and Drama, New York. (Prior to the official premiere, *Divertimento No. 15*—a revival of *Caracole* of 1952—was presented May 31, 1956, at the Mozart Festival in Stratford, Connecticut.)
PRINCIPAL DANCERS: Diana Adams, Melissa Hayden, Yvonne Mounsey, Patricia Wilde, Barbara Milberg, Nicholas Magallanes, Roy Tobias, Jonathan Watts.

The Unicorn, the Gorgon, and the Manticore
(*A Madrigal Fable*)
CHOREOGRAPHY: John Butler
MUSIC AND BOOK: Gian-Carlo Menotti
DECOR: Jean Rosenthal
COSTUMES: Robert Fletcher
PREMIERE: January 15, 1957, City Center of Music and Drama, New York. (Commissioned by the Elizabeth Sprague Coolidge Foundation in the Library of Congress, and first presented October 21, 1956, in the Coolidge Auditorium, Washington, D.C.)
DANCERS: Janet Reed (The Countess), Roy Tobias (The Count), Nicholas Magallanes (Man in the Castle—the Poet), Arthur Mitchell (The Unicorn), Eugene Tanner (The Gorgon), Richard Thomas (The Manticore), John Mandia (The Mayor), Wilma Curley (The Mayor's Wife), Jonathan Watts (The Doctor), Lee Becker (The Doctor's Wife).

The Masquers
CHOREOGRAPHY: Todd Bolender
MUSIC: Francis Poulenc
DECOR AND COSTUMES: David Hays
PREMIERE: January 29, 1957, City Center of Music and Drama, New York.
PRINCIPAL DANCERS: Melissa Hayden (A Young Woman), Jacques d'Amboise (A Soldier), Yvonne Mounsey (The Passerby), Charlotte Ray (A Friend of the Young Woman), Robert Barnett (The Boy She Meets), Jonathan Watts (Another Soldier).

Pastorale
CHOREOGRAPHY: Francisco Moncion
MUSIC: Charles Turner
DECOR: David Hays
COSTUMES: Ruth Sobotka
PREMIERE: February 14, 1957, City Center of Music and Drama, New York.
DANCERS: Allegra Kent, Francisco Moncion, Roy Tobias, Geralyn Donald, Barbara Fallis, Ruth Sobotka, Anthony Blum, Richard Rapp, Shaun O'Brien.

Square Dance
CHOREOGRAPHY: George Balanchine
MUSIC: Arcangelo Corelli and Antonio Vivaldi
PREMIERE: November 21, 1957, City Center of Music and Drama, New York.
PRINCIPAL DANCERS: Patricia Wilde and Nicholas Magallanes.

Agon
CHOREOGRAPHY: George Balanchine
MUSIC: Igor Stravinsky
PREMIERE: November 27, 1957, City Center of Music and Drama, New York.
DANCERS: Diana Adams, Melissa Hayden, Barbara Milberg, Barbara Walczak, Todd Bolender, Arthur Mitchell, Roy Tobias, Jonathan Watts, Roberta Lubell, Francia Russell, Dido Sayers, Ruth Sobotka.

Gounod Symphony
CHOREOGRAPHY: George Balanchine
MUSIC: Charles Gounod
(Symphony No. 1 in D major)
DECOR: Horace Armistead
COSTUMES: Karinska

Gounod Symphony (continued)
PREMIERE: January 8, 1958, City Center of Music and Drama, New York.
PRINCIPAL DANCERS: Maria Tallchief and Jacques d'Amboise.

Stars and Stripes
CHOREOGRAPHY: George Balanchine
MUSIC: Hershy Kay
(after music by John Philip Sousa)
DECOR: David Hays
COSTUMES: Karinska
PREMIERE: January 17, 1958, City Center of Music and Drama, New York.
PRINCIPAL DANCERS: Allegra Kent, Diana Adams, Robert Barnett, Melissa Hayden, Jacques d'Amboise.

Waltz Scherzo
CHOREOGRAPHY: George Balanchine
MUSIC: Peter Ilyich Tchaikovsky
COSTUMES: Karinska
PREMIERE: September 9, 1958, City Center of Music and Drama, New York.
DANCERS: Patricia Wilde and André Eglevsky.

Medea
CHOREOGRAPHY: Birgit Cullberg
MUSIC: Béla Bartók
(orchestration by Herbert Sandberg)
COSTUMES: Lewis Brown
PREMIERE: November 26, 1958, City Center of Music and Drama, New York. (Revival from the Royal Swedish Opera Ballet, Stockholm, 1954.)
PRINCIPAL DANCERS: Melissa Hayden (Medea); Jacques d'Amboise (Jason); Delia Peters, Susan Pillersdorf (Their Children); Shaun O'Brien (Creon, King of Corinth); Violette Verdy (Creusa, His Daughter).

Octet
CHOREOGRAPHY: William Christensen

MUSIC: Igor Stravinsky
PREMIERE: December 2, 1958, City Center of Music and Drama, New York.
DANCERS: Barbara Walczak, Dido Sayers, Roberta Lubell, Judith Green, Edward Villella, William Weslow, Robert Lindgren, Richard Rapp.

The Seven Deadly Sins
CHOREOGRAPHY: George Balanchine
MUSIC: Kurt Weill
DECOR AND COSTUMES: Rouben Ter-Arutunian
BOOK: Bertholt Brecht, translated by W. H. Auden and Chester Kallman
PREMIERE: December 4, 1958, City Center of Music and Drama, New York. (Revival from Les Ballets 1933.)
PRINCIPAL DANCER: Allegra Kent (Anna II).
PRINCIPAL SINGERS: Lotte Lenya (Anna I); Stanley Carlson, bass (Mother); Gene Hollman, bass (Father); Frank Porretta, tenor (Brother I); Grant Williams, tenor (Brother II).

Native Dancers
CHOREOGRAPHY: George Balanchine
MUSIC: Vittorio Rieti (Symphony No. 5)
DECOR: David Hays
GIRLS' COSTUMES: Peter Larkin
JOCKEY SILKS: H. Kauffman & Sons, Saddlery Co.
PREMIERE: January 14, 1959, City Center of Music and Drama, New York.
PRINCIPAL DANCERS: Patricia Wilde and Jacques d'Amboise.

Episodes (I)
CHOREOGRAPHY: Martha Graham
MUSIC: Anton von Webern
(*Passacaglia*, Opus 1; and Six Pieces for Orchestra, Opus 6; both 1909)

DECOR: David Hays
COSTUME DESIGN AND EXECUTION: Karinska
PREMIERE: May 14, 1959, City Center of Music and Drama, New York.
PRINCIPAL DANCERS: Martha Graham (Mary, Queen of Scots), Bertram Ross (Bothwell), Sallie Wilson (Elizabeth, Queen of England).

Episodes (II)

CHOREOGRAPHY: George Balanchine
MUSIC: Anton von Webern (Symphony, Opus 21; Five Pieces, Opus 10; Concerto, Opus 24; Variations for Orchestra, Opus 30; "Ricercata for Six Voices from Bach's *Musical Offering*")
DECOR: David Hays
COSTUME DESIGN AND EXECUTION: Karinska
PREMIERE: May 14, 1959, City Center of Music and Drama, New York.
PRINCIPAL DANCERS: Violette Verdy, Jonathan Watts, Diana Adams, Jacques d'Amboise, Allegra Kent, Nicholas Magallanes, Paul Taylor, Melissa Hayden, Francisco Moncion.

Night Shadow

(Later called *La Sonnambula*)
CHOREOGRAPHY: George Balanchine
MUSIC: Vittorio Rieti (after themes by Vincenzo Bellini)
DECOR AND COSTUMES: André Levasseur
PREMIERE: January 6, 1960, City Center of Music and Drama, New York. (Revived for this company by John Taras; world premiere by Ballet Russe de Monte Carlo, February 27, 1946, City Center of Music and Drama.)
PRINCIPAL DANCERS: Allegra Kent, Erik Bruhn, Jillana, John Taras, Suki Schorer, Edward Villella, and William Weslow.

Panamerica

CHOREOGRAPHY: George Balanchine, Gloria Contreras, Jacques d'Amboise, Francisco Moncion, John Taras
MUSIC: A series of short works by Latin-American composers Carlos Chávez, Luis Escobar, Alberto Ginastera, Julian Orbón, Juan Orrego Salas, Sivestre Revueltas, Hector Tosa, Heitor Villa-Lobos
DECOR: David Hays
COSTUMES: Karinska and Esteban Francés
PREMIERE: January 20, 1960, City Center of Music and Drama, New York.
PRINCIPAL DANCERS: Violette Verdy, Erik Bruhn, Patricia Wilde, Jillana, Edward Villella, Diana Adams, Nicholas Magallanes, Francisco Moncion, Maria Tallchief, Arthur Mitchell, Conrad Ludlow, Allegra Kent, Jonathan Watts, Roy Tobias.

Theme and Variations

CHOREOGRAPHY: George Balanchine
MUSIC: Peter Ilyich Tchaikovsky (Suite No. 3 in G)
COSTUMES: Karinska
PREMIERE: February 5, 1960, City Center of Music and Drama, New York. (World premiere by Ballet Theater, September 27, 1947.)
PRINCIPAL DANCERS: Violette Verdy and Edward Villella.

Pas de Deux (I)

CHOREOGRAPHY: George Balanchine
MUSIC: Peter Ilyich Tchaikovsky
COSTUMES: Karinska
PREMIERE: March 29, 1960, City Center of Music and Drama, New York.
DANCERS: Violette Verdy, Conrad Ludlow.

The Figure in the Carpet

CHOREOGRAPHY: George Balanchine
MUSIC: George Frederic Handel

The Figure in the Carpet
(continued)
(*Water Music* and *Royal Fireworks Music*)
BOOK: George Lewis
DECOR AND COSTUMES: Esteban Francés
PREMIERE: April 13, 1960, City Center of Music and Drama, New York.
PRINCIPAL DANCERS: Violette Verdy, Melissa Hayden, Jillana, Diana Adams, Patricia McBride, Mary Hinkson, Jacques d'Amboise, Edward Villella, Francisco Moncion, Arthur Mitchell, Nicholas Magallanes.

Monumentum pro Gesualdo
CHOREOGRAPHY: George Balanchine
MUSIC: Igor Stravinsky
(an arrangement for orchestra of three madrigals by Don Carlo Gesualdo)
DECOR: David Hays
PREMIERE: November 16, 1960, City Center of Music and Drama, New York.
PRINCIPAL DANCERS: Diana Adams and Conrad Ludlow.

Variations from Don Sebastian
(Later called *Donizetti Variations*)
CHOREOGRAPHY: George Balanchine
MUSIC: Gaetano Donizetti
DECOR: David Hays
WOMEN'S COSTUMES: Karinska
MEN'S COSTUMES: Esteban Francés
PREMIERE: November 16, 1960, City Center of Music and Drama, New York.
PRINCIPAL DANCERS: Melissa Hayden and Jonathan Watts.

Liebeslieder Walzer
CHOREOGRAPHY: George Balanchine
MUSIC: Johannes Brahms (Opus 52 and Opus 65)
DECOR: David Hays
COSTUMES: Karinska

PREMIERE: November 22, 1960, City Center of Music and Drama, New York.
DANCERS: Diana Adams and Bill Carter, Melissa Hayden and Jonathan Watts, Jillana and Conrad Ludlow, Violette Verdy and Nicholas Magallanes.

Jazz Concert
(a four-part program consisting of the ballets *Creation of the World, Ragtime, Les Biches,* and *Ebony Concerto*):

Creation of the World
CHOREOGRAPHY: Todd Bolender
MUSIC: Darius Milhaud
PREMIERE: December 7, 1960, City Center of Music and Drama, New York.
DANCERS: Patricia McBride, Conrad Ludlow, Janet Reed, Lois Bewley, Arthur Mitchell, Edward Villella.

Ragtime
CHOREOGRAPHY: George Balanchine
MUSIC: Igor Stravinsky
PREMIERE: December 7, 1960, City Center of Music and Drama, New York.
DANCERS: Diana Adams and Bill Carter.

Les Biches
CHOREOGRAPHY: Francisco Moncion
MUSIC: Francis Poulenc
PREMIERE: December 7, 1960, City Center of Music and Drama, New York.
PRINCIPAL DANCERS: Sara Leland and Anthony Blum.

Ebony Concerto
CHOREOGRAPHY: John Taras
MUSIC: Igor Stravinsky
PREMIERE: December 7, 1960, City Center of Music and Drama, New York.

DANCERS: Patricia McBride and Arthur Mitchell.

Modern Jazz:
Variants
CHOREOGRAPHY: George Balanchine
MUSIC: Gunther Schuller
(arrangement for orchestra, playing in the pit, and for the Modern Jazz Quartet, playing onstage)
PREMIERE: January 4, 1961, City Center of Music and Drama, New York.
PRINCIPAL DANCERS: John Jones (guest artist), Diana Adams, Melissa Hayden, Arthur Mitchell.

Electronics
CHOREOGRAPHY: George Balanchine
MUSIC: Remi Gassmann
(electronic work by Oskar Sala and the composer)
DECOR: David Hays
PREMIERE: March 22, 1961, City Center of Music and Drama, New York.
PRINCIPAL DANCERS: Diana Adams, Violette Verdy, Jacques d'Amboise, Edward Villella.

Valse et Variations
(Later called *Raymonda Variations*)
CHOREOGRAPHY: George Balanchine
MUSIC: Alexander Glazounov
(a score compiled from the ballet *Raymonda*)
DECOR: Horace Armistead
COSTUMES: Karinska
PREMIERE: December 7, 1961, City Center of Music and Drama, New York.
DANCERS: Patricia Wilde, Jacques d'Amboise; with Victoria Simon, Suki Schorer, Gloria Govrin, Carol Sumner, Patricia Neary; and Susan Keniff, Marlene Mesavage, Marnee Morris, Ellen Shire, Bettijane Sills, Lynda Yourth.

A Midsummer Night's Dream
CHOREOGRAPHY: George Balanchine
MUSIC: Felix Mendelssohn
(all incidental music composed for the several productions of the play, among them Opus 20 and Opus 61; as well as the following pieces: Overture to *Athalie*, Opus 74; Overture to *The Fair Melusine*, Opus 32; Overture to *The First Walpurgis Night*, Opus 60; Symphony No. 9 for Strings; and Overture to *Son and Stranger*, Opus 89)
DECOR: David Hays
COSTUMES: Karinska
PREMIERE: January 17, 1962, City Center of Music and Drama, New York.
PRINCIPAL DANCERS: Melissa Hayden (Titania), Conrad Ludlow (Cavalier to Titania), Edward Villella (Oberon), Arthur Mitchell (Puck), Patricia McBride (Hermia), Jillana (Helena), Nicholas Magallanes (Lysander), Bill Carter (Demetrius), Gloria Govrin (Hippolyta), Francisco Moncion (Theseus), Roland Vazquez (Bottom), Violette Verdy and Conrad Ludlow (*pas de deux* in Act 2).

Bugaku
CHOREOGRAPHY: George Balanchine
MUSIC: Toshiro Mayuzumi
DECOR: David Hays
COSTUMES: Karinska
PREMIERE: March 20, 1963, City Center of Music and Drama, New York.
PRINCIPAL DANCERS: Allegra Kent, Edward Villella.

Arcade
CHOREOGRAPHY: John Taras
MUSIC: Igor Stravinsky
(Concerto for Piano and Wind Instruments)

Arcade (*continued*)
DECOR: David Hays
COSTUMES: Ruth Sobotka
PREMIERE: March 28, 1963, City
Center of Music and Drama, New
York.
PRINCIPAL DANCERS: Suzanne
Farrell, Arthur Mitchell.

Movements for Piano and Orchestra
CHOREOGRAPHY: George Balanchine
MUSIC: Igor Stravinsky
(Movements for Piano and Orches-
tra, 1958–59)
PREMIERE: April 9, 1963, City
Center of Music and Drama, New
York.
PRINCIPAL DANCERS: Suzanne Farrell,
Jacques d'Amboise.

The Chase
(*The Vixen's Choice*)
CHOREOGRAPHY: Jacques d'Amboise
MUSIC: Wolfgang Amadeus Mozart
(Horn Concerto No. 3
in E flat, K. 447)
DECOR: David Hays
COSTUMES: Karinska
PREMIERE: September 18, 1963, City
Center of Music and Drama, New
York.
PRINCIPAL DANCERS: Allegra Kent
(The Vixen), André Prokovsky (The
Duke), Shaun O'Brien (A Wealthy
Friend).

Fantasy
CHOREOGRAPHY: John Taras
MUSIC: Franz Schubert
(*Fantasy* Piano Duet, Opus 103,
orchestrated by Felix Mottl)
PREMIERE: September 24, 1963, City
Center of Music and Drama, New
York.
PRINCIPAL DANCERS: Patricia
McBride and Edward Villella; Carol
Sumner, Marlene Mesavage, Robert
Rodham, Earle Sieveling.

Meditation
CHOREOGRAPHY: George Balanchine
MUSIC: Peter Ilyich Tchaikovsky
(from *Souvenir d'un lieu cher*, a set
of three pieces for violin and piano,
Opus 42, orchestrated by Alexander
Glazounov)
PREMIERE: December 10, 1963, City
Center of Music and Drama, New
York.
DANCERS: Suzanne Farrell, Jacques
d'Amboise.

Tarantella
CHOREOGRAPHY: George Balanchine
MUSIC: Louis Gottschalk
(*Grande Tarantelle*, reconstructed
and orchestrated by Hershy Kay)
COSTUMES: Karinska
PREMIERE: January 7, 1964, City
Center of Music and Drama, New
York.
DANCERS: Patricia McBride, Edward
Villella.

Quatuor
CHOREOGRAPHY: Jacques d'Amboise
MUSIC: Dimitri Shostakovich
(String Quartet No. 1)
PREMIERE: January 16, 1964, City
Center of Music and Drama, New
York.
DANCERS: Mimi Paul and Jacques
d'Amboise; Roland Vazquez and
Robert Maiorano.

Clarinade
CHOREOGRAPHY: George Balanchine
MUSIC: Morton Gould
(Derivations for Clarinet and Jazz
Band, 1954–55)
PREMIERE: April 29, 1964, New
York State Theater. (The music,
composed for Benny Goodman, was
played by him in the orchestra pit on
opening night. *Clarinade* was the
first new ballet staged at the New
York State Theater, Lincoln
Center.)

DANCERS: Gloria Govrin and Arthur Mitchell, Suzanne Farrell and Anthony Blum, with Bettijane Sills and Richard Rapp, Carol Sumner and Robert Rodham, and corps de ballet.

Dim Lustre

CHOREOGRAPHY: Antony Tudor
MUSIC: Richard Strauss (*Burleske* for Piano and Orchestra)
DECOR AND COSTUMES: Beni Montresor
PREMIERE: May 6, 1964, New York State Theater. (This ballet was originally created by Tudor for Ballet Theatre, October 20, 1943.)
PRINCIPAL DANCERS: Patricia McBride (The Lady with Him), Edward Villella (The Gentleman with Her), Robert Rodham (It Was Spring), Patricia Neary (She Wore Perfume), Richard Rapp (He Wore a White Tie).

Irish Fantasy

CHOREOGRAPHY: Jacques d'Amboise
MUSIC: Camille Saint-Saëns (from incidental ballet music for the opera *Henry VIII*)
DECOR: David Hays
COSTUMES: Karinska
PREMIERE: August 12, 1964, Greek Theater, Los Angeles. (New York premiere: October 8, 1964, New York State Theater.)
PRINCIPAL DANCERS: Melissa Hayden, André Prokovsky, and Anthony Blum, Frank Ohman.

Piège de Lumière

CHOREOGRAPHY: John Taras
MUSIC: Jean-Michel Damase
DECOR: Felix Labisse
COSTUMES: André Levasseur
BOOK: Philippe Hériat
SUPERVISION: David Hays
PREMIERE: October 1, 1964, New York State Theater. (This ballet was originally created by Taras for Grand Ballet du Marquis de Cuevas, December 23, 1952.)
PRINCIPAL DANCERS: Maria Tallchief (Queen of the Morphides), André Prokovsky (Iphias), Arthur Mitchell (Young Convict).

Ballet Imperial (II)

CHOREOGRAPHY: George Balanchine
STAGING: Frederic Franklin
MUSIC: Peter Ilyich Tchaikovsky (Piano Concerto No. 2 in G major)
DECOR: Rouben Ter-Arutunian
COSTUMES: Karinska
PREMIERE: October 15, 1964, New York State Theater. (This ballet was originally created by Balanchine for American Ballet Caravan, May 29, 1941.)
PRINCIPAL DANCERS: Suzanne Farrell, Patricia Neary, Jacques d'Amboise.

Pas de Deux and Divertissement

CHOREOGRAPHY: George Balanchine
MUSIC: Léo Delibes (from *Sylvia, La Source,* and *Naïla*)
COSTUMES: Karinska
PREMIERE: January 14, 1965, New York State Theater.
PRINCIPAL DANCERS: Melissa Hayden, André Prokovsky, Suki Schorer.

Shadow'd Ground

CHOREOGRAHY: John Taras
MUSIC: Aaron Copland (*Dance Panels,* 1962)
BOOK: Scott Burton
PRODUCTION (with photographic projections): John Braden
PREMIERE: January 21, 1965, New York State Theater.
PRINCIPAL DANCERS: Kay Mazzo, Robert Maiorano, Suki Schorer, Richard Rapp, Jillana, Roland Vazquez.

Harlequinade

CHOREOGRAPHY: George Balanchine
MUSIC: Riccardo Drigo

Harlequinade (*continued*)
DECOR AND COSTUMES: Rouben Ter-Arutunian
PREMIERE: February 4, 1965, New York State Theater.
PRINCIPAL DANCERS: Patricia McBride, Edward Villella, Suki Schorer, Deni Lamont, Gloria Govrin, Carol Sumner.

Don Quixote
CHOREOGRAPHY: George Balanchine
MUSIC: Nicolas Nabokov
DECOR AND COSTUMES: Esteban Francés (costumes executed by Karinska)
PREMIERE: May 28, 1965, New York State Theater. (Gala Benefit Preview, May 27, 1965, with George Balanchine in title role.)
PRINCIPAL DANCERS: Richard Rapp, Suzanne Farrell, Deni Lamont, Mimi Paul, Marnee Morris.

Variations
CHOREOGRAPHY: George Balanchine
MUSIC: Igor Stravinsky
(*Variations for Orchestra*, dedicated to the memory of Aldous Huxley)
PREMIERE: March 31, 1966, New York State Theater.
PRINCIPAL DANCER: Suzanne Farrell.

Summerspace
CHOREOGRAPHY: Merce Cunningham
MUSIC: Morton Feldman
DECOR AND COSTUMES: Robert Rauschenberg
SUPERVISION OF NEW YORK PRODUCTION: John Braden
PREMIERE: April 14, 1966, New York State Theater. (Revival from Merce Cunningham and his Dance Company, premiere, August 17, 1958, at the American Dance Festival, Connecticut College, New London, Connecticut.)
DANCERS: Anthony Blum, Kay Mazzo, Patricia Neary, Sara Leland, Deni Lamont, Carol Sumner.

Brahms-Schoenberg Quartet
CHOREOGRAPHY: George Balanchine
MUSIC: Johannes Brahms
(First Piano Quartet in G minor, Opus 25, orchestrated by Arnold Schoenberg)
DECOR: Peter Harvey
COSTUMES: Karinska
PREMIERE: April 21, 1966, New York State Theater. (Gala Benefit Premiere: April 19, 1966.)
PRINCIPAL DANCERS: Melissa Hayden, André Prokovsky, Gloria Govrin, Patricia McBride, Kent Stowell, Allegra Kent, Edward Villella, Suzanne Farrell, Jacques d'Amboise.

Divertimento No. 15 (II)
CHOREOGRAPHY: George Balanchine
MUSIC: Wolfgang Amadeus Mozart (K. 287)
DECOR: David Hays
COSTUMES: Karinska
PREMIERE: April 27, 1966, New York State Theater. (Revival of Balanchine's 1956 ballet of the same name.)
PRINCIPAL DANCERS: Melissa Hayden, Bettijane Sills, Sara Leland, Mimi Paul, Suki Schorer, Arthur Mitchell, Richard Rapp, Kent Stowell.

Jeux
CHOREOGRAPHY: John Taras
MUSIC: Claude Debussy
DECOR AND COSTUMES: Raoul Pène DuBois (costumes executed by Karinska)
PREMIERE: April 28, 1966, New York State Theater.
DANCERS: Melissa Hayden, Allegra Kent, Edward Villella.

Narkissos
CHOREOGRAPHY: Edward Villella
MUSIC: Robert Prince
DECOR AND COSTUMES: John Braden
PREMIERE: July 21, 1966, Saratoga

Springs Performing Arts Center.
(New York premiere: November 24,
1966, New York State Theater.)
PRINCIPAL DANCERS: Edward Villella
(Narkissos), Patricia McBride
(Echo Figure), Michael Steele
(Image-Nemesis Figure).

La Guirlande de Campra
CHOREOGRAPHY: John Taras
MUSIC: Georges Auric, Arthur
Honegger, Francis Poulenc, Ger-
maine Tailleferre, Daniel Lesur,
Alexis Roland-Manuel, and Henri
Sauguet, after a theme by André
Campra (written in 1717)
DECOR: Peter Harvey
COSTUMES: Peter Harvey and
Esteban Francés (the latter some
costumes taken from Balanchine's
The Figure in the Carpet)
PREMIERE: December 1, 1966, New
York State Theater. (A private
benefit performance was presented
April 19, 1966, at the same theater.)
PRINCIPAL DANCERS: Violette Verdy,
Melissa Hayden, Conrad Ludlow,
Mimi Paul, Patricia Neary, Marnee
Morris, Sara Leland, Suki Schorer,
Carol Sumner.

Prologue
CHOREOGRAPHY: Jacques d'Amboise
MUSIC: selected from keyboard works
of William Byrd, Giles Farnaby, and
others (arrangement and orchestra-
tion by Robert Irving)
DECOR AND COSTUMES: Peter Larkin
(costumes executed by Karinska)
PREMIERE: January 12, 1967, New
York State Theater.
PRINCIPAL DANCERS: Arthur Mitchell
(Othello), John Prinz (Iago), Frank
Ohman (Cassio), Mimi Paul
(Desdemona), Kay Mazzo (Emilia),
Marnee Morris (Allegra).

Trois Valses Romantiques
CHOREOGRAPHY: George Balanchine
MUSIC: Emmanuel Chabrier

COSTUMES: Karinska
PREMIERE: April 6, 1967, New York
State Theater.
PRINCIPAL DANCERS: Melissa
Hayden, Arthur Mitchell, and Gloria
Govrin, Marnee Morris, Frank
Ohman, and Kent Stowell.

Jewels
(a three-part program consisting of
Emeralds, Rubies, and *Diamonds*)
CHOREOGRAPHY: George Balanchine
MUSIC: Gabriel Fauré, from *Pelléas
et Mélisande* and *Shylock*
(*Emeralds*); Igor Stravinsky,
Capriccio for Piano and Orchestra
(*Rubies*); and Peter Ilyich
Tchaikovsky, from Symphony No.
3 in D major (*Diamonds*)
SCENERY: Peter Harvey
COSTUMES: Karinska
PREMIERE: April 13, 1967, New
York State Theater.
PRINCIPAL DANCERS: Violette Verdy,
Mimi Paul, Conrad Ludlow,
Francisco Moncion, Sara Leland,
Suki Schorer, and John Prinz
(*Emeralds*); Patricia McBride,
Edward Villella, and Patricia Neary
(*Rubies*); Suzanne Farrell and
Jacques d'Amboise (*Diamonds*).

Glinkaiana
CHOREOGRAPHY: George Balanchine
MUSIC: Mikhail Glinka
SCENERY AND COSTUMES: Esteban
Francés
PREMIERE: November 23, 1967,
New York State Theater.
PRINCIPAL DANCERS: Violette Verdy,
Paul Mejia; Mimi Paul, John
Clifford; Melissa Hayden; and
Patricia McBride, Edward Villella.

Metastaseis and Pithoprakta
CHOREOGRAPHY: George Balanchine
MUSIC: Iannis Xenakis
PREMIERE: January 18, 1968, New
York State Theater.
PRINCIPAL DANCERS: Suzanne Farrell
and Arthur Mitchell.

Haydn Concerto
CHOREOGRAPHY: John Taras
MUSIC: Franz Joseph Haydn
(Concerto for Flute and Oboe)
SCENERY AND COSTUMES: Raoul Pène
DuBois (costumes executed by
Karinska)
PREMIERE: January 25, 1968, New
York State Theater.
PRINCIPAL DANCERS: Kay Mazzo,
Patricia McBride, John Prinz, Earle
Sieveling.

Slaughter on Tenth Avenue
CHOREOGRAPHY: George Balanchine
MUSIC: Richard Rodgers
(from the musical On Your Toes)
NEW ORCHESTRATION: Hershy Kay
SCENERY: Jo Mielziner
COSTUMES: Irene Sharaff
PREMIERE: May 2, 1968, New York
State Theater.
PRINCIPAL DANCERS: Suzanne Farrell
and Arthur Mitchell.

Stravinsky: Symphony in C
CHOREOGRAPHY: John Clifford
MUSIC: Igor Stravinsky
COSTUMES: John Braden
PREMIERE: May 9, 1968, New York
State Theater.
PRINCIPAL DANCERS: Kay Mazzo,
Marnee Morris, Renee Estópinal,
Anthony Blum, John Prinz.

Tchaikovsky Suite No. 2
CHOREOGRAPHY: Jacques d'Amboise
MUSIC: Peter Ilyich Tchaikovsky
(Suite No. 2 for Orchestra)
PRODUCTION DESIGN: John Braden
PREMIERE: January 9, 1969, New
York State Theater.
PRINCIPAL DANCERS: Marnee Morris,
John Prinz; Allegra Kent, Francisco
Moncion; and Linda Merrill, John
Clifford.

Fantasies
CHOREOGRAPHY: John Clifford
MUSIC: Ralph Vaughan Williams

(**Fantasia on a Theme by Thomas
Tallis**)
COSTUMES: Robert O'Hearn
PREMIERE: January 23, 1969, New
York State Theater.
PRINCIPAL DANCERS: Sara Leland,
Kay Mazzo, Anthony Blum, Conrad
Ludlow.

La Source
CHOREOGRAPHY: George Balanchine
MUSIC: Léo Delibes
(from La Source and Naïla)
COSTUMES: Karinska
PREMIERE: February 5, 1969, New
York State Theater.
PRINCIPAL DANCERS: Violette Verdy,
John Prinz, and Suki Schorer.

Prelude, Fugue, and Riffs
CHOREOGRAPHY: John Clifford
MUSIC: Leonard Bernstein
PREMIERE: May 15, 1969, New York
State Theater. (Gala Benefit
Preview: May 8, 1969.)
PRINCIPAL DANCERS: Linda Merrill
and John Clifford.

Dances at a Gathering
CHOREOGRAPHY: Jerome Robbins
MUSIC: Frédéric Chopin (Mazurka
Op. 63, No. 3; Waltz Op. 69, No. 2;
Mazurka Op. 33, No. 3; Mazurka
Op. 6, No. 2 and No. 4; Mazurka Op.
7, No. 4 and No. 5; Mazurka Op. 24,
No. 2; Waltz Op. 42; Waltz
Op. 34, No. 2; Mazurka Op. 56, No.
2; Etude Op. 25, No. 4; Waltz Op.
34, No. 1; Waltz Op. 70, No. 2;
Etude Op. 25, No. 5; Etude Op. 10,
No. 2; Scherzo Op. 20, No. 1;
Nocturne Op. 15, No. 1—for solo
piano)
COSTUMES: Joe Eula
PREMIERE: May 22, 1969, New York
State Theater. (Gala Benefit
Preview: May 8, 1969.)
PRINCIPAL DANCERS: Allegra Kent,
Sara Leland, Kay Mazzo, Patricia
McBride, Violette Verdy, Anthony

Blum, John Clifford, Robert Maiorano, John Prinz, and Edward Villella.
PIANIST: Gordon Boelzner.

Pas de Deux (II)
CHOREOGRAPHY: Jacques d'Amboise
MUSIC: Anton von Webern
(Six Pieces for Orchestra)
PRODUCTION DESIGN: John Braden
PREMIERE: May 29, 1969, New York State Theater.
PRINCIPAL DANCERS: Deborah Flomine and Jacques d'Amboise.

Reveries
CHOREOGRAPHY: John Clifford
MUSIC: Peter Ilyich Tchaikovsky
(Suite No. 1, movements 1, 3, 4, and 6)
COSTUMES: Joe Eula
PREMIERE: December 4, 1969, New York State Theater.
PRINCIPAL DANCERS: Gelsey Kirkland, Johnna Kirkland, Anthony Blum, Conrad Ludlow, and Gloria Govrin.

In the Night
CHOREOGRAPHY: Jerome Robbins
MUSIC: Frédéric Chopin
(Nocturnes: Op. 27, No. 1; Op. 55, No. 1 and No. 2; and Op. 9, No. 2—for solo piano)
COSTUMES: Joe Eula
PREMIERE: January 29, 1970, New York State Theater.
PRINCIPAL DANCERS: Kay Mazzo and Anthony Bum; Violette Verdy and Peter Martins; and Patricia McBride and Francisco Moncion.
PIANIST: Gordon Boelzner.

Who Cares?
CHOREOGRAPHY: George Balanchine
MUSIC: George Gershwin (Lyrics: Ira Gershwin)
ORCHESTRATION: Hershy Kay
DECOR: Jo Mielziner
COSTUMES: Karinska

PREMIERE: February 5, 1970, New York State Theater.
PRINCIPAL DANCERS: Karin von Aroldingen, Patricia McBride, Marnee Morris, and Jacques d'Amboise.

Sarabande and Danse
CHOREOGRAPHY: John Clifford
MUSIC: Claude Debussy (orchestration by Maurice Ravel)
COSTUMES: Joe Eula
PREMIERE: May 21, 1970, New York State Theater.
PRINCIPAL DANCERS: Johnna Kirkland, Violette Verdy, John Clifford, Earle Sieveling.

Suite No. 3
CHOREOGRAPHY: George Balanchine
MUSIC: Peter Ilyich Tchaikovsky
SCENERY AND DESIGN: Nicolas Benois
PREMIERE: December 3, 1970, New York State Theater. (Including a revival of Balanchine's *Theme and Variations* of 1960.)
PRINCIPAL DANCERS: Karin von Aroldingen, Anthony Blum; Kay Mazzo, Conrad Ludlow; Marnee Morris, John Clifford; and Gelsey Kirkland, Edward Villella.

Kodály Dances
CHOREOGRAPHY: John Clifford
MUSIC: Zoltán Kodály
(*Dances of Galanta* and *Dances of Marosszék*)
COSTUMES: Stanley Simmons
PREMIERE: January 14, 1971, New York State Theater.
PRINCIPAL DANCERS: Johnna Kirkland, Anthony Blum, and Colleen Neary.

Four Last Songs
CHOREOGRAPHY: Lorca Massine
MUSIC: Richard Strauss
DECOR: John Braden
COSTUMES: Joe Eula
PREMIERE: January 21, 1971, New

Four Last Songs (*continued*)
York State Theater.
DANCERS: Robert Maiorano, Susan
Pilarre, Bonnie Moore, Meg Gordon,
Johnna Kirkland, Bryan Pitts, Lisa
de Ribere, Bonita Borne, Nolan
T'Sani.

Concerto for Two Solo Pianos
CHOREOGRAPHY: Richard Tanner
MUSIC: Igor Stravinsky
COSTUMES: Stanley Simmons
PREMIERE: January 21, 1971, New
York State Theater.
PRINCIPAL DANCERS: Gelsey
Kirkland, Colleen Neary, James
Bogan, John Clifford, David
Richardson, and Christine Redpath,
Giselle Roberge.

*Concerto for Jazz Band
and Orchestra*
CHOREOGRAPHY: George Balanchine
and Arthur Mitchell
MUSIC: Rolf Lieberman
PREMIERE: May 6, 1971, New York
State Theater. (One performance
only for the Benefit of the New York
City Ballet.)
DANCERS: The Dance Theater of
Harlem and the New York City
Ballet.

Octandre
CHOREOGRAPHY: Richard Tanner
MUSIC: Edgar Varèse
(*Octandre*, 1924, and *Intégrales*,
1925)
PREMIERE: May 13, 1971, New York
State Theater.
PRINCIPAL DANCERS: Johnna
Kirkland, Bryan Pitts, and Christine
Redpath.

The Goldberg Variations
CHOREOGRAPHY: Jerome Robbins
MUSIC: Johann Sebastian Bach
(For solo piano)
COSTUMES: Joe Eula
PREMIERE: May 27, 1971, New York

State Theater.
DANCERS: Karin von Aroldingen,
Renee Estópinal, Susan Hendl,
Gelsey Kirkland, Sara Leland,
Patricia McBride, Anthony Blum,
John Clifford, Peter Martins, Robert
Maiorano, Michael Steele, Helgi
Tomasson, Robert Weiss, Bruce
Wells.
PIANIST: Gordon Boelzner.

PAMTGG
CHOREOGRAPHY: George Balanchine
MUSIC: Roger Kellaway
(based on themes by Stan
Applebaum and Sid Woloshin)
DECOR: Jo Mielziner
COSTUME DESIGN: Irene Sharaff
PREMIERE: June 17, 1971, New York
State Theater.
PRINCIPAL DANCERS: Kay Mazzo,
Victor Castelli; Karin von
Aroldingen, Frank Ohman; and
Sara Leland, John Clifford.

Chopiniana
STAGING: Alexandra Danilova, after
Michel Fokine
MUSIC: Frédéric Chopin (Prelude
Op. 28, No. 7; Nocturne Op. 32, No.
2; Waltz Op. 70, No. 1; Mazurka
Op. 33, No. 3; Mazurka Op. 67, No.
3; repeat of Prelude Op. 28, No. 7;
Waltz Op. 64, No. 2; Waltz Op. 18,
No. 1—for solo piano)
PREMIERE: January 20, 1972, New
York State Theater.
PRINCIPAL DANCERS: Kay Mazzo,
Peter Martins, Karin von Aroldingen,
Susan Hendl.
PIANIST: Gordon Boelzner.

Watermill
CHOREOGRAPHY: Jerome Robbins
MUSIC: Teiji Ito
DECOR: Jerome Robbins
in association with David Reppa
COSTUMES: Patricia Zipprodt
PREMIERE: February 3, 1972, New
York State Theater.

DANCERS: Edward Villella and Penny Dudleston, Hermes Conde, Jean-Pierre Frohlich, Bart Cook, Tracy Bennett, Victor Castelli, Deni Lamont, Colleen Neary, Robert Maiorano.

Sonata
CHOREOGRAPHY: George Balanchine
MUSIC: Igor Stravinsky (a fragment of his first sonata for solo piano)
PREMIERE: June 18, 1972, New York State Theater.
DANCERS: Sara Leland, John Clifford.
PIANIST: Madeleine Malraux.

Scherzo Fantastique
CHOREOGRAPHY: Jerome Robbins
MUSIC: Igor Stravinsky
PREMIERE: June 18, 1972, New York State Theater.
PRINCIPAL DANCERS: Gelsey Kirkland, Bart Cook, and Bryan Pitts, Stephen Caras, Victor Castelli.

Symphony in Three Movements
CHOREOGRAPHY: George Balanchine
MUSIC: Igor Stravinsky
PREMIERE: June 18, 1972, New York State Theater.
PRINCIPAL DANCERS: Sara Leland, Marnee Morris, Lynda Yourth, Helgi Tomasson, Edward Villella, Robert Weiss, and Deborah Flomine, Johnna Kirkland, Delia Peters, Susan Pilarre, Giselle Roberge, Deni Lamont, Robert Maiorano, Frank Ohman, Earle Sieveling, Bruce Wells.

Violin Concerto
(later called *Stravinsky Violin Concerto*)
CHOREOGRAPHY: George Balanchine
MUSIC: Igor Stravinsky
PREMIERE: June 18, 1972, New York State Theater. (The music was first used for dancing by Balanchine, in a wholly different version, for the original Ballet Russe in 1941,

under the title *Balustrade*, with costumes and scenery by Pavel Tchelitchev.)
PRINCIPAL DANCERS: Karin von Aroldingen, Kay Mazzo, Jean-Pierre Bonnefous, Peter Martins.
VIOLINIST: Joseph Silverstein.

Symphony in E Flat
CHOREOGRAPHY: John Clifford
MUSIC: Igor Stravinsky (Opus 1)
COSTUMES: Stanley Simmons
PREMIERE: June 20, 1972, New York State Theater.
PRINCIPAL DANCERS: Gelsey Kirkland and Peter Martins.

Concerto for Piano and Winds
CHOREOGRAPHY: John Taras
MUSIC: Igor Stravinsky
(For piano, wind instruments, timpani, and string bass)
COSTUMES: Rouben Ter-Arutunian
PREMIERE: June 20, 1972, New York State Theater. (The music was first used for dancing by Taras, in a wholly different version, for the New York City Ballet in 1963, under the title *Arcade*.)
PRINCIPAL DANCERS: Bruce Wells, Robert Maiorano, Frank Ohman, Tracy Bennett, Victor Castelli, Peter Naumann.

Danses Concertantes
CHOREOGRAPHY: George Balanchine
MUSIC: Igor Stravinsky
DECOR AND COSTUMES: Eugene Berman (originally produced for the Ballet Russe de Monte Carlo)
PREMIERE: June 20, 1972, New York State Theater.
PRINCIPAL DANCERS: Lynda Yourth and John Clifford.

Octuor
CHOREOGRAPHY: Richard Tanner
MUSIC: Igor Stravinsky
(For wind instruments)
PREMIERE: June 21, 1972, New York

Octuor (*continued*)
State Theater.
DANCERS: Elise Flagg, Deborah
Flomine, Delia Peters, Lisa de
Ribere, Tracy Bennett, James Bogan,
Daniel Duell, Jean-Pierre Frohlich.

Serenade in A
CHOREOGRAPHY: Todd Bolender
MUSIC: Igor Stravinsky
(For solo piano)
COSTUMES: Stanley Simmons
PREMIERE: June 21, 1972, New York
State Theater.
PRINCIPAL DANCERS: Susan Hendl,
Robert Maiorano, Robert Weiss.
PIANIST: Madeleine Malraux.

*Divertimento from
"Le Baiser de la Fée"*
CHOREOGRAPHY: George Balanchine
MUSIC: Igor Stravinsky
PREMIERE: June 21, 1972, New York
State Theater.
PRINCIPAL DANCERS: Patricia
McBride, Helgi Tomasson, and
Bettijane Sills, Carol Sumner.

Scherzo à la Russe
CHOREOGRAPHY: George Balanchine
MUSIC: Igor Stravinsky
COSTUMES: Karinska
PREMIERE: June 21, 1972, New York
State Theater.
PRINCIPAL DANCERS: Karin von
Aroldingen and Kay Mazzo.

Circus Polka
CHOREOGRAPHY: Jerome Robbins
MUSIC: Igor Stravinsky
PREMIERE: June 21, 1972, New York
State Theater.
DANCERS: Jerome Robbins (Ring
Master) and children from the
School of American Ballet.

Scènes de Ballet
CHOREOGRAPHY: John Taras
MUSIC: Igor Stravinsky
COSTUMES: Karinska

PREMIERE: June 22, 1972, New York
State Theater.
PRINCIPAL DANCERS: Patricia
McBride and Jean-Pierre Bonnefous.

Duo Concertant
CHOREOGRAPHY: George Balanchine
MUSIC: Igor Stravinsky
(For violin and piano)
PREMIERE: June 22, 1972, New York
State Theater.
PRINCIPAL DANCERS: Kay Mazzo and
Peter Martins.
VIOLINIST: Lamar Alsop.
PIANIST: Gordon Boelzner.

The Song of the Nightingale
CHOREOGRAPHY: John Taras
MUSIC: Igor Stravinsky
COSTUME AND PROP DESIGN: Rouben
Ter-Arutunian
PREMIERE: June 22, 1972, New York
State Theater.
PRINCIPAL DANCERS: Gelsey
Kirkland, Elise Flagg, Penny
Dudleston, Francisco Moncion,
Peter Naumann.

Piano-Rag-Music
CHOREOGRAPHY: Todd Bolender
MUSIC: Igor Stravinsky
COSTUMES: Stanley Simmons
PREMIERE: June 23, 1972, New York
State Theater.
PRINCIPAL DANCERS: Gloria Govrin
and John Clifford.
PIANIST: Madeleine Malraux.

Dumbarton Oaks
CHOREOGRAPHY: Jerome Robbins
MUSIC: Igor Stravinsky
COSTUMES: Patricia Zipprodt
PREMIERE: June 23, 1972, New York
State Theater.
PRINCIPAL DANCERS: Allegra Kent
and Anthony Blum.

Ode
CHOREOGRAPHY: Lorca Massine
MUSIC: Igor Stravinsky

(Elegiacal Chant in Three Parts for Orchestra, 1943)
PREMIERE: June 23, 1972, New York State Theater.
PRINCIPAL DANCERS: Colleen Neary, Christine Redpath, Robert Maiorano, Earle Sieveling.

Pulcinella
CHOREOGRAPHY: George Balanchine and Jerome Robbins
MUSIC: Igor Stravinsky
(after Giambattista Pergolesi)
SCENERY AND COSTUMES: Eugene Berman
PREMIERE: June 23, 1972, New York State Theater.
PRINCIPAL DANCERS: Violette Verdy, Edward Villella; Francisco Moncion, Michael Arshansky, Shaun O'Brien; George Balanchine, Jerome Robbins.

Choral Variations on Bach's "Vom Himmel Hoch"
CHOREOGRAPHY: George Balanchine
MUSIC: Igor Stravinsky
(For mixed chorus and orchestra)
SCENERY: Rouben Ter-Arutunian
PREMIERE: June 25, 1972, New York State Theater.
PRINCIPAL DANCERS: Karin von Aroldingen, Melissa Hayden, Sara Leland, Violette Verdy, Anthony Blum, Peter Martins.

Requiem Canticles
CHOREOGRAPHY: Jerome Robbins
MUSIC: Igor Stravinsky
(For contralto, bass soloists, chorus, and orchestra)
PREMIERE: June 25, 1972, New York State Theater.
PRINCIPAL DANCERS: Merrill Ashley, Susan Hendl, Robert Maiorano, Bruce Wells.

Concerto No. 2
(later called *Tchaikovsky Concerto No. 2*)
CHOREOGRAPHY: George Balanchine

MUSIC: Peter Ilyich Tchaikovsky
(For solo piano)
PREMIERE: January 12, 1973, New York State Theater. (This ballet is a reworking of Balanchine's *Ballet Imperial* of 1964.)
PRINCIPAL DANCERS: Patricia McBride, Peter Martins, Colleen Neary, Tracy Bennett, Victor Castelli, Suzanne Erlon, Marjorie Spohn.
PIANIST: Gordon Boelzner.

A Beethoven Pas de Deux
CHOREOGRAPHY: Jerome Robbins
MUSIC: Ludwig van Beethoven
(Four Bagatelles for solo piano)
COSTUMES: Florence Klotz
GALA BENEFIT PREVIEW: May 16, 1973, New York State Theater. (For one performance only; premiere January 10, 1974.)
DANCERS: Violette Verdy and Jean-Pierre Bonnefous.
PIANIST: Jerry Zimmerman.

Cortège Hongrois
CHOREOGRAPHY: George Balanchine
MUSIC: Alexander Glazounov
(from *Raymonda*)
DECOR AND COSTUMES: Rouben Ter-Arutunian
PREMIERE: May 17, 1973, New York State Theater. (Gala Benefit Preview, May 16.)
DANCERS: Melissa Hayden and Jacques d'Amboise; Karin von Aroldingen and Jean-Pierre Bonnefous.

An Evening's Waltzes
CHOREOGRAPHY: Jerome Robbins
MUSIC: Serge Prokofiev (from *Suite of Waltzes*)
DECOR AND COSTUMES: Rouben Ter-Arutunian
PREMIERE: May 24, 1973, New York State Theater.
DANCERS: Patricia McBride and Jean-

An Evening's Waltzes (continued)
Pierre Bonnefous; Christine Redpath and John Clifford; Sara Leland and Bart Cook.

Four Bagatelles
CHOREOGRAPHY: Jerome Robbins
MUSIC: Ludwig van Beethoven
COSTUMES: Florence Klotz
PREMIERE: January 10, 1974, New York State Treater. (Gala Benefit Preview as *A Beethoven Pas de Deux*, May 16, 1973.)
DANCERS: Gelsey Kirkland, Jean-Pierre Bonnefous.
PIANIST: Jerry Zimmerman.

Variations pour une Porte et un Soupir
CHOREOGRAPHY: George Balanchine
SONORITY: Pierre Henri
DECOR AND COSTUMES: Rouben Ter-Arutunian
PREMIERE: February 17, 1974, New York State Theater.
DANCERS: Karin von Aroldingen, John Clifford.

Dybbuk
(later called *The Dybbuk Variations*)
CHOREOGRAPHY: Jerome Robbins
MUSIC: Leonard Bernstein
DECOR: Rouben Ter-Arutunian
COSTUMES: Patricia Zipprodt
PREMIERE: May 16, 1974, New York State Theater. (Gala Benefit Preview, May 15.)
PRINCIPAL DANCERS: Patricia McBride, Helgi Tomasson, Bart Cook, Victor Castelli, Tracy Bennett, Hermes Condé.
SINGERS: David Johnson (baritone), John Ostendorf (bass).

Bartók No. 3
CHOREOGRAPHY: John Clifford
MUSIC: Béla Bartók (Piano Concerto No. 3)

COSTUMES: Ardith Haddow
PREMIERE: May 23, 1974, New York State Theater. (First presented March 27, 1974, by Los Angeles Ballet Theater.)
PRINCIPAL DANCERS: Debra Austin, Muriel Aasen, Wilhelmina Frankfurt, Sara Leland, Anthony Blum.

Saltarelli
CHOREOGRAPHY: Jacques d'Amboise
MUSIC: Antonio Vivaldi (Concerto in D minor; Concerto Grosso in D minor, Op. 3, No. 11)
DECOR AND COSTUMES: John Braden
PREMIERE: May 30, 1974, New York State Theater.
PRINCIPAL DANCERS: Merrill Ashley, Christine Redpath, Francis Sackett.

Coppélia
CHOREOGRAPHY: George Balanchine (after Marius Petipa)
MUSIC: Léo Delibes
SCENARIO: Charles Nuitter (after E. T. A. Hoffmann's *Der Sandmann*)
DECOR AND COSTUMES: Rouben Ter-Arutunian
PREMIERE: July 17, 1974, Performing Arts Center, Saratoga Springs, New York. (Gala New York Benefit Preview, November 20, 1974.)
PRINCIPAL DANCERS: Patricia McBride (Swanilda/Coppélia), Helgi Tomasson (Franz), Shaun O'Brien (Dr. Coppélius).

Sinfonietta
CHOREOGRAPHY: Jacques d'Amboise
MUSIC: Paul Hindemith (Sinfonietta in E)
PRODUCTION DESIGN: John Braden
PREMIERE: January 9, 1975, New York State Theater.
PRINCIPAL DANCERS: Christine Redpath, Colleen Neary, Bart Cook, Francis Sackett.

The Spellbound Child
CHOREOGRAPHY: George Balanchine
MUSIC: Maurice Ravel
(*L'Enfant et les Sortilèges*)
DECOR AND COSTUMES: Aline Bernstein
BOOK: From a poem by Colette
PREMIERE: November 20, 1946, Central High School of Needle Trades, New York.
PRINCIPAL DANCERS: Gisella Caccialanza, Ruth Gilbert, Georgia Hiden, Tanaquil LeClercq, Elise Reiman, Beatrice Tompkins, Paul d'Amboise, William Dollar (title role sung by Joseph Connoly).
REVIVAL: May 15, 1975, as *L'Enfant et les Sortilèges*, New York State Theater.
DECOR AND COSTUMES: Kermit Love
SUPERVISING DESIGNER: David Mitchell
PRINCIPAL DANCERS: Paul Offenkranz, Marnee Morris, Christine Redpath, Jean-Pierre Frohlich, Tracy Bennett, Colleen Neary.

Sonatine
CHOREOGRAPHY: George Balanchine
MUSIC: Maurice Ravel
PREMIERE: May 15, 1975, New York State Theater. (Gala Benefit Preview, May 14, 1975.)
DANCERS: Violette Verdy, Jean-Pierre Bonnefous.
PIANIST: Madeleine Malraux.

Concerto in G
(later called *In G Major*)
CHOREOGRAPHY: Jerome Robbins
MUSIC: Maurice Ravel (Piano Concerto in G major)
DECOR AND COSTUMES: Rouben Ter-Arutunian
PREMIERE: May 15, 1975, New York State Theater. (Gala Benefit Preview, May 14, 1975.)
PRINCIPAL DANCERS: Suzanne Farrell, Peter Martins.
PIANIST: Gordon Boelzner.

Introduction and Allegro for Harp
CHOREOGRAPHY: Jerome Robbins
MUSIC: Maurice Ravel (For harp, string quartet, flute, and clarinet)
COSTUMES: Arnold Scaasi
PREMIERE: May 22, 1975, New York State Theater.
PRINCIPAL DANCERS: Patricia McBride, Helgi Tomasson.
HARPIST: Cynthia Otis.

Schéhérazade
CHOREOGRAPHY: George Balanchine
MUSIC: Maurice Ravel
PREMIERE: May 22, 1975, New York State Theater.
PRINCIPAL DANCERS: Kay Mazzo, Edward Villella.

Alborada del Gracioso
CHOREOGRAPHY: Jacques d'Amboise
MUSIC: Maurice Ravel
COSTUMES: John Braden
PREMIERE: May 22, 1975, New York State Theater.
PRINCIPAL DANCERS: Suzanne Farrell, Jacques d'Amboise.

Ma Mère l'Oye (Fairy Tales for Dancers)
(later called *Mother Goose*)
CHOREOGRAPHY: Jerome Robbins
MUSIC: Maurice Ravel
SCENARIO: Maurice Ravel, based on fairy tales by Charles Perrault and others
COSTUMES: Stanley Simmons
PREMIERE: May 22, 1975, New York State Theater.
PRINCIPAL DANCERS: Muriel Aasen, Delia Peters, Tracy Bennett, Deborah Koolish, Richard Hoskinson, Matthew Giordano, Colleen Neary, Jay Jolley, Daniel Duell.

Daphnis and Chloe
CHOREOGRAPHY: John Taras
MUSIC: Maurice Ravel
COSTUMES AND PRODUCTION DESIGN: Joe Eula

Daphnis and Chloe (continued)
PREMIERE: May 22, 1975, New York State Theater.
PRINCIPAL DANCERS: Peter Martins, Nina Fedorova, Karin von Aroldingen, Peter Schaufuss.

Le Tombeau de Couperin
CHOREOGRAPHY: George Balanchine
MUSIC: Maurice Ravel
PREMIERE: May 29, 1975, New York State Theater.
DANCERS: Judith Fugate, Jean-Pierre Frohlich, Wilhelmina Frankfurt, Victor Castelli, Muriel Aasen, Francis Sackett, Susan Hendl, David Richardson, Marjorie Spohn, Hermes Condé, Delia Peters, Richard Hoskinson, Susan Pilarre, Richard Dryden, Carol Sumner, Laurence Matthews.

Pavane
CHOREOGRAPHY: George Balanchine
MUSIC: Maurice Ravel ("Pavane pour une Infante Défunte")
PREMIERE: May 29, 1975, New York State Theater.
DANCER: Patricia McBride.

Une Barque sur l'Océan
CHOREOGRAPHY: Jerome Robbins
MUSIC: Maurice Ravel
COSTUMES: Parmelee Welles
PREMIERE: May 29, 1975, New York State Theater.
DANCERS: Victor Castelli, Daniel Duell, Laurence Matthews, Jay Jolley, Nolan T'Sani.

Tzigane
CHOREOGRAPHY: George Balanchine
MUSIC: Maurice Ravel
COSTUMES: Joe Eula
PREMIERE: May 29, 1975, New York State Theater.
PRINCIPAL DANCERS: Suzanne Farrell, Peter Martins.
VIOLINIST: Lamar Alsop.

Gaspard de la Nuit
CHOREOGRAPHY: George Balanchine
MUSIC: Maurice Ravel
DECOR AND COSTUMES: Bernard Daydé (execution supervised by David Mitchell)
PREMIERE: May 29, 1975, New York State Theater.
PRINCIPAL DANCERS: Colleen Neary, Victor Castelli, Karin von Aroldingen, Nolan T'Sani, Sara Leland, Robert Weiss.
PIANIST: Jerry Zimmerman.

Sarabande and Danse (II)
CHOREOGRAPHY: Jacques d'Amboise
MUSIC: Claude Debussy (orchestrated by Maurice Ravel, 1923)
COSTUMES: John Braden
PREMIERE: May 29, 1975, New York State Theater.
PRINCIPAL DANCERS: Colleen Neary, Bart Cook, Kyra Nichols, Francis Sackett.

Chansons Madécasses (*Songs of the Madegasque*)
CHOREOGRAPHY: Jerome Robbins
MUSIC: Maurice Ravel
PREMIERE: May 29, 1975, New York State Theater.
DANCERS: Patricia McBride, Helgi Tomasson, Debra Austin, Hermes Condé.
SINGER: Gwendolyn Killebrew (mezzo-soprano).

Rapsodie Espagnole
CHOREOGRAPHY: George Balanchine
MUSIC: Maurice Ravel
COSTUMES: Michael Avedon
PREMIERE: May 29, 1975, New York State Theater.
PRINCIPAL DANCERS: Karin von Aroldingen, Peter Schaufuss, Nolan T'Sani.

The Steadfast Tin Soldier
CHOREOGRAPHY: George Balanchine
MUSIC: Georges Bizet

DECOR AND COSTUMES: David
Mitchell
PREMIERE: July 30, 1975, Perform-
ing Arts Center, Saratoga Springs,
New York.
DANCERS: Patricia McBride, Peter
Schaufuss.

Chaconne
CHOREOGRAPHY: George Balanchine
(staged by Brigitte Thom)
MUSIC: Christoph Willibald von
Gluck (ballet music from "Orpheus
and Eurydice")
COSTUMES: Karinska
PREMIERE: January 22, 1976, New
York State Theater.
PRINCIPAL DANCERS: Suzanne Far-
rell, Peter Martins, Susan Hendl,
Jean-Pierre Frohlich.

Union Jack
CHOREOGRAPHY: George Balanchine
MUSIC: Hershy Kay (adapted from
traditional British sources)
DECOR AND COSTUMES: Rouben Ter-
Arutunian
PREMIERE: May 13, 1976. (Gala
Benefit Preview, May 12, 1976.)
PRINCIPAL DANCERS: Helgi Tomas-
son, Jacques d'Amboise, Sara Leland,
Kay Mazzo, Peter Martins, Karin
von Aroldingen, Suzanne Farrell,
Jean-Pierre Bonnefous, Patricia
McBride.

Other Dances
CHOREOGRAPHY: Jerome Robbins
MUSIC: Frédéric Chopin
PREMIERE: November 26, 1976,
New York State Theater. (Gala
Benefit Preview, May 9.)
DANCERS: Suzanne Farrell, Peter
Martins.

Bournonville Divertissements
CHOREOGRAPHY: August Bournon-
ville (staged by Stanley Williams)
MUSIC: S. Holger Paulli, Hans

Christian Lumbye, Edvard Helsted,
J. Paulli
COSTUMES: Ben Benson (after
original designs)
PREMIERE: February 3, 1977, New
York State Theater.
PRINCIPAL DANCERS: Daniel Duell,
Nichol Hlinka, Patricia McBride,
Helgi Tomasson, Merrill Ashley,
Robert Weiss, Kyra Nichols, Peter
Martins, Suzanne Farrell, Adam
Lüders, Colleen Neary.

Etude for Piano
CHOREOGRAPHY: George Balanchine
MUSIC: Alexander Scriabin
COSTUMES: Christine Giannini
PREMIERE: June 4, 1977, Spoleto
Festival USA, Charleston, South
Carolina.
NEW YORK CITY BALLET PREMIERE:
June 17, 1977, New York State
Theater.
DANCERS: Patricia McBride, Jean-
Pierre Bonnefous.

Vienna Waltzes
CHOREOGRAPHY: George Balanchine
MUSIC: Johann Strauss, Jr., Franz
Lehár, Richard Strauss
SCENERY: Rouben Ter-Arutunian
COSTUMES: Karinska
PREMIERE: June 23, 1977, New York
State Theater.
PRINCIPAL DANCERS: Karin von
Aroldingen, Sean Lavery, Patricia
McBride, Helgi Tomasson, Sara
Leland, Bart Cook, Kay Mazzo,
Peter Martins, Suzanne Farrell,
Jorge Dunn.

Ballo della Regina
CHOREOGRAPHY: George Balanchine
MUSIC: Giuseppe Verdi (from *Don
Carlos*)
COSTUMES: Ben Benson
PREMIERE: January 12, 1978, New
York State Theater.
PRINCIPAL DANCERS: Merrill Ashley,
Robert Weiss.

Calcium Light Night
CHOREOGRAPHY: Peter Martins
MUSIC: Charles Ives
SET: Steven Rubin
PREMIERE: January 19, 1978, New York State Theater.
DANCERS: Daniel Duell, Heather Watts.

Kammermusik No. 2
CHOREOGRAPHY: George Balanchine
MUSIC: Paul Hindemith
COSTUMES: Ben Benson
PREMIERE: January 26, 1978, New York State Theater.
PRINCIPAL DANCERS: Karin von Aroldingen, Colleen Neary, Adam Lüders, Sean Lavery.

Tricolore
CHOREOGRAPHY: Peter Martins—Part I; Jean-Pierre Bonnefous—Part II; Jerome Robbins—Part III

MUSIC: Georges Auric
SCENERY AND COSTUMES: Rouben Ter-Arutunian
PREMIERE: May 18, 1978, New York State Theater.
PRINCIPAL DANCERS: Colleen Neary, Adam Lüders, Merrill Ashley, Sean Lavery, Karin von Aroldingen.

A Sketch Book
CHOREOGRAPHY: Jerome Robbins—Parts I, III, and IV; Peter Martins—Part II
MUSIC: George Frederic Handel and Heinrich von Biber (Part I); Gioacchino Rossini (Part II); Georg Philipp Telemann (Part III); Giuseppe Verdi (Part IV)
PREMIERE: June 8, 1978, New York State Theater.
PRINCIPAL DANCERS: Daniel Duell, Heather Watts, Sean Lavery, Joseph Duell, Kyra Nichols, Peter Martins.

INDEX

The text of this book was set in various weights of Electra, a typeface designed by William Addison Dwiggins. The book was composed, printed, and bound by American Book–Stratford Press, Saddle Brook, New Jersey. Typography and binding design by Camilla Filancia